DREAMS
OF NATIONHOOD

American Jewish Communists and the Soviet
Birobidzhan Project, 1924-1951

JEWISH IDENTITIES IN POST MODERN SOCIETY

Series Editor: Roberta Rosenberg Farber – Yeshiva University

Editorial Board:
Sara Abosch – University of Memphis
Geoffrey Alderman – University of Buckingham
Yoram Bilu – Hebrew University
Steven M. Cohen – Hebrew Union College – Jewish Institute of Religion
Bryan Daves – Yeshiva University
Sergio Della Pergola – Hebrew University
Simcha Fishbane – Touro College
Deborah Dash Moore – University of Michigan
Uzi Rebhun – Hebrew University
Reeva Simon –Yeshiva University
Chaim I. Waxman – Rutgers University

Dreams of Nationhood:
American Jewish Communists and the Soviet
Birobidzhan Project, 1924-1951

Henry Felix Srebrnik

Boston 2010

Library of Congress Cataloging-in-Publication Data

Srebrnik, Henry Felix.
  American Jewish communists and the Soviet Birobidzhan project, 1924-1951 / Henry Felix Srebrnik.
     p. cm. -- (Jewish identities in post modern society)
  Includes bibliographical references and index.
  ISBN 978-1-61811-817-2
  1. Jews--United States--Politics and government--20th century. 2. Jewish communists--United States--History--20th century. 3. Communism--United States--History--20th century. 4. Icor. 5. Birobidzhan (Russia)--History. 6. Evreiskaia avtonomnaia oblast (Russia)--History. I. Title.
  E184.J4S74 2010
  973'.04924--dc22
                              2010024428

Copyright © 2010 Academic Studies Press
All rights reserved

Cover and interior design by Adell Medovoy

Published by Academic Studies Press in 2010

28 Montfern Avenue
Brighton, MA 02135, USA
press@academicstudiespress.com
www.academicstudiespress.com

TABLE OF CONTENTS

Abbreviations	*vii*
List of Illustrations	*ix*
Preface	*xiii*
Introduction: American Jews, Communism, the ICOR and Birobidzhan	1
The Formation of Ambijan	29
The "People's Delegation" and the Popular Front, 1935-1939	55
Wartime Aid to the Soviet Union: the ICOR	83
Wartime Aid to the Soviet Union: Ambijan	101
The Postwar Orphans' Campaign and the Ambijan-ICOR Merger	119
The Glory Years, 1946-1948	139
Ambijan and the Creation of Israel	165
The Gathering Storm: McCarthyism, Cold War, and Decline	189
Islands of Resistance, 1949-1950	215
Conclusion: From Hope to Hoax	229
Appendix: Paul Novick's 1936 Visit to the Jewish Autonomous Region	249
Appendix: George Koval	253
Selected Bibliography	255
Index	283

Abbreviations and Acronyms

ACWA	Amalgamated Clothing Workers of America
Ambijan	American Committee for the Settlement of Jews in Birobidjan
Artef (Yiddish)	Workers Theater Group (*Arbeter Teater Farband*)
Comintern	Communist (Third) International
CPSU	Communist Party of the Soviet Union
CPUSA	Communist Party of the United States of America
FBI	Federal Bureau of Investigation
GEZERD (Yiddish)	Association for the Settlement of Jewish Toilers on the Land (*Alfarbandishe Gezelshaft farn Aynordenen Oyf Erd Arbetndike Yidn*)
ICOR (Yiddish)	Association for Jewish Colonization in the Soviet Union (*Gezelshaft far Yidishe Kolonizatsye in Ratn-Farband*)
ILGWU	International Ladies' Garment Workers' Union
ITO (Yiddish)	Jewish Territorialist Organization (*Yidishe Teritorialistishe Organizatsye*)
IWO	International Workers Order (*Internatsyonaler Arbeter Ordn*)
JAFC	Jewish Anti-Fascist Committee in the Soviet Union (*Yevreysky Antifashistsky Komitet*)
JAR	Jewish Autonomous Region
JPC	Jewish Peoples Committee
Joint	American Jewish Joint Distribution Committee
JPFO	Jewish People's Fraternal Order (*Yidishn Fraternaln Folks-ordn*)

Abbreviations and Acronyms

KOMERD (Yiddish)	Committee for the Settlement of Jewish Toilers on the Land (*Komitet farn Aynordenen Oyf Erd Arbetndike Yidn*)
KOMZET (Russian)	Committee for the Settlement of Jewish Toilers on the Land (*Komitet po Zemel'nomu Ustroistvu Trudyaschikhsya Evre'ev*)
ORT	World Union of Societies for Promotion of Artisanal and Agricultural Work Among the Jews (World ORT Union)
OZET (Russian)	Association for the Settlement of Jewish Toilers on the Land (*Obschestvennyi Komitet po Zemel'nomy Ustroistvu Evreiskikh Trudyaschikhsya*)
Proletpen (Yiddish)	Proletarian Writers Union (*Proletarisher Shrayber Fareyn*)
UJA	United Jewish Appeal
USSR	Union of Soviet Socialist Republics
WC	Workmen's Circle (*Arbeter Ring*)
Yevsektsiya (Russian)	Jewish Section of the Soviet Communist Party (*Yevreyskaya Sektsiya*)
YKUF	World Jewish Cultural Union (*Alveltlekher Yidisher Kultur Farband*)

List of Illustrations

Map of Birobidzhan, 1941, from Universal Jewish Encyclopedia, 1941	....*preface, page 28*
Lord Marley, from Birobidjan: A New Hope for Oppressed European Jews	....*chapter 1, page 53*
Cover of Biro Bidjan as I Saw It, 1934, by Lord Marley	....*chapter 1, page 53*
B.Z. Goldberg, Schottenstein-Jesselson Library of the Herbert D. Katz Center for Advanced Judaic Studies at the University of Pennsylvania, Philadelphia	....*chapter 1, page 54*
Pamphlet advertising Anna Louise Strong lecture, Feb. 6, 1936, Russian Relief Collection, Yeshiva University Archives, New York	....*chapter 1, page 54*
Cover of Ambijan pamphlet Birobidzhan: The Jewish Autonomous Territory	....*chapter 1, page 54*
Chicago Ambijan Invitation for Lord Marley Dinner, November 1936, Chicago Jewish Archives, Spertus Institute of Jewish Studies, Chicago	....*chapter 2, page 81*
Invitation for the People's Delegation, Los Angeles, May 1936, YIVO Institute for Jewish Research, New York	....*chapter 2, page 81*
Delegates to the Plenum of the ICOR National Executive, New York, Feb. 28, 1937, Nailebn-New Life, April 1937	....*chapter 2, page 81*
Cover of Nailebn-New Life, April 1938 (English side)	....*chapter 2, page 82*
Cover of Nailebn-New Life, April 1938 (Yiddish side)	....*chapter 2, page 82*
Shloime Almazov, Nailebn-New Life, April 1939	....*chapter 2, page 82*
Professor Charles Kuntz, Nailebn-New Life, June 1940	....*chapter 3, page 100*

LIST OF ILLUSTRATIONS

Shloime Mikhoels (on left) at the gravesite of Sholem Aleichem, New York, 1943 (B.Z. Goldberg's son Mitchell is at the right), Schottenstein-Jesselson Library of the Herbert D. Katz Center for Advanced Judaic Studies at the University of Pennsylvania, Philadelphia	....chapter 3, page 100
Watches for the Red Army, Ambijan Bulletin, April 1943	....chapter 4, page 118
Ad for Maud's Summer-Ray, New Masses, June 3, 1941	....chapter 4, page 118
Ambijan National Conference, Nov. 25-26, 1944, Ambijan Bulletin, June 1945	....chapter 4, page 118
Chicago Ambijan Leadership, Sentinel, Chicago, May 16, 1946	....chapter 5, page 138
Senator Claude Pepper on cover of Sentinel, Chicago, June 20, 1946	....chapter 5, page 138
National Conference for Birobidzhan, March 9-10, 1946, Ambijan Bulletin, April 1946	....chapter 5, page 138
Ad for Einstein Fund Dinner, Sentinel, Chicago, Dec. 4, 1947	....chapter 5, page 163
Flyer advertising concert for Birobidzhan, Town Hall, New York, May 1947, YIVO Institute for Jewish Research, New York	....chapter 6, page 164
Flyer advertising Bronx Ambijan Concert for 20th Anniversary of Birobidzhan, April 1948, YIVO Institute for Jewish Research, New York	....chapter 6, page 164
Gina Medem, from A Lebnsveg	....chapter 7, page 187
Chicago Ambijan telegram to David Ben-Gurion, May 12, 1948, Chicago Jewish Archives, Spertus Institute of Jewish Studies, Chicago	....chapter 7, page 187
Andrei Gromyko on cover of flyer for American-Soviet-Palestine Friendship Dinner, 1947, Schottenstein-Jesselson Library of the Herbert D. Katz Center for Advanced Judaic Studies at the University of Pennsylvania, Philadelphia	....chapter 7, page 188
Paul Novick, courtesy Jewish Currents	....chapter 8, page 214

Albert Einstein on cover of Ambijan Bulletin, January-February 1950 ....chapter 8, page 214

Flyer advertising Ambijan conference celebrating 15th anniversary of Birobidzhan as a Jewish Autonomous Region, 1949 (English side), YIVO Institute for Jewish Research, New York ....chapter 9, page 227

Flyer advertising Ambijan conference celebrating 15th anniversary of Birobidzhan as a Jewish Autonomous Region, 1949 (Yiddish side), YIVO Institute for Jewish Research, New York ....chapter 9, page 228

Preface

The American Jewish Communist movement, active within the Jewish community for some three decades, included two left-of-center movements whose main aim was to provide support for the Soviet project to establish a Jewish socialist republic in the Birobidzhan region in the far east of the Soviet Union. The first of these groups, the Association for Jewish Colonization in the Soviet Union, or the ICOR (transliterated acronym for *Yidishe Kolonizatsye Organizatsye in Ratn-farband* or Organization for Jewish Colonization in Soviet Russia, which it also called itself in English), was founded in 1924, and was active within the immigrant working class milieu; its members were to a large extent first and second generation Yiddish-speaking Jews of east European origin. In addition to aiding Jewish settlers in Birobidzhan, the ICOR had a number of clearly defined political goals: the defense of the Soviet Union, which, it claimed, was in the process of solving the "national question" and eliminating anti-Semitism; the struggle against fascism, especially, after 1933, in Nazi Germany; and opposition to Zionism, an ideology deemed inimical to the Jewish working class. As well, the ICOR championed the political views and advanced the goals of the Communist Party of the U.S.A. (CPUSA) on behalf of policies that it perceived as beneficial to the Jewish working class.

The second group, the American Committee for the Settlement of Jews in Birobidjan, or Ambijan, was founded in 1934 as a popular front group catering to native-born, English-speaking, middle-class Jews. When, in response to the increasing menace of Nazism and fascism, the international Communist movement sought broader alliances, Ambijan began to recruit members from the wealthier and longer-established German-Jewish community. As a result, Ambijan was more liberal and inclusive in its political orientation than was the ICOR, which made little secret of its pro-Soviet and left-wing outlook. In its early years, Ambijan avoided ideological debates concerning the establishment of socialism in the Soviet Union; instead, the group emphasized the need for rescue and rehabilitation efforts on behalf of Jews threatened by fascism in Europe. Nonetheless, there was some overlap in the leadership of the two organizations, and both were controlled by Communists. In 1946 the two organizations merged; they survived another five years before disbanding in the face of American government harassment during the early years of the Cold War and the increasing evidence of anti-Semitic repression in the Soviet Union itself.

The activities of Ambijan and the ICOR must be studied against the larger backdrop of the politics of the Soviet Union during this era. In 1928, the Soviet government approved the choice of Birobidzhan in the far east of the country as a national Jewish unit. Here Jews would possess their own administrative, educational and judicial institutions, and would function in their own language, Yiddish. Support for this enterprise was sought from a wide array of Jewish groups in North America, some of which responded favorably to Soviet requests for aid. Primarily, though, most of the people committed to the rebuilding of Jewish life within a Soviet framework were ideologically and organizationally tied to the newly-formed Communist Party of the United States, and they founded groups such as Ambijan and the ICOR.

My interest in these two movements has been long-standing. Some 40 years ago I was a graduate student in the Contemporary Jewish Studies program at Brandeis University in Waltham, Massachusetts. Like many people caught up in the New Left politics of the time, I became increasingly interested in the Old Left, and especially in its Jewish component. Brandeis, which had been founded as a Jewish institution in 1948, counted among its faculty many liberals and also some academics whose careers had been damaged by McCarthyism. The university library contained an excellent collection of left-wing Jewish materials, and while enrolled in a course on American Jewish history I came across an incomplete run of *Nailebn-New Life*, a bilingual English-Yiddish periodical published by the ICOR. I wrote a lengthy paper on the group for a course in American Jewish history taught by the late Leon Jick, and published a piece on Birobidzhan for the Boston *Jewish Advocate* in 1972.

After graduating from Brandeis in 1973, I went on to research Jewish Communists in England for a PhD completed at the University of Birmingham, but I retained my interest in the pro-Birobidzhan movement. Eventually I decided to revisit the subject and examine the scholarship of the succeeding 30 years. It turned out that almost nothing had been written. So, although much had changed since the early 1970s--the Soviet Union had vanished, the American Old and New lefts had both expired--this topic still awaited its chronicler. I began to research the ICOR and a sister movement, Ambijan. Until 1935 the ICOR operated as a single organization in both Canada and the United States, so I researched both simultaneously. I soon realized that the material would fill more than one volume, and I decided that I would first write a comprehensive history of the Canadian movement, from its origins in the 1930s through its demise in 1951. That book was published in 2008.[1]

These and other Jewish left movements served as a cultural and educational home and a support system, both political and personal, to assist newly arrived immigrants who found themselves in an unfamiliar new country, whose language they had not yet mastered. Immigrants could even choose their doctors and dentists from among the many professionals who joined these groups. Most of the people involved remain obscure, yet the issues they grappled with, and the ideas and theories they espoused, had immense consequences. They generated ideas, programs, and visions that later became the commonplaces of social policy in America.

These two organizations were for some three decades central to the concerns of a large portion of the American Jewish community. They attracted thousands of members, and created branches and divisions in tens of cities across America. Millions of dollars were raised by them, especially in the 1941-1949 period. Ambijan and the ICOR addressed all of the major issues facing American Jews at the time: domestic anti-Semitism; the debates over socialism and attitudes towards the Soviet Union, with its own large Jewish community; and the creation of Israel. In that brief conjuncture between 1941 and 1949—when the Soviet Jewish emissaries Shloime Mikhoels and Itsik Fefer visited the United States; when the Soviets defeated Hitler; and when Israel was founded— these movements were "front row center" and, I submit, very important opinion shapers within the American Jewish community. Many important figures were supporters of Ambijan and the ICOR, including the scientist Albert Einstein; explorer Vilhjalmur Stefansson; the artists Marc Chagall and Molly Picon; U.S. vice-president Henry Wallace; a number of U.S. senators, including Alben Barkley, Warren Magnusson and Claude Pepper, as well as many governors, mayors and other officials; and Soviet diplomat Andrei Gromyko.

This is why I have tried to meticulously document the minutiae of their political lives as well as more important events. If much of this book seems a compendium of names, places, and dates, then that is intentional. I have not been able to live with or among the people about whom I write, as those who were involved in the Jewish Communist movement are by now almost all deceased or, if living, well into their 90s, with their political activities long behind them. Therefore, I have had to depend on their written accounts rather than, except in a few cases, oral interviews or participant observation. Out of necessity, then, my methodology has involved a form of "historical immersion." I have read their newspapers cover to cover, including not only the news stories, editorials, belles lettres, poems, and organizational notices, but also the (fascinating) advertisements, the brief notices, and other ephemera, in order to "inhabit" their world and to locate meaning within the context of their own political culture. To quote Clifford Geertz, I have sought "to converse with them." My descriptions have been cast "in terms of the constructions…they use[d] to define what happened to them."[3]

This book offers no new theoretical constructs or analyses; rather, it documents, through the use of previously unread material, a narrative history of these movements. This is their story, told largely through their eyes (and words). My main objective has been to describe their work and to present this archival research to the scholarly community. It is a narrowly-focused monograph: it looks at the organizational and institutional history of two groups that were "limbs" on a bigger "body" of Communist front groups. The larger history of the important fronts, and also of the Communist Party itself, has been—and continues to be—written, So there is no need to repeat it here.

I should also at this point emphasize that this is not a history of the Birobidzhan project itself. There are numerous works, in English, French, Hebrew, Russian and Yiddish, about the history of the Jewish Autonomous Region (JAR) within the USSR, and I therefore saw little need to replicate these. I point readers to a few of them in my endnotes and bibliography.

Nor is this a book describing the debate in the larger Jewish community of America regarding the Birobidzhan project, including the debates over Yiddish vs. Hebrew. I address these issues mainly from the viewpoint of the ICOR and Ambijan. Many works have dealt with these debates from "the other side." There is a wealth of material on non- and anti-Communist reaction to, and dismissal of, Birobidzhan, among the relief agencies, Judaic organizations, the various Zionist movements, and the social democrats centered around the Jewish Labor Committee and the *Forverts*; they have all already had their say in many articles and books, and rightly so! My purpose is not to revisit these polemics, but to present, for the historical record, the pro-Communist views.

During the quarter century in which Birobidzhan figured prominently in American Jewish Communist propaganda, the image of the Jewish Autonomous Region shifted over time: from its role as a Jewish national unit and counter to Zionism in the 1920s to a refuge from Nazism in the 1930s; from a vehicle by which to secure financial support for the Soviet struggle in World War II to a vision of the JAR as part of a post-war Jewish revival after the destruction of the Holocaust; and finally, as a partner with the new Jewish State of Israel in creating an independent Jewish future after 1948. After 1951, with the demise of Ambijan, it largely disappeared from view, even among most Jewish Communists.

As my bibliography indicates, a number of books and articles have been written about the American Jewish Communists and their support organizations by scholars such as Paul Buhle, Gennady Estraikh, Roger Keeran, Harvey Klehr, Arthur Liebman, Tony Michaels, Paul Mishler, Arthur Sabin, David Shuldiner, Daniel Soyer, Zosa Szajkowski, and Thomas Walker; and by former activists such as Melech Epstein, Kalmen Marmor, Gina Medem, and Paul Novick. There are also works, in English, about Birobidzhan itself, by, among others, Chimen Abramsky, Zvi Gitelman, Allan Laine Kagedan and Robert Weinberg. But no academic treatments of Ambijan and the post-1935 ICOR exist,[3] despite the significant role they played in the American Jewish left subculture for almost two decades. My research aims to rectify this major gap in our knowledge of the Jewish left, and in this book I examine the history and political activities between

1934 and 1951 of these two left-of-center movements.

The introduction offers an overview of the groups that constituted, often in an informal rather than "official" manner, the American Jewish Communist movement during this period, including the ICOR. Chapter one introduces the American Committee for the Settlement of Jews in Birobidjan (Ambijan) and charts early attempts to facilitate migration to the Jewish Autonomous Region, while chapter two discusses the attempt by both the ICOR and Ambijan to create a "people's delegation" to visit Birobidzhan in order to facilitate immigration. Chapters three through five provide a detailed examination of the work to help Soviet Jewry during World War II, including the scheme to settle Jewish Holocaust orphans in Birobidzhan after 1945 and the amalgamation of the ICOR and Ambijan into one organization. The next two chapters examine the postwar successes of Ambijan, and its work between 1946 and 1950 on behalf of the struggle to create the new state of Israel as well as its continuing support of the JAR. Chapter eight examines the demise of Ambijan due to rising anti-Soviet sentiment during the McCarthy era, even though, as chapter nine explains, "islands of pro-Soviet resistance" remained. The conclusion describes the domestic and international context in which the organization was terminated in 1951.

Unfortunately, perhaps due to their fears of political persecution during the McCarthy era, very few members of either Ambijan or the ICOR have left us personal letters or other ephemera of their daily lives. I have examined the written material bequeathed to us (much of it in Yiddish) by the two organizations in their own and sister American publications, including journals, books, magazines and pamphlet literature; especially important were the magazines *Ambijan Bulletin, ICOR, Jewish Life, Nailebn-New Life* and *Soviet Russia Today.*

I have also made use of the extensive Federal Bureau of Investigation (FBI) files on Ambijan and the ICOR, obtained under the Freedom of Information/Privacy Acts. These in a sense provide a "counterpoint" to the self-image held by the activists and ordinary members of the movement; they provide us with a narrative of the activities of Ambijan and the ICOR, from the point of view of the increasingly suspicious, dominant American culture. The FBI files also include information that the Ambijan and ICOR activists would have preferred to conceal not only from the larger public, but from their own membership.

My research has entailed the collection of primary and secondary data in various public libraries and archives. The YIVO Institute for Jewish Research in New York is the most important repository of materials produced by the American Jewish pro-Communist left. YIVO has five archival boxes of papers concerning Ambijan and the ICOR, including the correspondence, reports, manuscripts, and press clippings of Abraham Jenofsky, the last executive secretary of the two U.S. organizations. It also houses several thousand letters, diaries, reports, manuscripts, and press clippings, of Kalmen Marmor, the prominent Jewish Communist active in the ICOR and the Ambijan Committee. Included in this collection is Marmor's personal correspondence with Reuben Brainin and Khaim Zhitlovsky, among others, who were active in the pro-Birobidzhan movement.

The Tamiment Institute at the Elmer Holmes Bobst Library, New York University, an important repository of materials about the labor movement, holds materials relating to the International Workers Order and other radical and socialist organizations. The Reference Center for Marxist Studies in New York contains a very substantial literature about the CPUSA; it has on file Communist Party periodicals such as the *Communist, New Masses* and *Political Affairs*. The Ben-Zion Goldberg (Benjamin Waife) papers are housed at the Schottenstein-Jesselson Library of the Herbert D. Katz Center for Advanced Judaic Studies at the University of Pennsylvania in Philadelphia and contain materials relating to the ICOR and Ambijan, as well as other people and groups involved with the support of the Birobidzhan project, including the American Committee of Jewish Writers, Artists and Scientists. Papers relating to the work of the ICOR and Ambijan in Chicago, including correspondence and papers of Harry D. Koenig and Ethel Osri, are housed at the Chicago Jewish Archives, Asher Library, Spertus Institute of Jewish Studies, Chicago. The Jewish Division of the New York Public Library has a substantial collection of books and periodicals about the American Jewish Communist movement, as well as copies of the *Ambijan Bulletin*. The Russian Relief Collection in the Yeshiva University Archives, New York, contains material on the ICOR and Ambijan movements. The Vilhjalmur Stefansson Collection, at the Baker Memorial Library, Dartmouth College, Hanover, NH, contains a wealth of materials on the Arctic explorer, who was involved with many pro-Communist organizations, including Ambijan. The Jewish Historical Society of the Upper Midwest in Minneapolis has files on the local ICOR and Ambijan organizations. The Jewish Public Library Archives in Montreal include a large collection of materials concerning the noted Hebraist Reuben Brainin, later active in many pro-Soviet organizations. The United States National Archives in College Park, MD, is the repository for FBI surveillance files on Ambijan and the ICOR. I have also made use of materials at the Butler Library, Columbia University, New York; Goldfarb Library, Brandeis University, Waltham, MA; Jewish Theological Seminary Library, New York; and the University of Illinois Library, Urbana-Champaign, IL.

I would like to thank the staffs of all the archives and libraries mentioned above. As well, I thank the Chicago Jewish Archives, Schottenstein-Jesselson Library, Yeshiva University Archives, and YIVO Institute for allowing me to reprint illustrations. (All other pictures are in my personal possession.) As well, the staff of the Interlibrary Loan divisions of the MacKimmie Library, University of Calgary, Calgary, Alberta, and the Robertson Library, University of Prince Edward Island, Charlottetown, PEI, provided prompt and courteous service in obtaining journal articles and books for me as needed.

I also wish to acknowledge the help and encouragement of colleagues and friends, past and present, including Irving Abella, Michael Birkner, Paul Boudreau, Robert Brym, Gennady Estraikh, Irene Gammel, Jonathan Goldstein, Irving Hexham, Matthew Hoffman, Joshua Rubenstein, Shloime Perel, Howard Segal, David Shneer, Gerald Tulchinsky, Robert Weinberg, and David Weinberg. Finally, I thank my wife Patricia Thomas Srebrnik, whose unstinting support and painstaking editorial work has enabled me to complete this book. Any errors in fact or interpretation are, of course, my own.

This study has benefitted from grants from the Social Sciences and Humanities Research Council of Canada and from the University of Prince Edward Island, and I thank them for their support.

All translations from the Yiddish, unless otherwise indicated, are my own. A note regarding orthography: For the transliteration of article and book titles and names into the Roman alphabet, I have used a modified version of the standard YIVO-based system, except in the case of figures whose names, rendered into Roman characters, often appeared in English-language publications; there I have kept to the familiar spelling, for example, Kuntz, not Kunts. I have also used the conventional spelling of place names, even when transliterating from the Yiddish – so, for example, Bronx, not Bronks, Chicago, not Shikago, Cleveland, not Klivland, Philadelphia, not Filadelfia, Los Angeles, not Los Andzheles. If a journal or newspaper was bilingual and had a proper name in both English and Yiddish, I have used the English spelling – so, for example, *Nailebn-New Life*, not *Naylebn–New Life*. Finally, in the interests of consistency, I have used the acronym ICOR or Icor, this being the organization's own Roman alphabet transliteration, even when I was quoting from Yiddish sources, though in those instances it should rightly read IKOR or Ikor. Finally, a note regarding the spelling of the word Birobidzhan. The modern transliteration from the Russian for the Jewish Autonomous Region is Birobidzhan or Biro-bidzhan; when transliterating from Yiddish, I also spell it Birobidzhan or Biro-bidzhan. But during the 1920s to the 1950s it was usually written in English characters as Birobidjan or Biro-bidjan, and I have retained that spelling when quoting directly from English-language sources of the time.

This study is a cautionary tale, for it illustrates how otherwise intelligent, critical people were misled by an unscrupulous, indeed murderous, regime, and placed their hopes for a better world in the hands of people who turned out to be political criminals, even sociopaths. It is the story of people who accepted as truth the lies and fantasies spun by cynical propagandists, and who put their trust in those who were building not socialism but gulags. Of course, I speak with the advantage of hindsight: while I have tried to sympathize with the members of Ambijan and the ICOR, as I re-construct their stories, I know in advance the wrong roads they will follow, the terrible mistakes they will make, the Soviet lies and deceptions they will take at face value and swallow whole.

Even so, and also taking into account that they were thousands of miles removed from the utopia in which they had invested all their political hopes, I still cannot understand how so many well-educated people, well aware of the shortcomings of their own society, could so completely take leave of their critical faculties and suspend all disbelief when it came to judging the Soviet Union. True, as the book illustrates, there were the occasional skeptics who voiced their concerns, and no doubt others silently quit the movement. When reading their internal documents, one finds more questioning and even dissention than they acknowledged in their "public" postures. Most, however, were still won over by the propaganda emanating from the USSR and by the reassurances of the Ambijan and ICOR leadership. After all, since the Soviet Union was a closed society and there was so little information about Birobidzhan, they basically had to take what they were told on faith. If I were less sympathetic, I might describe theirs as a form of "willful blindness," a term used by lawyers to describe a situation where people intentionally allow themselves to be deceived or deluded.[4]

This book is dedicated to my late parents Edward and Esther and to those of their families, from Częstochowa, Poland, who died *oyf kidush hashem* in the Holocaust. I was born in that city soon after the war and I too am a *tshenstokhover yid*.

Endnotes

1 *Jerusalem on the Amur: Birobidzhan and the Canadian Jewish Communist Movement, 1924-1951* (Montreal: McGill-Queen's University Press, 2008).
2 Clifford Geertz, "Thick Description: Towards an Interpretive Theory of Culture," in Clifford Geertz, ed. *The Interpretation of Cultures: Selected Essays* (New York: Basic Books 1973), 13, 15, 18.
3 As the ICOR was a unified North American movement until 1935, the first three chapters of my book *Jerusalem on the Amur* describes its work in the United States as well as in Canada during its first decade.
4 As Gennady Estraikh has noted, "American Communist journalists took everything emanating from Moscow at face value and repeated it to their super-credulous Yiddish readers." Gennady Estraikh, *Yiddish in the Cold War (Studies in Yiddish 7)* (London: Legenda, 2008), 17.

INTRODUCTION:
AMERICAN JEWS, COMMUNISM, THE ICOR AND BIROBIDZHAN

For much of the 20th century, Jews comprised a disproportionate component of the American left. Before World War I, the Jewish Socialist Federation, claiming 14,000 members, was a significant segment of the Socialist Party. Jews by the tens of thousands worked in the "needle trades" and belonged to trade unions such as the Amalgamated Clothing Workers of America (ACWA), the International Ladies' Garment Workers' Union (ILGWU),[1] and the International Fur and Leather Workers' Union.[2] They also belonged to fraternal orders such as the Workmen's Circle or *Arbeter Ring*; and they provided the readership for mass-circulation socialist newspapers such as the *Forverts*, edited by Abe Cahan. They gave the Socialist Party their votes as well as their intellectual support: in 1914, 1916 and 1920, they elected Meyer London to Congress from New York's 12th Congressional district on Manhattan's Lower East Side. As a major portion of the city's electorate, in 1917 they provided the strong backing that enabled Morris Hillquit to capture 22 per cent of the vote in New York City's mayoralty campaign, and they also helped elect for the Socialists seven aldermen, ten state assemblymen, and a municipal judge. A constant influx from tsarist Russia of Bundists (the Jewish social democratic party in the Russian Empire), socialist revolutionaries, and other radicals, particularly after the 1905 Russian Revolution, constantly fed the socialist springs in New York and elsewhere. Jewish left-wingers were usually more internationally minded in their concerns than were native-born American socialists.

The Russian Revolution of 1917 and the formation of the Communist, or Third, International (Comintern) two years later resulted in a split within the Socialist Party (SP). A number of radical groups quit or were expelled, and after a confusing period of organizational and ideological competition, including the formation of two pro-Soviet parties, the Communist Labor Party and the Communist Party of America, they had by 1922 united into a Communist Party, which had received the imprimatur of the Comintern. Most of the members of the SP's Jewish Socialist Federation bolted to join the new party; as a result, during the 1920s, some established Jewish socialists, including Alexander Bittelman, Shakhno Epstein, Louis Hendin, Paul (Pesach) Novick, Moissaye Olgin, J.B. Salutsky (later J.B.S. Hardman), Alexander Trachtenberg, and many others, began their careers as Jewish Communists. For some, this would be a lifelong vocation. Bittelman and Epstein began publishing a weekly, the *Emes*, for the new Jewish section of the party; Bittelman also edited the journal *Der Kamf*. A daily newspaper, the *Frayhayt*, was created in 1922. It became the *Morgn Frayhayt* in 1929.[3] The paper's founding editor was Moissaye Olgin, born near Kiev in 1878. He had become a Bundist and had studied at the University of Kiev and the University of Heidelberg before arriving in the U.S. in 1915; he obtained a PhD at Columbia University three years later. In 1920-21 Olgin visited the new Soviet Russia. His experience there did much to convert him from a left Socialist to an orthodox Communist.[4] He was an early organizer in the Jewish section of the party, and a long-time member of the National Committee of the CPUSA. Olgin was also for many years the American correspondent for *Pravda*, the Soviet Communist Party daily.

Described by its founders as a "Communistic fighting newspaper" that was "upheld by the...Jewish revolutionary workers," the *Frayhayt* was pledged to support revolutionary unionism, proletarian culture, the unity of black and white workers, and, of course, defense of the USSR, especially in its attempts to renew Jewish life along productive lines. It opposed, on the other hand, "sweat shops and union misleaders," "socialist renegades," and "fascistic Zionism."[5] The *Frayhayt* counted 22,000 readers by 1925, making it the largest of the nine daily Communist papers then published in the United States; it had more readers than did the English-language *Daily Worker*, which it predated by two years.[6] Finally, the Jewish Communists founded an "earnest theoretical journal for Marxism-Leninism," *Der Hamer*, under the editorship of Leon Talmy (original name, Leyzer Talmonovitsky) in 1926.[7]

The Jewish community of the time, mainly proletarianized newcomers from eastern Europe, provided a framework of experience upon which this radical minority "could construct a role of great importance"; as Paul Buhle has recounted, "a Messianic radicalism among the immigrant Jewish workers...allowed Communism to appeal to some of the deepest traditions of the community."[8] The world of Jewish socialism was a secular one and its discourse radical; even so, its roots lay deep within the Jewish tradition, which, although far from monolithic, has always aspired to improve the world. Though there was much in Jewish life that the Jewish Socialists opposed, from Orthodox Judaism to Zionism, such people did not turn to Communism because they were alienated from the Jewish world, but rather because "of their urge to act for the sake of an improved society and to better the condition of the Jewish workers."[9] This "messianic" aspect of their ideology would also revise the old Judaic ideal of a return to the "Land of Israel," by substituting Soviet Russia for Israel as the new "promised land." Such people "were imbued with a semi-religious attitude to the USSR," which had become for them "a dreamland of freedom and equality."[10]

For some Jews growing up in this period, notes Ezra Mendelsohn,

"Jewishness was synonymous with political radicalism," an integral part of their culture. The economic depression also resulted in a process of radicalisation for many Jews, as socio-economic mobility was blocked and many became proletarianized. "The 1930s were the heyday of the formation of the radical Jewish cosmopolitan (or universalist) intelligentsia," a group not very interested in specifically Jewish politics and culture. They wanted to create a society "where Jew and gentile could meet as absolute equals, sharing the same ideals of brotherhood and universalism."[11] Many Jews on the left had internalized the derogatory view of traditional Jewish culture as outmoded; Jews, they asserted, had to be "liberated" from their ghettoized existence and become an economically "healthy" and "productive" people.

The Communist movement attracted urban, professional and intellectual elements, and Jews were heavily represented in all three categories, so, as Melech Epstein has noted, "a unique environment favored its spread" among Jews.[12] At its zenith, the CP's influence on significant elements within American Jewry "exceeded anything experienced in other ethnic communities," Henry Feingold has asserted.[13] It was estimated that Jews constituted some 15 per cent of the newly-created CPUSA; in some cities, a majority of CPUSA members were Jewish.[14] By 1931, at least 19 per cent of the party was Jewish, and its largest district, New York, was overwhelmingly Jewish in membership. An even higher proportion of Communist officials were Jews: between 1921 and 1938, "no Central Committee had fewer than a one-third Jewish membership; most were about 40 per cent Jewish."[15] According to some estimates, during the 1930s and 1940s, "about half of the Party's membership was composed of Jews, many with an East European socialist background."[16]

Jack Stachel, the party's national organizational secretary, who was himself Jewish, told the sixth convention of the CPUSA in 1929 that in Los Angeles "practically 90 per cent" of the membership was Jewish.[17] "From its formation in 1919 and throughout much of the 1920s, the Communist Party of Los Angeles was based among the Jews of Boyle Heights"; they worked in the needle trades and as store owners. Many Jewish Communists were later active in the communities of Echo Park and Silver Lake.[18] In Philadelphia, the Communist movement drew the bulk of its members from Jewish immigrants or their children, who lived in "left-wing strongholds" such as West Philadelphia and Strawberry Mansion. According to Paul Lyons, in the 1930s, 75 per cent of the membership of District Three of the CPUSA, which included Philadelphia, was Jewish; as one former leader stated, "The Jews dominated the district."[19] In Chicago, a city of more than 3,376,438 in 1930, less than ten percent of the population was Jewish. Of these approximately 300,000 Jews, about 135,000, or 45 per cent, were foreign-born; they constituted a mere 4 per cent of the entire Chicago population. Yet in 1931, 22 per cent of the 1,936 members of the Chicago CP were foreign-born Jews. On Chicago's West Side, with its heart along Roosevelt Road, Jews had developed "a rich leftist enclave complete with newspapers, theaters, and restaurants." There were 13 Jewish International Workers Order branches in the city.[20]

Communists soon realized that "front groups"—which were less centralized and hierarchical than the CPUSA—were an effective means of attracting supporters for their causes; some who joined the front groups would eventually become full-fledged members of the Party.[21] As the National Groups Commission of the CPUSA itself stated in October 1946, "Auxiliary mass organizations of a fraternal, cultural, or relief character, organizations called into existence to meet special needs and problems of a nationality group, can function most effectively and properly when organized as nationality groups in character, composition, and leadership...In such organizations the political and organizational unity of the American working class can be achieved and is being achieved by the work of its vanguard, the Communists."[22] So, although "nominally independent," they were "organized around single-issue or special-interest concerns, in which the Communists exercised effective organizational control."[23] Their programs were often framed with help from CP leaders. "Party membership was not openly discussed, and influence was exerted through the established Communist procedure of a clandestine fraction, which met secretly to plan strategy."[24] Typically, the president was a well-regarded public figure not openly identified as a Communist; indeed, sympathetic liberal "fellow-travelers" were preferred to doctrinaire socialists or social democrats, who were more likely to voice ideological concerns regarding events in Soviet Russia. However, the secretary, paid functionaries and most members of the executive committee, who ran the group's day-to-day activities, were CP members. And the party members "always had the power to set limits in the fronts."[25] Other criteria by which front organizations could be identified included the following: if their meetings were addressed by, and their publications were open to contributions from Communists; if they cooperated with the CP in its campaigns and activities; if their publications advertised CP activities or those of other front groups; if funds were collected on behalf of the CP; if they received favorable publicity in the Communist press; and if they were uncompromisingly loyal to the Soviet Union and the CP line.

As Michael Denning has noted, the popular front of the 1930s was a radical social movement uniting industrial unionists, Communists, independent socialists, community activists and anti-fascists. The front organizations were "not mere façades," he has argued, but were rather "built on the characteristic form of American radical politics, the voluntary reform association." They were sustained by "a movement culture, a world of working-class education, recreation, and entertainment built by the Communist Party, the new industrial unions, and the fraternal benefit lodges, particularly those of the International Workers Order (IWO)."[26]

In fact, the IWO, "the largest, most successful left-wing organization in modern American history,"[27] would become "the most conspicuously successful Communist front in the United States."[28] It "was led by extremely capable, articulate, and politically committed men and women." Max Bedacht, who was a onetime secretary of the CPUSA, an editor of the *Communist*, and a member of the party's Politburo, became the IWO's general secretary after 1933; William Weiner, a financial secretary and treasurer of the CP, became its president in 1931.[29] As Bedacht himself reminded the party's extraordinary national conference in July 1933, "Without these mass organizations the Party could not have leadership over these masses in permanent organizational form."[30]

By the early 1920s in the Jewish community "one could observe a new, well-organized Communist wing with its own Yiddish journals."[31] In his study of the American Jewish left, Arthur Liebman has referred to the various Jewish fraternal orders, newspapers, and unions grouped around the Communist Party as having constituted a distinct "Jewish Left subculture." He suggests that "the social walls around the Yiddish-speaking Communist party members...were thicker than those of the English-speaking members. Their immersion in Yiddish culture effectively cut them off from American life [and] from non-party members in the Yiddish-speaking community."[32] They had undertaken a radical reformulation of their Jewish identification, and their "culture-within-a-culture" provided a "lifelong set of continuities" for those who chose to remain within it, "insulating them from the vagaries of a world in flux," according to David Shuldiner.[33] Robert Snyder remarks that,"[F]using radical and ethnic culture, they created an alternative to mainstream culture that reinforced their political commitments."[34] As Robbie Lieberman has observed, "One did not have to be a Communist [Party member] in order to adopt or maintain a left-sectarian view in the early 1930s nor to experience one's connection to the Left as a defining aspect of life." The Jewish Communist movement provided the symbols, rituals, ideas, and commitments around which to organize one's life.[35]

In the Jewish Communist left subculture, there was an entire panoply of front groups, often with specialized functions, many operating primarily in Yiddish. These groups were active among the highly intellectual, urban, and still largely proletarian or petty-bourgeois Jewish population. They were particularly effective in appealing to immigrants who were traumatized by the rough-and-tumble world of North American capitalism, and who may have retained revolutionary traditions from their east European homeland. The front groups regarded the Bolshevik revolution and the state thus created as the first steps toward the eventual realization of socialism worldwide, and thus of Jewish liberation from persecution. They judged the Soviet Union from the vantage point of Jewish politics, and supported it because they believed that the elimination of anti-Semitism was an inexorable consequence of socialist construction.

According to the CPUSA's internal organ, the *Party Organizer*, in 1930 there were 7,500 members in Yiddish-language organizations under party control, and another 6,100 in organizations "influenced" by the party.[36] The most important of these groups was the Jewish Section of the IWO (in Yiddish, the *Internatsyonaler Arbeter Ordn*).

It had its origins in the Jewish People's Fraternal Order (JPFO) or *Der Yidishn Fraternaln Folks-ordn*, founded in October 1929 when 15,000 dissidents in 108 Workmen's Circle branches, plus minorities from another 22 branches, split off from the national organization. This splinter group denounced the Circle, which, they stated, had been originally "created under the flying banner of the class-struggle," but had now been transformed into "an organization serving the interests of capitalism."[37] A year later the JPFO cooperated with other CP-dominated ethnic fraternal benefit societies in forming the IWO. The JPFO, which retained its separate identity while functioning as the Jewish Section of the IWO, published a Yiddish monthly, *Der Funk*, and by 1935 operated over 148 schools, including five high schools, which enroled 8,000 students. Kalmen Marmor, director of their school system, announced at a convention held in Philadelphia in May 1930 that the schools would raise children "in the spirit of the class struggle, in Yiddish," by teaching them to support strikes, picket lines, and mass demonstrations.[38] By 1938, the Jewish section of the IWO counted 36,000 members in 260 branches--about one-third the total IWO membership. As a fraternal society that also provided affordable health insurance and medical and death benefits for its members, the IWO Jewish section "provided an important vehicle for recruitment."[39] Even in December 1940, when the fortunes of Jewish Communists were at their lowest during the period of the Hitler-Stalin Pact, the JPFO still had 32,548 members, according to a CPUSA report to the Comintern.[40]

Another group of great importance was the Jewish Workers Society, which operated many workers' clubs. In 1924 it began construction of a $4 million "red city" of 750 co-operative apartments, the United Workers Cooperative Colony, or the "Coops," on Allerton Avenue in the East Bronx, New York. Wrote one woman who grew up there: "A couple of thousand people, including hundreds of children of all ages, lived there as one great family."[41] In this self-contained world, with its own IWO schools, libraries, a youth center with 15 clubs, cultural activities and stores, "the most important day of the year was neither Yom Kippur [the Jewish Day of Atonement] nor Christmas but May Day."[42] This area, as Beth Wenger has observed, was "a haven for political radicalism," which so permeated the neighborhood that "it became part of the rhythm of daily life."[43]

Cultural and intellectual organizations proliferated in the Jewish Communist movement. There was the Artef *(Arbeter Teater Farband)*, the Workers Theater Group founded in 1925, with Kalmen Marmor as chair. There was the Proletpen *(Proletarisher Shrayber Fareyn)*, the left-wing writers' group headed in the U.S. by Shloime Almazov, Paul Yuditz, and A. (Isaac) Raboy, that had split from the I.L. Peretz Writers Club in 1929 and became the American branch of the Moscow-based International Union of Revolutionary Writers. And there was the Jewish Workers' University, founded in 1926 to prepare an intelligentsia for the workers movement and train teachers for the school system of the Jewish Section of the IWO. Israel Ber Bailin headed the Workers' University until 1933, by which time it comprised 26 professors and 625 students. Bailin then became editor of *Der Hamer*, taking over from Talmy when the latter left for the Soviet Union, and remaining as editor until that journal was discontinued in 1939.[44] Choruses were another "of the principal cultural activities of Jewish radicals in the United States": the Communists ran many choruses, including the *Frayhayt Gezang Fareyn*, affiliated with the newspaper; one of its founders and leaders, Jacob Schaefer, was a central figure in the Composers Collective of the Workers Music League.[45] As well, the Jewish Communists operated camps, including Kinderland, Lakeland, *Nitgedeiget*, and Unity, all near New York City.[46] Jewish Communism was indeed a "cradle to the grave" movement.

A national conference of the language bureaus of the CPUSA, meeting in Pittsburgh on September 22-23, 1936, recognized the need to build popular front movements among ethnic groups. "All our language Bureaus are orientating on penetrating broader masses, on breaking their isolation, on changing their methods of work and doing away with the remnants of sectarianism." The party's Jewish Bureau was mentioned by name as one that had learned this lesson.[47] In August 1937, the Jewish Bureau of the New York State CP began publishing an English-language monthly, *Jewish Life*, because, wrote the Communist Party theoretician V.J. Jerome, the party now realized that Jews and other minorities were "national groups" and not merely "immigrants speaking foreign tongues." The CP, declared Jerome, "furnishes a program for struggle for the rights of the Jews...*as a national group*."[48] In 1938, the newly-founded American section of the YKUF *(Yidisher Kultur Farband)* or World Jewish Cultural Union, founded in Paris in 1937, began publishing a serious literary journal, *Yidishe Kultur*. Jewish Communists went to great lengths to portray themselves as proud, ethnically-conscious Jews: in December 1938, the Jewish Bureau convened a national conference that formally acknowledged the importance of Jewish culture, and in the summer of 1939 its secretary, Joseph Sultan, declared that Jewish culture was closely connected to the interests of the Jewish people.[49] Communism would provide the framework for defining a class-centered form of ethnic identity.[50]

In the 1930s, with the growth of fascism in Europe, "tens of thousands of Jews throughout the country were drawn to Communist-front organizations, particularly to the various 'anti-Fascist' groups."[51] As Ellen Schrecker put it, "the Party's single most effective recruiter, by far, was Adolf Hitler."[52] The struggle against Nazism became for many Jews "the emotional and moral center of radicalization," and their anti-fascist ideological inclinations led many towards eventual institutional affiliation with the CP.[53] Public opinion polls indicated that "during the 1930s, American Jews had a more favorable opinion of the Soviet Union than did the general population," and, "when pushed to choose Communism or fascism, American Jews overwhelmingly leaned toward the former, not necessarily from real conviction, but rather in a clear rejection of the intense anti-Semitism of Nazi Germany."[54]

The increased strength of fascist regimes in Europe, where Jews were economically trapped and physically threatened, made the USSR appear ever more as the only beacon of hope. The new Labor Zionist periodical *Jewish Frontier*, in its December 1934 editorial statement, observed that, with the rise to power of Hitler, "many modern Jews find themselves turning hopefully to Soviet Communism," feeling "a specific sympathy" towards a country engaged in a "vigorous fight for racial and national equality and where every vestige of anti-Semitism is staunchly repressed."[55] James Waterman Wise, son the head of the American Jewish Congress, Rabbi Stephen S. Wise, wrote in the October 29, 1935 issue of the Communist magazine *New Masses* that in the "widening and strengthening of the united front against fascism in every guise and form," American Jews must "write themselves down as Communists."[56]

The CP-dominated Jewish Peoples Committee (JPC), formed in 1936, engaged in various protests on behalf of German and Polish Jews and claimed that the more moderate Jewish organizations were too fearful of domestic anti-Semites to engage in bold action. At its national conference held in Washington on November 20, 1937, and attended by 1,000 delegates, it passed a resolution appealing to the U.S. government "to intercede in behalf of the down-trodden Polish Jews."[57] Its "national unity" congress in March 1938 in New York was attended by 2,000 people. New York Congressmen Vito Marcantonio and William I. Sirovich were among the speakers. William Weiner of the IWO was elected president of the JPC and the Hebraist Reuben Brainin its honorary president. The delegates called on the U.S. Congress to outlaw anti-Semitism and other forms of discrimination.[58] The ICOR and Ambijan would both become bright stars in this American Jewish Communist galaxy, especially once the Soviets decided on the far eastern region of Birobidzhan as a site to provide Jews with their own political entity, and later to enable a Zionist-style "ingathering of the exiles" by the rescue of Jews threatened by fascist regimes in Europe.

The Birobidzhan project is probably best understood in the context of that form of Jewish nationalism known as territorialism, a doctrine that contended that Jewish self-determination could be realized in places other than the Land of Israel. From the time of the great upheavals in Russia's Pale of Settlement in the late 19th century, these proposals addressed the problems of Jewish emancipation, anti-Semitism, lack of civil rights, and cultural exclusion. The solutions included emigration to and the settlement of Jews in rural, agricultural areas in parts of Angola, Argentina, Australia, Brazil, British Guiana, Canada, Cyprus, Ecuador, Surinam, and elsewhere, and even the creation of a Jewish polity in Uganda. Many of these projects were promoted by the International Territorialist Organization, founded by Israel Zangwill in 1905 and disbanded in 1925; and the Freeland League for Jewish Colonization, founded in London in 1935.[59]

Socialist territorialists sought safe havens not just to escape oppression in Europe, but also as a means towards the economic "rehabilitation" of the Jewish people, who, in their view, needed to "normalize" through the pursuit of agricultural and industrial labor rather than remain "non-productive" middlemen and traders. So the Jewish settlement in Birobidzhan would arouse widespread interest among those who sought in Jewish territorialism and colonization a solution to statelessness, including many who were otherwise not enamoured of the Soviet state or Communist ideology. Support for the enterprise was sought, and received, from a wide array of Jewish groups, especially those without strong links to Zionism and the Jewish enterprise in Palestine. Bourgeois liberals, secular Yiddishists, non-Zionists and advocates of Jewish territorialism, along with Communists, responded to Soviet requests for aid and "raised money, held meetings, and issued publications."[60]

Vladimir Lenin had acknowledged Jews as a legitimate nationality, so in the years following the Bolshevik Revolution, the Soviet regime decided to set aside specific territory for those Jews who wished to build a collective Jewish socialist life. The People's Commissariat of Nationalities, as well as the *Yevsektsiya*, the Jewish Section of the Communist Party of the Soviet Union (CPSU), had been established to deal with such issues.[61] Mikhail Kalinin, chair of the Central Executive Committee of the Supreme Soviet of the Soviet Union from 1919 to 1946, was convinced that Jews should enjoy a measure of territorial concentration somewhere in the Soviet Union, in order to develop as a full-fledged nationality, and two agencies were created to advance this cause. The Committee for the Settlement of Jewish Toilers on the Land (KOMZET in Russian, KOMERD in Yiddish), a government body formed on August 20, 1924, was attached to the Presidium of the Soviet of Nationalities, and chaired by Peter G. Smidovitch. The ostensibly non-governmental Association for the Settlement of Jewish Toilers on the Land (OZET in Russian, GEZERD in Yiddish), was created on January 27, 1925, and soon chaired by the noted Jewish Bolshevik Shimen Dimanshtein of the *Yevsektsiya*. The economist Yuri Larin, who was the first chair of the GEZERD, and the Soviet Commissars for Foreign Trade and for Foreign Affairs, Leonid Krassin and Georgi Chicherin, were also involved, a clear indication that the Soviet government attached great importance to an organization that was making an appeal to world Jewry to aid in the "renewal" of Jewish life. Kalinin told the first GEZERD congress in November 1926 that the Jews, like all small peoples "deprived of the opportunities for national evolution," were threatened by assimilation and national erosion: "The Jewish people now faces the great task of preserving its nationality. For this purpose a large segment of the Jewish population must transform itself into a compact farming population, numbering at least several hundred thousand souls." [62]

The Bolsheviks did their utmost to facilitate the social rehabilitation of the Jewish petty bourgeoisie by promoting the formation of artisanal co-operatives, and by encouraging the constitution of Jewish agricultural collectives in areas of heavy Jewish population destined to become autonomous regions. The focus at first was on settlements in Belarus, Ukraine and, especially, the Crimea. With the establishment of the Jewish autonomous national districts—Kalinindorf, Stalindorf, and Nayslatopol in the Ukraine; plus Fraydorf and, later, Larindorf in the Crimea—Jews were settled in agricultural colonies. The campaign to settle déclassé Jews on the soil was widely publicized in the United States and elsewhere.[63] The American Jewish Joint Distribution Committee (the "Joint") and the World Union of Societies for Promotion of Artisanal and Agricultural Work Among the Jews (World ORT Union), already active in helping poor Jews in eastern Europe, provided money for projects in the Soviet settlements. The American Jewish Joint Agricultural Corporation (the "Agro-Joint") had been formed by the Joint in 1924 specifically to aid Jewish farmers in the Soviet Union.[64]

Felix Warburg, chair of the Joint, had been active in the work for Russian Jews in the 1920s, providing a gift of $400,000 at a meeting of the

Joint in Philadelphia on September 12-13, 1925. Dr. Joseph A. Rosen, the Joint's specialist on Jewish colonization in the USSR, told the gathering that "the Jews in Russia, under the present Government, feel safer now than under any other Government."⁶⁵ Rosen had been instrumental in convincing the Joint to form the Agro-Joint, which provided aid to the KOMERD in creating Jewish agricultural colonies in the southern Ukraine and Crimea in the 1920s and 1930s.⁶⁶ In 1927, Warburg visited the Jewish agricultural colonies in the Crimea and Ukraine and wrote to James N. Rosenberg, the chair of the Agro-Joint, that he was "profoundly impressed" by the "rapid progress" being made, thanks to the "splendid understanding and assistance" of the Soviets. Jews had fully vindicated themselves as farmers, he declared, and he became "an enthusiastic believer in the land settlement work."⁶⁷

Rosenberg told the *New York Times* after returning from a visit to the Soviet Union in June 1926 that "These Jews, hitherto herded in ghettos, are eagerly seizing the chance now given them to settle on the soil, the same as other Russians."⁶⁸ The newspaper called him "the American father of the back-to-the-soil movement among the Jews of the former Pale of Settlement." Rosenberg noted that since 1923, more than 100,000 Jews had settled on more than one million acres in the Crimea, Ukraine and White Russia. He said that "The Jewish farmer destroys a thousand blind prejudices against the Jew" and "is an irrefutable demonstration of the Jewish aptitude for a hardy, natural life of productive toil." In any case, with immigration to the U.S. curtailed, the economically "surplus" Jewish population in Russia "has no outlet at present. Only the soil available within Russia can absorb would-be emigrants."⁶⁹

When the writer Elias Tobenkin visited the Soviet Union in 1933, he was especially impressed with the Jewish settlements in the Crimea. "The dream of a Jewish republic on the shores of the Black Sea won the sympathy of Jews the world over. American Jews responded with utmost generosity," he wrote. With the help of the Agro-Joint, the farms were a great success.⁷⁰ William Zukerman, too, touted the success of the Crimean settlements. The Crimea had an excellent geographic location, enjoying good transportation by land or sea. Near major centers of population, it was itself more sparsely populated and, being almost an island, isolated enough to become a compact Jewish-majority territory. Its excellent climate and soil made it "the California of Russia," Zukerman exclaimed. The Crimea also appealed to Jews abroad. Non-Zionist organizations such as the ORT and the Joint "flocked to the banner of Crimea" and answered the GEZERD's appeals for funds. Jewish nationalists, including Folkists, Bundists and territorialists, approved of the idea, while some Zionists saw it as a "second Palestine, a Zion of the Diaspora." A few even dreamt of a "Greater Zionism" embracing both the Crimea and Palestine.⁷¹

But a Jewish Crimea was not to be. Land was in great demand in the European areas of the USSR, and Jews faced hostility from native Tatars and Ukrainians.[72] So the *Yevsektsiya* and GEZERD began to look for larger, more remote areas in which to settle Jews. The plan was to move as many Jews as possible to a parcel of rich, entirely undeveloped land on the easternmost borders of Siberia where, freed from the bourgeois trades of the shtetl, they would form collective farms and transform themselves into a strapping class of Soviet peasantry. Their presence in the east would also help safeguard against a Chinese or Japanese invasion. Some considered the project a shrewd means by which to neutralize Zionist sentiments among the Jewish masses in the old Pale of Settlement. Thousands of Soviet Jews would see an opportunity to escape poverty and anti-Semitic violence and become part a longstanding dream: a Jewish homeland—but in the USSR. The development of a national area for Jews might also help reduce anti-Semitism in the cities in Belarus, European Russia, and Ukraine where Jews competed with other nationalities for scarce resources.

On March 28, 1928, the Soviet government approved the choice of Birobidzhan, a sparsely populated area of 13,895 square miles (36,490 square kilometers) in the Amur-Ussuri district of the Far Eastern Territory of the USSR, as a national Jewish unit, administratively and territorially, for "contiguous Jewish settlements."[73] Jews in Birobidzhan were to have their own administrative, educational and judicial institutions. They would function in their own language, Yiddish. In fact, most Soviet Jews were wary of settling a region thousands of miles from traditional centers of Jewish life, nor did most wish to be territorially segregated; this reminded them too much of "the dreaded Pale."[74] Still, some Jewish settlers began moving to Birobidzhan in late 1928 and various communes were established, including Waldheim, Icor and Birefeld.[75] Furniture, chalk and brick factories were built. By 1932, 25,000 Jews lived in the region. And even before the formation of Ambijan, some pro-Soviet Jews from abroad began to take an interest in immigrating to the new Jewish territory, especially as the worldwide Depression deepened in the early 1930s.[76]

On May 7, 1934, in an effort to make the project more attractive, Moscow declared Birobidzhan a Jewish Autonomous Region (*Oblast*) of the Far Eastern Territory of the Russian Soviet Federative Socialist Republic, with the promise that when Jews numbered at least 100,000, or formed a majority of the total population, Birobidzhan would become a full-fledged Soviet republic, on a par with others such as Armenia or Georgia. Mikhail Kalinin went further, predicting that "In ten years time Biro-Bidzhan will become the most important guardian of the Jewish-national culture and those who cherish a national Jewish culture must link up with Biro-Bidzhan...We already consider Biro-Bidzhan a Jewish national state."[77] In December 1934, a Soviet was convened and elected a government for the region. On August 29, 1936, the presidium of the central executive committee of the USSR adopted a decree which named Birobidzhan the cultural center for all Soviet Jews.[78] Birobidzhan was now a "Jewish National state," an historic confirmation of Stalinist nationality policy and proof that Jews could master agricultural work. The "burning desire for the creation of a homeland," stated the decree, "has found fulfilment." Birobidzhan was becoming a center of national Jewish culture "for the entire Jewish toiling population," including Jews abroad.[79]

These announcements created great excitement among pro-Soviet Jews in the United States. On December 21, 1924, at a conference held in New York City, the ICOR had been founded by a group of Jewish Communists and Left Poale (socialist) Zionists, its symbol a sickle superimposed on a sheaf of wheat. Having learned of Soviet plans to settle Jews on the land, the Jewish section of the CPUSA had decided to provide help "in a truly brotherly manner" by forming a non-partisan broad mass organization. When the newly-created executive committee met on December 29, Jews in thirteen cities were already involved with the ICOR.[80] Its first offices were at 46 Canal Street in Manhattan, then at 112 East 19th Street until 1928, when the organization moved to 799 Broadway. The ICOR's first national secretary was Dr. Elias (Elye) Wattenberg, then a Left Poale Zionist. His successor was Leon Talmy, a member of the CP. Ab. Epstein, a former top-ranking official with the Workmen's Circle who had become a Communist, was the national organizer. The titular head of the organization was Dr. Charles Kuntz. There were similar organizations in Europe, South America, South Africa, and even Palestine.[81]

The ICOR operated as a North American organization, with branches in Canada as well as the United States, until 1935. I have described its American activities from 1924 until 1935 in my book *Jerusalem on the Amur*, a study of the pro-Birobidzhan movement in Canada, so there is no need to repeat that history here.

The ICOR had four main ideological objectives. First and foremost, the organization sought to assist the pioneers of Birobidzhan in building a socialist Jewish republic. Secondly, the ICOR worked to persuade American Jews to sympathize with and defend the Soviet Union, the only country in the world that was well on the way towards eliminating anti-Semitism. The organization's third objective was to help the Jewish masses in various capitalist countries who were being victimized by pogroms, persecution and fascism. Finally, the ICOR sought to make Jews understand that Zionism, too, was a capitalist ideology, and was thus fatally flawed: because Zionism was actually in league with the genuine enemies of the Jewish people, the Jewish settlement in Palestine was unjust and was certain to end in failure. This last theme was particularly emphasized during the very left-wing phase of the world Communist movement between 1928 and 1935; it became less pronounced after 1935, during the anti-Nazi popular front period.[82]

So, while Communists continued to attack Zionism in party publications, the less openly pro-Communist Jewish organizations began to water down their anti-Zionism in the later 1930s, especially following the seventh congress of the Comintern held in Moscow in the summer of 1935. As the 1930s progressed, and the politics of the popular front replaced the extreme left sectarianism of the earlier period, there would be fewer and fewer allusions to the pernicious fascism of the Zionists.

While the Joint and others who had been enthusiastic about the European Jewish farming colonies were wary of the idea of settling Jews in an inhospitable area of the far east, the ICOR threw its support behind the new Birobidzhan project, which, it informed American Jews, was no mere colonisation attempt aimed at "normalising" Jewish life but part of that rapid and radical reshaping of Soviet society proclaimed by CPSU general secretary Joseph Stalin when he announced the first Five-Year Plan in 1928. The ICOR sent an "experts commission" to Birobidzhan in the summer of 1929 to study the economic feasibility of the region. After six weeks travelling throughout the territory by train, boat, wagon, and on horseback, the commission returned with a glowing report.[83] Leon Talmy, now the national secretary of the ICOR, was a member of the expedition and in 1931 published a book about his trip.[84] The ICOR, stressed Charles Kuntz, "fully envisages the socialist reconstruction, the wholesale regeneration of Jewish life in the Soviet Union and the significance of Birobidjan in this respect." As it would be the "workers and peasants that build the new socialist order in the Soviet Union," Kuntz was certain that "the poorer classes" of American Jews would "rally round the ICOR."[85] The ICOR would remain a CP-dominated front group on the immigrant Jewish left until its amalgamation with Ambijan in 1946.

ICOR activities were intertwined with those of other CP movements and groups. In 1933 Marmor, who had already integrated the study of the ICOR into the IWO curriculum, suggested to another Communist, Shloime Almazov, who had replaced Talmy as the national secretary of the ICOR, that children in the IWO school system should develop contacts with Birobidzhan school children.[86] The Allerton Avenue "Coops" had their own ICOR branch: Abraham Olken, the secretary of the New York City ICOR Committee, in November 1932 described the ICOR branch there as a club where every evening people met to drink tea, socialize, meet friends, discuss politics, and play chess or dominoes. Every Monday there was a cultural evening, with lectures on various issues, debates, and readings.[87] Ernie Rymer, in an article on the 50th anniversary of the Coops, noted the existence of the ICOR group, which "worked in the 1920s and 1930s to stimulate interest in the Soviet Union and to help its industrialization."[88] Amy Swerdlow, a "red diaper baby" who also grew up in the co-operatives and whose father was a CPUSA functionary, recalls that at Camp Kinderland, "we made a yearly symbolic pilgrimage to Birobidzhan, which we situated in an isolated part of the camp grounds and where we held a picnic and sang Russian and Yiddish songs."[89] Bert Steinberg, who attended IWO *shules*, also spent summers at Kinderland, where "I learned about Birobidjan…and sang the *'Internationale'*—in Yiddish."[90] The ICOR's journal noted that in the summer of 1928 the camp held two "ICOR days," August 11-12, at which Ab. Epstein, the ICOR national organizer, organized a concert together with the teachers.[91]

A number of noted Jewish personalities were involved with the ICOR. The *maskil* Reuben Brainin, born in Lyadi, Belarus in 1862, and well-known in Hebraist and Zionist circles before World War I, was one mainstay. He was favorably impressed by Soviet plans for Jewish rehabilitation during visits to the USSR in 1926 and 1930. While he continued to support the settlement of Jews in Palestine, he explained, the Soviet experiment was of more significance, since it was destined to solve the problems of three million Jews.[92] Brainin joined the ICOR and praised its leadership, "which undertakes both the ideas and the practical work necessary for building up a Jewish socialist republic."[93] He became a well-known figure at gatherings on behalf of Birobidzhan until his death in November 1939.[94]

Charles Kuntz, also a former *maskil*, was born in 1869 in a village near Kiev, and arrived in the United States in 1895. He had become a scholar and remained aloof from Jewish life until the 1917 revolution awakened in him a socialist and Jewish sensibility.[95] "He looked at the Soviet Union through the lenses of a social utopia," observed Melech Epstein. "The Communist movement knew how to attract men of standing like Kuntz; they were immensely valuable as fronts."[96] Indeed, according to Brainin, it had been his "old friend, Professor Kuntz," who "opened my eyes to the truth" regarding Soviet Russia.[97] Kuntz became active in Ambijan after the ICOR was merged with the former organization in 1946. He died in 1953.[98]

Khaim Zhitlovsky, the proponent of secular Jewish diaspora nationalism and of Jewish nationhood reconstituted on a productive socialist agricultural basis, also provided invaluable help to the ICOR. Born in 1865 in what is now Belarus, Zhitlovsky was involved with Russian populists and Socialist Revolutionaries in Russia. After he made his home in the United States in 1908, he exercised a major influence on the immigrant Jewish community. Zhitlovsky was a *narodnik* (Russian populist) and a champion of the theory that "healthy" nations required a class of agriculturalists. He had been at the first Zionist Congress in Basle in 1897, but had rejected Zionism and become a territorialist. Zhitlovsky, whose relationship with the Jewish Communist left was a lengthy yet problematic one, was attracted by Soviet promises to promote a secular Yiddish culture in the new socialist state because for him, "language and culture were virtually indistinguishable."[99] After 1936, he endorsed the Birobidzhan project, convinced that the Soviets had finally solved the Jewish problem. He joined the ICOR in 1938.[100] Zhitlovsky died while on a cross-country speaking tour of Canada and the United States in May 1943.[101]

Paul Novick, too, was of immeasurable value to the ICOR. Born in Brest-Litovsk in 1891, Novick had come to the United States in 1913. Following the March 1917 revolution in tsarist Russia, he returned to eastern Europe and worked on newspapers in Kiev, Minsk, Vilnius and Warsaw before coming back to New York in 1920. Novick helped found the *Frayhayt* in 1922 and became its editor after Moissaye Olgin's sudden death in November 1939. Novick was an activist in the ICOR. In time he became a member of the executive of the JPFO; of the YKUF; of the American Committee of Jewish Writers, Artists and Scientists; and of Ambijan. He was also a founding editor of *Jewish Life*, predecessor of *Jewish Currents*.[102] When Novick died, aged 97, in 1989, he had outlived the *Frayhayt*, which expired September 11, 1988, by almost a year.[103]

Sholem Aleichem's son-in-law B.Z. Goldberg, a noted Yiddish journalist, also did much work for the ICOR and contributed articles favorable to the Birobidzhan project. Born in 1895 in Olshani, near Vilnius, Goldberg, whose real name was Ben-Zion Waife, came to the U.S. as a boy in 1907. He was the managing editor of *Der Tog*, the prestigious and non-partisan New York Yiddish daily, for 15 years; his daily column dealt with foreign affairs. In 1934, Goldberg spent four months in the Soviet Union, becoming the first foreign journalist to visit Birobidzhan. He remarked, in an interview with the *New York Times*, that the Soviet project was superior to the Zionist enterprise in Palestine, in that Birobidzhan was three times as large as Palestine; had no Arab problem; and would be protected by the Soviet military. Yet, he reassured non-Communist Jews that the Soviet Jewish territory would not be a competitor to Zionism; indeed, he joked, Orthodox Jews and capitalists would not immigrate to Birobidzhan so long as "they can go to Tel Aviv and make money."[104] Goldberg's stature in the Jewish community provided the ICOR, and later Ambijan, with much-needed credibility.[105] He died in Tel Aviv in December 1972 at age 78, a year after *Der Tog-Morgn Zhurnal* ceased publication.[106]

Gina Medem also worked tirelessly on behalf of the ICOR and later Ambijan. According to Israel Ber Bailin, Medem was "an *exceptional* orator," an artist and sculptor of words, "an ambassador of the people to the people."[107] Born in 1886 in Tomashov, Poland, she had joined the Bund and had married its chief theoretician, Vladimir Medem, who died in 1923, a year after they both arrived in New York. Gina Medem became a Communist after visiting the Soviet Union in 1926. As a foreign correspondent for the *Frayhayt*, Medem travelled to the new Jewish region in 1929, 1931, and 1933. After visiting Birobidzhan in 1931, she published "The Taiga Calls" in the March 1932 issue of the *ICOR* journal. She spoke of being "amazed" by the progress she observed after a hiatus of just two years. The Jewish population had increased, and the pulse of life had so changed that "it was almost impossible to recognize it." Forests had been cleared, crops planted, industries developed, communities built. This was a land where the worker was the boss and where the mandate to build socialism lay in the hands of the workers and peasants.[108] When Medem next visited Birobidzhan in 1933, she observed that more Soviet youths had arrived to industrialize the region as part of the five year plan. Medem found it hard to say goodbye to these "warm comrades" and to the beautiful countryside, rivers, and hills of Birobidzhan. She died in Los Angeles in 1977, aged 89.[109]

Endnotes

1 In 1995, the ACWA and ILGWU amalgamated into the Union of Needletrades, Industrial and Textile Employees (UNITE). A merger with the Hotel Employees and Restaurant Employees International Union in 2004 created UNITE HERE.
2 In 1955, as a result of persistent harassment, this Communist-controlled union joined the Amalgamated Meat Cutters and Butcher Workmen union.
3 See Tony Michels, *A Fire in Their Hearts: Yiddish Socialists in New York* (Cambridge, MA: Harvard University Press, 2005), 217-250, for the movement of Jewish socialists into the newly formed Communist movement.
4 Olgin would visit the USSR again in 1924, 1931 and 1934. Daniel Soyer, "Soviet Travel and the Making of an American Jewish Communist: Moissaye Olgin's Trip to Russia in 1920-1921," *American Communist History* 4, 1 (June 2005): 1-20.
5 "Yidishe prese in amerike," *Icor yor-bukh - ICOR Year Book 1932* (New York: National Executive Committee of the ICOR, 1932), 192 [Yiddish section].

INTRODUCTION

6   Zosa Szajkowski, *Jews, Wars, and Communism*. Vol. I: *The Attitude of American Jews to World War I, the Russian Revolutions of 1917, and Communism (1914-1945)* (New York: Ktav, 1972), 415. For more on the *Frayhayt* and other Yiddish-language Communist publications, see Gennady Estraikh, "The Yiddish-Language Communist Press," in Dan Diner and Jonathan Frankel, eds., *Dark Times, Dire Decisions: Jews and Communism* (*Studies in Contemporary Jewry* 20) (New York: Oxford University Press, 2004): 62-82; Gennady Estraikh, *In Harness: Yiddish Writers' Romance with Communism* (Syracuse, NY: Syracuse University Press, 2005); and Gennady Estraikh, *Yiddish in the Cold War*.
7   "Yidishe prese in amerika," *Icor yor-bukh - ICOR Year Book 1932*, 193 [Yiddish section].
8   Paul Buhle, "Jews and American Communism: The Cultural Question," *Radical History Review* 23 (Spring 1980): 11, 14. "Utopian and quasi-messianic visions were...endemic to the East European [Jewish] style of politics," notes Jonathan Frankel in "Modern Jewish Politics East and West (1840-1939): Utopia, Myth, Reality," in Zvi Gitelman, ed., *The Quest for Utopia: Jewish Political Ideas and Institutions Through the Ages* (Armonk, NY: M.E. Sharpe, 1992), 84.
9   Bat-Ami Zucker, "The 'Jewish Bureau': The Organization of American Jewish Communists in the 1930s," in Michael J. Cohen, ed., *Modern History: Bar-Ilan Studies in History III* (Ramat-Gan, Israel: Bar-Ilan University Press, 1991), 146.
10 Gennady Estraikh, *Yiddish in the Cold War*, 4.
11 Ezra Mendelsohn, *On Modern Jewish Politics* (New York: Oxford University Press, 1993), 87-88, 94-96.
12 Melech Epstein, *The Jew and Communism: The Story of Early Communist Victories and Ultimate Defeats in the Jewish Community, U.S.A. 1919-1941* (New York: Trade Union Sponsoring Committee, 1959), ix.
13 Henry L. Feingold, *The Jewish People in America*. Vol. IV: *A Time For Searching: Entering the Mainstream 1920-1945* (Baltimore: Johns Hopkins Press, 1992), 223.
14 Theodore Draper, *American Communism and Soviet Russia: The Formative Period* (1960; New York: Vintage edition, 1986), 191.
15 Harvey Klehr, *The Heyday of American Communism: The Depression Decade* (New York: Basic Books, 1984), 163. Klehr lists 10 Jews among the 27 most important CPUSA leaders between 1921 and 1961. Harvey Klehr, *Communist Cadre: The Social Background of the American Communist Party Elite* (Stanford, CA: Hoover Institution Press, 1978), 110. He also notes that foreign-born Jews were typically more assimilated, educated and middle-class than foreign-born non-Jews, so had the requisite skills to rise to leadership positions in the party. Many also had emerged from the ranks of activists in the garment unions. Harvey Klehr, "Immigrant Leadership in the Communist Party of the United States of America," *Ethnicity* 6 (March 1979): 41-42.
16 Guenter Lewy, *The Cause that Failed: Communism in American Political Life*

(New York: Oxford University Press, 1990), 295. As many as 100,000 Jews may have passed through the party during that period. On 307-308 Lewy provides figures for total CPUSA membership between 1919 and 1988.

17 J[ack] Stachel, "Organization Report to the Sixth Convention of the Communist Party of the U.S.A.," *The Communist* 8, 4 (April 1929): 179-189, and 8, 5 (May 1929): 234-249.

18 Daniel Hurewitz, *Bohemian Los Angeles and the Making of Modern Politics* (Berkeley, CA: University of California Press, 2007), 155. This remained true into the 1950s. See Gerald Horne, *Class Struggle in Hollywood 1930-1950: Moguls, Mobsters, Stars, Reds, and Trade Unionists* (Austin, TX: University of Texas Press, 2001), 63, 88-90; and George J. Sanchez, "'What's Good for Boyle Heights Is Good for the Jews': Creating Multiculturalism on the Eastside during the 1950s," *American Quarterly* 56, 3 (September 2004): 633-661.

19 Paul Lyons, *Philadelphia Communists, 1936-1956* (Philadelphia: Temple University Press, 1982), 21-34, 54, 58, 71-78, 113.

20 Randi Storch, *Red Chicago: American Communism at its Grassroots, 1928-35* (Urbana, IL: University of Illinois Press, 2007), 39-41, 54-55.

21 Judy Kutulas, *The Long War: The Intellectual People's Front and Anti-Stalinism, 1930-1940* (Durham, NC: Duke University Press, 1995), 2, 132.

22 "Communist Work Among the American Jewish Masses," *Political Affairs* 25, 11 (November 1946): 1041.

23 Maurice Isserman, *Which Side Were You On? The American Communist Party During the Second World War* (Middletown, CT: Wesleyan University Press, 1982), 20. Isserman notes that the term "Communist front" became a pejorative phrase often used by their opponents to discredit the politics of such organizations. Communists usually preferred the terms "auxiliary organizations" and "mass organizations." See also Draper, *American Communism and Soviet Russia*, 171-185. His own experiences in one front organization are described on ix-xi.

24 Andrew Hemingway, *Artists on the Left: American Artists and the Communist Movement 1926-1956* (New Haven: Yale University Press, 2002), 86. This is not to say that the non-Communists in fronts were simply "dupes of Party manipulation." For many "social liberals," Hemingway reminds us, "it was possible to see the Soviet Union as embodying certain shared progressive values whatever the deformities of its political system" (195-196).

25 Kutulas, *The Long War*, 105. For more on the concept of the "fellow-traveler," and Communist attitudes towards such people, see David Caute, *The Fellow-Travellers: A Postscript to the Enlightenment* (New York: Macmillan, 1973), 1-12.

26 Michael Denning, *The Cultural Front: The Laboring of American Culture in the Twentieth Century* (London: Verso, 1996), 4, 63, 67. Denning, too, prefers to see non-Communist activists in front organizations as "independent leftists who worked with Party members" as equals in a "broad and tenuous left-wing alliance" (5-6).

27 Arthur J. Sabin, *Red Scare in Court: New York versus the International Workers Order* (Philadelphia: University of Pennsylvania Press, 1993), 351.

28 David Caute, *The Great Fear: The Anti-Communist Purge Under Truman and Eisenhower* (New York: Simon and Schuster, 1978), 173. Apart from its Jewish section, the IWO included Russian, Spanish, Croatian, Finnish, Italian, Greek, Hungarian, Polish, Romanian, Serbian, Slovak and Ukrainian nationality sections.

29 Roger Keeran, "National Groups and the Popular Front: The Case of the International Workers Order," *Journal of American Ethnic History* 14 (Spring 1995): 33-39. For an overview of the IWO's first two decades, see Sabin, *Red Scare in Court*, 1-24; another history, emphasizing its ethnic diversity, is Thomas J. E. Walker, *Pluralistic Fraternity: The History of the International Worker's Order* (New York: Garland, 1991).

30 Max Bedacht, "Work in Mass Organizations," *Party Organizer* 6, 8-9 (August-September 1933): 79.

31 Henry L. Feingold, *Zion in America: the Jewish Experience from Colonial Times to the Present* (New York: Hippocrene Books, 1974), 278-279.

32 Arthur Liebman, *Jews and the Left* (New York: John Wiley, 1978), 26-33, 314-315, 520. For more on the concept of "Jewish Communism" as an ethno-social movement, see Henry Felix Srebrnik, *London Jews and British Communism, 1935-1945* (London: Vallentine Mitchell, 1995), 11-19; and Henry Felix Srebrnik, *Jerusalem on the Amur*, 7-11. See also Henry Srebrnik, "'Next Year in Birobidzhan!' The Messianic Rhetoric of Jewish Communists in the Search for a New Zion," in Ulrich van der Heyden and Andreas Feldtkeller, eds., *Border Crossings: Explorations of an Interdisciplinary Historian. Festschrift for Irving Hexham* (Stuttgart: Franz Steiner Verlag, 2008): 305-317.

33 David P. Shuldiner, *Of Moses and Marx: Folk Ideology and Folk History in the Jewish Labor Movement* (Westport, CT: Bergin & Garvey, 1999), 21, 24, 34.

34 Robert Snyder, "The Paterson Jewish Folk Chorus: Politics, Ethnicity and Musical Culture," *American Jewish History* 74 (September 1984): 27.

35 Robbie Lieberman, *"My Song is My Weapon": People's Songs, American Communism, and the Politics of Culture, 1930-1950* (Urbana, IL: University of Illinois Press, 1989), 15-16.

36 "Shortcomings of Party Fractions in Language Work," *Party Organizer* 3, 4 (June-July 1930): 10. This same article listed 60,000 Jews as belonging to organizations "under enemy leadership."

37 Milton Doroshkin, *Yiddish in America: Social and Cultural Foundations* (Rutherford, NJ: Fairleigh Dickinson University Press, 1969), 166. Some of the Workmen's Circle's schools had already become affiliated with the Jewish section of the CP a few years earlier.

38 Epstein, *The Jew and Communism*, 259; Keeran, "National Groups and the Popular Front," 31. See also Bat-Ami Zucker, "American Jewish Communists and Jewish Culture in the 1930s," *Modern Judaism* 14, 2 (May 1994): 179-180; Klehr, *The Heyday of American Communism*, 382-385; David Leviatin,

Followers of the Trail: Jewish Working-Class Radicals in America (New Haven: Yale University Press, 1989), 27-30; Liebman, *Jews and the Left*, 310-325.

39   Fraser M. Ottanelli, *The Communist Party of the United States: From the Depression to World War II* (New Brunswick, NJ: Rutgers University Press, 1991), 126.

40   John Earl Haynes and Harvey Klehr, "The CPUSA Reports to the Comintern: 1941," *American Communist History* 4, 1 (June 2005): 52.

41   Ruth Pinkson, "The Life and Times of an Elderly Red Diaper Baby," in Judy Kaplan and Linn Shapiro, eds., *Red Diapers: Growing Up in the Communist Left* (Urbana, IL: University of Illinois Press, 1998), 232. Labor Zionists, trade unionists and Bundists in the Workmen's Circle also created cooperative housing in the Bronx, building the Farband Houses, the Amalgamated Cooperative Houses, and the Sholem Aleichem Cooperative. These housing cooperatives included libraries, theaters and concerts, cooperative grocery stores where the residents shopped, cafeterias where they snacked, and nursery schools that minded and molded their children while they worked. The houses retained their radical Jewish character through the 1950s. See Richard Plunz, "Reading Bronx Housing, 1890-1940," in Timothy Rub, ed., *Building a Borough: Architecture and Planning in the Bronx, 1890-1940* (New York: Bronx Museum of the Arts, 1986): 30-76.

42   Deborah Dash Moore, *At Home in America: Second Generation New York Jews* (New York: Columbia University Press, 1981), 80. See also Murray Schumach, "Reunion Hails Bronx Housing Experiment of 20's," *New York Times*, May 2, 1977, 37. To gain a sense of the intense cultural, political and social life in this self-contained community as recalled by former residents, see also Vivian Gornick, *The Romance of American Communism* (New York: Basic Books, 1977), 53-59, 147-148; Liebman, *Jews and the Left*, 307-310; and Michal Goldman, "A World in the World: Living in the Coops," *Jewish Currents* 57, 6 (November-December 2003): 24-25, 48.

43   Beth S. Wenger, *New York Jews and the Great Depression: Uncertain Promise* (New Haven: Yale University Press, 1996), 93. See also 110-115 for a description of Communist grass-roots mobilization around rent strikes and other protests in these Jewish neighborhoods during the Depression.

44   These organizations are described in the section on "Yidishe arbeter organizatsyes in amerike," *Icor yor-bukh - ICOR Year Book 1932*, 178-191 [Yiddish section]. Bailin died in Los Angeles on April 29, 1961. Shloime Almazov called on all ICOR members to help build the Artef, which was "our" theater, the only "proletarian art theater in Yiddish in America." "In der icor bavegung," *ICOR* 7, 8 (September 1934): 16. For Artef, see Edna Nahshon, *Yiddish Proletarian Theatre: The Art and Politics of the Artef, 1925-1940* (Westport, CT: Greenwood Press, 1998). For Proletpen, see Amelia Glaser and David Weintraub, eds., *Proletpen: America's Rebel Yiddish Poets* (Madison, WI: University of Wisconsin Press, 2005).

45   Shuldiner, *Of Moses and Marx*, 105; David K. Dunaway, "Unsung Songs

of Protest: The Composers Collective of New York," *New York Folklore* 5 (Summer 1979): 5.

46 Leviatin, *Followers of the Trail*, 32-33, 280-282; Paul C. Mishler, *Raising Reds: The Young Pioneers, Radical Summer Camps, and Communist Political Culture in the United States* (New York: Columbia University Press, 1999), 83-108.

47 "Decisions of the National Conference of Language Bureaus," *Party Organizer* 9, 11 (November 1936): 16.

48 V. J. Jerome, "A Year of 'Jewish Life'," *The Communist* 17, 9 (September 1938): 850-852, 856-858 (emphasis in original). Jerome in 1935 had become editor of *The Communist* (which later became *Political Affairs*) and held that position until 1955. He was also the cultural commissioner of the Communist Party. *Jewish Life* re-emerged in November 1946 under the imprimatur of the Morning Freiheit Association.

49 Zucker, "American Jewish Communists," 181.

50 Paul C. Mishler, "Red Finns, Red Jews: Ethnic Variation in Communist Political Culture During the 1920s and 1930s," *YIVO Annual* 22 (1995): 142, 147.

51 Howard M. Sachar, *A History of the Jews in America* (New York: Alfred A. Knopf, 1992), 433-434.

52 Ellen W. Schrecker, *No Ivory Tower: McCarthyism and the Universities* (New York: Oxford University Press, 1986), 35.

53 Lyons, *Philadelphia Communists*, 24-25.

54 Philip Rosen et al, "Philadelphia Jewry, the Holocaust, and the Birth of the Jewish State. Section I: Philadelphia Jewry and the Holocaust," in Murray Friedman, ed., *Philadelphia Jewish Life, 1940-1985* (Philadelphia: Temple University Press, 2003), 5.

55 "What We Stand For," in [Hayim Greenberg, ed.], *Jewish Frontier Anthology 1934-1944* (New York: Jewish Frontier Association, 1945), 3-5.

56 James Waterman Wise, "Are Jews Communists?" *New Masses* 17, 5 (Oct. 29, 1935): 10. An editorial in the Communist *New Masses* had already noted that Waterman Wise had accepted that Jews needed to align themselves with the forces opposing fascism. "Jewry at the Crossroads," *New Masses* 11, 4 (April 24, 1934): 6. Stephen Wise, however, was never a friend of the Communists. See Zosa Szajkowski, *Jews, Wars, and Communism*. Vol. I: 421-422.

57 "Ask U.S. to Protest for Jews in Poland," *New York Times*, Nov. 20, 1937, 7; "Hull Gets Plea for Jews," *New York Times*, Nov. 21, 1937, section 1, 7.

58 "War on Anti-Semitism Held Universal Cause, *New York Times*, March 13, 1938, section 1, 35; "Ban on Anti-Semitism Sought in Congress," *New York Times*, March 14, 1938, 8.

59 For an ideological and historical summary, see Isaak N. Steinberg, "Territorialism: A History of the Movement," in Basil J. Vlavianos and Feliks Gross, eds., *Struggle for Tomorrow: Modern Political Ideologies of the Jewish People* (New York: Arts Inc., 1954), 112-129; and Michael C. Astour, *Geshikhte fun der frayland-lige un funem teritorialistishn gedank* (Buenos Aires: Freeland League, 2 vols, 1967). Steinberg was a major figure in the League.

60 Nora Levin, *The Jews in the Soviet Union Since 1917* (New York: New York University Press, 1988). Vol. I, 291.
61 For the *Yevsektsiya*, see Zvi Gitelman, *Jewish Nationality and Soviet Politics: The Jewish Sections of the CPSU, 1917-1930* (Princeton, NJ: Princeton University Press, 1972); and Mordechai Altshuler, "The Attitude of the Communist Party of Russia to Jewish National Survival, 1918-1930," *YIVO Annual of Jewish Social Science* 14 (1969): 68-86.
62 Chimen Abramsky, "The Biro-Bidzhan Project, 1927-1959," in Lionel Kochan, ed., *The Jews in Soviet Russia Since 1917*, 3rd ed. (London: Oxford University Press, 1978), 69.
63 Jonathan Dekel-Chen, " 'New' Jews of the Agricultural Kind: A Case of Soviet Interwar Propaganda," *Russian Review* 66, 3 (July 2007): 424-450.
64 See Jonathan Dekel-Chen, *Farming the Red Land: Jewish Agricultural Colonization and Local Soviet Power, 1924-1941* (New Haven: Yale University Press, 2005).
65 "Gives $1,000,000 for Jewish Relief," *New York Times*, Sept. 14, 1925, 21. See also *Founding a New Life for Suffering Thousands: Report of Dr. Joseph A. Rosen on Jewish Colonization Work in Russia* (New York: United Jewish Campaign, 1925). The journalist Louis Fischer called Rosen "a Russian intellectual turned dirt farmer in Minnesota." Louis Fischer, "Forward to the Soil!" *Menorah Journal* 11, 2 (April 1925): 176. For more on Rosen's work with the Joint and other relief organizations in the Soviet Union in the 1920s and 1930s, see Allan L. Kagedan, "American Jews and the Soviet Experiment: The Agro-Joint Project, 1924-1937," *Jewish Social Studies* 43, 2 (Spring 1981): 153-164; and Zosa Szajkowski, *Jews, Wars, and Communism.* Vol. IV: *The Mirage of American Jewish Aid in Soviet Russia 1917-1939* (New York: privately printed, 1977), especially 88-93. Rosen's wife was a strong supporter of the USSR and "Rosen's attitude to the Soviet regime was a mixture of friendliness and criticism," notes Szajkowski (91). Rosen, an anti-Zionist and territorialist, was born in Moscow in 1877 and came to the U.S. in 1903. He died in 1948.
66 *United Jewish Campaign News* 1, 4, New York, October 1926.
67 "Laud Jewish Colonization," *New York Times*, May 22, 1927, Section 1, 31; "Warburg Reports Colonies Thriving," *New York Times*, May 24, 1927, 7; "Warburg Pledges $1,000,000 to Fund," *New York Times*, April 25, 1928, 16. See further Ron Chernow, *The Warburgs: The Twentieth-Century Odyssey of a Remarkable Jewish Family* (New York: Vintage, 1994).
68 "Pictures the Jews on Russian Farms," *New York Times*, June 29, 1926, 9. "The land settlement is so successful that even Orthodox Jews who never knew anything about farming are eager to settle the land," he remarked. *Jewish Colonization in Soviet Russia* (New York: ICOR, [1927], [4-5]. See also Moses A. Leavitt, *The JDC Story: Highlights of JDC Activities 1914-1952* (New York: American Jewish Joint Distribution Committee, 1953), 9-10.
69 Isaac Don Levine, "$40,000,000 to Settle Jews on Russian Land," *New York Times*, July 29, 1928, Section 7, 16. Rosenberg said that by 1930 the Agro-

Joint had spent $8 million in the Soviet Union. "Says 3,000,000 Jews Will Stay in Russia," *New York Times*, Feb. 26, 1930, 6. The wealthy Chicago Jewish merchant and philanthropist Julius Rosenwald in 1928 pledged $5 million for Joint-sponsored Jewish settlement projects in the Soviet Union. A vice-president of the anti-Zionist American Jewish Committee, he stated that he preferred Jewish colonization even in Birobidzhan to Palestine, "for at least there they remain in their native country." Zosa Szajkowski, *Jews, Wars, and Communism*. Vol. I, 427. See also Yehuda Bauer, *My Brother's Keeper: A History of the American Jewish Joint Distribution Committee, 1929-1939* (Philadelphia: Jewish Publication Society, 1974), 100-102; Lawrence P. Bachmann, "Julius Rosenwald," *American Jewish Historical Quarterly* 64, 1 (September 1976): 89-105; Priscilla Roberts, "Jewish Bankers, Russia, and the Soviet Union, 1900-1940: The Case of Kuhn, Loeb and Company," *American Jewish Archives* 49, 1-2 (1997): 9-37; and Jerome C. Rosenthal, "Dealing with the Devil: Louis Marshall and the Partnership Between the Joint Distribution Committee and Soviet Russia," *American Jewish Archives* 39, 1 (April 1987): 1-22.

70 Elias Tobenkin, *Stalin's Ladder: War & Peace in the Soviet Union* (New York: Minton, Balch and Co., 1933), 153-168, 172-182.

71 William Zukerman, "The Jewish Colonization Movement in Soviet Russia," *Menorah Journal* 21, 1 (April-June 1933): 74-76, 79.

72 Still, by 1930, some 231,000 Jews were engaged in agricultural activities throughout the Soviet Union. Robert Weinberg, "Jews into Peasants? Solving the Jewish Question in Birobidzhan," in Yaacov Ro'i, ed., *Jews and Jewish Life in Russia and the Soviet Union* (London: Frank Cass, 1995), 90.

73 Two excellent overviews of the entire project are provided by Allan Laine Kagedan, *Soviet Zion: The Quest for a Russian Jewish Homeland* (New York: St. Martin's Press, 1994); and Robert Weinberg, *Stalin's Forgotten Zion: Birobidzhan and the Making of a Soviet Jewish Homeland. An Illustrated History, 1928-1996* (Berkeley: University of California Press, 1998). See, as well, Alan L. Kagedan, "Birobidzhan," *Central Asian Survey* 12, No. 2 (July 1993): 87-94; and the entry "Birobidjan," written by Avrahm Yarmolinsky, then head of the Slavonic Division of the New York Public Library, in the *Universal Jewish Encyclopedia* of 1941 (New York: Ktav, 1969 reprint edition), 372-378.

74 George St. George, *Siberia: The New Frontier* (New York: David McKay Co., 1969), 323. Noting Jewish reluctance, a journalist from the *Yevsektsiya*'s newspaper *Der Emes* observed in April 1928, "the Jews raise their hands easily for Biro-Bidjan, but not their feet." Abramsky, "The Biro-Bidzhan Project, 1927-1959," 72.

75 For a detailed description of Jewish toponymy in Birobidzhan, and the changes made to place names through the years, see Boris Kotlerman, "Jewish Names on the Map of Birobidzhan," in Aaron Demsky, ed., *These Are the Names: Studies in Jewish Onomastics*. Vol. 4 (Ramat Gan, Israel: Bar-Ilan University Press, 2003), 109-126.

76 See Leon Talmy, "Biro-bidzhan 1928-1931," *Icor yor-bukh - ICOR Year Book 1932*, 15-18 [Yiddish section].
77 Quoted in Abramsky, "The Biro-Bidzhan Project, 1927-1959," 74-75. The American support groups, not realizing Kalinin was just a figurehead by now, paid far too much attention to his pronouncements.
78 Gennady Estraikh, "Yiddish Language Conference Aborted," *East European Jewish Affairs* 25, 2 (Winter 1995): 91-92.
79 Quoted in Melech Epstein, *The Jew and Communism*, 309-310.
80 "In di shtet," *ICOR* 1 (March 1925): 14; "Barikht fun sekretar E. Vatenberg," *ICOR* 2-3 (April-May 1925): 7; *"Icor" Bulletin* No. 1 (April 1925): 8; Ab. Epstein, "Zibn yor ICOR geshikhte," *Icor yor-bukh - ICOR Year Book 1932*, 46 [Yiddish section].
81 Benjamin Pinkus, *The Jews of the Soviet Union: The History of a National Minority* (Cambridge: Cambridge University Press, 1988), 65; Allan Laine Kagedan, *Soviet Zion*, 22-23.
82 See my article "'An Enemy of the Jewish Masses': The ICOR and the Campaign Against Zionism, 1924-1935," in August Grabski, ed., *Lewica Przeciwko Izraelowi: Studia O Zydowskim Lewicowym Antysyjonizmie / Rebels against Zion: Studies on Jewish Left Anti-Zionists* (Warsaw: Jewish Historical Institute, 2010): 93-116.
83 *Barikht fun der amerikaner icor ekspertn-komisye* (New York: ICOR 1930); *Report of the American Icor Commission for the Study of Biro-Bidjan and its Colonization* (New York: ICOR, 1930). See also *Di ershte trit fun biro-bidzhan* (New York: ICOR, 1929).
84 Leon Talmy, *Oyf royer erd: Mit der 'icor'-ekspeditsye in biro-bidzhan*. New York: Frayhayt 1931.
85 Charles Kuntz, "Biro-Bidjan in Socialist Construction," *Icor yor-bukh - ICOR Year Book 1932*, x [English section].
86 Epstein, *The Jew and Communism*, 259; letter from Kalmen Marmor to Shloime Almazov, New York, May 31, 1933, and letter from Shloime Almazov to Kalmen Marmor, New York, June 1, 1933; in the Kalmen Marmor papers, 1873-1955, RG205, Microfilm group 495, folder 545 "Icor-korespondents, 1930-1937";YIVO Institute for Jewish Research, New York [hereafter YIVO]. For more on Marmor, see his autobiography, *Mayn lebns-geshikhte*, 2 vols. (New York: YKUF Farlag, 1959).
87 A. Olken, "Vos tut zikh in di new yorker icor brentshes," *ICOR* 5, 10 (November 1932): 14. Even the Farband Houses, the Amalgamated Cooperative Houses, and the Sholem Aleichem Cooperative had ICOR sections.
88 Ernie Rymer, "50th Anniversary of Workers Cooperative Colony," *Frayhayt*, May 1, 1977, 15.
89 Letter from Amy Swerdlow to the author, New York, May 21, 1996.
90 Bert Steinberg, "Living a Secular Jewish Life," *Jewish Currents* 54, 9 (October 2000): 19. Steinberg is a former president of the Society for Humanistic Judaism.

91 "Barikht fun new yorker 'icor' komitet farn yor 1928," *ICOR* 2, 2 (February-March 1929): 21.

92 Anita Shapira, "'Black Night—White Snow': Attitudes of the Palestinian Labor Movement to the Russian Revolution, 1917-1929," in Ezra Mendelsohn, ed., *Essential Papers on Jews and the Left* (New York: New York University Press, 1997), 260.

93 Reuben Brainin, "Bagrisung fun khaver brainin bay der natsyonaler konvenshon fun icor in marts, 1935," in Reuben Brainin, *Umshterblekhe reyd vegn birobidzhan un vegn der sotsyalishtishe leyzung fun der natsyonaler frage* (New York: ICOR, 1940), 13 [Yiddish].

94 "Reuben Brainin, 77, Noted Writer, Dies," *New York Times*, Dec. 1, 1939, 23. See also the obituary "Reuben brainin geshtorbn," *Kanader Adler*, Montreal, Dec. 1, 1939, 1-2, and the article by the noted historian of Canadian Jewry, B.G. Sack, "Reuben brainin: a por verter tsu zayn farlust," *Kanader Adler*, Montreal, Dec. 1, 1939, 4.

95 This information comes from a pamphlet printed by the ICOR on the occasion of Kuntz's 75th birthday in 1944, entitled "Prof. Charles Kuntz *President* Icor Association, Inc." with his picture above the title. It is in the Morris Stern papers, RG231, Box 1, unnamed folder; YIVO.

96 Melech Epstein, *The Jew and Communism*, 173-174.

97 Brainin, "Bagrisung...," 13 [Yiddish].

98 Kuntz's personal papers have never been located; his great-great nephew, University of Oregon historian Daniel Rosenberg, speculates that any papers Kuntz may have preserved would have been passed on to a political associate rather than to a family member. E-mail letter to the author from Professor Daniel Rosenberg, University of Oregon, Eugene, OR, March 8, 2004.

99 Matthew Hoffman, "From Pintele Yid to Racenjude: Chaim Zhitlovsky and Racial Conceptions of Jewishness," *Jewish History* 19, 1 (March 2005): 75. For more appraisals of Zhitlovsky's role, see Max Rosenfeld, "Zhitlovsky: Philosopher of Jewish Secularism," in Morris U. Schappes et al, *"Jewish Currents" Reader* (New York: Jewish Currents, 1966), 78-89; Emanuel S. Goldsmith, *Architects of Yiddishism at the Beginning of the Twentieth Century: A Study in Jewish Cultural History* (Rutherford, NJ: Fairleigh Dickinson University Press, 1976), 161-181; Jonathan Frankel, *Prophecy and Politics: Socialism, Nationalism, and the Russian Jews, 1862-1917* (Cambridge: Cambridge University Press, 1981), 258-287; and David H. Weinberg, *Between Tradition and Modernity: Haim Zhitlowski, Simon Dubnow, Ahad Ha-Am, and the Shaping of Modern Jewish Identity* (New York: Holmes & Meier, 1996), 83-144.

100 Shloime Almazov remembered, when he had become the national secretary of the ICOR, visiting Zhitlovsky's home in Croton-on-Hudson in New York State to convince him to join the ICOR. S. Almazov, *Mit dem vort tsum folk: derfurungen fun a lektor* (New York: YKUF Farlag, 1947), 52-53.

101 Nakhman Meisel, "Di letste rayzeh fun dr. khaim zhitlovsky," *Vochenblat*, Toronto, 3 June 1965, 5.

102 Sid Resnick, "Pesekh Novick: Redakter fun der 'Morgn-Frayhayt'," *Di Pen* 30 (January 1997): 1-8; Harvey Klehr and John Earl Haynes, *The American Communist Movement: Storming Heaven Itself* (New York: Twayne Publishers, 1992), 100.

103 "*Morgn Freiheit*, April 2, 1922 -- Sept. 11, 1988," *Jewish Currents* 42, 11 (November 1988): 3; Morris U. Schappes, "Paul Novick: In Sorrow and Pride," *Jewish Currents* 43, 11 (November 1989): 5; Peter B. Flint, "Paul Novick is Dead; Editor, 97, Helped Start Yiddish Daily," *New York Times*, Aug. 22, 1989, D3.

104 "Soviet Colony is Held No Blow at Zionism," *New York Times*, Dec. 20, 1934, 20.

105 "A fellow-traveler sui generis," Goldberg, who was sympathetic to the USSR but never officially linked with Communism, "was the perfect propagandist as far as the Soviet Union was concerned." Shimon Redlich, *Propaganda and Nationalism in Wartime Russia: The Jewish Antifascist Committee in the USSR, 1941-1948* (Boulder, CO: East European Quarterly, 1982), 108-109.

106 "B.Z. Goldberg, Columnist, Dies; Wrote for Yiddish Papers Here," *New York Times*, 30 December 1972, 24.

107 I.B. Bailin, "Gina Birenzweig un Gina Medem (eynike kharakter-shtriken)," in Gina Medem, *A Lebnsveg: Oytobyografishe notitsn* (New York: Gina Medem Bukh-komitet, 1950), 7 (emphasis in original).

108 Gina Medem, "Di taiga ruft," *ICOR* 5, 3 (March 1932): 7-8; Gina Medem, "Nokh amol birobidzhan," *Icor yor-bukh - ICOR Year Book 1932*, 66-69 [Yiddish section].

109 Gina Medem, *Lender, Felker, Kamfn* (New York: Gina Medem Bukh-komitet, 1963), 211-213, 237-239, 246. She died January 29, 1977, and her obituary can be found in the *Frayhayt*, Feb. 20, 1977, 15. See also in the same issue, 10, a eulogy by I. E. Rontch, "Di Literarishe yerushe fun Gina Medem." Irena Klepfisz asserts that Medem's "silence on the drastic change in Jewish life and her continued admiration for the Soviets," even after 1956, is "dumbfounding." Despite the destruction of Yiddish and Birobidzhan by Stalin, "she has no words of protest or regret." She was unable to give up her politics, even though, as Klepfisz speculates, she would never have settled in Stalinist Russia because "Her Medem name, and her Jewishness would have imprisoned her, most likely killed her." Irena Klepfisz, "Di Mames, Dos Loshn/The Mothers, the Language: Feminism, Yidishkayt, and the Politics of Memory," *Bridges: A Journal for Jewish Feminists and Our Friends* 4, 1 (Winter/Spring 1994): 27-33.

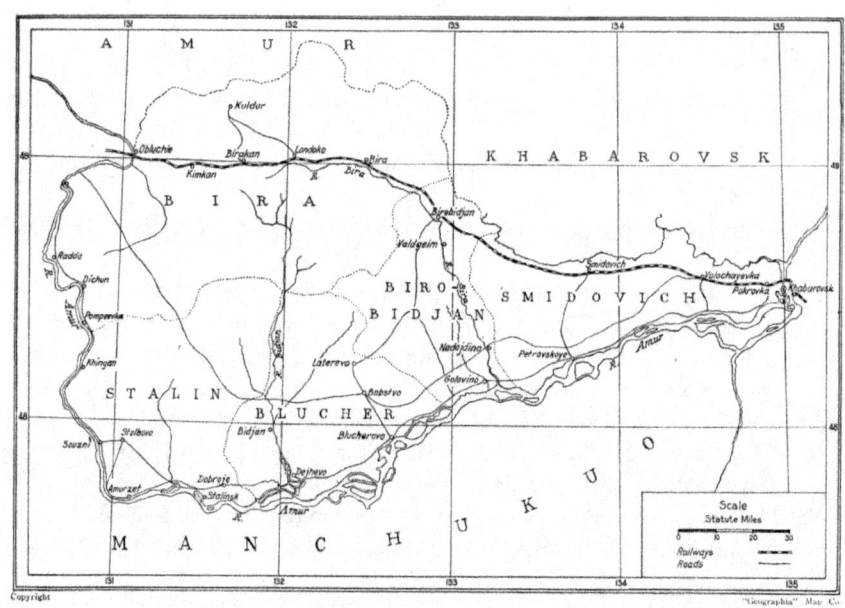

Map of Birobidzhan, 1941, from *Universal Jewish Encyclopedia*, 1941

The Formation of Ambijan

Faced with the Nazi challenge following Hitler's accession to power in Germany, Stalin began to view the United States as a potential Soviet ally against Germany and Japan; as Earl Browder, then general secretary of the CPUSA, later remarked, the party "rapidly moved out of its extreme leftist sectarianism...towards the broadest united front tactics of reformism for strictly limited immediate aims."[1] The ICOR and Ambijan would prosper in this climate and succeed "in stirring up a great deal of interest for the Jewish region in the Soviet far east."[2]

In particular, the notion that Birobidzhan might serve as a place of political sanctuary, a potential haven from racial persecution for European Jews, as well as a center of Jewish economic and cultural regeneration, became more pronounced. This theme would become especially prevalent in Ambijan, a popular front organization more concerned with "anti-fascist" politics and the rescue of European Jewry than with programs for "socialist construction."

The idea of Birobidzhan as a refuge for non-Russian Jews had been broached even before 1933. In 1928, the pro-Soviet journalist Louis Fischer asserted that "Jews are not hard to find who are intrepid enough even to face the long journey to Bira-Bidzhan [sic] and the adventurous prospects that face them there"; he thought it "not inconceivable that there will also be recruits from Poland." In 1932 Fischer again wondered whether "Biro-Bidjan was perhaps conceived as a colony for Jews from Poland, Rumania, and Lithuania." But he dismissed the idea, declaring that "the consummation of that plan is very distant."[3] The *New York Times* was also skeptical: an article in 1932 suggested that "It is premature, to say the least, to expect that an independent Jewish republic will be established on Soviet soil in the near future."[4]

The journalist William Zukerman, who wrote for the Yiddish daily *Morgn Zhurnal*, had also heard that Birobidzhan would be opened by the Soviet government "as a place of immigration for Jews from outside the Soviet Union" and he was certain that this would meet with "an enthusiastic response from Jewish workers outside Russia." He stated in 1932 that "this project has its resemblances to Zionism. There is a striking family likeness between the Kalinin and the Balfour declarations; between the Jewish National Home in Palestine and the Jewish National Republic in Siberia." But "the Jewish National Home in Soviet Russia is being built without all those grave problems which have confronted Zionism since the Balfour Declaration."[5]

Until now, Zukerman wrote a year later, the Jewish colonization movement in Russia had "lacked its Palestine," that is, a geographic location on which to focus its efforts. The Birobidzhan project, he asserted, would not merely solve Jewish economic problems; it would also be a means of preserving national life: "It is this spiritual undercurrent of the movement that is as much responsible for its popularity among Jews as the economic reconstruction which it brings." Birobidzhan, unlike the Crimea, was almost uninhabited and belonged to no one nationality. Zukerman speculated that Birobidzhan could serve as a destination for east European Jews, who could settle there "without raising any racial complications at all."

Zukerman was not blind to Birobidzhan's drawbacks. Its great distance from European Russia made for social isolation: "A Jewish settler is bound to feel exiled in a place like that," he worried. Were the Soviets interested merely in developing the area as a bulwark against a possible Japanese invasion?"[6]

Journalist Abraham Revutsky warned the readers of the *Menorah Journal* in 1929 that "current rumours describing Bira-Bidzhan [sic] as a sort of new Eldorado are greatly exaggerated." Previous attempts to settle the area with serfs or Cossacks in the 19th century had failed, he noted; the "winter and summer are both colder than Winnipeg," and the clay soil was not very good. Like Zukerman, he wondered if the main impetus for the scheme was to keep out Chinese settlers or Japanese troops. Revutsky concluded that "Those who have rushed Jewish settlers into this enterprise without proper investigation and preparation have not acted in a thoroughly impartial and scientific manner."[7] Zukerman and Revutsky's fears were realized when in 1931 the Japanese invaded and conquered Manchuria, creating the puppet state of Manchukuo in February 1932. Not coincidentally, the USSR elevated Birobidzhan to the status of a full-fledged autonomous region of the Russian Soviet Federative Socialist Republic on May 7, 1934.

Probably the most prominent non-Jewish champion of the Birobidzhan scheme was the British fellow-traveler Dudley Leigh Aman, First Baron Marley. Born in 1884, he had been trained as an army officer and was wounded in France as a major in the Royal Marine Artillery during World War I. He became a Fabian socialist and joined the British Labour Party after the war. He ran for election to the House of Commons (and lost) five times between 1922 and 1929, but he was elevated to the House of Lords by Ramsay MacDonald's Labour government in 1930. Marley was Undersecretary of State for War in 1930-31, and became a deputy speaker and chief Labour Party whip in the upper chamber.[8]

By the early 1930s Lord Marley was involved in pro-Communist activities in England, including a stint as head of the Paris-based World

The Formation of Ambijan

Relief Committee for the Victims of German and Austrian Fascism. The committee had been formed in May 1933 by Willi Münzenberg, one of Stalin's chief propagandists in the West, and was an outgrowth of another of Münzenberg's fronts, Workers International Relief. Münzenberg established numerous fronts for the Moscow-dominated Comintern during his career before he mysteriously died after the Nazis conquered France in 1940.[9]

In 1934 the Labour Party placed the World Relief Committee on its list of proscribed Communist auxiliaries, over the objections of left-wing party members like Marley and Harold Laski, who maintained that it was "pursuing the non-political objective of aiding the distressed."[10] This did not seem to faze Marley, who brazenly denied any connection between the Committee and the Comintern. In September 1936 he was elected a member of the presidium of the International Conference Against Racial Discrimination and Anti-Semitism, another Communist-inspired front that met in Paris. As a result of his affiliations with Communist-inspired groups, Marley finally lost the chief whip's position in 1937, though he remained deputy speaker of the House of Lords until 1941.[11] An alleged former Comintern agent who was interviewed in Paris in January 1951 told the FBI that Marley "had a direct contact with the Comintern" in the 1930s. In 1932 he had attended an anti-imperialist conference in Shanghai, and returned to Britain via the Soviet Union. While in Moscow, Marley had been prevailed upon to help the cause of colonization in Birobidzhan.[12]

Marley had already been very active with the World ORT Union, as chairman of the Parliamentary Advisory Council of the British ORT Federation, and had visited Poland and the Soviet Union on behalf of the ORT. In January 1933 he had come to New York to open a three-week campaign, which took him to seven other American and four Canadian cities, to raise $500,000 for the organization. He noted that in the Soviet Union the ORT was helping retrain "economically bankrupt and helpless" Jews to enable them to work in agriculture and industry. He was greeted with great enthusiasm by the Jewish communities that hosted him and his farewell reception was attended by some 3,000 people.[13] So it was no great leap to lend his talents to a territorialist project to rehabilitate the Jewish people.

The ICOR published two editions of his pamphlet *Biro Bidjan as I Saw It* in 1934 and 1935. Marley had visited Birobidzhan in October 1933 and, like many others, compared it favorably to Palestine, because in Birobidzhan, the number of Jews who could be received "*is quite unlimited.*" In language reminiscent of early Zionist accounts of Palestine, he wrote that "there is no problem of an existing local population to be dealt with." However, Marley noted, the Zionists had in fact been wrong about Palestine, where "there is a widespread and increasingly bitter opposition on the part of the Arab population." And while in Birobidzhan the Soviet government offered settlers free transport and free land, in Palestine the British were now discouraging the immigration of Jewish refugees. Indeed, Marley claimed to have interviewed a number of Jews who had come from Palestine and "who preferred the conditions of Biro-Bidjan."

Marley described the sites he had visited, noting that there were now 50 collective farms in the region, as well as new industries. He noted that the language of instruction in the schools was Yiddish, with Russian as a second language. Marley stated that Birobidzhan's "soil is fertile and produces good crops." There was also "plenty of water." The climate, he added, "is extremely healthy. In summer it is hot, but not too hot for comfort; in winter it is cold with snow but with a brilliant sunshine similar to conditions in Switzerland." Marley noted that settlers need not be Communists but "should be ready to work in a collective spirit for the good of the community...rather than for private profit or personal gain."

As a former army officer, Marley also rejected any possibility of a Japanese attack on Birobidzhan from their newly-conquered Chinese province of Manchuria. The part of Birobidzhan on the Amur that faced Manchukuo on the Japanese side of the river was "entirely unsuitable for military advance," he declared, nor would the Japanese air force "waste their time in bombing operations on open fields or small farm villages." His pamphlet concluded by stating that *"Biro-Bidjan has immense possibilities for Jewish colonization and I hope that my Jewish friends will cease any campaign of misrepresentation of conditions in Biro-Bidjan until they have seen for themselves what those conditions are."*[14]

An "anti-fascist" fellow-traveler, Marley was a prototype of the semi-distinguished people who often were titular heads of Communist groups. He proved to be an immense asset to both the ICOR and Ambijan when they decided to broaden their base of support in line with the Comintern's new "popular front" strategy after 1935. Linking Marley to the Birobidzhan project "was an extremely shrewd choice" on the part of Münzenberg, notes Nicole Taylor. Marley had exactly the combination of authority and disarming directness to appeal to the American Jewish public. "American audiences adored this charming, six-foot, silver-haired Englishman. As a parliamentarian, Marley gave the project the gravitas it needed. As a military man, he was able to set off claims that the Jewish Autonomous Region would be a target of attack in the event of war."[15] His ostensible expert military knowledge when it came to assessing Birobidzhan's safety was often repeated by other Communists.

The Formation of Ambijan

The ICOR's work was soon supplemented by a new organization. On February 27, 1934, the American Committee for the Settlement of Jews in Birobidjan, or Ambijan, was conceived at a meeting held at the Ritz-Carleton Hotel in New York. William W. Cohen, a prominent banker, stockbroker, communal worker and former Democratic Congressman from New York—he represented the 17th Congressional district of Manhattan from 1926 to 1928—would later remark that Birobidzhan "first dawned upon me" as "a haven for Jews in distress" at the end of 1933, "shortly after Germany had fallen into the grip of fascism and a kind of cannibalistic anti-Semitism was let loose upon the Jews of that country." Cohen, who had visited the USSR in 1931, contacted Lord Marley during the latter's February 1934 12-city nationwide coast-to-coast tour on behalf of victims of German Nazism, and invited him to the Ritz-Carleton meeting. There, Marley provided a first-hand account of the Birobidzhan region and suggested that a provisional committee be formed to explore the settlement of foreign Jews in Birobidzhan. Cohen was satisfied that "if and when permission to settle non-Russian Jews in Birobidjan could be obtained, this new Jewish Autonomous Region would present an exceptional haven for the salvage and rehabilitation of many thousands of Jews suffering in the infernos of central and eastern Europe." [16]

Ambijan began operating on September 23, 1935, when it set up shop at 285 Madison Avenue, New York, as a "non-partisan and non-sectarian" organization. Membership in the organization cost $5. Marley was made the honorary president, and Cohen became founding president. Among the vice-presidents were B.Z. Goldberg, associate editor of the Yiddish daily *Der Tog*; Jacob Mordecai (J.M.) Budish; Franklin S. Harris, president of Brigham Young University in Provo, Utah, who had led the 1929 ICOR expedition to Birobidzhan; Jacob G. Lipman, a professor at the Rutgers College of Agriculture in New Jersey; and James Waterman Wise, the editor of the liberal periodical *Opinion: A Journal of Jewish Life and Letters*. Max Levin became chair of the Board of Governors, Edward I. Aronow was the secretary-treasurer and John Lyons the executive secretary. Others on the Board of Governors included Joseph A. Marcus, chair of the Campaign committee; Dr. Julius Hammer, head of the Finance committee; Gerson C. Young, chair of the Speakers committee; Jack Schreiber, head of the Membership committee; Sol Low, head of the Landsmanshaft committee; Mrs. Lonnie Levin, chair of the Women's committee, and Miles M. Sherover, chair of the Foreign Contacts committee. There were also a number of trade divisions, including Wine and Liquor, Graphic Arts, Fur, Ladies' Apparel, Woolens and Clothing, and Lawyers'. [17]

Franklin S. Harris, an agronomist, was one of the country's leading soil scientists and director of the American Society of Agricultural Engineering. Upon his return from Birobidzhan to the U.S. in the fall of 1929, he had referred to the region in glowing terms in a radio address entitled "Jewish Colonization in Biro-Bidjan," broadcast over Washington radio station WOL on October 29. "Never, in all history, has yet such an opportunity dawned upon the toiling Jewish people" for the building of "a creative, productive community and building it on the basis of real equality of opportunity," he remarked. The expedition he led in 1929 had found a region with 10 million acres of fertile land, abundant sunshine, and a growing season similar to that of the northern U.S., one particularly well suited to the cultivation of root crops and legumes, including soy beans and rice. It was also well adapted to the livestock industry, particularly dairy farming. There was an abundance of mineral resources and forest products. As for transportation, he noted that the Trans-Siberian Railroad served the region, and the rivers flowing into the Amur would allow transportation by water to the Pacific Ocean.[18]

B.Z. Goldberg had visited Birobidzhan in the summer and autumn of 1934, as part of a four-month sojourn in the Soviet Union. Upon his return to the U.S., he emphasized the region's potential in Jewish as well as economic terms, in articles published in *Der Tog* and in numerous Anglo-Jewish newspapers.[19] Goldberg was "carried away by the almost boundless enthusiasm everywhere in evidence." In Birobidzhan the Jew "can call the very land his own. He is earning it by the sweat of his brow and the frost-bites on his ears." Goldberg was certain the region would become a full-fledged republic by 1936.[20] "Already, it has a warm, specifically Jewish atmosphere. Yiddish has a much more creative role here than in any other part of the Soviet Union. Assimilationist influences are altogether absent," Goldberg told a meeting at the New School for Social Research in New York on December 26, 1934. "A large audience listened to and enthusiastically received his comprehensive report," Ambijan later reported.[21]

Ambijan managed to attract middle class and even quite wealthy people "far removed from left-wing tendencies," including non-Jews.[22] FBI director J. Edgar Hoover later noted that Ambijan was reportedly formed "mainly for the purpose of breaking down the alleged hostility of the majority of the upper middle class Jews toward the Soviet Union."[23] One of the participants who attended the inaugural February 27, 1934 meeting was the German Jewish investment banker Felix Warburg. He spoke of the great possibilities inherent in Birobidzhan and stressed the need for the development of a "pioneering spirit" in young Jews, in order to make them suitable as settlers. Warburg noted that conditions in Palestine were "complicated," whereas "the

Russian Government has been fair to the Jewish people."[24] James N. Rosenberg, vice-president and chair of the Board of Directors of the Joint and chair of the Agro-Joint, was another prominent supporter of Ambijan. Clearly, Ambijan would be able to attract wealthy American Jewish philanthropists already involved with territorialist projects to ameliorate the condition of impoverished Jews in eastern Europe.

Another person whose fame and stature proved an invaluable resource for the leadership of Ambijan was the prominent Arctic explorer, scientist and author Vilhjalmur Stefansson. He became a vice-president of Ambijan in 1936 and was particularly active in the organization during World War II.[25] Born in 1879 in Arnes, Manitoba, a small Icelandic immigrant community some 50 miles north of Winnipeg, in western Canada, he grew up in North Dakota, where his family had moved soon after his birth. Stefansson was a world-famous figure. During various Arctic expeditions in Alaska and Canada, undertaken between 1906 and 1918, he had discovered hitherto unknown islands. He had written ethnological descriptions of Inuit life in the far north. He was a tireless advocate of northern colonization. Stefansson was well-known on the lecture circuit, and many of his books were best-sellers.[26] After 1918 he lived mainly in New York, where he met, hired as a librarian, and in 1941 married Evelyn Schwartz Baird, who was 34 years his junior. An art student and the daughter of a left-wing Hungarian Jewish immigrant family, she would also be active in Ambijan.

Many of Stefansson's rivals and enemies in Canada tried to discredit him as a publicity-seeking charlatan whose claims about the possibilities of life in the Arctic were overly rosy.[27] The Soviets, however, adopted many of Stefansson's ideas and published his books in translation in the 1930s.[28] He, in turn, began "extolling the achievements of the Soviets in the development of their northern regions."[29] Stefansson, as president of the Explorers Club of New York, was particularly impressed by Soviet efforts to open an Arctic sea route between the Atlantic and Pacific Oceans.[30] At the annual dinner of the Explorers Club in 1937, Stefansson called the Soviet exploits at the North Pole the "outstanding exploring event" of the year.[31] When the Soviets unveiled their Arctic Pavilion at the New York World's Fair in 1939, Stefansson considered this "fitting, and most instructive to the United States and to Canada," since only the Soviet Union "carries forward the ideas and practices of frontier development."[32] By now involved with various pro-Soviet front groups, and given his propensity for combining pro-Soviet politics with expertise in far northern exploration and settlement, it was perhaps only natural that Stefansson would become linked to a project that involved the taming of a largely uninhabited wilderness at the far eastern edge of Siberia.

The supporters of the Birobidzhan project also made use of the various "celebrities" on the pro-Communist left: on February 6, 1936, for instance, Anna Louise Strong, the "Famous Journalist and Author, Editor, 'Moscow News', Recently returned from [the] Soviet Union," spoke about "Biro-Bidjan as I Saw It" to an ICOR-sponsored gathering at Webster Hall, New York.[33] Strong, who had been in Birobidzhan in April of 1935, described to her audience the post-1917 history of Soviet nationalities policy and the country's struggle against all forms of racism and national oppression. Jews were not attracted to Birobidzhan because they were oppressed; far from it. They had the same rights as all Soviet citizens. However, only in Birobidzhan would they have the "final" expression of their nationality, in a place where they would form a majority and be able to exercise self-determination. Strong had been able to speak with Professor Joseph Lieberberg, head of the Birobidzhan government, whom she described as "one of the most brilliant men I have ever met."[34] Strong also published articles on Birobidzhan in venues such as *Asia*, an ostensibly independent magazine that hewed the Comintern line on the colonial world. There, she informed readers that Birobidzhan was being settled by Jewish pioneers who "want to express themselves, in schools, courts, theaters, government, not only as Soviet citizens but also as Jews."[35]

Behind the scenes, it was the Russian-born and Russian-speaking J.M. Budish, a member of the CPUSA, who was the important moving force behind Ambijan. Budish had been a founding member of the ICOR, and had already been supporting Birobidzhan in ICOR publications.[36] He was employed by the Amtorg Trading Corp., which represented Soviet interests in the U.S.[37] As chair of Ambijan's administrative committee, his negotiations with Soviet officials in Moscow, and his contacts with the newly-arrived Soviet ambassador to the United States, Alexander M. Troyanovsky, would provide much of the material for Ambijan's propaganda efforts in the 1930s.

The U.S. had recognized the Soviet regime in 1933, and in 1934 Troyanovsky became the new Soviet ambassador to Washington.[38] The ambassador, who had been to Birobidzhan in 1934, met with an Ambijan delegation on May 19, 1935. He told them he had been impressed with the enthusiasm of the Jewish pioneers in Birobidzhan, and he conveyed from Moscow the news that the Soviet government would admit a "certain number" of non-Russian Jews to settle in the JAR. He was certain that Ambijan would be able to make the necessary arrangements to facilitate such settlement. Ambijan in turn promised Troyanovsky that Jewish supporters of Birobidzhan would supply $150 in cash, and passage to the Soviet border, to every eligible Jewish family wishing to immigrate to Birobidzhan from a country neighboring the USSR, and a further $200 after their arrival.

Budish and Miles M. Sherover of the Ambijan Board of Directors travelled to Moscow in the summer of 1935 to negotiate with the GEZERD and KOMERD regarding the role Ambijan would play. Budish travelled on to Birobidzhan in September to speak to local authorities, and published an account of his trip in the ICOR magazine *Nailebn-New Life*. Impressed by the JAR's size, he noted that it would take seven hours by express train to traverse the territory from west to east. He was also proud to see that the signs in the train stations were printed in Yiddish. Budish found the capital city, Birobidzhan, in the midst of a "feverish" but carefully planned building boom. Wide avenues were replacing narrow streets. Hospitals, schools, theaters, libraries, cultural centers, factories, warehouses, shops, restaurants, houses, apartments, office buildings, even newspaper kiosks, were all under construction; many of the new structures "would not have been out of place in America," he stated.

Budish was pleased to receive an affirmative answer when he asked whether the Soviets would allow non-Soviet Jews to settle in Birobidzhan: On October 10, the GEZERD officially authorized Ambijan to move forward. Settlers would be selected who would be "best adapted for pioneering conditions" and they would be assured of a home and livelihood when they arrived. In its 1935 statement of purpose, Ambijan had explained that it wished to study and facilitate the settlement in Birobidzhan of such Jews living in countries "whose conditions make it necessary for them to leave their present homelands, and who, by their training, vocation, and inclination, may be fit for settlement in Birobidjan." It had now received permission from the Soviet government to assist destitute non-Russian Jewish families who would be selected chiefly from Poland, Lithuania, Romania and Germany; the selection of immigrants would be carried out by Ambijan representatives in co-operation with Soviet officials. In Birobidzhan, the settlers would be absorbed into collectives and other co-operative enterprises. Ambijan would provide $350 for each family chosen, to cover costs of transportation and relocation.[39]

Ambijan confidently assured prospective members that Birobidzhan was well on its way to becoming a "prosperous agricultural-industrial state." The greatest difficulties having "already been left behind," the new Jewish republic would soon be open for "mass immigration of Jewish pioneers from other parts of the U.S.S.R. and from other countries."[40] William W. Cohen and Sol Low travelled to Washington to meet with Troyanovsky and informed him that Ambijan had received official authorization to go forward with the plan. They expressed their appreciation for the "generous attitude" shown by the Soviet government in permitting the immigration and in granting these settlers "the same privileges and exemptions as native settlers."[41]

Even before the final go-ahead from the GEZERD, Ambijan had begun its work. On August 22, 1935, it held a meeting at the Hotel Astor to further discuss the possibilities of Jewish immigration to Birobidzhan; speakers included Benjamin Brown, Gerson C. Young, James Waterman Wise, and Max Levin. Brown, a marketing specialist and sales director of the Utah Poultry Producers Cooperative Association, had been part of the 1929 ICOR expedition to Birobidzhan. The speakers pointed out that "Jews would find no hostile population in Biro-Bidjan, which would offer them a safe haven."[42] On October 10, Cohen sent Vilhjalmur Stefansson a letter outlining the goals of the Committee and informing him that "A number of prominent Jews and non-Jews" had already lent their names as sponsors.[43] A month later, John Lyons circulated a letter inviting members and friends of Ambijan to a reception to receive "confidential reports of the official arrangements with the Soviet Government made with our Committee" and to make plans for upcoming activities, including a dinner for Ambassador Troyanovsky on November 19.[44] A press release was issued by Lyons after the meeting, announcing that arrangements had been worked out with the Soviet authorities whereby destitute Jewish families in European countries would be assisted to establish themselves in Birobidzhan "at very little cost." The only payments necessary within the USSR would be the sum of $200 per family, and Ambijan would raise an additional $150 per family to get them to the Soviet Union. "Thus, for an outlay of $350.00, it will be possible to save a destitute family of five persons now living in Poland, Lithuania, Roumania or Germany, and to start it on the road to an independent livelihood and permanent security."[45] A follow-up luncheon at the Bankers' Club on December 17 was organized, Cohen wrote to Stefansson, "to acquaint our sponsors with the progress made by our Committee, and to announce the generous conditions outlined to us by the Soviet Government regarding the admission of non-Russian Jews into Birobidjan, the newly created Jewish Autonomous Territory." Jean J. Arens, the Soviet consul general in New York, addressed the guests and pledged his cooperation in facilitating the work of the committee. He was glad, he said, to speak about "a work of peace, of good-will, of humanity, which is built on the principle of equality between nations and races." He predicted "that in about ten years hence Biro-bidjan will be the cultural center of the Jewish masses."[46]

Ambijan's literature stressed the need to select settlers to Birobidzhan who would be sufficiently strong and healthy to adapt to its climate and engage in physical labor. Stefansson disagreed; his own experiences growing up on the frontier and working with people in the severe conditions of the Arctic had taught him that "good health and bodily strength, while desirable, are secondary. The chief thing is mental attitude....What you need for Birobidjan, then, is not the physiologically hardy but the psychologically adaptable," people whose courage could not be broken. In a letter written in early January 1936 he urged Cohen to select families "who want to go, who think they are going to like it when they get there, and who expect to succeed."[47] Cohen, impressed with the advice, invited Stefansson to his home on Central Park West to meet privately with a group of men interested in the project. Cohen also asked Stefansson to speak to an audience of "about 300 or 400 persons" at the Hotel Astor on February 4; Ambijan wanted them to "understand that the problems of weather in Birobidjan, or, rather climate, can be easily answered by an expert."[48]

A pamphlet published by the Committee in early 1936 stated that "already 100,000 Jews in Poland have signified their desire to emigrate" to "the vast, undeveloped, and as yet sparsely populated Jewish Autonomous Territory," a region larger than Belgium and Holland combined or "over three times the area of the state of New Jersey," and in latitude "no further from the equator than Paris or Montreal." Despite the difficulties attendant on the settling of a virgin land, "there are undoubtedly enormous opportunities for the development of agriculture and industry in Birobidjan on a large scale."[49]

By early 1936 the organization had a full slate of activities scheduled. The *Ambijan Bulletin* of February 14 listed lectures, luncheons, and rummage sales at various clubs, temples and synagogues. Among those lecturing at Ambijan events were James Waterman Wise; Professor Horace M. Kallen of the New School for Social Research; and Rabbi Ira Eisenstein of the Society for the Advancement of Judaism, who was the son-in-law of Rabbi Mordecai Kaplan and a founder of the Reconstructionist movement in Judaism. William Cohen, Judge Jeremiah T. Mahoney, former justice of the Supreme Court of New York, and Charles Recht, who since 1922 had served as an attorney for the Soviet government and was a member of Ambijan's Board of Directors, all broadcast over radio station WEVD, the station owned by the *Forverts*, whose call letters were derived from the initials of the famed socialist Eugene Victor Debs.[50]

Recht, who was closely associated with the Amtorg Trading Corp., addressed the issue in terms of the economic plight the Jews had found themselves in after World War I and the revolution in Russia. These events had "dealt a death blow to the remnants of the pre-war economic system, based largely on handicraft and small-scale industry, petty trade and comparatively primitive methods in agriculture." The resulting distress of east European Jews in the Baltic states, Poland and Romania "cannot be remedied except by mass immigration" or "ultimate extinction," he prophesized. But in the new Soviet state, the authorities took steps not only to politically enfranchise the Jews, "but also to effect their re-education along occupational lines and their absorption into the productive life of the new Russia." This "nurture and encouragement" led to a cultural and economic renascence among the Jewish masses. As for Birobidzhan, it was the culmination of the principles that had been designed to finally answer the "Jewish Question" in the Soviet Union, the response to those of its Jewish citizens who desired to establish a Jewish state "on soil unencumbered with old hostilities."[51] Recht, who was also a member of the ICOR, visited Birobidzhan in 1936 and declared it "a success." The fertility of the land and its industrial possibilities "have been found to be ample to support and give a rich livelihood to millions of inhabitants in the future," including immigrants from foreign lands. For the Jews of the world, concluded Recht, Birobidzhan constituted "a sacred trust." It provided "not only an answer to many of the arguments of the anti-Semite, but in the world arena Biro-Bidjan may well become the shield against the attack of the Jew-baiter and the Jew-hater."[52]

Cohen told the *New York Times* that Ambijan would hold a major dinner for Troyanovsky at the Hotel Astor in New York on March 11, to mark the initial step in raising $350,000. He assured the newspaper that "when the Jewish population attains a figure of 50,000 the territory will become a Jewish republic." James Waterman Wise, Wall Street lawyer and social reformer George Gordon Battle, Vilhjalmur Stefansson, U.S. senator Elbert D. Thomas of Utah, and New York State Supreme Court justice Mitchell May all spoke at the dinner, at which the invited guests, who included, apart from pro-Soviet sympathizers, men such as pro-Zionists Jacob de Haas and Horace M. Kallen, were told that the plight of Jews in some parts of Europe was "distressing beyond description." They were living lives that "dooms them to slow extinction from undernourishment and starvation." Their only salvation lay through emigration. "Unfortunately, the possible outlets, even including Palestine, are extremely limited. It is therefore of the greatest historical significance that the Soviet Government has generously agreed, in response to the urgent requests of [Ambijan] and other organizations of similar aim, to open the gates of the new Jewish Autonomous Territory in the U.S.S.R. to Jewish emigrants from other lands." Ambijan was authorized to arrange for the settlement of 1,000 families in Birobidzhan in 1936; these settlers would even be eligible for "full-fledged citizenship."[53]

Troyanovsky in his speech at the dinner remarked that "in our country there is no Jewish problem. All nationalities enjoy equality and liberty." He added that "we are happy that anti-semitism has almost completely disappeared in our country, and our young generation especially is completely free from any trace of the anti-semitic spirit." With the creation of the JAR, "the Jewish people have acquired their own state organization as a basis for national culture." He emphasized that the USSR desired as settlers those who would be able to withstand life under pioneering conditions. He thanked Ambijan for "making all the necessary arrangements to assist these emigrants to establish themselves in the Jewish Territory."[54] In an address in Chicago, he declared that anti-Semitism "is looked upon as a barbarity in our country."[55]

New York politicians joined in the praise. Democratic Congressman Emanuel Celler, who represented the 10th Congressional district, encompassing parts of Brooklyn and Queens, hoped the Soviet decision to allow 1,000 Jewish families from outside the country to move to Birobidzhan "will be the beginning of a movement that will help tens of thousands of Jews to find a haven of refuge." These Jews "will be taken out of their misery and transferred to a country where they will enjoy economic security and equality of opportunity." They would have self-government and the use of their own language, Yiddish. "Never in the history of the world has such a glorious opportunity been offered to the Jews." Samuel Levy, the Manhattan borough president, stated his gratification at the lack of anti-Semitism in the Soviet Union, and added that Ambijan's cause was "deserving of the support of every American."[56]

Vito Marcantonio, who represented the 20th Congressional district of East Harlem for the CP-influenced American Labor Party (ALP), also chimed in: In a radio address he delivered over WHN on August 22, 1936, Marcantonio expressed his admiration "for the splendid way in which Russia has solved its problem of racial and national minorities." There was, he stated, "absolute equality" for all peoples of the Soviet Union, and "it is especially gratifying to know that there is no anti-Semitism in present-day Russia." He referred to Birobidzhan as "immense" and said that, given its resources, it could "easily" support several million people. The new Russia, "freed from the plague of anti-Semitism, is ready to receive Jewish immigrants into Biro-Bidjan from other lands which have fallen victims to the curse of anti-Semitism."[57]

At a meeting held at the Hotel Edison, New York, on September 20, and attended by 450 delegates representing 250 Jewish organizations, Ambijan launched a campaign to raise $500,000 to settle 1,000 families and 500 individuals in Birobidzhan. Charles Recht, recently returned from Birobidzhan, asserted that much had been accomplished in the past two years. Despite an acute shortage of housing, manpower and machinery, "they are doing miracles."[58] Budish appealed to all concerned to raise the necessary funds as soon as possible in order to meet the initial quota quickly. Jewish Welfare funds in Cincinnati, Omaha and Passaic, NJ, had already sent money. "This will pave the way for the securing of permission for the settlement in Birobidjan of larger numbers in the succeeding years."[59] Sixty Ambijan members met at the Hotel Astor on October 3 to announce that Ambijan would be receiving full cooperation from the Soviets in settling Russian and non-Russian Jews in Birobidzhan. Miles M. Sherover, president of the Soviet-American Securities Corp., who had visited the USSR along with Budish a year earlier, reported that 4,000 non-Russian Jews had already been permitted to settle in Birobidzhan in 1936.[60] William Cohen again assured his audience that in Birobidzhan Jews could look forward to "freedom of spirit, comfort, and the opportunity to work," in a place where "a Jew may hold his head up" and no longer suffer humiliation. He called on American Jews to aid as many of the downtrodden Jews in Europe as possible "to find relief in this haven of refuge called Biro-Bidjan."[61] Writing in *Nailebn-New Life*, Cohen later asserted that there was "no vestige of persecution or discrimination against Jews in the Soviet Union."[62]

The publicity campaign received wide attention; the Soviets even began to produce films about Birobidzhan as a means of appealing to American Jews. In 1935 movie-goers in New York could be enlightened by a Yiddish "talkie" entitled *Biro-Bidzhan*, produced by Soyuzkino News and directed by Mikhail Slutsky, which opened on April 6 at the Acme Theater, 14th Street and Union Square. "Come see the life of the Jewish pioneers in Biro-Bidzhan! Come see the way the Jewish Autonomous Territory in Biro-Bidzhan is being built! Come see how the settlers begin to take their first steps on the soil of Biro-Bidzhan. Come see how they are building, come see the golden ears of corn in their fields," stated a notice in the *ICOR* monthly.[63] Another Soviet movie, *Iskateli Schastya (Seekers of Happiness)*, also known in the United States as *Birobidjan: A Greater Promise*, was made by the director Vladimir Korsh-Sablin in Belarus in 1936 for Belgoskino and released in the U.S. that same year. Its plot was based on a group of Jews who, "passionately dreaming of working the Soviet land...in their new homeland, Birobidzhan," immigrate to the new Jewish autonomous region.[64] "It contrasted the character of the *luftmensch*, who was interested in get-rich-quick schemes...with honest Jews, who wanted to take advantage of the opportunity offered by the Soviet Union and live a rich and happy life on a collective farm."[65] The movie "received

The Formation of Ambijan

an extraordinary amount of publicity in the English-language *Moscow Daily News*."[66] The Hollywood trade newspaper *Variety*, in its review, asserted that it was directed to Jews outside Russia: "Obviously the film, on behalf of the Soviet, is inviting Jews outside of Russia to settle and develop the wild Birobidjian [sic] country, which in case of war with Japan could become among Russia's first lines of defense."[67]

In September of 1936, Marley returned to the U.S. for three months, and succeeded in raising large sums for Birobidzhan. His first event was a dinner at the Hotel Astor on September 22, attended by 300 people, at which Marley spoke of the indescribably bad condition of Jews in Poland.[68] At Marley's farewell dinner held at the Hotel Commodore on December 22, attended by over 1,000 guests, George Gordon Battle announced that the Soviet government would authorize the admittance of 2,000 families and 500 individuals from Poland in 1937, almost double the original quota.[69] Over $100,000 was pledged, a sum, editorialized the Washington-based *National Jewish Ledger*, which reflected "the new attitude toward Birobidjan on the part of American Jewry," who had come to recognize that this was "the only place of Jewish refuge where the government is ready to help in a material way." The paper excused the delays in settling foreign Jews in the region by explaining that the Soviet government was unwilling "to be stampeded into a mass movement before Birobidjan is ready to absorb foreign Jewish immigrants."[70]

Ambijan's fifty-page *Year Book* commemorating Marley's farewell dinner was full of testimonials and letters of support, including one from Stefansson, who was now also listed as a member of Ambijan's Board of Directors and Governors: "The Birobidjan project seems to me to offer a most statesmanlike contribution to the problem of the rehabilitation of eastern and central European Jewry. I sincerely hope that your movement attains the success it merits."[71] Even some religious figures supported the idea. Rabbi Philip S. Bernstein of Temple B'rith Kodesh in Rochester, NY, who wrote a column entitled "The Jewish Scene" in the national Anglo-Jewish press, advised readers not to oppose the project on ideological grounds, despite the Soviet government's views on religion. He added that if Jews with Communist sympathies preferred Birobidzhan to Palestine, "that is their rightful privilege."[72] Another rabbi, Solomon B. Freehof of Temple Rodef Shalom in Pittsburgh, also endorsed the idea, noting that it had two advantages: First, Birobidzhan "is no crowded land with ancient inhabitants," and second, "it is in Russia—the one land in the world where anti-Semitism is a crime."[73]

Lonnie Levin, chair of Ambijan's Women's Division, gave a luncheon on March 20, 1937 at the Hotel Astor in New York. Vilhjalmur

Stefansson addressed the gathering, explaining that although Birobidzhan was not a utopia, for "the stricken Jews of Poland, Roumania, Lithuania, and other European countries, Birobidjan would already represent an advance to a higher standard of living, to say nothing of the immeasurably greater degree of security and hope for the future." Stefansson's speech was carried on radio station WMCA in New York.[74]

At its annual meeting held at the Hotel Astor on October 7, 1937, Ambijan added Battle, Justice Mitchell May, and Congressmen Emanuel Celler and William I. Sirovich, to its list of vice-presidents.[75] Sirovich, a Democrat representing Manhattan's 14th Congressional district, had visited the Soviet Union in 1931 and 1933. He stated that "once a Jew has made up his mind to establish a group life, Birobidjan is the answer to his prayer."[76]

Endnotes

1 Earl Browder, "The American Communist Party in the Thirties," in Rita James Simon, ed., *As We Saw the Thirties: Essays on Social and Political Movements of a Decade* (Urbana, IL: University of Illinois Press, 1967), 237.
2 Melech Epstein, *Jewish Labor in U.S.A.: An Industrial, Political and Cultural History of the Jewish Labor Movement, 1882-1914* (New York: Ktav, 1969), 257.
3 Louis Fischer, "Progress in the Colonies," *Menorah Journal* 15, 4 (October 1928): 343, 345; Louis Fischer, "The Jews and the Five-Year Plan," the *Nation* 134, 3490 (May 25, 1932): 599.
4 "Soviet Jewish Plan Lags," *New York Times*, Sept. 30, 1932, 14.
5 William Zukerman, "A Jewish Home in Russia," the *Nation* 134, 3488 (May 11, 1932): 540. The Labor Zionist periodical *Jewish Frontier* also called Birobidzhan "a Soviet edition" of Zionism. "What We Stand For," in [Hayim Greenberg, ed.], *Jewish Frontier Anthology 1934-1944*, 3-5.
6 William Zukerman, "The Jewish Colonization Movement in Soviet Russia," *Menorah Journal* 21, 1 (April-June 1933): 73-74, 77-81.
7 Abraham Revutsky, "Bira-Bidzhan: A Jewish Eldorado?" *Menorah Journal* 16, 2 (February 1929): 158-168.
8 "Obituary: Lord Marley," *Times*, London, March 3, 1952, 6.

9   For more on this amazing political propagandist, see Stephen Koch, *Double Lives: Stalin, Willi Münzenberg and the Seduction of the Intellectuals* (New York: Enigma Books, 2004); and Sean McMeekin, *The Red Millionaire: A Political Biography of Willy Münzenberg, Moscow's Secret Propaganda Tsar in the West, 1917-1940* (New Haven: Yale University Press, 2003). Much has been published about the Comintern. See E.H. Carr, *Twilight of the Comintern, 1930-1935* (New York: Pantheon Books, 1983); Duncan Hallas, *The Comintern* (London: Bookmarks, 1985); Kevin McDermott and Jeremy Agnew, *The Comintern: A History of International Communism from Lenin to Stalin* (New York: St Martin's Press, 1996); and Tim Rees and Andrew Thorpe, eds., *International Communism and the Communist International, 1919-43* (New York: St Martin's Press, 1998). See also Jane Degras, ed., *The Communist International 1919-1943 Documents*. Vol. III: *1929-1943* (London: Oxford University Press, 1965).
10 John F. Naylor, *Labour's International Policy: The Labour Party in the 1930s* (London: Weidenfeld and Nicolson, 1969), 80-81.
11 Nicole Taylor, "The Mystery of Lord Marley," *Jewish Quarterly* 198 (Summer 2005): 67-69.
12 FBI report from Edward Scheidt, Special Agent in Charge, New York, to Director, FBI, March 1, 1951, originally in NY File 100-42538. File 100-99898, Section 6, Freedom of Information/Privacy Acts [hereafter FOIPA] No. 416152, Ambijan. The informant had served the Comintern between 1928 and 1938.
13 "Lord Marley Here to Work for ORT," *New York Times*, Jan. 26, 1933, 19; "Lord Marley Asks for Support for ORT, *New York Times*, Jan. 30, 1933, 3; "Lord Marley Pleads for Relief for Jews," *New York Times*, Feb. 15, 1933, 19; "Hail Lord Marley for His Aid to Jews," *New York Times*, March 11, 1933, 15; "Marley Lauds ORT Work," *New York Times*, March 13, 1933, 16; "Marley Off, Finds We Are Still Rich," *New York Times*, March 18, 1933, 15.
14 Lord Marley, *Biro Bidjan as I Saw It* (New York: ICOR, 1934): 2-15 (emphasis in original).
15 Nicole Taylor, "The Mystery of Lord Marley," 68.
16 William W. Cohen, "Foreword," in *Birobidjan: A New Hope for Oppressed European Jews: Year Book of the American Committee for the Settlement of Jews in Birobidjan, Published on the Occasion of the Farewell Dinner Rendered to the Right Honorable Lord Marley at the Hotel Commodore* (New York: Ambijan, Dec. 22, 1936), 1. Ambijan took note of Marley's "eminence as a thinker and leader in contemporary liberal thought," his "nobility of mind and purposes" and "his efforts in the cause of the liberation of the oppressed, his unceasing advocacy of social justice." He symbolized "the hoped-for solution of the problems of the persecuted Jews in central and eastern Europe." "Lord Marley," in *Birobidjan: A New Hope for Oppressed European Jews*, 3. For details of Marley's 1934 American trip, see the *New York Times*: "Lord Marley Here to Assail Hitler," Feb. 7, 1934, 4; "Lord Marley Plea Aids Nazi Victims," Feb.

8, 1934, 5; "Lord Marley Calls Hitler Peace Threat," Feb. 25, 1934, section 2, 3; and "Act to Help Jews Settle in Russia," Feb. 28, 1934, 6. Among the sponsors of Marley's trip was Columbia professor John Dewey.

17   Harry G. Kriegel of the Graphic Arts Division pledged to raise at least $35,000 and Victor A. Fischel of the Wine and Liquor Trade Division the same amount. Outside of New York, the most extensive work had been done in Chicago and New England. The New England division, headed by Isaac S. Kibrick, Thomas Small, Solomon Agoos, and Albert Weschler, had already made plans to raise $25,000. J. M. Budish, "The American Birobidjan Committee," in *Birobidjan: A New Hope for Oppressed European Jews*, 14, 17-18; "Our Co-Workers Say," in *Birobidjan: A New Hope for Oppressed European Jews*, 20; letterhead on Ambijan stationery; membership application; circular letter written by John Lyons, New York, Nov. 11, 1935, in the Russian Relief Collection, Box 2, Birobidzhan folder, Yeshiva University Archives, New York [hereafter Yeshiva]. Julius Hammer was the father of Armand Hammer, the well-known pro-Soviet entrepreneur with many business interests in the USSR; Lyons hosted a radio show on WEVD, and served as secretary of a Workmen's Circle branch.

18   The transcript of his address was published in the ICOR pamphlet *Biro-Bidjan and You* (New York: Astoria Press, 1929).

19   See, for instance, "They Preserve Judaism in Russia," *Jewish Criterion*, Pittsburgh, Nov. 2, 1934, 31-32. "The houses which the colonists occupy today ...are not very magnificent, mere peasants' cottages; but in comparison with those first living-quarters they are palatial."

20   B.Z. Goldberg, "Judea a la Soviet or The Jews Go Back to the Wilderness or A Jewish Homeland in the Making," typed mss., [1935], 2-5, 7; in the B.Z. Goldberg papers, Box 61, Articles on the Soviet Union, folder "The Jews Go Back to the Wilderness," Schottenstein-Jesselson Library at the Herbert D. Katz Center for Advanced Judaic Studies, University of Pennsylvania, Philadelphia [hereafter B.Z. Goldberg papers].

21   *Birobidjan: The Jewish Autonomous Territory* (New York: American Committee for the Settlement of Jews in Birobidjan (Ambijan), 1936), 8, 30. But see his description of the 1934 trip in B.Z. Goldberg, *The Jewish Problem in the Soviet Union: Analysis and Solution* (New York: Crown, 1961), 170-189. Written when he was no longer a pro-Soviet sympathizer, but a socialist Zionist, Goldberg acknowledged that he had faced difficulties when he tried to visit the Icor commune. "Most of the Birobidjan propaganda was directed at the Jews of the Western world....In the view of the Soviet leaders, the Jews could be instrumental in helping them attain their objective of better public relations with the West," he admitted (193).

22   Melech Epstein. *Pages from a Colorful Life: An Autobiographical Sketch* (Miami Beach: Block Publishing, 1971), 105. Robert Weinberg called Ambijan "a Communist front organization." *Stalin's Forgotten Zion*, 56. Ambijan was "more sophisticated" than the ICOR and able to recruit "unsuspecting

dupes," whereas the latter was "a crude Communist front that used insulting rhetoric against the very Jews that it wanted to influence." Herbert Romerstein and Eric Breindel, *The Venona Secrets: Exposing Soviet Espionage and America's Traitors* (Washington, DC: Regnery Publishing, 2000), 397.

23 Memo from John Edgar Hoover to Lawrence M.C. Smith, Chief, Special War Policies Unit, Washington, June 22, 1943. A report to Hoover from an informant in New York, dated Oct. 20, 1943, noted that most of the top members of Ambijan were not Communists, but that the rank-and-file membership had a large percentage of Communists, who were "the most active workers in the Ambijan activities." File 100-99898, Section 1, FOIPA No. 416152, Ambijan.

24 "Act to Help Jews Settle in Russia," *New York Times*, Feb. 28, 1934, 6; Felix Warburg, "Offers Tremendous Possibilities," *Ambijan Bulletin* 3, 2 (February 1944): [7]. Warburg was, like many in the German Jewish elite in America, a non-Zionist, someone who believed in Jewish settlement, but not necessarily a Jewish state, in Palestine. See further Raphael Medoff, "Felix Warburg and the Palestinian Arabs: A Reassessment," *American Jewish Archives* 54, 1 (2002): 11-36; Bauer, *My Brother's Keeper*, 100-102.

25 See the letter from J.M Budish, then chair of the Administrative Committee of Ambijan, to Vilhjalmur Stefansson, New York, Nov. 5, 1936, in which Budish informed Stefansson that Stefansson had been elected a vice-president of Ambijan at the organization's annual meeting of October 25, 1936, held at the Hotel Astor, New York. Stefansson Correspondence, MSS 196, Box 40, 1936--USSR Folder; in the Stefansson Collection, Baker Memorial Library, Dartmouth College, Hanover, NH [hereafter Stefansson Collection].

26 See, for instance, Vilhjalmur Stefansson, *My Life with the Eskimo* (New York: Macmillan, 1913); Vilhjalmur Stefansson *The Friendly Arctic: The Story of Five Years in Polar Regions* (New York, Macmillan, 1921); Vilhjalmur Stefansson, *Hunters of the Great North* (New York: Harcourt, Brace, 1922); Vilhjalmur Stefansson, *The Northward Course of Empire* (New York: Harcourt, Brace, 1922); Vilhjalmur Stefansson, *The Adventure of Wrangel Island* (New York: Macmillan, 1925); Vilhjalmur Stefansson, *Unsolved Mysteries of the Arctic* (New York: Macmillan, 1938). These books went through many editions and were translated into German, Hungarian, Icelandic, Russian, Spanish and Swedish.

27 "Egotistical, iconoclastic, and dogmatic, he was always convinced that his way was the right way." Pierre Berton, *Prisoners of the North* (Toronto: Doubleday Canada, 2004), 66. This did not endear him to many people. "Stefansson was, and is, more than an eminent Canadian. He was one of the most widely known personalities in the Canada and the world of the 1920s." Yet while "regarded as a folk hero" in both the U.S. and Russia, he received little recognition in Canada. Richard J. Diubaldo, *Stefansson and the Canadian Arctic* (Montreal: McGill-Queen's University Press, 1978), 1-2, 4.

28 "Stefansson's books so altered their idea of the Arctic that they started a

movement toward the North Pole which somewhat resembled our celebrated advance on the Klondike." Robert Lewis Taylor, "Profiles: Klondike Stef--I," *New Yorker* 17, 36 (Oct. 18, 1941): 26. This was the first of a two-part profile of Stefansson published by Taylor in the *New Yorker*. The second piece appeared the following week.

29 D.M. LeBourdais, *Stefansson: Ambassador of the North* (Montreal: Harvest House, 1963), 183-184. See also Earl P. Hanson, *Stefansson: Prophet of the North* (New York: Harper, 1941), 179, 210-214.

30 Vilhjalmur Stefansson, "A Prophecy Fulfilled," *Soviet Russia Today* 6, 5 (July 1937): 8. An accompanying photo showed Stefansson with Soviet ambassador Alexander A. Troyanovsky and New York consul general Jean J. Arens at a ceremony at the Explorers Club. Arens, who served as consul general in New York from June 1935 after a previous posting as a counsellor at the Soviet embassy in Paris, was recalled to the Soviet Union in January 1937 and, even after denouncing "Trotskyism," disappeared into Stalin's gulags. "Soviet Consul is Shifted," *New York Times*, May 29, 1935, 6; "Soviet Shifts Arens from his Post Here," *New York Times*, Jan. 31, 1937, Section 1, 25; "Red Leaders Feared Victims of Clean-Up," *New York Times*, Nov. 30, 1937, 5. *Soviet Russia Today* was until 1939 the organ of the Friends of the Soviet Union.

31 "Stefansson Hails Russian Exploits," *New York Times*, Jan. 9, 1938, Section 1, 35.

32 "Soviet Pavilion Hails Arctic Feats," *New York Times*, June 12, 1939, 10; Vilhjalmur Stefansson, "The Friendly Soviet Arctic," *Soviet Russia Today* 8, 4 (July 1939): 17-19.

33 Flyer announcing her appearance; Russian Relief Collection, Box 2, Birobidzhan folder, Yeshiva.

34 Anna Louise Strong, "Biro-Bidjan as I Saw It," *Nailebn-New Life* 10, 3 (March 1936): 12-14 [English section] and *Nailebn-New Life* 10, 4 (April 1936): 10-11 [English section].

35 Anna Louise Strong, "Birobidjan," *Asia* 36, 1 (January 1936): 41-42. The daughter of a Nebraska minister, Strong earned a Ph.D. in philosophy at the University of Chicago, became a journalist, and participated in the 1919 Seattle General Strike. She later moved to Moscow and helped found the English-language *Moscow News*. No mention is made of her talks on Birobidzhan or of Strong's articles about the region in the comprehensive biography of her life written by Tracy B. Strong and Helen Keyssar, *Right in her Soul: The Life of Anna Louise Strong* (New York: Random House, 1983), though the authors provide otherwise detailed descriptions of Strong's various lecture tours in the United States over the decades.

36 See J.M. Budish, "Di rizige sotsyalistishe boyung inm sovyetn farband," *Icor yor-bukh - ICOR Year Book 1932*, 19-23 [Yiddish section].

37 According to Russian historian Svetlana Chervonnaya, Budish, who spoke English, German, French and Russian, was a senior economist at Amtorg and

was on their list of American employees in 1936 and 1937. "Foreign nuclei of VCP (b) [Zagranichnye yacheiki VKP (b)]", in the RGASPI [Rossiiskii gosudarstvennyi arkhiv sotsial'no-politicheskoi istorii - Russian State Archive of Social and Political History], fond 17, description 36, file 327. E-mail letter from Svetlana Chervonnaya to the author, Moscow, August 16, 2005. (The VCP (b) was the Soviet Communist Party; the RGASPI is now the main depository for documentation relating to the history of socialism and the records of the CPSU and its predecessors.) The ICOR and Ambijan could not directly send cash or goods to Birobidzhan, but had to go through Amtorg, which did all the buying for Birobidzhan. This information is contained on p. 9 of a 17-page report dated Sept. 7, 1944 submitted by E.E. Conroy, Special Agent in Charge, originally in NY File 100-14454. File 100-2074, FOIPA Release of Organization for Jewish Colonization. Budish died in 1966. "Jacob M. Budish, 80, a Labor Economist," *New York Times*, June 7, 1966, 47.

38 The ICOR published a profile of Troyanovsky. Samuel Sachs, "The First Soviet Ambassador to the United States," *ICOR* 7, 1 (January 1934): 23.
39 J.M. Budish, "A grus fun der yiddisher autonomer teritorye," *Nailebn-New Life* 9, 7 (November 1935): 32-33 [Yiddish section]; *Birobidjan: The Jewish Autonomous Territory*, 7-10; J. M. Budish, "The American Birobidjan Committee," in *Birobidjan: A New Hope for Oppressed European Jews*, 14-15; "Application for Membership"; Russian Relief Collection, Box 2, Birobidzhan folder, Yeshiva.
40 *Birobidjan: The Jewish Autonomous Territory*, 30.
41 "Jews to be Settled in Soviet Territory," *New York Times*, Oct. 29, 1935, 14.
42 "Jews Weigh Soviet Haven," *New York Times*, Aug. 23, 1935, 13. Benjamin Brown at this time had also sponsored a Zionist youth group who had settled on agricultural land near Trenton, NJ, in preparation for making *aliyah* to Palestine. Stanley Bero, "Back to the Land," *Jewish Standard*, Toronto, Aug. 17, 1934, 3, 8.
43 Letter from William W. Cohen to Vilhjalmur Stefansson, New York, Oct. 10, 1935; Stefansson Correspondence, MSS 196, Box 38, 1935--USSR Folder; Stefansson Collection.
44 "Soviet to Aid Jews," *New York Times*, Oct. 4, 1935, 18; Circular letter signed by John Lyons, New York, Nov. 11, 1935; Russian Relief Collection, Box 2, Birobidzhan folder, Yeshiva.
45 Press release in the Philip Sandler papers, RG420, Box 4, "Materyaln vegn der ICOR kampanye far a folks-delegatsye," YIVO.
46 "Plans Made to Aid Jewish Settlers," *New York Times*, Dec. 18, 1935, 32; J. M. Budish, "The American Birobidjan Committee," in *Birobidjan: A New Hope for Oppressed European Jews*, 15; Cohen afterwards told Stefansson that the explorer's presence "helped to make it a success." Letters from William W. Cohen to Vilhjalmur Stefansson, New York, Dec. 9 and Dec. 24, 1935; Stefansson Correspondence, MSS 196, Box 38, 1935--USSR Folder;

CHAPTER ONE

Stefansson Collection.

47. Letter from Vilhjalmur Stefansson to William W. Cohen, Jan. 2, 1936; Stefansson correspondence, MSS 196, Box 40, 1936--USSR Folder, Stefansson Collection.

48. Letters from William W. Cohen to Vilhjalmur Stefansson, New York, Jan. 7, 1936, Jan. 17, 1936 and Jan. 27, 1936; Stefansson correspondence, MSS 196, Box 40, 1936--USSR Folder, Stefansson Collection.

49. *Birobidjan: The Jewish Autonomous Territory*, 6, 13.

50. Eisenstein and Budish were also scheduled to speak about Birobidzhan to a gathering of the Association of Reform Rabbis at the Hotel Taft on March 10, 1936; Kallen and Eisenstein also were to speak at the S.A.J. [Society for the Advancement of Judaism] Temple on West 86th St., New York on March 7 and March 15, respectively. *Ambijan Bulletin*, Feb. 14, 1936.

51. Charles Recht, "The Jewish Question Answered," in *Birobidjan: A New Hope for Oppressed European Jews*, 12-13.

52. Charles Recht, "Is Biro-Bidjan a Success?" *Nailebn-New Life* 10, 9 (September 1936): 5-6 [English section]. Recht, born in 1887 in what is now the Czech Republic, was, according to an FBI report, considered "a key figure in Communist activities in the New York area." This information is contained on p. 23 of a 33-page report dated Nov. 5, 1944 submitted by E.E. Conroy, Special Agent in Charge, originally in NY File 100-42538. File 100-99898, Section 1, FOIPA No. 416152, Ambijan.

53. "Jews Hail Compact for Colony in Soviet," *New York Times*, March 1, 1936, 5; "Jews' Plight Laid to Trade Crises," *New York Times*, March 12, 1936, 15; J. M. Budish, "The American Birobidjan Committee," in *Birobidjan: A New Hope for Oppressed European Jews*, 15; flyer announcement of the dinner; Russian Relief Collection, Box 2, Birobidzhan Folder, Yeshiva.

54. "The Soviet Ambassador Speaks on Biro-Bidjan," *Nailebn-New Life* 10, 4 (April 1936): 6-9 [English section].

55. *Birobidjan: The Jewish Autonomous Territory*, 18.

56. "Prominent Leaders Appraise Birobidjan," in *Birobidjan: A New Hope for Oppressed European Jews*, 34-35.

57. Vito Marcantonio, "Anti-Semitism and Biro-Bidjan," *Nailebn-New Life* 10, 9 (September 1936): 11-12 [English section]. Many articles and books have appeared about Marcantonio. One full-length biography is by Gerald Meyer, *Vito Marcantonio: Radical Politician, 1902-1954* (Albany, NY: State University of New York Press, 1989). See also Kenneth Waltzer, "The Party and the Polling Place: American Communism and the American Labor Party in the 1930s," *Radical History Review* 23 (Spring 1980): 104-129; and Kenneth Waltzer, "The FBI, Congressman Vito Marcantonio, and the American Labor Party," in Athan G. Theoharis, *Beyond the Hiss Case: The FBI, Congress, and the Cold War* (Philadelphia: Temple University Press, 1982): 176-214.

58. "Jews Seek $500,000 for Resettlement," *New York Times*, Sept. 21, 1936, 40; "Review of the Year 5697," in Harry Schneiderman, ed., *American Jewish Year*

Book 5698 (September 6, 1937 to September 25, 1938). Vol. 39 (Philadelphia: Jewish Publication Society of America, 1937): 246-247.

59 J. M. Budish, "The American Birobidjan Committee," in *Birobidjan: A New Hope for Oppressed European Jews*, 18-19; letter from J.M. Budish to Vilhjalmur Stefansson, New York, Nov. 5, 1936; Stefansson correspondence, MSS 196, Box 40, 1936--USSR Folder, Stefansson Collection.

60 "Soviet to Aid Jews," *New York Times*, Oct. 4, 1936, 18. Sherover, born in Cracow in 1896, came to the U.S. in 1903. A confidential 1944 FBI report called him "a man with a shady reputation" who had also been employed by the Amtorg Trading Corp. This information is contained on p. 24 of a 33-page report dated Nov. 5, 1944 submitted by E.E. Conroy, Special Agent in Charge, originally in NY File 100-42538. File 100-99898, Section 1, FOIPA No. 416152, Ambijan.

61 W.W. Cohen, "The Autonomous Jewish Territory in Biro Bidjan is a Shining Light," *Nailebn-New Life* 10, 11 (November 1936): 8 [English section].

62 W.W. Cohen, "'No Vestige of Anti-Semitism in the U.S.S.R.'," *Nailebn-New Life* 11, 11 (November 1937): 33 [English section].

63 "A toki fun biro-bidzhan in acme teater," *ICOR* 8, 4 (April 1935): 25. This was the last issue of the *ICOR*; it was succeeded by the new ICOR magazine, *Nailebn-New Life* in May 1935.

64 Arkady Vaksberg, *Stalin Against the Jews*, translated from the Russian by Antonia W. Bouis (New York: Alfred A. Knopf, 1994), 66.

65 Peter Kenez, "Jewish Themes in Stalinist Films," *Judaism* 45, 3 (Summer 1996): 283.

66 James Hoberman, *The Red Atlantis: Communist Culture in the Absence of Communism* (Philadelphia: Temple University Press, 1998), 85.

67 "Film Reviews," *Variety*, July 1, 1936, 25; October 21, 1936, 23.

68 "Lord Marley Honored Here," *New York Times*, Sept. 23, 1936, 7. He spoke on behalf of the ORT two nights later and also on Dec. 19 and Dec. 24. "American Advice Held Need for Jews," *New York Times*, Sept. 25, 1936, 19; "Polish Jews' Plight Seen Getting Worse," *New York Times*, Dec. 20, 1936, Section 1, 2; "$10,000 Pledged for ORT," *New York Times*, Dec. 27, 1936, 31. Felix Warburg attended the Sept. 22 reception for Marley "to see what he was saying about refugees and Russia." Quoted in Zosa Szajkowski, *Jews, Wars, and Communism*. Vol. IV, 161.

69 "Birobidjan Project Gets New Impetus," *New York Times*, Dec. 23, 1936, 12.

70 "$100,000 for Birobidjan," *National Jewish Ledger*, Washington, DC, Jan.1, 1937, 6.

71 "Prominent Leaders Appraise Birobidjan," in *Birobidjan: A New Hope for Oppressed European Jews*, 36.

72 Rabbi Philip S. Bernstein, "The Paradox of Biro-Bidjan," *National Jewish Ledger*, Washington, DC, Jan. 15, 1937, 6. Bernstein also wrote for the *Nation*, *Harper's* and other magazines. He was a Jewish chaplain for the U.S. military in World War II and later helped Holocaust survivors in Europe.

73 Quoted in *Birobidjan: The Jewish Autonomous Territory in the U.S.S.R.* (New York: American Committee for the Settlement of Jews in Birobidjan, [1936]).
74 Letter from Lonnie R. Levin to Vilhjalmur Stefansson, New York, Feb. 18, 1937; letter from J.M. Budish to Vilhjalmur Stefansson, March 25, 1937; "Material for Dr. Vilhjalmur Stefansson", 4; "Today on the Radio" schedule; all in Stefansson correspondence, MSS 196, Box 43, 1937--USSR A-B Folder, Stefansson Collection.
75 Untitled pamphlet in the Russian Relief Collection, Box 2, Birobidzhan folder, Yeshiva. May had been a congressman in 1898-1900, and was appointed to the New York State Supreme Court in 1922.
76 "Prominent Leaders Appraise Birobidjan," in *Birobidjan: A New Hope for Oppressed European Jews*, 35.

Lord Marley, from *Birobidjan: A New Hope for Oppressed European Jews*

Cover of *Biro Bidjan as I Saw It*, 1934, by Lord Marley

B.Z. Goldberg, Schottenstein-Jesselson Library of the Herbert D. Katz Center for Advanced Judaic Studies at the University of Pennsylvania.

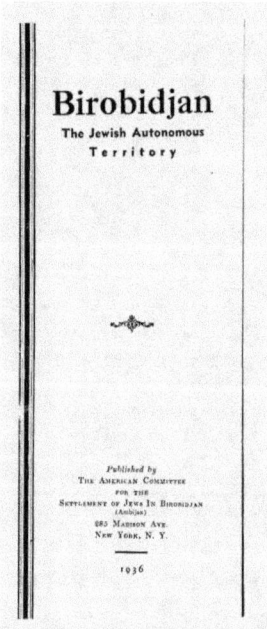

Cover of Ambijan pamphlet
Birobidzhan: The Jewish Autonomous Territory

Philadelphia Pamphlet advertising Anna Louise Strong lecture, Feb. 6, 1936, Russian Relief Collection, Yeshiva University Archives, New York

The "People's Delegation" and the Popular Front, 1935-1939

In 1935 the ICOR began making plans to send a "people's delegation" to Birobidzhan to facilitate implementation of the plan to settle European Jews there. Fifteen of the 50 delegates would be ICOR members. The membership endorsed the idea at the organization's sixth national convention, held on February 8-10, 1935, in New York.[1] The plan was eliciting, according to the ICOR's new magazine, *Nailebn-New Life*, "colossal interest throughout the country."[2] Ambijan, too, soon took up the idea of sending a delegation.

Shloime Almazov reported to a plenum of the ICOR national executive committee held in New York on October 27 that the GEZERD had received the idea favorably and would give the delegation its fullest cooperation. It was essential that ICOR assemble a representative delegation that would include members from all sectors of Jewish society. *Morgn Frayhayt* writer and ICOR activist Moishe Katz suggested that apart from the 15 ICOR representatives, 10 be selected from fraternal organizations, 10 from *landsmanshaftn*, and 10 from unions; the remaining five should be artists, writers or professionals. The delegation, which would also be bringing to Birobidzhan a "People's Book" of greetings from the broad masses of American Jews and their organizations, "will see with its own eyes the manner in which the one and only Jewish autonomous territory in the world is being created." The book, for which 250,000 signatures would be collected, would find a permanent home in the new Jewish State Museum in the Jewish Autonomous Region. Upon its return, the delegation would regale the Jewish masses of America with its impressions of the JAR.[3]

In order to attract participants, a Sponsors Committee of the People's Delegation to Biro-Bidjan was set up, with the Yiddish playwright Leon Kobrin as chair and Shloime Almazov as secretary. The Yiddish novelist Joseph Opatoshu and poets Abraham Reisen and Zishe Weinper were members, as were the Communists and fellow-travelers Abraham Olken, Leon Dennen, Charles Kuntz, James Waterman Wise, Moishe Nadir, Reuben Brainin and son Joseph, Rubin Saltzman of the IWO, J.M. Budish, Louis Hyman, Max Levin, Ab. Epstein and Melech Epstein. Its sponsors included Mike Gold, then editor of *New Masses*; New York state congressmen William I. Sirovich and Vito Marcantonio; Norman Thomas of the Socialist Party; professor Franklin S. Harris of Brigham Young University; professors John Dewey, Franz Boas, Lowell P. Beveridge and Gardner Murphy of Columbia University; law professor Louis Warsoff of Brooklyn College; Robert K. Speer, education professor at New York

University; journalists William Edlin, editorial writer for *Der Tog* and a founder of the Workmen's Circle; and Dr. Alexander Mukdoni (Macdony) of the Yiddish daily *Morgn Zhurnal*; the actress Molly Picon; rabbis Ira Eisenstein and Mordecai Kaplan; Harry F. Ward, president of the American League Against War and Fascism; Roger Baldwin of the American Civil Liberties Union; and numerous other rabbis, academics, artists, union leaders, and journalists.[4]

"It is certain that a delegation of representatives of American Jewry to Biro-Bidjan is of great significance at the present time," declared the committee. Such a delegation would bring back "an authentic report" and "thus help to satisfy the widespread and constantly increasing interest now being manifested within the American Jewish community." As well, the delegation would demonstrate the friendship of the Jewish masses in this country "towards the pioneering work" in Birobidzhan, where some 50,000 Jews were projected to settle in the territory's capital city, Birobidzhan, over the next five years. The committee invited organizations representing Jewish workers, professionals, the middle-class, and fraternal groups to participate.[5] A press release sent out by the New York Committee of the People's Delegation to Biro-Bidjan called on ICOR members in their respective cities to create "people's committees" to organize conferences to choose the delegates. It would also be necessary to raise $350 to cover the expenses of each of the delegates, who would travel to Birobidzhan in September 1936.[6]

A major conference that drew 300 delegates from 200 organizations was held at the Hotel Pennsylvania in New York on May 17, 1936 under the auspices of Ambijan. Speakers included William W. Cohen, B.Z. Goldberg, and Justice Mitchell May, who remarked that "in the Soviet Union the Jew is considered an equal citizen and there the immigrant will have every opportunity to build a secure home and a peaceful life." Another conference to select delegates was called for May 24, 1936 at the Hotel Astor. Dr. A.I. Fisher, secretary of the New York City Committee of the People's Delegation to Biro-Bidjan, called on the Jews of America to send representatives to the conference to avail themselves of "this historic opportunity" to help in the building of Birobidzhan, a territory "larger than Holland and Belgium, and three times that of New Jersey," and already populated by 20,000 Jews. The conference drew 370 delegates from 184 organizations and called on all Jews to familiarize themselves with the way the three million Soviet Jews were transforming themselves into a productive people.[7]

Each participating group was able to nominate five members to be among those who would eventually be elected to the people's delegation from New York City; altogether, 50 people were nominated for the six positions that were allocated to the city. Almazov, reporting on the event, claimed that the Hotel Astor meeting represented 125,000 Jews, including 55,000 in workers' organizations. There were Jews from all walks of life—members of the Workmen's Circle, rabbis, Communists, union officials, refugees from Germany, women from synagogue sisterhoods. These diverse groups had come together, he declared, because they realized that Birobidzhan was a beacon of light in a world where the crisis of capitalism increased the levels of anti-Semitism day by day. The USSR was the only exception to the increasing dangers facing Jews, and Birobidzhan was progressing with the full support of all the various national groups in "the greatest country on earth."[8]

A pamphlet released to publicize the efforts quoted Edward E. Grusd, editor of the *B'nai B'rith Magazine*: "Those Jews who still believe in the value of prayer should thank God that in today's mad world there is a Biro-Bidjan—a great land beckoning to them, challenging their best energies and talents. In these days of distress for Israel, Biro-Bidjan may well turn out to be their one sure haven." B.Z. Goldberg remarked that "Biro-Bidjan will be a great, complete and prosperous Jewish state whether we will it or not. If we join hands with the pioneers today, we can exert an influence over the state tomorrow."[9]

There was considerable activity across the country; an editorial in *Nailebn-New Life* indicated that by June 1936, conferences called for the purpose of forming the people's delegation had taken place in New York, Boston, Chicago, Cleveland, Detroit, Philadelphia, Pittsburgh, and Los Angeles, as well as other locales. The editorial declared that "there are thousands who are eager to get the great honor of being on the first People's delegation from the Jewish people in America to the first and only Jewish Autonomous Territory in the world." By August, Buffalo, Washington, Cincinnati, Hartford, and Minneapolis-St. Paul had joined the list.[10]

In New York itself the various ICOR branches were being mobilized. Morris Stern of the Yiddish Cultural Branch, headquartered in the Bronx, was asked by Almazov to attend a meeting on October 24, 1935 of the special committee formed by the national executive to begin organizing for the people's delegation.[11] The ICOR club in the "Coops" on Allerton Avenue in the East Bronx held a conference on March 1, 1936, at which ICOR national organizer Ab. Epstein gave a lengthy speech outlining the progress being made in Birobidzhan. The conference resolved to support the creation of the people's delegation and help elect delegates. It also pledged to find 5,000 signatories for the "People's Book."[12]

In Buffalo, Rose and Samuel Obletz, respectively secretary and president of the local ICOR, welcomed delegates to a conference on May 17 to organize on behalf of the people's delegation. Support in the city came from many local Jewish organizations. Rabbis Morris Adler of

Temple Emanuel and Reuben J. Magil of Temple Beth El lent their names, as did Julian Park, a dean at the University of Buffalo.[13] At the June 12 gathering, Rose Oblentz was nominated as a delegate. In her acceptance speech, she called this moment "a peak of utter joy and happiness" and spoke of a trip she had recently taken to the Soviet Union: there she had observed a new world being planned and constructed "for the purpose of bringing joy of living into the life of all the people." She contrasted this to the "misery of the masses of people" she saw in France, Germany, Finland, Turkey, Greece, Egypt and Palestine.[14]

In Detroit, which would have two representatives on the people's delegation, 25 "mass organizations" attended a conference on January 12. B.Z. Goldberg spoke to an audience of 900 as support for the people's delegation grew.[15] On February 9, a similar conference held in Cleveland resolved to help raise money and signatories for the "People's Book" that would accompany the mission.[16] In Cincinnati, many of the faculty at the Hebrew Union College expressed their support for the people's delegation, including the noted historian Jacob Raider Marcus, who was elected a delegate from that city.[17]

On June 8, Boston held its initial conference, attended by 95 people. Professor Kuntz addressed the gathering, speaking about his work in Birobidzhan. The meeting organized an action committee to ask all Jewish organizations in the city to nominate members for election to the people's delegation at a forthcoming nomination conference. On July 15, the conference, attended by 101 delegates, nominated 13 people.[18]

Pittsburgh held its meeting to nominate candidates on June 21. Economics Professor Nathan Miller of the Carnegie School of Technology spoke of the importance of sending a delegation to Birobidzhan and the gathering heard from a number of speakers.[19] In Milwaukee, a conference took place on June 26.[20] On July 4, in St. Paul, MN, a conference was convened to elect the one representative for the region. It chose Dr. Victor E. Levine, chair of the Department of Biological Chemistry at Creighton University in Omaha.[21]

Ambijan and the ICOR enjoyed considerable support in Chicago, which was to send three delegates to Birobidzhan. We have a considerable amount of information about the pro-Birobidzhan movement in the city, as the minutes of the Ambijan organization were deposited in the Chicago Jewish Archives at the Spertus Institute of Jewish Studies. Dean Edith Abbot and professors A.J. Carlson, Louis Wirth, and F.L. Schuman of the University of Chicago had become members of the Sponsors Committee for the People's Delegation to Biro-Bidjan, along with judges Harry M. Fisher and Samuel Heller, and rabbis G. George Fox of the South Shore Temple and Nathan Budzinsky of the B'nai Moshe Synagogue. Also involved were the actor Jacob Ben-Ami; attorney Jacob G. Grossberg, one of the founders of the American Jewish Congress; prominent Chicago Jews such as Dr. George Halperin, Bernard Horwich, Dr. Harry Richter, Dr. Ben Zion Wolf of the Polish Jewish Farband; and a number of Jewish journalists. On January 19, a conference was held to promote the people's delegation. A total of 128 delegates from 74 *landsmanshaftn*, synagogues, Jewish clubs, and other organizations were in attendance.

In February, attorneys Grossberg and Harry D. Koenig met with prominent Jews to form a Chicago Division of Ambijan. Among these were Nicholas J. Pritzker, Dr. Julius Schaffner, and Harry Zarbin, who had returned from a visit to Birobidzhan and described the region in glowing terms. Sol Low came from New York to help organize the division, which was addressed by James Waterman Wise. Grossberg became honorary chairman of the new division, with Isadore Isenberg as president. Koenig and another attorney, Solomon Jesmer, became vice-presidents; Jesmer, who was Russian-born and a Communist, was active in arranging tours to the Soviet Union. Zarbin served as the treasurer, and Schaffner as the financial secretary. Others active in the organization included Charles J. Komaiko, Bernard J. Hecker, Rubin Shapiro, and Arthur Weinreb. At a conference on May 10, 20 people were nominated for Chicago's three positions on the Birobidzhan delegation.[22]

The Chicago Ambijan held a banquet for 500 guests at the Medinah Club on June 28. Saul Wagman, a Warsaw Jewish journalist, described the sad plight of Polish Jewry and urged those in attendance to support Ambijan's program: "Only the American Jews can help their suffering brethren." Other speakers included Professor Ernest Burgess of the University of Chicago and rabbis George Fox and Jacob Singer of Temple Mizpah. Commented one participant, "I was thrilled to the depths of my being by the addresses of prominent sponsors of this cause."[23] On July 26, a "day of festivities" marked the election of the three Chicago delegates to the people's committee. Those selected were Municipal Judge Samuel Heller, Dr. George A. Berd, and Dr. J. Rubin.[24]

Chicago's Anglo-Jewish newspaper, the *Sentinel*, published articles and letters from enthusiastic supporters of Ambijan. One contributor remarked on "the high character of the sponsorship, here and elsewhere." Another asserted that Ambijan's efforts would "transmit a ray of sunshine to those of our coreligionists who are forced to exist in darkness and misery" in Europe. Still, there remained some skepticism: In a letter to the *Sentinel*, Grossberg rebuked those members of the community who were maliciously impugning Ambijan's purposes and motives. He considered their attempts to discredit Ambijan "an unpardonable disservice to their persecuted and despairing brethren in Poland and elsewhere."[25]

In a letter published in August in the mass circulation magazine *News-Week*, Harry Koenig wrote that Jewish settlers in Birobidzhan, including some from outside the Soviet Union, were "busily engaged in developing the territory, rich in large deposits of coal, iron ore, graphite, limestone, marble, gold, and other minerals; valuable varieties of timber; hot sulphur springs, etc." According to Koenig, the climate was "healthful," with "abundant sunshine most of the year," while the summers were warm and "sufficiently long" to produce a variety of good crops. "The possibilities of this territory as a haven of refuge for European Jews was first brought up by Lord Dudley Marley, a member of the British Parliament, about two years ago," wrote Koenig. He hoped that the Chicago Ambijan would by the end of 1937 grow to 1,000 members: "We are confident of raising many thousands of dollars for the purpose of settling our needy brethren across the seas, in Birobidjan."

On November 29, the Chicago group sponsored a banquet at the Palmer House in honor of Lord Marley. An audience of over 600 "listened with rapt attention to the gifted orator." Among the guests were judges Harry M. Fisher, Samuel Heller, and Joseph Sabath; Representative Adolph J. Sabath of Chicago's 5th Congressional district; and Edward J. Kelly, mayor of Chicago. Judge Fisher said that he was "an old-time Zionist" but did not find "any conflict between Birobidjan and Palestine." He pointed to the equality of Jews in the Soviet Union and said that in his opinion the Soviet Constitution "was not a mere document but a living reality." Koenig noted that the group had enlisted the aid of many rabbis, who had "espoused our cause to their congregations."[26] The Chicago division held its second annual dinner on June 20, 1937 at the Standard Club. The guest of honor was Charles Recht, recently returned from a trip to Birobidzhan. He would provide the "latest first hand information on the new historic movement which may affect the destinies of the millions of European Jews."[27]

One of Ambijan's preeminent supporters in Los Angeles was Judge Isaac Pacht, a member of its Board of Directors. He called Lord Marley a man of courage "in espousing the cause of racial tolerance, neighborliness and understanding."[28] But it was the Los Angeles City Committee of the ICOR that provided most of the publicity for the people's delegation project. In 1936, the Los Angeles Committee had 12 branches, including three youth branches, with some 1,200 members.[29] Nathan Krupin, secretary of the Committee, called this a defining moment in the organization's history. The people's delegation to Birobidzhan would bring back news of the tremendous progress being made in Birobidzhan, and combat the "poison" being spread about the USSR by the bourgeois Jewish press. As well, the publicity surrounding the proposed delegation and the "People's Book" would enable ICOR activists throughout the country to mobilize support from other organizations in order to raise some $50,000 for cultural institutions in Birobidzhan, including the purchase of a modern printing press. "We now face a test. Will we fulfil our mission? This depends upon us."[30]

A leaflet circulated to Jewish organizations in Los Angeles by the ICOR noted that Birobidzhan "was being built with the widest possible help of the government and the peoples of the Soviet Union." A new Jewish way of life was developing, with its own culture and a self-sufficient economy, and the fact that 4,000 Jews from Poland might be allowed to settle in Birobidzhan had increased the level of interest. An organizational meeting of 55 people, representing an array of unions, ICOR and IWO branches, *lansdmanshaftn*, and cultural groups, was held on March 31 in order to convene a conference to choose the two delegates that Los Angeles was allotted on the people's delegation; a second conference took place on May 19.[31]

Writing in *Nailebn-New Life*, Krupin congratulated the members of the ICOR in Los Angeles for their commitment on behalf of the organization. The ICOR occupied "an honored place" among the Jewish organizations in the city. "It is our warmest wish," Krupin declared, "that when the delegation returns after having seen with their own eyes the achievements, not only will they themselves become committed friends of Birobidzhan," but "will also help make it popular among the broadest Jewish masses, so that Birobidzhan will not be only a project of the ICOR, but for all Jewish strata. At that point the delegation will have accomplished its historical mission." The Los Angeles ICOR cautioned that the work of the People's Conference must not terminate with the election of delegates to travel to Birobidzhan; the Conference must also continue to organize against the treatment of Jews in fascist countries.[32]

One member of the Los Angeles Executive Committee of the People's Conference for a People's Delegation to Birobidzhan, Dr. William Ostrowsky, asserted that in this time of fascism and anti-Semitism "there is only one ray of hope for the Jewry of the world....It is not the Promised Land of the Bible—it is the Jewish Autonomous Province, the future Jewish Socialist Soviet Republic," now "the talk of the world and the hope of millions of Jews in many lands." Most miraculous "is the transformation in the settlers themselves. The Jew of yesterday, who lived by his wit, by barter, and anything but productive labor has suddenly been transformed. He has now become productive, lives by his own labors, and builds with the sweat of his brow his glorious future in his own state—a socialistic state....Even his physique is changing—his back is straightening, his muscles are hardening, and gone is the frightened and worried look."[33]

The Philadelphia Jewish community faced an anti-Semitism that was at its height between 1930 and 1940. In reaction, most Philadelphia Jews supported the Democratic Party and many more were brought into association with liberal-left causes.[34] The papers of Philip Sandler, the secretary of the Philadelphia City Committee ICOR, are deposited at the YIVO Institute in New York and provide a rich record of the day-to-day affairs of the city's branches.[35]

Philadelphia's Communist milieu was extremely Jewish, and this was the atmosphere in which fronts such as the ICOR operated.[36] The local Jewish newspaper, the *Yidishe Velt-Jewish World*, had expressed its support for the ICOR-supported projects in Russia almost as soon as the organization was formed. A "People's Committee for Building up of Biro-Bidjan" organized a conference at the YMHA Building in January 1936; the Philadelphia community was informed that "the vast majority of Jews from various European lands now look upon Biro-Bidjan as their primary hope." The committee called on the Philadelphia Jewish "mass organizations," "organized Jewish workers," and other bodies, to *"Come see for yourselves the building of Birobidzhan!"*[37] In turn, the committee formed an "Initiative Committee for a People's Delegation to Biro-Bidzhan," with Dr. M.V. Leof, who had visited the Soviet Union and had spoken to many prominent people about Birobidzhan, as president; Ber Eppelbaum, a well-known Yiddish writer, as secretary; and Philip Sandler as organizer. The Committee would select the three delegates from Philadelphia who would become part of the 50-person group that would travel to Birobidzhan. Some non-Communists, such as assistant district attorney Abraham Berkowitz, who was elected vice-president, and a number of Yiddish journalists, including David B. Tierkel, managing editor of the Philadelphia edition of *Der Tog*, also became involved; they emphasized that the committee should be non-partisan.

It was decided to go ahead with a major conference on June 14. Sandler wrote Almazov on April 28, pleased that a number of prominent Philadelphians were showing interest in the project. He also told the national secretary that he had participated in a symposium on Birobidzhan and Palestine organized by the Jewish National Workers Alliance (Labor Zionist *Farband*) and "it looks like I did a good job." A meeting was organized by Leof at the Benjamin Franklin Hotel on May 13 to bring people up to date on the work done and make further plans. Eppelbaum reported on the meetings that had already been held and plans were made to publicize the June 14 conference.[38]

The committee produced a brochure that stated that the Soviets had declared Birobidzhan open for emigration "for a vast number of Jewish families from countries outside of Russia." As fascism persecuted Jews and drove them from their homes in Europe, Birobidzhan "is rapidly becoming not only a beacon light for a new life but a haven of refuge for the Jewish wanderer." It would be able to accommodate *"hundreds of thousands of Jews."* It was the duty of Jews to help prepare Birobidzhan for a large immigration "of our people from the countries where they are now subjected to persecution and oppression."[39] The June 14 meeting attracted more than 300 delegates representing 90 organizations to which 35,000 Jews belonged. There was great enthusiasm: Leof told the delegates that, if he were only younger, he would abandon his medical practice and devote himself "with all my energy to Birobidzhan."[40] Such pro-Birobidzhan scenes were played out in many Jewish communities.

By summer, the nomination process was over. The August 1936 issue of *Nailebn-New Life* listed the names of nominees from Boston, Chicago, Cleveland, and Pittsburgh. Among these were Rabbi George Fox (Chicago), industrialist and ICOR stalwart Joseph Morgenstern (Cleveland), Professor Nathan Miller (Pittsburgh), and Alexander Brin, publisher of the *Jewish Advocate* (Boston).[41] The ICOR claimed that at the various mass meetings, symposia and debates, over a quarter million Jews took part in the voting to select delegates, including 45,000 in New York City, despite the opposition of social democrats in the Workmen's Circle and *Forverts*. "We have lived to see a great moment, when the Jewish masses can send their representatives to see with their own eyes, the way yesterday's beaten and oppressed" Jews had now become "the builders of their own land."[42]

The September issue of *Nailebn-New Life* ran photos of 23 of the people elected to the people's delegation from various cities; another five were featured in October.[43] Among the six elected from New York City were Congressman William I. Sirovich and James Waterman Wise.[44] Even the World Jewish Congress held in August 1936 in Geneva adopted resolutions in support of groups active in helping Jews to settle in Birobidzhan.[45] But the date for the departure of the people's delegation, which had been scheduled for September, was now postponed until December.[46]

In the meantime, the ICOR involved itself with another project to garner publicity for Birobidzhan among the Jews of America. In August 1934, to commemorate the granting of full autonomous status to Birobidzhan, the predominantly Jewish New York branch of the John Reed Clubs, the main American organization for Communist and other pro-Soviet writers and artists, had set up a Birobidzhan art committee and informed the ICOR that it was launching a drive to collect artworks for the new Birobidzhan State Museum: "We plan to hold an exhibition of the accepted works at the time of the session of the forthcoming Icor convention, and another exhibition in Moscow, before shipment to Biro-Bidjan."[47] The project gained impetus in November 1935, when two New York artists formed the ICOR Art Committee. Frank C. Kirk, a well-known New York painter born in Zhitomir, Ukraine in 1889, who came to the U.S. in 1910, became secretary of this committee; the chair was the sculptor Adolf Wolff. Chapters in Chicago and Philadelphia also contributed their efforts and by March 1936, 203 works of art by 119 artists (about half of them non-Jews) had been assembled to present to the museum. Included were works by Julius Bloch, Yosl Cutler, Todros Geller, Maurice Glickman, Minna Harkavy, Frank Horowitz, Morris Kantor, Yasuo Kuniyoshi, Louis Lozowick, Zuni Maud, William Meyerowitz, Jose Clemente Orozco, Alexander Portnoff, Mitchell Siporin, Moses and Raphael Soyer, Max Weber, and William Zorach. (Two of the paintings were portraits of Charles Kuntz.) The catalogue of the exhibition noted that "Over one hundred artists of every school and tendency have extended the hand of solidarity to the people of Birobidjan."[48]

Kuntz expressed his pleasure that artists were "increasingly moving closer to ICOR because of their growing interest in Biro-Bidjan."[49] He called this "fitting gift" an "expression of friendship." Almazov congratulated the artists involved for "blazing the trail for closer cultural ties between the masses in this country and the Jewish pioneers in Birobidjan." He hoped that the collection would serve as the nucleus for "an important Art Museum" in Birobidzhan. *Morgn Frayhayt* editor Moissaye Olgin considered the collection of paintings, sculptures and etchings to be an expression of gratitude to the Soviet system "for what it has done by way of liberating the oppressed nationalities in general, the Jews in particular." For those Jews who had grown up under the tsars and now witnessed the new life under the Soviets, "the change seems little short of miraculous," an "historic romance more gripping than any product of the playwright's mind." He declared that the exhibition "will go down in history as a great link between America and the Soviets, between the progressive intellectuals of America and the liberated Jews."[50]

In March, the collection was exhibited in New York and in April it travelled to Boston, where it was part of an ICOR convention."[51] The works, accompanied by Kirk, were then shipped to Moscow in late December and remained on display at the Museum of Modern Western Art for six weeks; the exhibition received critical acclaim and was judged "a tremendous success."[52] However, the works never reached their final destination in Birobidzhan and their fate remains unknown.[53]

The Soviets, along with Ambijan and the ICOR, had tried to enlist the support of the Joint for their proposal to allow foreign Jews to immigrate to Birobidzhan. Dr. Joseph A. Rosen, the American Jewish Joint Distribution Committee's specialist on Jewish colonization in the USSR, had at first been skeptical concerning Birobidzhan.[54] But with Hitler's accession to power in Germany, he became more amenable and considered devoting Agro-Joint funds to the project. [55] He may even have "tried—but ultimately failed—to stir support in Washington for a major resettlement of German Jews in the Jewish Autonomous Region in Birobidzhan with hints that the project would reverse the recent decline of American exports to Russia."[56]

In December 1936, at a conference held by the Joint, Rosen described his

The "People's Delegation" and the Popular Front, 1935-1939

visit to Birobidzhan in the summer of 1936. Although Rosen acknowledged that there were "very great potential possibilities for immigration from outside of Russia," he noted that "due to the present complicated international situation, not a single family from abroad has been settled yet." He added that if the situation were to change, the Joint would be ready to do its part. The *Forverts* was, as usual, quick to pounce. In an editorial of December 16, entitled "Biro-Bidzhan," it quoted Rosen and concluded that the enthusiastic publicity grossly exaggerated the actual achievements in Birobidzhan. Indeed, sneered the *Forverts*, the project was little more than a propaganda device to provide favorable publicity for the Jewish Communists in America.

The ICOR countered with its usual claims: anti-Semitism had been abolished in the Soviet Union, and Birobidzhan, with an area as big as Belgium and Holland combined, was moving from strength to strength: already it contained 25,000 Jews, including settlers from "all the countries in the world." With its wealth of natural resources, it was suitable for fishing, farming and mining, and the capital city, Birobidzhan, now boasted many cultural, educational and literary institutions. Adolph Held, the prominent Jewish socialist who was president of the Forward Association, had himself visited Birobidzhan on behalf of the ORT in the summer of 1936 and "had seen with his own eyes foreign-born Jews, who are now fortunate people in the Jewish Autonomous Territory." Why then, asked the ICOR, was the *Forverts* so intent on besmirching Birobidzhan? Obviously because it was "obsessed with blind hatred for the Soviet Union." How long, asked the ICOR, would the Jewish masses allow themselves to be mocked?[57]

At the plenum of the national executive committee of the ICOR, which met in New York on February 28, 1937, delegates passed a resolution expressing their hope that the Soviet Union would "as quickly as possible be able to open its gates to proletarian Jews from European countries."[58] Almazov, for one, in public remained confident that all was well. He stated that the JAR's budget had increased five-fold over the previous three years and that 17,000 newcomers, including 1,000 Jewish families from outside the Soviet Union, would settle in Birobidzhan during the course of the year. The Soviet government's third Five-Year Plan projected a total of 150,000 Jews in the JAR by the end of 1942, with 60,000 living in the capital city. Given the deep interest of the entire USSR in the success of the region, Birobidzhan would soon assume its rightful place as a full-fledged Soviet Socialist Republic. It would become "a bee-hive of cultural activities" and "grow into a center of Jewish culture serving the needs not only of its own population but of the 3,000,000 [Jewish] people in the Soviet Union."[59] As late as August 1937, Ambijan would publish a 29-page pamphlet entitled *The Promise of Birobidjan*.[60]

Privately, however, the Jewish Communists began to sense that something was amiss; despite the reams of propaganda, the actual settlement of the 1,000 non-Russian Jewish families seemed stalled. In a letter to the KOMERD, Ambijan impressed upon the authorities in charge of the project in Moscow the urgency of the situation of European Jewry and appealed to them to accelerate the process. Ambijan's work, it stressed, which even at the best of times faced "very serious odds and ruthless opposition" within the American Jewish community, had of late become "greatly handicapped by the delays in starting the settlement of the initial quota of 1,000 families"; this delay was "perplexing and distressing."[61] Budish and George Segal, an Ambijan vice-president, were sent to Russia to investigate, and met with KOMERD and GEZERD officials in Moscow on May 19, May 25, June 5 and June 9 of 1937. They reported on their findings to an Ambijan board meeting on August 4. Soviet officials had assured them that the problems were logistical in nature and would be rectified: more funds would be appropriated to improve transportation to Birobidzhan and to accelerate construction of decent housing for incoming settlers. These provisions would make it possible to absorb increasing and substantial numbers of non-Russian, as well as Russian, Jews. The Committee then sent a letter to S.E. Chutzkayev, chair of KOMERD, noting "with gratitude" that their fears had been allayed.[62] Aaron Lipper, chair of the budget and policy committee, visited Moscow a few months later and also conferred with Chutzkayev. He had stated a year earlier that thousands of east European Jews were "clamoring for settlement in Birobidjan. For them it spells 'HOPE' and a 'PROMISED LAND'." Upon his return, Lipper told an Ambijan dinner that it was only the lack of housing facilities that had so far prevented an influx of non-Russian Jews to Birobidzhan; this, Soviet officials assured him, would be remedied within six months. Cohen, Goldberg, and Stefansson, all of whom also spoke at the dinner, were no doubt relieved to hear this.[63] Cohen looked forward "to a speedy elimination of the difficulties that are making some delay in the beginning of such settlement."[64]

Regional Ambijan chapters were also becoming disquieted by what appeared to some members to be foot-dragging on the part of the Soviets. In Chicago, a new 18-member executive board, with Harry Koenig as president and Arthur Weinreb as treasurer, had been voted into office on June 30, 1937. On July 7 the board received a communication from J.M. Budish, who had just returned from the Soviet Union. According to Budish, Soviet officials had told him that "due to international complications," they were unable to make definite promises. Budish himself hoped that settlement of immigrants might begin in 1938. Expressing their concern, the Chicago executive asked Budish to visit Chicago to elaborate; executive director Maurice E. Moore travelled to New York to arrange the visit.

Meanwhile, the Chicago leadership was visited by Aaron Lipper on July 14. Lipper explained that "the failure of the movement thus far to settle distressed non-Russian Jews in Birobidjan" was due to "international difficulties demanding the attention of the Russian Government." He assured the board that settlement projects had not been abandoned and that the USSR fully expected "to live up to its agreement" with Ambijan. Still, some members felt that solicitations for contributions might be discontinued "until the general situation is clarified." Indeed, the July 21 executive board meeting was told that some organizations that had been collecting money for Ambijan were keeping these funds "under lock and key until the beginning of immigration."

Jacob Grossberg, however, implored his fellow members not to lose heart. Grossberg insisted that despite the current difficulties, "the groundwork for settlement in Birobidjan" was being laid: "what is impossible of performance today may become easy of accomplishment tomorrow." Grossberg remarked that the Zionists in Palestine faced even greater problems. He then "made an impassioned plea to go forward with Birobidjan as by far the easiest road to the solution of the Jewish problem." According to the minutes of the July 21 meeting, the board "was deeply inspired by Mr. Grossberg's words."[65]

Budish arrived in Chicago on July 30 and met with the executive board at the Palmer House Hotel a day later. Many members were in a pessimistic mood: Bernard J. Hecker, chair of the Trades, Professionals and Landsmanshaftn division, felt that the delays in settlement "spelled the complete failure of all our efforts," while Philip A. Klapman, the recording secretary, wondered why a shortage of housing should in itself "result in refusal of Soviet officials to commit themselves as to the time when settlement may begin."

Budish replied that the lag in immigration was not due to lack of interest on the part of the Soviets, but rather to two other factors: a continuing housing shortage in the JAR, and the strained international situation. "World peace is imperative for the project," he said. Much work had already been done to build up Birobidzhan; efforts would now be made "to accelerate progress." Based on his talks with officials in Moscow, Budish was certain that "Russia remained determined to begin non-Russian colonization as soon as circumstances made that possible." He beseeched his listeners to continue their work, "so that when the doors to Birobidjan are opened and money is needed immediately," Ambijan would be ready to provide funds.

Though some on the executive board remained skeptical, Jacob Grossberg thanked Budish for his "kindness and generosity" in "clearing up certain misunderstandings as regards to the present position of the Soviet Government." Harry Zarbin, too, remained committed: "There is no alternative to Birobidjan, for where is the Jew to go today? What country is today willing to grant him an asylum?" He concluded that "Birobidjan is the greatest gift and the greatest opportunity that has fallen into the lap of Jews. Birobidjan is the spiritual life and the spiritual hope of an oppressed people. We must not quit and we must not falter today." Such remarks carried the day, leaving Budish "confident that the Chicago organization can and will go forward to ultimate victory."[66]

Though Budish during his visit to Chicago had hinted obliquely at "ignorance, indolence and sabotage" as being partly responsible for the problems in Birobidzhan,[67] the Ambijan and ICOR activists in America were still not apprised of the real situation in the Soviet Union, despite telltale hints about "investigation commissions" looking into governance in Birobidzhan. A rising tide of xenophobia and nationalism had begun to engulf the country. Stalin's great purges, which had already begun, would prevent immigration from outside, thereby relegating the project to allow foreigners into Birobidzhan into a political limbo.

The Jewish Autonomous Region was particularly hard-hit; in three successive purges between 1936 and 1938, the political and cultural leadership of the region was decimated. Professor Joseph Lieberberg, chair of the region's Soviet, was arrested in August 1936; the First Secretary of the region's CP, Matvei Khavkin, was arrested in the fall of 1937. Minor functionaries were accused of being counter-revolutionaries, Zionists, separatists and conspirators.[68] As well, charges of Jewish nationalism, Zionism, espionage on behalf of Germany and Japan, and other counter-revolutionary activities were laid against most former members of the *Yevsektsiya*, GEZERD and KOMERD, who disappeared into the gulags of the secret police. Both the GEZERD and the KOMERD were liquidated in 1938. The general suppression of Jewish culture in the Soviet Union was underway. The "people's delegation" was quietly shelved. This was no time to allow foreign Communists and pro-Soviet sympathizers to visit Birobidzhan.[69]

News of the purges appeared in the *New York Times* of March 7, 1937, in an article by Elias Tobenkin, who had lived in the Soviet Union in 1933 and had also visited Birobidzhan in 1935 on behalf of the Joint's Joseph A. Rosen. Tobenkin's initial impressions of Birobidzhan had been quite favorable, but following the stories of purges in the region, he became more cautious. According to his report, the arrests in Birobidzhan had set back plans to elevate the JAR into an autonomous republic early in 1938. Tobenkin said that most of the 19,000 Jews in the region, nearly half living in the city of Birobidzhan, had been motivated to move there by a mixture of nationalist feelings and a desire to escape the "drab ghetto surroundings" they left behind. Birobidzhan was part of the territory "which militarists in Japan covet" and this was part of the reason the

Soviets were settling the region "with feverish haste." But he noted that Birobidzhan was becoming an important center of industry in the Soviet far east: "Some of these factories are operating with machines supplied with money collected by American Jews."[70]

Tobenkin's article was quite positive in tone, but this did not prevent J.M. Budish from publishing a rejoinder in the *Times* three weeks later. Budish praised Tobenkin for providing facts about Birobidzhan's "rapid progress," which "should go far to do away with many of the old prejudices" and make it clear that it was "entirely fit for mass colonization of a people like the Jews." However, Budish felt that Tobenkin had exaggerated the danger of an invasion by Japan, and he repeated Lord Marley's argument that Birobidzhan was about the safest place in the Soviet far east. Significantly, however, Budish said nothing about the people's delegation that had been scheduled to travel to Birobidzhan.[71]

A delegation of Ambijan leaders met with Troyanovsky at the Soviet embassy in Washington on December 2, 1937. The Soviet ambassador told Aaron Lipper, Max Levin and George Segal that the policy of the Soviet government to admit a certain number of non-Russian Jews to Birobidzhan remained in force but that there was a delay due to a lack of housing materials and "other temporary special conditions in the Far East, with which we are all familiar."[72] A widespread pro-Japanese espionage network had been discovered in the region, he stated, forcing a halt to immigration.[73]

Almazov told the delegates at a plenary session of the ICOR national executive held at the Hotel McAlpin in New York on May 8, 1938 that patience was required when it came to the issue of the people's delegation. The ICOR's enemies had used the delay to smear the ICOR and slander the Soviet Union, he declared, but the delegation, or at least a part of it, would still eventually visit Birobidzhan. The region "was not being built in a day," and there would be plenty of time for future delegations to travel there.[74] And when the ICOR celebrated the 10th anniversary of the 1928 establishment of Birobidzhan as a Jewish settlement at the Manhattan Opera House in New York on April 17, the "People's Book" was presented to Soviet ambassador Troyanovsky, who would send it on to Birobidzhan.[75]

In June 1938 the *New York Times* reported that 17 people had been shot as "spies" and "wreckers" in Birobidzhan. In October it reported that a few weeks earlier, a "separatist conspiracy" had been uncovered in Birobidzhan: Jewish conspirators had operated schools "for spies and wreckers in the interests of an unnamed power."[76] *Nailebn-New Life* now carried articles that spoke of the "wreckers" who had engaged in "sabotage" and had tried to destroy the works of those building the JAR: the USSR had no choice but to screen visitors carefully, lest they prove to be spies for Japan or other fascist powers.[77]

On the 10th anniversary of the establishment of Birobidzhan, Khaim Zhitlovsky had called it "the foremost event in the modern history of the Jewish people" and "an example of how the Jewish question ought to be solved in all countries containing a large population of Jews." All Jews, stated Zhitlovsky, should hope that the development of Birobidzhan be as speedy and as successful as possible and that Birobidzhan should become in the next five to ten years a "miracle among the nations."[78] But Zhitlovsky in late 1938 admitted that direct help to Birobidzhan had of late ceased, as a result of the "uncertain world political situation." (Zhitlovsky was probably referring to the fact that the Joint had terminated all its projects in the USSR in the summer of 1938.) He was careful to explain this did not mean that the Soviet government was averse to accepting help from those who did not meddle in its politics. As for the fact that it was not admitting foreign Jews, this too was blamed on the international situation, which required a high degree of screening of potential immigrants. When this uncertain period had passed, Zhitlovsky wrote, "the Soviet state will open the doors to Biro-bidzhan." After all, he argued, immigration to Palestine had also been curtailed, but this did not make its supporters lose hope in the Zionist cause.[79] These arguments were repeated throughout the Jewish Communist movement. The Reuben Brainin ICOR branch in the Jamaica neighorhood of Queens, New York, in a flyer celebrating the 10th anniversary of Birobidzhan printed in early March 1938, noted that the "uncertain conditions now prevailing in the far east" had made it impossible to settle Jews from Germany, Poland and Romania in Birobidzhan.[80]

Paul Novick, who had visited Birobidzhan in 1936,[81] now insisted that it had never been the intention of the Soviet government to turn Birobidzhan into a "Red Palestine" that would gather Jews "from the so-called Diaspora into its borders." He conceded that the Soviets had granted the requests of Ambijan and the ICOR to permit some Polish Jews to settle in the Jewish Autonomous Region, and that it was due to "strained international relations" that the plan did not materialize. For example, the Japanese threat to the Soviet far east after 1931 had necessitated the transfer of resources from industrial and agricultural projects, to military defense. "There are still difficulties which some people choose to overlook."[82]

The ICOR also was forced to counter accusations that the whole people's delegation campaign had been a fraud designed simply to raise money. Philip Sandler in a letter dated May 1, 1937 asked Almazov what had happened to the money collected in Philadelphia. Since the delegation had never left, many participating organizations wanted their money back. In a response written May 8, Almazov acceded to the request to refund the $500 that had been sent to the New York office to cover the expenses of the Philadelphia delegates who had been selected to go to Birobidzhan. Not wishing to admit the project was dead, Almazov added: "We trust that you will have the money ready at any moment when the delegation will have to go to Biro-Bidjan. We may say, in this connection, that we expect the delegation to go very shortly.

"Trusting that our decision to refund the money will dispel any further misapprehensions on the part of your people who gave credence to the malicious accusations of the enemies of Biro-Bidjan that the money was misappropriated, and being certain that after the delegation will go to Biro-Bidjan, there will be even further strengthened the confidence in our work for Biro-Bidjan." Sandler then sent out form letters to the organizations involved, telling them that the committee was ready to refund their money but asking them, should it be financially feasible, to leave the money with the committee for the time being, in case the delegation to Birobidzhan might soon leave.[83]

Ambijan chapters also faced a crisis of confidence. In February 1937, Harry Koenig in Chicago wrote to Budish to explain that unless actual immigration to Birobidzhan were to commence, there would be no point in organizing a dinner to feature Soviet ambassador Troyanovsky: "we feel that we have nothing to sell to the public" and "Troyanovsky's coming here would have a rather empty meaning, at this time." In his response, Budish was forced to agree that it would be wise to postpone any visit by Troyanovsky until the national office was able to ascertain from Moscow that "a long-range plan... for the settlement of a substantial number of Jews from Eastern and Central Europe during a period of five years or so" was being formulated.[84]

Since immigration to Birobidzhan remained at a standstill, the Chicago Ambijan finally decided, at an executive meeting held on February 20, 1939, to recommend to the full membership that the organization turn over its remaining funds to the ORT, which "most nearly represents the aims and purposes for which Ambijan was organized." At the general meeting held on March 1, a telegram was read from Budish endorsing the decision to turn the remaining funds over to the ORT; the Chicago Ambijan, though not officially disbanded, ceased to function.[85] Such retrenchment took place in chapters across the country.

In June of 1939—at a time when Stalin had begun to reassess his relationship with the western powers and was moving towards a rapprochement with Hitler—the national organization itself suspended all activity.[86] At a meeting on June 14, it decided that some of the funds it had raised should be turned over to the ORT, since Ambijan could no longer pursue its goal of settling foreign Jews in Birobidzhan. After all, unlike the Joint, the World ORT Union had enthusiastically endorsed the Birobidzhan project at a meeting of its Executive Committee in Paris in January 1934 and thereafter provided the JAR with machinery, raw materials, and training courses for would-be settlers.[87] The Russian-born lawyer Jacob Broches Aronoff, a prominent member of Ambijan, was on the ORT's Board of Directors.[88] And, as noted earlier, Lord Marley was very active in the organization.[89] Shloime Almazov noted in 1940 that Ambijan had finally refunded some of the $30,000 it had collected to donors and had turned the rest over to the ORT.[90]

J. M. Budish in later years admitted that Ambijan was compelled to suspend all activities for the immediate settlement of non-Russian Jews in Birobidzhan in early 1938, due to the "tense" international situation that eventually "culminated in World War II."[91] The ICOR also tried to shift some of the blame onto the Polish government, which, it stated, had not allowed Soviet officials into Poland to select prospective settlers.[92] But despite these revisions of history, the whole matter of the people's delegation remained an embarrassing incident, one that the enemies of the Birobidzhan project would not let them forget.[93] However, pro-Soviet sympathizers continued to insist that the Jewish Autonomous Region would eventually become a refuge for east European Jews fleeing Nazism.[94] Only after World War II did Budish himself admit that only about 100 refugee families were actually settled before 1939.[95]

Endnotes

1 "Deklaratsye fun der 6-ter konvenshon funm icor," *ICOR* 8, 3 (March 1935): 3-4; S. Almazov, "Di 'Icor'-konvenshon un vos hot zi uns gelernt," *ICOR* 8, 3 (March 1935): 5-6; "Barikht fun der 6-ter natsyonaler yubili-konvenshon fun dem 'icor'," *ICOR* 8, 3 (March 1935): 7; "Barikht fun der natsyonaler ekzekutiv fun 'icor' tsu der 6-ter konvenshon," *ICOR* 8, 3 (March 1935): 8-22; "Konvenshon rezolutsyes," *ICOR* 8, 3 (March 1935): 24-25; "Vendung fun der natsyonaler ekzekutiv tsu ale icor tuer," *ICOR* 8, 3 (March 1935): 26.

2 "Editoriyale notitsn," *Nailebn-New Life* 9, 2 (June 1935): 3; "In der icor bavegung," *Nailebn-New Life* 9, 2 (June 1935): 37.

3 S. Almazov, "Barikht fun der natsyonaler ekzekutiv fun icor tsum plenum, gehalten in new york, okt. 27tn, 1935," *Nailebn-New Life* 9, 7 (November 1935): 52-54 [Yiddish section]; "Editorials," *Nailebn-New Life* 9, 8 (December 1935): 4 [Yiddish section]; "Protokol fun icor plenum," *Nailebn-New Life* 9, 8 (December 1935): 29-30 [Yiddish section]; S. Almazov, "Di folks-delegatsye keyn biro bidzhan," *Nailebn-New Life* 10, 1 (January 1936): 7-8 [Yiddish

section]; "Immediate and Important Tasks," *Nailebn-New Life* 10, 3 (March 1936): 3 [English section]; S. Almazov, "The People's Delegation to Biro-Bidjan," *Nailebn-New Life* 10, 4 (April 1936): 5 [English section].

4   "Sponsors of the People's Delegation to Biro-Bidjan," *Icor yor-bukh - ICOR Year Book 1936 Icor yor-bukh - ICOR Year Book 1936* (New York: National Executive Committee of the ICOR, 1936), 5 [English section]. See also the letter from Ab. Epstein to William Edlin, New York, Dec. 5, 1935, encouraging him to work with the People's Delegation; in United States Territorial Collection, RG251, Box 8, folder 82 "Letter from Icor," YIVO. One signatory, Harry Elmer Barnes, then with the New York *World-Telegram*, in later life would become a darling of Holocaust revisionists. Ab. Epstein died in May 1943. Leah Steinberg, "Ab. Epstein un zayne baytrog tsum yidishn lebn in amerike," *Nailebn-New Life* 17, 7 (July 1943): 20.

5   "A Call for a People's Delegation to Biro-Bidjan," *Icor yor-bukh - ICOR Year Book 1936*, 4 [English section].

6   Undated press release from the New York Committee of the People's Delegation to Biro-Bidjan; in the Philip Sandler papers, RG420, Box 4, "Materyaln vegn der ICOR kampanye far a folks-delegatsye," YIVO.

7   Letter from the New York City Committee of the People's Delegation to Biro-Bidjan to William Edlin, New York, May 13, 1936; letter from Shloime Almazov to Morris Stern, May 19, 1936; in the Morris Stern papers, RG231, Box 1, unnamed folder, YIVO; "Rezolutsye vegn der folks-delegatsye keyn biro bidzhan," *Nailebn-New Life* 10, 6 (June 1936): 32 [Yiddish section]. Dr. A. I. Fisher was also chair of the English Division of the New York City ICOR. See his letter to Reuben Brainin, New York, March 8, 1937, asking Brainin to contribute to a forthcoming booklet on Birobidzhan; Group II, Box b., folder 26, "Brainin and the USSR – ICOR – Announcements & Flyers," Reuben Brainin Collection, Jewish Public Library Archives, Montreal [hereafter JPL].

8   S. Almazov, "A groyser farnem arum a groyser oyfgabe," *Nailebn-New Life* 10, 6 (June 1936): 7-8 [Yiddish section].

9   The quotes by Goldberg and Grusd are from "Biro-Bidjan," undated pamphlet circulated to publicize the "New York City Conference for a People's Delegation to Biro-Bidjan," in United States Territorial Collection, RG117, Box 57, folder "Birobidzhan," YIVO.

10 "The People's Delegation to Biro-Bidjan is Taking Shape," *Nailebn-New Life* 10, 6 (June 1936): 3 [English section]; S. Almazov, "A Truly Representative Delegation to Biro-Bidjan," *Nailebn-New Life* 10, 8 (August 1936): 15 [English section].

11 Letter from Shloime Almazov to Morris Stern, New York, Oct. 23, 1935; in the Morris Stern papers, RG231, Box 1, unnamed folder, YIVO. Stern, a jeweler in the Bronx, was born in Pinsk, Belarus, in 1884 and had become active in Branch 24 of the Workman's Circle in New York. A friend of Zhitlovsky's, he would become a member of the New York Committee in 1936, and by 1941 he would be national treasurer of the ICOR. Later prominent in Ambijan, he

was also active in the Jewish Council for Russian War Relief during World War II. Stern died Sept. 6, 1949. "Troyer rezolutsyes," *Nailebn-New Life* 22, 8 (September-October 1949): 22.

12 "Barikht fun icor konferents in der kooperativer kolonye," *Nailebn-New Life* 10, 4 (April 1936): 34 [Yiddish section].

13 Temple Beth Zion's youth group also supported the plan, but its rabbi, Joseph L. Fink, did not. "News from the English-Speaking Branches of the 'Icor'," *Nailebn-New Life* 10, 6 (June 1936): 11-12 [English section]; "An Open Letter to Rabbi Fink," *Nailebn-New Life* 10, 6 (June 1936): 13 [English section].

14 Rose Obletz, "It is a Great Privilege to be a Member of the People's Delegation to Biro-Bidjan," *Nailebn-New Life* 10, 7 (July 1936): 5 [English section].

15 "In der icor bavegung," *Nailebn-New Life* 10, 3 (March 1936): 28 [Yiddish section]; "Di biro bidzhan folks-konferents in detroit," *Nailebn-New Life* 10, 7 (July 1936): 37 [Yiddish section].

16 "Cleveland konferents far dem folks-delegatsye keyn biro bidzhan," *Nailebn-New Life* 10, 3 (March 1936): 30 [Yiddish section].

17 Dovid Shvay, "Di kompanye far der folks-delegatsye farkhapt di yidishe masn," *Nailebn-New Life* 10, 7 (July 1936): 20 [Yiddish section].

18 "Bostoner konferents far folks-delegatsye keyn biro bidzhan," *Nailebn-New Life* 10, 7 (July 1936): 36 [Yiddish section]; "A Letter from Boston," *Nailebn-New Life* 10, 8 (August 1936): 14 [English section].

19 "Pittsburg konferents far biro bidzhan delegatsye," *Nailebn-New Life* 10, 7 (July 1936): 38 [Yiddish section].

20 "Konferents far biro bidzhaner folks-delegatsye in milwaukee, wisc." *Nailebn-New Life* 10, 8 (August 1936): 29 [Yiddish section].

21 "News from the English-Speaking Branches of the 'Icor'," *Nailebn-New Life* 10, 8 (August 1936): 8-9 [English section].

22 Sponsors Committee for People's Delegation to Biro-Bidjan, "Chicago Sponsors Committee of the People's Delegation to Biro-Bidjan," New York, Jan. 17, 1936; in the Philip Sandler papers, RG420, Box 4, "Materyaln vegn der ICOR kampanye far a folks-delegatsye," YIVO; "Chicago halt op a konferents oyf tsu shikn a delegatsye keyn biro-bidzhan," *Nailebn-New Life* 10, 3 (March 1936): 32 [Yiddish section]; Harry D. Koenig, "Birobidjan Over Chicago," in *Birobidjan: A New Hope for Oppressed European Jews*, 21, 37; S[olomon] Jesmer, "Ambijan," in J. I. Fishbein, ed., *The Sentinel Presents 100 Years of Chicago Jewry* (Chicago: Sentinel Publishing Co., 1948): 101, 112; Louis S. Berlin, "Biro-Bidjan: A Potential Jewish Republic," *Sentinel*, Chicago, Nov. 12, 1936, 3; "Ambijan President Appoints Committees," *Sentinel*, Chicago, Dec. 24, 1936, 13.

23 "Rally for Biro-Bidjan at Conference and Dinner," *Sentinel*, Chicago, July 2, 1936, 22; Bertha Loeb Lang, "This Busy World," *Sentinel*, Chicago, July 9, 1936, 14; "Dinner in Honor of Delegates Attending Ambijan Conference of Jewish Organizations of the Middle West," pamphlet in Collection No. 20: Chicago Chapter, American Birobidjan Committee, Series B. Papers of Ethel Osri (From Collection No. 82). Folder 10: Programs and Brochures, 1936-48;

Chicago Jewish Archives, Asher Library, Spertus Institute of Jewish Studies, Chicago [hereafter Chicago Jewish Archives].

24   "Di konferents in chicago far der folks-delegatsye keyn biro bidzhan," *Nailebn-New Life* 10, 7 (July 1936): 37 [Yiddish section]; Sh. Secular, "Arum der folks-delegatsye keyn biro bidzhan in chicago," *Nailebn-New Life* 10, 8 (August 1936): 13-14 [Yiddish section]; "Chicago Representatives to the National Biro-Bidjan Delegation Elected," *Sentinel*, Chicago, Aug. 6, 1936, 19.

25   A. A. Freedlander, "Biro-Bidjan's Claims," *Sentinel*, Chicago, June 25, 1936, 4; Louis S. Berlin, "Biro-Bidjan: A Potential Jewish Republic," *Sentinel*, Chicago, Nov. 12, 1936, 3; letter to the editor from Jacob G. Grossberg, *Sentinel*, Chicago, Jan. 28, 1937, 17.

26   Letter to the editor from Harry D. Koenig, Chicago, *News-Week*, Aug. 29, 1936: 2; Harry D. Koenig, "Birobidjan Over Chicago," in *Birobidjan: A New Hope for Oppressed European Jews*, 21, 37. Koenig erroneously listed the dinner as having taken place on Nov. 2.

27   "Second Annual Dinner of the American Committee for the Settlement of Jews in Birobidjan Chicago Division," pamphlet in Collection No. 20: Chicago Chapter, American Birobidjan Committee, Chicago Jewish Archives, Series B. Papers of Ethel Osri (From Collection No. 82). 10. Programs and Brochures, Chicago Jewish Archives.

28   "Our Co-Workers Say," in *Birobidjan: A New Hope for Oppressed European Jews*, 20.

29   *Suvenir-program: Folks-konferents far a folks delegatsye keyn biro bidzhan - Souvenir Program: Peoples' Conference for a Delegation to Biro-Bidjan* (Los Angeles: ICOR, 1936), [5, 7, 9, 12, 15] [English section]; [4-5, 11] [Yiddish section].

30   N. Krupin, "Di historishe misye fun der folks-delegatsye," *Nailebn-New Life* 10, 2 (February 1936): 13 [Yiddish section].

31   *Suvenir-program*, [17] [English section]; "Los Angeles folks-konferents far a folks-delegatsye keyn biro bidzhan," *Nailebn-New Life* 10, 5 (May 1936): 36 [Yiddish section]; undated circular brochure from Chaim Shapiro and Dr. W. Ostrowsky of the Los Angeles ICOR; letters from Dr. W. Ostrowsky to various organizations, Los Angeles, April 20, 1936, May 26, 1936, June 16, 1936; in the Philip Sandler papers, RG420, Box 4, "Materyaln vegn der ICOR kampanye far a folks-delegatsye," YIVO.

32   Nathan Krupin, "Der icor—a breyte gezelshaflekhe organizatsye," *Suvenir-program*, [4] [Yiddish section]; Nathan Krupin, "Di brentshes fun 'icor' in los angeles ba der arbet," *Nailebn-New Life* 10, 6 (June 1936): 36 [Yiddish section].

33   Dr. W. Ostrowsky, "Our Delegation to Biro-Bidjan," *Suvenir-program*, [1] [English section].

34   Murray Friedman, "From Outsiders to Insiders? Philadelphia Jewish Life, 1940-1985," in Murray Friedman, ed., *Philadelphia Jewish Life*, xxv, xxxii.

35   Sandler, born in Lithuania in 1905, had come to the U.S. at the age of 10, and was a Yiddish journalist, writing for the *Morgn Frayhayt* and other left-wing papers. He broke with the pro-Soviet movement after 1956, became a labor Zionist, and

wrote for the *Forverts* and other Yiddish periodicals. He died in 1981.

36 Lyons, *Philadelphia Communists, 1936-1956*, 60-61, 64 lists many of the front groups that operated in Philadelphia and helped make the Philadelphia CP a "small but important part" of New Deal and Popular Front politics, but he makes no mention of the ICOR or Ambijan. By 1929, Strawberry Mansion was 80 per cent Jewish and 34 per cent foreign born. Paul Lyons, "Philadelphia Jews and Radicalism: The American Jewish Congress Cleans House," in Murray Friedman, ed., *Philadelphia Jewish Life*, 58. Following the war, neighborhoods such as Strawberry Mansion and West Philadelphia emptied of Jews, who began moving into suburban areas. This pattern was repeated in most American cities.

37 Conference announcement, in English and Yiddish (emphasis in original); Russian Relief Collection, Box 2, Birobidzhan folder, Yeshiva.

38 Letter from Philip Sandler to ICOR members, Philadelphia, Feb. 4, 1936 and numerous other letters to various individuals sent in January and February 1936; letters from Shloime Almazov to Philip Sandler, New York, March 20, April 29, May 22 and May 29, 1936; letters from Philip Sandler to Shloime Almazov, Philadelphia, April 28, May 4, and May 28,1936; minutes of the meetings of the Initiative Committee for a People's Delegation to Biro-Bidzhan; in the Philip Sandler papers, RG420, Box 4, "Materyaln vegn der ICOR kampanye far a folks-delegatsye," YIVO.

39 Initiative Committee for a People's Delegation to Biro-Bidzhan, "A ruf... tsu ale yidishe organizatsyes!"; in the Philip Sandler papers, RG420, Box 4, "Materyaln vegn der ICOR kampanye far a folks-delegatsye," YIVO (emphasis in original).

40 N. Wagner, "Di bavegung arum der folks-delegatsye in philadelphia," *Nailebn-New Life* 10, 7 (July 1936): 18-19 [Yiddish section].

41 "Balloting for the People's Delegation to Biro-Bidjan," *Nailebn-New Life* 10, 8 (August 1936): p. 18 [English section].

42 S. Almazov, "45,000 shtimen far biro bidzhaner folks-delegatsye in new york aleyn," *Nailebn-New Life* 10, 8 (August 1936): 4-5 [Yiddish section]; S. Almazov, *Ten Years of Biro-Bidjan 1928-1938*, translated from the Yiddish by Nathan Farber (New York: ICOR, May 1938), 28.

43 "Mitglider fun der folks-delegatsye keyn biro-bidzhan," *Nailebn-New Life* 10, 9 (September 1936): 15-18 [Yiddish section] and *Nailebn-New Life* 10, 10 (October 1936): 37 [Yiddish section].

44 "To Visit Biro-Bidjan," *New York Times*, July 25, 1936, 14; "Der fayerung fun der new yorker folks-delegatsye far biro bidzhan," *Nailebn-New Life* 10, 9 (September 1936): 29 [Yiddish section].

45 Zosa Szajkowski, *Jews, Wars, and Communism*. Vol. I, 428.

46 "In der icor bavegung," *Nailebn-New Life* 10, 10 (October 1936): 30 [Yiddish section].

47 "John reed club shaft a zamlung fun kuntstverk far dem yidishn muzey in biro bidzhan," *ICOR* 7, 8 (September 1934): 17; "John Reed Club to Present

Collection of Art to Jewish Museum in Biro-Bidjan," *ICOR* 7, 8 (September 1934): 27. See also "Art Collection for Biro Bidjan," *Nailebn-New Life* 10, 1 (January 1936): 13 [English section]. The project has been described in Andrew Weinstein, "From International Socialism to Jewish Nationalism: The John Reed Club Gift to Birobidzhan," in Matthew Baigell and Milly Heyd, eds., *Complex Identities: Jewish Consciousness and Modern Art* (New Brunswick, NJ: Rutgers University Press, 2001): 142-161; and Nikolai Borodulin, "American Art for Birobidzhan," *Jews in Eastern Europe* 3, 49 (Winter 2002): 99-108. For more on Communist Jewish artists, see Ezra Mendelsohn, "Jews, Communism, and Art in Interwar America," in Dan Diner and Jonathan Frankel, eds., *Dark Times, Dire Decisions: Jews and Communism* (*Studies in Contemporary Jewry* 20) (New York: Oxford University Press, 2004): 99-132.

48 Quoted in "The First Museum of Art in Biro-Bidjan," *Nailebn-New Life* 9, 8 (December 1935): 6 [English section].

49 Charles Kuntz, "The Art Collection for Biro-Bidjan," *Nailebn-New Life* 10, 6 (June 1936): 8 [English section].

50 Charles Kuntz, "Birobidjan and Culture," 3; Shloime Almazov, "To the Artists' Committee Arranging the Collection for the Birobidjan Museum," 3; and Moissaye J. Olgin, "The Splendid Example of the American Artists," 4, in *Biro-Bidjan: Exhibition of Works of Art Presented by American Artists to the State Museum of Biro-Bidjan* (New York: Art Committee of ICOR, 1936).

51 "Boston Greets Art Collection for Biro-Bidjan," *Nailebn-New Life* 10, 4 (April 1936): 13 [English section].

52 Frank C. Kirk, "Mit der 'icor' kunst-oysshtelung in moskve," *Nailebn-New Life* 11, 6 (June 1937): 20 [Yiddish section].

53 Robert Weinberg, *Stalin's Forgotten Zion*, 52, 57.

54 "Dr. Rosen Skeptical About Siberian Plan," *New York Times*, Feb. 12, 1928, Section 3, 8.

55 Zosa Szajkowski, *Jews, Wars, and Communism*. Vol. IV, 179-185.

56 Jonathan Dekel-Chen, "An Unlikely Triangle: Philanthropists, Commissars, and American Statesmanship Meet in Soviet Crimea, 1922-37," *Diplomatic History* 27, 3 (June 2003): 373.

57 *Lost zikh mer nit narn!! Bakent zikh mit di emest'e faktn! Entfert di felsher!* (New York: National Executive of the ICOR, December 1936). Rosen's comments are contained in a letter to S. Almazov, New York, Dec. 17, 1936 and along with the *Forverts* editorial, are reprinted in this pamphlet.

58 "Protokol fun 'icor'-plenum," *Nailebn-New Life* 11, 4 (April 1937): 29 [Yiddish section].

59 S. Almazov, "Biro-Bidjan Marches On!" *Nailebn-New Life* 11, 2 (February 1937): 5 [English section]; S Almazov, " 'The Shape of Things to Come' in Birob-Bidjan," *Nailebn-New Life* 11, 8 (August 1937): 57-9 [English section]. As was typical with these sorts of articles, Almazov provided very detailed facts and figures regarding the agricultural, cultural and industrial development plans for the JAR.

60 *The Promise of Birobidjan: Summary of Proceedings of Meeting of Board of Governors, Directors, Chairmen of Divisions, and Sponsors of the American Committee for the Settlement of Jews in Birobidjan Held at the Aldine Club, New York City, August 4, 1937* (New York: American Committee for the Settlement of Jews in Birobidjan, 1937).

61 "Statement by the American Committee for the Settlement of Jews in Birobidjan to be Delivered by our Delegation to the Soviet Government through the KOMZET," New York, April 12, 1937, 4-5; Stefansson correspondence, MSS 196, Box 43, 1937--USSR A-B Folder, Stefansson Collection.

62 *The Promise of Birobidjan*, 8-19; letter from Ambijan to KOMZET, Aug. 4, 1937; Stefansson correspondence, MSS 196, Box 43, 1937--USSR A-B Folder, Stefansson Collection.

63 "Our Co-Workers Say," in *Birobidjan: A New Hope for Oppressed European Jews*, 20 (emphasis in original); "Reports on Birobidjan," *New York Times*, Dec. 5, 1937, 39. Lipper, a lawyer by profession and in the Brooklyn Division of Ambijan, was president of Kay Manufacturing Corp., a maker of steel products, based in Brooklyn. He died in 1939. "Aaron Lipper, Headed Steel Products Firm," *New York Times*, Nov. 23, 1939, 27.

64 W.W. Cohen, "'No Vestige of Anti-Semitism in the U.S.S.R.'," *Nailebn-New Life* 11, 11 (November 1937): 33 [English section].

65 "List of Officers and Executive Board, Chicago Division, American Birobidjan Committee," June 30, 1937; Minutes, July 7, 1937; July 14, 1937, July 21, 1937; Collection No. 20: Chicago Chapter, American Birobidjan Committee, Chicago Jewish Archives. Series A. Minutes 1. Minute Book 1936-1939, Chicago Jewish Archives.

66 Minutes, July 31, 1937; Collection No. 20: Chicago Chapter, American Birobidjan Committee, Chicago Jewish Archives. Series A. Minutes 1. Minute Book 1936-1939, Chicago Jewish Archives.

67 Minutes, July 31, 1937; Collection No. 20: Chicago Chapter, American Birobidjan Committee, Chicago Jewish Archives. Series A. Minutes 1. Minute Book 1936-1939, Chicago Jewish Archives.

68 See Robert Weinberg, "Purge and Politics in the Periphery: Birobidzhan in 1937," *Slavic Review* 52, 1 (Spring 1993): 13-27. The repression also extended to many Birobidzhan writers, who would spend years in Stalin's camps and prisons. Leonid Shkolnik, "Birobidzhan: Jewish Autonomy--To Be or Not to Be?" translated from the Russian by Michael Sherbourne, *Jewish Quarterly* 37 (Winter 1990-91): 21-23. Shkolnik was editor of the Yiddish newspaper *Birobidzhaner Shtern*.

69 Melech Epstein asserted that the entire plan had never lived up to expectations in any case, and that instead of the 250,000 signatures the ICOR hoped to gather for the People's Book, only some 50,000 were collected. Melech Epstein, *The Jew and Communism*, 314-315. *Nailebn-New Life* snuck this fact into an otherwise very positive article about the book. Charles Rubin, "The Book of Hope and Joy," *Nailebn-New Life* 11, 8 (August 1937): 11-12 [English section].

70　Elias Tobenkin, "Biro-Bidjan Heads Held as Plotters," *New York Times*, March 7, 1937, section 2, 7; Zosa Szajkowski, *Jews, Wars, and Communism*. Vol. IV, 163-164.
71　J.M. Budish, "Birobidjan Called Place of Promise," *New York Times*, March 28, 1937, section 2, 3.
72　"Reassuring Statement by Ambassador Troyanovsky on the Settlement of Non-Soviet Jews in Biro-Bidjan," *Nailebn-New Life* 12, 3 (March 1938): 11 [English section].
73　Joseph Nedava, *Trotsky and the Jews* (Philadelphia: Jewish Publication Society of America, 1972), 215.
74　"Barikht fun der natsyonaler ekzekutiv fun 'icor' tsum plenum," *Nailebn-New Life* 12, 6 (June 1938): 25 [Yiddish section].
75　S. Almazov, "Der 'icor' un biro-bidzhan," *Nailebn-New Life* 12, 4 (April 1938): 14-15 [Yiddish section]. *Nailebn-New Life* 12, 5 (May 1938): 3 [English section] published a photo of Troyanvsky receiving the "People's Book." The ambassador declared that "the Jewish problem in general can be solved only by the general efforts of civilized nations to defeat contemporary reaction." The attempts to destroy the USSR on the part of fascism had failed, he reassured the celebrants, and the forces of reaction would be defeated by the masses. "Troyanovsky Scores Persecution of Jews," *New York Times*, April 18, 1938, 15.
76　"Jewish Soviet State Suffers First Purge," *New York Times*, June 15, 1938, 4; "Soviet Disenfranchises 321," *New York Times*, Oct. 3, 1938, 7.
77　N. Bigler, "Biro-Bidjan Grows Strong," *Nailebn-New Life* 12, 9 (October 1938): 11-12 [English section]; Nikolai S. Bigler was a Birobidzhan deputy to the Supreme Soviet of the Russian Soviet Federative Socialist Republic.
78　Khaim Zhitlovsky, "Keyn beserer entfer oyf der yiddisher frage ken gor nit gemolt zayn," *Nailebn-New Life* 12, 4 (April 1938): 9 [Yiddish section].
79　Dr. Khaim Zhitlovsky, "Vos der morgn ken brengen," *Nailebn-New Life* 12, 10 (November 1938): 13 [Yiddish section]. This was a reprint of an article he had published in *Der Tog* on Oct. 23, 1938.
80　"10 yor biro-bidzhan: grandyezer kontsert arandzhirt fun reuben brainin icor, jamaica"; Group II, Box b., folder 28, "Reuben Brainin ICOR of Jamaica Branch (Long Island) – Flyers," Reuben Brainin Collection, JPL.
81　See his book, *Yidn in biro-bidzhan: A bazukh in der yidisher autonomye gegnt* (New York: ICOR, 1937).
82　Paul Novick, "The N.Y. Times Falls Victim to Anti-Biro-Bidjan Propaganda," *Nailebn-New Life* 13, 2 (February 1939): 5-6 [English section].
83　Letter from Philip Sandler to Shloime Almazov, Philadelphia, May 1, 1937; letter from Shloime Almazov to Philip Sandler, New York, May 8, 1937; undated circular letter from Philip Sandler to participating organizations in the Initiative Committee for a People's Delegation to Biro-Bidzhan; in the Philip Sandler papers, RG420, Box 4, "Materyaln vegn der ICOR kampanye far a folks-delegatsye," YIVO. Many Jews did in fact call Ambijan's campaign to

resettle Polish Jews in Birobidzhan a "fund-raising gimmick." Salo W. Baron, *The Russian Jew Under Tsars and Soviets* (New York, Macmillan, 1976), 198.

84 Letter from Harry Koenig to J.M. Budish, Chicago, Feb. 4, 1937; letter from J.M. Budish to Harry Koenig, New York, Feb. 11, 1937; Collection No. 20: Chicago Chapter, American Birobidjan Committee, Series C. Other Organizational Records. Folder 14: Files of Harry Koenig, Chicago Jewish Archives.

85 Minutes, Feb. 20, 1939; March 1, 1939; Collection No. 20: Chicago Chapter, American Birobidjan Committee, Chicago Jewish Archives. Series A. Minutes 1. Minute Book 1936-1939, Chicago Jewish Archives.

86 "The American Committee for the Settlement of Jews in Birobidjan," circular letter to all members, [late October, 1941]; Stefansson correspondence, MSS 196, Box 56, 1941--USSR General Folder, Stefansson Collection.

87 For the ORT's efforts in Birobidzhan, see Leon Shapiro, *The History of ORT: A Jewish Movement for Social Change* (New York: Schocken Books, 1980), 156-160; and Alexander Ivanov, "Facing East: the World ORT Union and the Jewish Refugee Problem in Europe, 1933-38," *East European Jewish Affairs* 39, 3 (December 2009): 369-388. For a brief history of the ORT's work during the 1920s and 1930s, see also Sarah Kavanaugh, *ORT and the Rehabilitation of Holocaust Survivors* (London: Vallentine Mitchell, 2008).

88 See pp. 1-2 of the 24-page FBI report of Sept. 19, 1945, submitted by E.E. Conroy, Special Agent in Charge, originally in NY File 100-42538. File 100-99898, Section 1, FOIPA No. 416152, Ambijan.

89 Alexander Ivanov, "Facing East," 372-376, 379.

90 S. Almazov, "An Open Letter to Rabbi David Aronson in Minneapolis, Minn.," *Nailebn-New Life* 14, 5 (June 1940):12 [English section]. The ORT however had also been forced to terminate its activities in the Soviet Union by the end of 1938.

91 J.M. Budish, "To the Members and Friends of Ambijan," *Ambijan Bulletin* 2, 3 (April 1943): 5; "Birobidjan—Jewish Autonomous Region and Post-War Rehabilitation of the Jews," *Ambijan Bulletin* 3, 2 (February 1944): [10-14].

92 S. Almazov, "An Open Letter to Rabbi David Aronson in Minneapolis, Minn.," 12 [English section].

93 Melech Epstein, *The Jew and Communism*, 313-317.

94 See, for example, the book by two pro-Soviet fellow-travelers, Raymond Arthur Davies and Andrew J. Steiger, *Soviet Asia: Democracy's First Line of Defense* (New York: Dial Press, 1942), who repeated a Soviet claim that Birobidzhan had been "preparing to receive 50,000 immigrants by 1940," and that many east European Jews fleeing Hitler did find a haven there following the Nazi invasion of the USSR in 1941 (282).

95 J.M. Budish, "National Conference Rallies American Jews to Birobidjan," *Ambijan Bulletin* 5 (September 1946): 4.

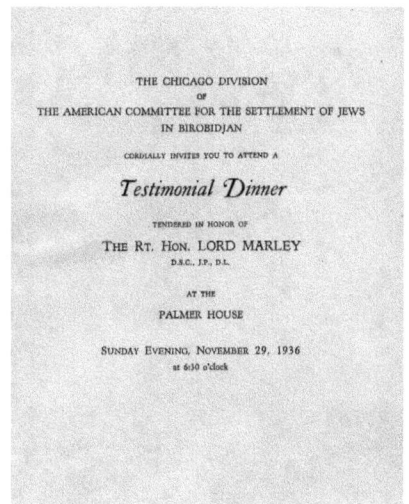 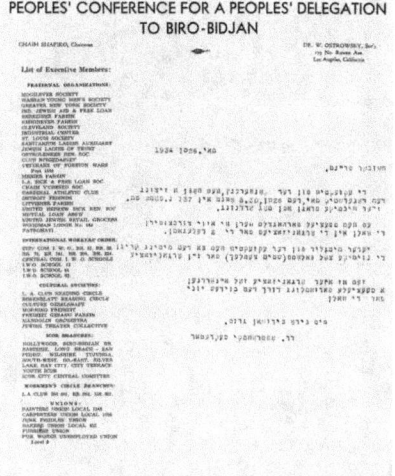

Chicago Ambijan Invitation for Lord Marley Dinner, November 1936, Chicago Jewish Archives, Spertus Institute of Jewish Studies, Chicago

Invitation for the People's Delegation, Los Angeles, May 1936, YIVO Institute for Jewish Research, New York

Delegates to the Plenum of the ICOR National Executive, New York, Feb. 28, 1937, *Nailebn-New Life*, April 1937

Cover of *Nailebn-New Life*, April 1938 (English side)

Cover of *Nailebn-New Life*, April 1938 (Yiddish side)

Shloime Almazov, *Nailebn-New Life*, April 1939

Wartime Aid to the Soviet Union: the ICOR

Despite setbacks related to the "people's delegation" campaign, both the ICOR and Ambijan had grown in the post-1934 period, when fear of German Nazism and relatively latitudinarian Popular Front politics drove or enticed many Jews into their ranks. Before the war, Ambijan claimed 1,000 members in eight branches, while the ICOR counted 12,000 in 110 branches.[1] But the entire Jewish Communist movement suffered a tremendous jolt when the Treaty of Non-Aggression between Germany and the Soviet Union, better known as the Molotov-Ribbentrop or Hitler-Stalin Pact, was signed on August 23, 1939, and Poland was subsequently partitioned between the two countries. From September 3, 1939, when Great Britain and France declared war on Germany, until June 22, 1941, when Nazi Germany attacked the USSR, Communists directed much of their venom, not at Hitler's Germany, but at Britain and France. As Maurice Isserman has observed, there were occasions in the fall of 1939 when official party pronouncements "left listeners with the impression that the Nazis were in some ways preferable to the Allies. Hitler, after all, had made his peace with the Soviet Union, while British and French intentions remained unclear and seemed to hold a more sinister potential."[2] British and French imperialism was denounced more vigorously than fascism and the now-partitioned Poland was dismissed as nothing more than an artificial entity. The CPUSA opposed assistance to Britain and France or any American military involvement in the war.

The party's official support of the treaty between Germany and the Soviet Union caused especial consternation among Jewish Communists. Melech Epstein recalled "spontaneous stirrings" in ICOR branches, and letters of protest from individual members appeared in the newspapers. Epstein was among the thousands who quit the CPUSA; Moishe Nadir and other literary figures broke off their association with the *Morgn Frayhayt*; the ICOR hobbled along, while Ambijan was forced to cease operations entirely for a few years.[3] In early 1941, B.Z. Goldberg and 11 other fellow-travelers were expelled from the *Y.L. Peretz Shrayber Fareyn*, the writers' union, for their pro-Soviet leanings. Goldberg also lost his daily column at the Yiddish daily *Der Tog* and was forced to resign as managing editor; he was now blamed for having allowed the publication, while he was managing editor, of articles by Communists.[4]

Shloime Almazov recalled that when news broke of the pact, the telephone in his office at the ICOR rang constantly and hundreds of telegrams poured in from those seeking explanations. The ICOR leadership struggled to come to terms with these developments, and ICOR members needed "nerves of iron" to withstand the accusations now hurled against the Soviet Union. Almazov set out to on a nation-wide tour to defend the pact; he argued that the USSR, far from becoming Hitler's ally, was in fact buying time and deflecting an Anglo-French scheme to turn Hitler eastwards. Almazov, met by tremendous hostility, wrote that "the power of the misleaders and the purveyors of falsehood was very strong." In some of the cities he visited the ICOR could not manage to rent a hall; in other cities, printers refused to print tickets for the meetings.[5] Circulation of the *Morgn Frayhayt* fell drastically, and Jewish Communists feared for their safety as street speakers.[6] By the end of 1940, the ICOR faced financial ruin. Almazov announced he would be resigning as secretary. Dr. Lewis Schatzov stepped down as treasurer, replaced by Morris Stern. Charles Kuntz remained the national chair.[7] Until the debts were paid, the printers refused to send out ICOR publications, including *Nailebn-New Life*, to subscribers.[8] While the organization was able to publish an issue of *Nailebn-New Life* in April, the magazine once again suspended publication, and no further numbers would be printed until the issue of October-November 1941. As well, the organization soon moved to smaller quarters at Rooms 213-214, One Union Square West.[9]

Of course everything changed after Hitler's invasion of the USSR on June 22, 1941. Almost immediately following the invasion, the ICOR went into high gear. A resolution pledging "full and unstinting support to the Soviet Union in its struggle to defend its land, its people and its freedom" was adopted at a mass meeting called by the American Council on Soviet Relations in New York on July 2. Charles Kuntz told the 8,000 people who had come to Madison Square Garden that this was no longer an "imperialist war," but one between the fascist forces on one side and the peoples' forces on the other side, and the leadership in this will rest with the Soviet Union." Extraordinary meetings of the ICOR national executive and the new national administrative committee were held on July 9 and 28 to prepare for the coming months.[10]

The ICOR now proclaimed itself, on its new letterhead, an "Association for Information on the Economic, Cultural, and Social Life of the Jews the World Over."[11] At its national conference, held on October 25-26, 1941 in New York, the new national secretary, Abraham Jenofsky, admitted that in the previous two years the ICOR "had lost sight of its primary goal, to bring clarity to the Jewish masses regarding the building of Jewish life in the Soviet Union, regarding the solution of the national question in the Soviet Union, in particular as it affected Jews."

Jenofsky told the delegates that the six million Jews in the Soviet Union had been a ray of hope for all of the 17 million Jews in the world. "We looked up to them and gained some consolation for the thousands of years of suffering that Jews had endured in their history, for the suffering that the 600,000 Jews had endured in Nazi Germany. Now, we are dealing not with hundreds of thousands, but millions of Jews living under the heel of the wild animal, Hitler. Now we are speaking about the fate of the entire Jewish people." The Red Army and Soviet government were battling to save the world from Hitlerism. "Our brothers and sisters are fighting, hundreds of thousands of heroes are putting their lives on the line to defend the Soviet Union and to free the world from this great disaster....With their blood they are redeeming the honor of the Jewish people and its past, present and future." In August the Jewish Anti-Fascist Committee (JAFC) had been formed in Moscow. American Jews must respond to their appeals for aid, they must heed the calls of David Bergelson, Ilya Ehrenburg and others, as the Jews of England and Palestine have already done, declared Jenofsky. The ICOR called on all Jewish organizations in the country, regardless of ideology, to join together: "there is a blaze burning in the world and we must all unite to help douse it."

Jenofsky took note of the straitened financial situation in which the ICOR had of late found itself, but emphasized that with the new world situation, it was imperative to rebuild the organization, especially in cities such as Chicago, Philadelphia, Los Angeles, and Boston, as well as in smaller centers. The tens of thousands of activists and sympathizers had to be brought back into the organization. Khaim Zhitlovsky had now become the honorary president; Sholem Levine and Jennie Posner were vice-presidents, and Morris Stern the treasurer.[12] The national committee in early 1942 decided to "prepare a working apparatus to be in a position to tackle the important activities of the ICOR." The first step would be to reach those members of the ICOR that had dropped out and induce them to return, and to start a drive among American Jews for new members. Morris L. Olken was appointed the national organizer to help increase the ICOR's membership.[13]

A delegation from the ICOR visited the Soviet embassy in the autumn of 1941 to promise $50,000 in assistance to the "heroic fighters" of the Red Army; some of the money would be dedicated to building a field hospital. The ICOR called on its supporters to declare their solidarity with the Soviet Union, and ICOR groups throughout the country began to raise money. The Los Angeles ICOR announced it would seek $2,000 from its members; Boston aspired to raise twice that amount.[14]

Jenofsky embarked on a tour of 14 cities to encourage ICOR branches to mobilize their membership and raise their level of fund-raising. The well-being of the Soviet Union and its Jewish population had always been of especial importance to the ICOR, Jenofsky declared. Now that the USSR was in a life-and-death struggle against Nazism, it was imperative that the two largest Jewish communities in the world, in America and the USSR, make common cause to defeat the enemy.[15]

In Los Angeles, on May 10, 1942, 1,000 people rallied to hear B.Z. Goldberg; $700 was raised at this event. Goldberg spoke at three other venues while in the city, to raise another $300. Individual ICOR branches were also collecting funds, bringing in another $2,000, so that by the end of the month a total of $3,000 had been raised. At a meeting of the national executive in New York on July 13, the ICOR announced that it had sent $15,000 for the field hospital to the Jewish Council for Russian War Relief, which the ICOR had helped create in February 1942. Meanwhile, on May 24, the JAFC in Moscow urged western Jewish communities to send funds to pay for 500 airplanes and 1,000 tanks. On August 13, the ICOR launched a new campaign to raise enough money to buy, as its share, one new tank and one new airplane.[16]

This pro-Soviet enthusiasm did not go unnoticed. Already, on May 11, an FBI informant had advised the Bureau that the Communist Party had been instructed to work among the Jewish population on behalf of the Soviet Union.[17] That July, in New York, FBI Agent P. E. Foxworth filed a detailed 32-page report on the ICOR. He noted that the organization, which opposed Zionism, was primarily interested in advancing the Soviet cause. Foxworth concluded that "Communist controlled" ICOR was being used by the CPUSA to disseminate propaganda and recruit new members: according to one of his informants, who was a member both of the Bronx CP and of the Sholem Aleichem ICOR branch, CP members were told that they should actively recruit for the party at the local level, in the ICOR branches.[18] A few months later, an FBI memo to Director J. Edgar Hoover warned that the ICOR "may attempt penetration into wider circles of the Jewish community." The report stated that, while there was no harm in the ICOR raising money for the Soviet Union, a "line should be drawn somewhere" regarding the amount of help citizens should be able to give to other countries, "even if friendly." In any event, "for the sake of national security" the ICOR should continue to be monitored.[19]

The national executive and the New York City ICOR Committee met on September 14. Dr. Lewis Schatzov, chair of the New York City committee, asserted that by supplying the Red Army with 500 aircraft and 1,000 tanks, Jews would fulfil their duty and earn the right to make their case for Jewish rights at a peace conference following the victory."[20] Three days later, Jenofsky announced that the ICOR had already raised $7,000 towards the purchase of a tank, and another $1,600 for the Jewish Council for Russian War Relief; altogether, $17,000 had been sent to the Council.[21]

At the national conference, held on October 10-11, and attended by 189 delegates from 116 organizations, plus another 1,200 guests, national secretary Jenofsky stated that the attack by the Nazis on the Soviet Union had caused tremendous destruction to communities that had been built up by the Soviets. The self-governing Crimean colonies that Jews had created were now destroyed. "These colonies are close to us, because the 'Icor' had assisted in their development. Now the murderous Nazis are spreading death and destruction as they trod that earth."

Jenofsky told his listeners that the Soviets had been rescuing not only Soviet Jews but also refugees from Nazi-occupied lands: Jews from Poland, Romania and the Baltic states had been removed to Tashkent, Samarkand and Alma-Ata in central Asia. More than a million Jews were now in Uzbekistan, he said.

The ICOR was also intent on reminding President Roosevelt of his promise to open a second front, as requested by Soviet Foreign Minister Vyacheslav Molotov. One way to do this was by organizing people to send letters and telegrams to the president. Jenofsky asserted that the fate of enslaved Europe and the entire Jewish people rested on the outcome of the ongoing battle at Stalingrad. At a time when 90 percent of Hitler's armies were occupied in the east, the opening of a second front could mean defeat for Germany within a few months. The ICOR, he emphasized, needed to draw even more attention to this "burning issue."

Jenofsky assured the delegates that "we are certain that the time will come when the contribution of the 'Icor' to Jewish organizational life will be recognized with a special place of honor in the general history of our people. The 'Icor' will be included among the pioneers who helped to reconstruct Jewish life on a healthy basis."[22] The organization also changed its fund-raising focus: Maxim Litvinov, who had become Soviet ambassador to Washington in December 1941, had suggested that the ICOR might find more useful ways to help the Red Army than by purchasing a tank; the national executive therefore decided to launch a new campaign to raise $15,000 to buy 10 mobile x-ray units.[23]

On December 20, the ICOR sponsored a concert at the Manhattan Center in celebration of the Soviet Union's 25th anniversary. One of the speakers was Rabbi Abraham Bick. Bick, who was head of the Warsaw Center in New York, president of the Union of American Jews of Ukrainian Descent, and rabbi at the Haym Solomon Congregation in New York, had become an important supporter of the ICOR's work and a contributor to *Nailebn-New Life*. Given his familiarity with rabbinic and Khasidic literature, Bick could in one sentence, as Nakhman Meisel observed, combine an adage from the *Mishnah* [rabbinical commentaries] with a quote from Lenin, an illustration from a Polish *magid* [preacher] with an aphorism from Maxim Gorky.[24] Obviously he would be an asset during this period of "rapprochement" with Zionists and religious Jews.

Bick called the Soviet Union the "pillar" in the fight against fascism. It was only fitting that the Jews should take part in the heroic struggle by the Red Army. Jews had a long tradition of fighting and dying, as martyrs, for their beliefs. On the 25th anniversary of the Soviet Union, concluded Bick, "regardless of our political or religious affiliations, we Jews must acknowledge that it is thanks to the Russian Revolution and the Soviet regime that we have become the equals of all other citizens and peoples in that sixth of the world that was once the imperium of pogroms."[25]

The 15th anniversary of Birobidzhan as an area for Jewish settlement was observed by ICOR branches throughout the country. In February 1943, with the assistance of Ambijan, the ICOR organized a jubilee committee of 150 "prominent personalities" from all walks of life to plan the celebrations which would be held at the Manhattan Center, New York, on April 25. Some 3,000 people attended the event, including diplomats from Soviet Russia, Czechoslovakia, Norway and Greece. One of the speakers was Judge Anna Kross, who pointed out that the anniversary fell in 1943 during another great festival of freedom, Passover. The Soviet vice consul in New York, Mikhail S. Vavilov, spoke of the "noble activities of the Jewish Americans in…helping the heroic Russian people." Paul Novick recalled his visit to Birobidzhan in 1936. He told his listeners that the Soviet Union had not simply given the Jews Birobidzhan, but had also provided them with the means to develop the region. "What an example to the world!"[26]

National organizer Morris Olken attended other celebrations in an array of cities, including Milwaukee, Chicago, Toledo, Cincinnati, Minneapolis-St. Paul, and Trenton, NJ. He found great enthusiasm everywhere, with packed lecture halls, banquets, good publicity on the radio and in the newspapers (including some interviews with Olken himself), support from many prominent Jewish personalities, the enrolment of many new ICOR members, and generous donations to the ICOR campaigns on behalf of Russian war relief. It was apparent, concluded Olken, that the Jews of America had rallied behind the Soviet Union and were aware of the importance of Birobidzhan.[27]

Khaim Zhitlovsky, who had joined the editorial board of *Naileben-New Life*, continued to advance the ICOR's cause, stressing the need for Jewish unity. He stated that the interests of the Jewish people at this critical moment required that all socialists, *"with all their heart,"* support the Soviets in their struggle against Nazism. Zhitlovsky described himself as a "friend" of Stalin's Russia and considered the Soviet leader's position on the national question to be the correct one; he predicted that the USSR would eventually evolve into a more democratic federal state. "The world front for universal peace and progress is now in the Soviet Union."[28]

Zhitlovsky also chided those leftists who refused to join with other, non-socialist Jews at a time when all Jews faced the danger of genocide. He reminded them of the call from the JAFC for "all of their Jewish brothers throughout the world" to unite to fight Hitlerism. Jewish unity was a necessity during this world war, he contended, and the main duty of Jews at this time was to march together "with our brothers" in the Soviet Union.[29]

No other Jewish community, he wrote, could match that of the Soviet Union. They need not fear anti-Semitism and pogroms, which had been completely uprooted. They were free of economic uncertainty; and thanks to the Bolshevik Revolution, they had not only the theoretical legal opportunity, but also the actual concrete ability and means to preserve their national culture. This goal entailed the creation of Jewish national districts in the European parts of the country and the granting of a specific territory for Jewish national, political and cultural self-determination in Birobidzhan. Thus, "they stood at the *highest level* when compared to other Jewish communities" and enjoyed *"the happiest"* Jewish national existence. In the Soviet Union, Jews were "reconstructing their lives on a productive socialist basis, and were granted equal respect alongside all the other peoples of the country."[30]

Zhitlovsky spoke for many Jews when he announced on February 23, 1943 that "Our Jewish people now has *two* countries in which a new Jewish life is being built, a *normal* life," one where Jews would live in Jewish towns and Jewish cities, "just like all the other peoples on earth. The two countries are Birobidzhan and *erets yisroel*." In both, he declared, Jewish life would become "normalized." The two should not be regarded as antagonistic alternatives; each could become "a fortress for our national survival and for the normal development of our own national culture." True, Zhitlovsky acknowledged, Birobidzhan still had far fewer Jews than the Palestine *yishuv*, but it was only 15 years old, whereas the modern Zionist settlement of *erets yisroel* had begun as far back as the arrival of the first pioneers in 1882. "Every Jewish accomplishment in both countries gives us courage in the struggle for our survival, elevates the prestige of our people in the eyes of the non-Jewish world, and strengthens our desire for the complete national liberation of our people, with the complete rights and strengths of membership in the fraternal family of nations. May the Jewish nation of Birobidzhan have long life and mature in freedom!"[31]

By now the full scope and magnitude of the Holocaust had become known. Paul Novick wrote in the January 1943 *Nailebn-New Life* that millions of Jews were dead or in the process of being murdered. Half the Jews of Poland had already perished, as had all the Jews in Bessarabia. Novick called on all Jews to do their utmost to save those who still lived, by agitating for a second front in western Europe. He speculated that if a second front had been promptly opened, the Nazis might already have been defeated, and the imprisoned Jews freed. Meanwhile, the Nazis were "exterminating" the Jewish population of one occupied country after another. "Again and again we must say, we must shout…*Time is working for Hitler and against our brothers and sisters. Every day, every hour works against them.*"³²

The Jewish Communists linked Hitler's genocide to their own pro-Soviet stance. When Max Levin and Abraham Jenofsky wrote, in English and Yiddish, *A Call to Jewish Landsmanschaften, Societies, Orders, Auxiliaries, Trade Unions, Synagogues, Congregations, Cultural Institutions, Etc. to Celebrate 15 Years of Biro-Bidjan*, they declared that Hitler's mass murders could be stopped only by Soviet arms. "At a time when millions of Jews are faced with extermination at the hands of bloody Hitlerism, when two million of our brothers and sisters have already been slaughtered and millions more face hunger, humiliation and death; when the sky is overcast with a dread thundercloud which threatens to drown the world in Jewish blood," they declared, "the Soviet Union, with its mighty Red Army, with our own Jewish heroes in their midst, stands out like a tower of light, a beacon of hope for the Jewish people and the whole civilized world."³³

This theme became more pronounced in mid-1943, when the American Committee of Jewish Writers, Artists and Scientists sponsored the visit to North America of two of the most preeminent members of the JAFC: Shloime Mikhoels, the actor, and Itzik Fefer, the poet. The Committee's officers were Khaim Zhitlovsky, chair; B.Z. Goldberg, secretary; and Sholem Asch, president. Paul Novick, Shloime Almazov, Dr. Raphael Mahler, and the Joint's Joseph A. Rosen were also members, alongside such luminaries as Albert Einstein, the Committee's honorary president; Professor Franz Boas; the writers Lion Feuchtwanger and Waldo Frank; the actor Maurice Schwartz; and the artist Marc Chagall. Chagall, when he arrived in New York from France in 1941, was already a prominent figure on the pro-Communist left.³⁴ Despite this long list of officers and celebrities, the Committee was actually run by Joseph Brainin, a Communist and the son of Reuben Brainin.³⁵

Mikhoels and Fefer arrived in the United States on June 17 and left on October 20. Their tour included, apart from New York, stops in Newark, Boston, Philadelphia, Washington, Milwaukee, Cincinnati, Cleveland, Detroit, Chicago, Pittsburgh, Los Angeles, and San Francisco; the pair also visited Britain, Canada and Mexico. Rabbi Stephen S. Wise, president of the American Jewish Congress, introduced them to the 50,000 people that thronged the Polo Grounds in Manhattan on July 8. Also seated on the dais was Nahum Goldmann, president of the World Jewish Congress. The program opened with the playing of the "Star-Spangled Banner," the Zionist hymn "Hatikvah," and the "Internationale." Among the artists participating that night were Larry Adler, Eddie Cantor and Paul

Robeson, who sang Russian and Yiddish songs. The main theme was the call for the opening of a second front in Europe; Fefer pointed out that Jews in Europe were being saved from extermination by the Soviet government.[36]

Their stay in the U.S. received prominent coverage in the JAFC's Moscow-based Yiddish newspaper, *Eynikayt*. In Chicago, they were greeted by the mayor, Edward J. Kelly, as well as by delegates from 140 Jewish organizations. The visit made a "colossal impression." In Boston, they were introduced by the Yiddish actor Maurice Schwartz at a mass meeting in Symphony Hall. Some 10,000 people turned out at a gathering in their honor in Philadelphia, and special editions of the local Yiddish papers were printed. In Los Angeles, Judge Isaac Pacht was their host at a meeting where 7,000 people gave them "stormy ovations." In Hollywood, they met with actors Eddie Cantor, Charlie Chaplin, John Garfield, Paul Muni and Edward G. Robinson; with writers Theodore Dreiser, Thomas Mann, and Upton Sinclair; and with studio heads David O. Selznick and Harry and Jack Warner. The Warners' studio produced a record of their Los Angeles speeches.[37]

Mikhoels told Brainin, who headed up the official national reception committee and also accompanied the two Soviet guests to Albert Einstein's home in Princeton, NJ, that the Jews in the Red Army were displaying "epic heroism" and "yield to no one in bravery, courage and willingness to give their lives for the people… Only the total extermination of Fascists can bring back peace and security." Fefer added that, "History will measure the participation of peoples in this mainly in terms of the number of Fascist beasts annihilated!"[38]

While Mikhoels and Fefer were in New York, the ICOR leadership basked in their reflected glory. The two Soviet Jews appeared on the Yiddish covers of the July, August and September 1943 issues of *Nailebn-New Life* as well as the cover of the June-July 1943 *Yidishe Kultur* (where they were pictured standing at Sholem Aleichem's grave in New York).[39] At an August 12 gathering of the ICOR membership at the Hotel Edison, New York, Mikhoels shared a table with Abraham Jenofsky and Morris L. Olken. Editorials in *Nailebn-New Life* proclaimed that Mikhoels and Fefer embodied "the best of Soviet Jewry." They had come to America to encourage "the maximum unity possible" among the Jews, in order to fight the common enemy, Hitlerism. How envious the naysayers at the anti-Soviet *Forverts* must have felt at such a display of enthusiasm and unity, crowed the editors of *Nailebn-New Life*.[40]

Some 500 ICOR activists attended the August 12 reception at the Hotel Edison. "Dear Icor friends, to us you are considered closer than a brother or a sister," Mikhoels declared. "Greetings from the war front, where our people stand united with the other Soviet peoples against the enemy, whose name will be erased forever from the history of the world. In our country everyone is familiar with the activities of the Icor. In you we have faithful friends, you have helped us with deeds and without any complaints. We know with what energy you took part in spreading the significance of Birobidzhan. You in the Icor have done much in helping build Birobidzhan." Mikhoels also explained that the Soviet government had been planning to make Birobidzhan a full-fledged Soviet republic but had been forced to delay this due to the war.[41]

Their visit, noted Chagall's biographer, had a mass appeal: "It was a combination of nostalgia for the old country, belief in the utopian Soviet propaganda from a distance, and gratitude to the Soviets who had saved at least a million and a half Jews from the Nazis."[42] Nakhman Meisel wrote that it surpassed all expectations—despite the cavilling of their misguided detractors at the *Forverts*. Mikhoels and Fefer had met with Jews and non-Jews from all walks of life—altogether, Meisel estimated, they had probably spoken to some 200,000 people. They brought with them a message "from our brothers, fighting heroically on the front." Meisel was also impressed by the fact that their tour was conducted in Yiddish. He hoped that their trip would result in a stronger relationship between the Jews of America and Russia, and that the unity they promoted so effectively would enable Jews to speak with a strong voice at the peace talks that would follow the ultimate defeat of Hitlerism.[43] Morris Olken, too, noted that the "triumphant tour of the Soviet Jewish delegation" was helping to cement unity between the U.S. and the USSR.[44] "American Jewry greeted the dear guests with open arms and took them into their hearts," Moishe Katz told the readers of the Moscow *Aynikayt*. During their hundreds of meetings with people from all walks of life, they brought to America the "fighting spirit of Soviet Jewry" while also raising, through their magnificent speeches, the prestige of the Yiddish language.[45]

The ICOR held a national plenum at the Pythian Plaza in New York on January 30, 1944. The delegates were reminded by Jenofsky that the visit of Mikhoels and Fefer had been a great success. This momentous event had created a closer physical and spiritual bond between two-thirds of the Jewish people. "Only a very small reactionary element on the Jewish street," centered around the *Forverts*, had put their own selfish politics and "zoological hatred" of the Soviet Union ahead of the interests of the Jewish people, by rejecting the message brought by the Soviet emissaries. "We believe, however," Jenofsky stated, that the influence of the naysayers "will disappear"; Jews "will realize that their politics is false and destructive." The historic gathering in the Polo Grounds, and the other events across the United States, Mexico and Canada, demonstrated the fervent desire of the Jews of America for friendship with their brothers and sisters in the Soviet Union. The ICOR had played an important role in preparing and organizing the tour. As a result, the ICOR, an old friend of the Soviet Union, was lauded with compliments "which ought to make every Icorist feel proud."

Over the previous 15 months the ICOR had carried out three major campaigns on behalf of aid to the Soviet army: First, it had raised $15,000 for the purchase of 10 mobile X-ray units. Then it had distinguished itself in a campaign to raise money to fund a room in Leningrad Military Hospital 1117 in honor of Khaim Zhitlovsky, who had died the previous May. That campaign had gone extremely well: $20,000 was raised, enough money to fund two rooms at the hospital. The third campaign, on behalf of "National War Relief," was for the most part confined to New York, and netted $5,000. All told, announced Jenofsky, in the past two years the amounts raised by the ICOR for the Red Army and for Russian war relief had totalled almost $100,000. "Today we have committees and branches in 50 cities, across 20 states. *Nailebn* is sent out to 153 cities and towns in the country." Jenofsky informed the delegates that the ICOR had proposed to the authorities in Birobidzhan a plan to assist in further developing the territory following the war.[46]

A celebration of the tenth anniversary of the Jewish Autonomous Region was held at Town Hall, New York, on May 14. It featured a concert conducted by Vladimir Heifetz and two theatrical performances by the Artef company, entitled "A Yid fort keyn Biro-Bidzhan" and "A Khaseneh in Biro-Bidzhan." A day earlier, Jenofsky had discussed the forthcoming anniversary celebration on New York radio station WHOM. He stated that "Birobidzhan is now preparing to accept a few thousand war orphans and in the near future Birobidzhan will admit thousands of refugees who will settle there and build a happy future."[47]

On December 25, 1944, the ICOR marked 20 years of existence at Town Hall in Manhattan. Similar celebrations were held in other cities across the country, bringing in large donations. At the New York gathering, in front of 1,500 people, "It can be stated with confidence," Jenofsky asserted, "that the Icor will take a prominent place in the reconstruction and rehabilitation work after the war." He noted that the national executive of the ICOR had approached the Birobidzhan administration to seek their permission to help settle several hundred war orphans in Birobidzhan. Jenofsky also reminded his listeners of the role played by the ICOR during the visit of the two Soviet emissaries in the summer of 1943. He recalled the "hearty and brotherly" greetings Mikhoels had conveyed to the ICOR from Jews in the Soviet Union. Soviet Consul General Eugene (Evgeny) D. Kisselev also spoke at the meeting, and Jenofsky's appeal for donations brought in $4,665.[48]

As the war wound down, the ICOR began publicizing stories about

CHAPTER THREE

Birobidzhan's educational, industrial and technical advances during the war years. "The interest of the Jews of America towards Biro-Bidzhan grows from day to day," stated Jenofsky.[49] At the end of hostilities in 1945 the ICOR published a pamphlet by Alexander Bakhmutsky, the secretary of the Birobidzhan CP, translated into English, entitled "New Achivements in Birobidjan." Bakhmutsky's article reiterated the by now clichéd descriptions of progress in Birobidzhan: the construction of scores of factories since 1934, the provision of newly built transport and communication systems, and the rapid development of agriculture. Now, he added, Birobidzhan was allocating about three million rubles to build two homes for orphaned children.[50]

ENDNOTES

1 "Jewish National Organizations," in Harry Schneiderman, ed., *American Jewish Year Book 5700 (September 14, 1939 to October 2, 1940)*. Vol. 41(Philadelphia: Jewish Publication Society of America, 1939): 450, 471-472.
2 Maurice Isserman, *Which Side Were You On?*, 45-46.
3 Melech Epstein, *The Jew and Communism*, 369. Epstein describes the disarray in the ranks of the Communist Party and its various Jewish front groups on 349-370.
4 "Strike on 'The Day'," *New Masses* 38, 10 (February 25, 1941): 21; Nathaniel Buchwald, "Dark is 'The Day'," *New Masses* 39, 2 (April 1, 1941): 11-12; Melech Epstein, *The Jew and Communism*, 376; Shimon Redlich, *Propaganda and Nationalism in Wartime Russia*, 110. Goldberg later claimed that his policy had been "to oppose the pact but not make it an excuse for an abusive campaign against the Soviet Union." Typewritten mss. in the B.Z. Goldberg papers, Box 72, Personal Matters, folder "Biography – BZG."
5 S Almazov, *Mit dem vort tsum folk*, 299-304. The Los Angeles ICOR did manage to hold a "mass meeting" on Oct. 24, 1939 at the Embassy Auditorium. See Louis G. Reynolds, *The Pact and the Jew: How it Has Affected the Destiny of 5,000,000 Jews* (Los Angeles: City Committee ICOR, [1939]). But by spring 1940 in Philadelphia, *Brit Akhim*, an organization previously sympathetic to the ICOR, refused to allow its auditorium to be used for ICOR events. S. Almazov, "A briv vos veyst di meyshim fun di fashistishe farfirer oyf der yidisher gas," *Neilebn-New Life* 14, 5 (June 1940): 22 [Yiddish section].

6   Paul Buhle, *Marxism in the United States: Remapping the History of the American Left*, 2nd ed. (London: Verso, 1991), 134.
7   See the letter from Morris Stern to the members of the Yiddish Cultural Branch of the ICOR, New York, Dec. 31, 1940, informing them, with regret, of Almazov's impending departure as secretary; in the Morris Stern papers, RG231, Box 1, unnamed folder, YIVO. *Nailben* attributed his resignation to ill-health. "Der icor far naye oyfgabn un arbeter-formen," *Nailben-New Life* 15, 1 (March 1941): 4-5 [Yiddish section]. According to an FBI informant, Almazov officially resigned at a national executive committee meeting on Jan. 17, 1941. Supposedly he was slated for special work on behalf of the National Council of Jewish Communists. This information is contained on pp. 5-6 of an 8-page FBI report dated Aug. 5, 1947, submitted by Edward Scheidt, Special Agent in Charge, originally in NY File 100-14454. File 100-2074, FOIPA Release of Organization for Jewish Colonization.
8   Letter from G. Alman to Morris Stern, New York, [April 1941]; in the Morris Stern papers, RG231, Box 1, unnamed folder, YIVO. Gabriel Alman served as temporary national secretary. He had been appointed as ICOR field organizer in 1938. "G. Alman Appointed Field Organizer," *Nailebn-New Life* 12, 3 (March 1938): 14 [English section].
9   For details of the ICOR's situation during the 1939-1941 period, see my article " 'The Jews Do Not Want War!': American Jewish Communists Defend the Hitler-Stalin Pact, 1939-1941," *American Communist History* 8, 1 (June 2009): 49-71.
10 "8,000 at Meeting Urge Aid to Russia," *New York Times*, July 3, 1941, 5; Circular letter from G. Alman, New York, July 5, 1941; in the Morris Stern papers, RG231, Box 1, unnamed folder, YIVO.
11 The national executive committee held a meeting at its old offices at 799 Broadway and decided on the change of name. The actual application for a Certificate of Change of Name was filed on Dec. 16, 1941, and the ICOR became known as the "Icor Association for Information on the Economic, Cultural, and Social Life of the Jews the world Over, Inc." This information is contained on p. 11 of a 32-page FBI report dated July 27, 1942, submitted by P.E. Foxworth, Special Agent in Charge, originally in NY File 100-14454. File 100-2074, FOIPA Release of Organization for Jewish Colonization.
12 "Barikht far dem natsyonaln komitet fun dem 'icor'," New York, Oct. 25-26, 1941, mss; in the Abraham Jenofsky papers, RG734, Box 1, folder 6, YIVO.
13 FBI report from P.E. Foxworth, Assistant Director, New York, April 7, 1942, to Director, FBI, containing a March 31 informant's communication, originally in File 100-13257. File 100-2074, FOIPA Release of Organization for Jewish Colonization; "M.L. Olken – natsyonaler organayzer fun icor," *Nailebn-New Life* 16, 9 (September 1942): 3. Olken (sometimes Olkin) was born in Russia in 1901 and came to the U.S. in 1910. He died in 1953. See "Abraham Olkin," *Jewish Life* 7, 9 (July 1953): 19.
14 A. Jenofsky, "Der 'icor' bay der arbet," *Nailebn-New Life* 15, 3 (October-

November 1941): 14-16; A. Jenofsky, "Der 'icor' bay der arbet," *Nailebn-New Life* 15, 4 (December 1941): 15; "Di 'icor' aktsye far der royter armey," *Nailebn-New Life* 16, 1 (January 1942): 3.

15 A. Jenofsky, "Der 'icor' bay der arbet," *Nailebn-New Life* 16, 4 (April 1942): 15; A. Jenofsky, "Der 'icor' ibern land – zayn funktsye un oyfgabn," *Nailebn-New Life* 16, 5 (May 1942): 7, 16; A. Jenofsky, "Di icor kampanye farn feld-shpitol," *Nailebn-New Life* 16, 6 (June 1942): 12.

16 N. Krupin, "Der icor in los angeles vayst dem vayg," *Nailebn-New Life* 16, 7 (July 1942): 14; "Icor haybt on a kampanye tsu shafn tanken un eroplanen far der royter armey," *Nailebn-New Life* 16, 8 (August 1942): 2; "Icor Briefs," *Nailebn-New Life* 16, 8 (August 1942): 14.

17 This information is contained on p. 14 of a 17-page report dated Sept. 7, 1944 submitted by E.E. Conroy, Special Agent in Charge, originally in NY File 100-14454. File 100-2074, FOIPA Release of Organization for Jewish Colonization.

18 This information is contained on pp. 1, 16, 31-32 of a 32-page report dated July 27, 1942, submitted by P.E. Foxworth, Special Agent in Charge, originally in NY File 100-14454. File 100-2074, FOIPA Release of Organization for Jewish Colonization.

19 FBI Memo of Jan. 2, 1943, regarding the ICOR and *Nailebn*. File 100-2074, FOIPA Release of Organization for Jewish Colonization.

20 Undated letters [probably mid-August and early September 1942] from Abraham Jenofsky, Charles Kuntz and Dr. L. Schatzov, chair of the New York City ICOR Committee, to Morris Stern, New York; in the Morris Stern papers, RG231, Box 1, unnamed folder, YIVO; Dr. L. Schatzov, "Di itstike lage un der icor," *Nailebn-New Life* 16, 9 (September 1942): 10; M.L. Olken, "The Icor and its Immediate Tasks," *Nailebn-New Life* 16, 10 (October 1942): 23-24.

21 The Los Angeles ICOR had donated $3,500. "Der icor bay der arbet," *Nailebn-New Life* 16, 10 (October 1942): 19.

22 "Barikht far dem natsyonaln komitet fun 'icor'," and "Organizatsye plan far vayterdike arbet," New York, Oct. 10-11, 1942, mss; in the Abraham Jenofsky papers, RG734, Box 1, folder 6, YIVO. The cover of the Yiddish side of the September 1942 issue of *Nailebn-New Life* was illustrated with a painting of the destroyed Jewish colonies in the Crimea drawn by Frank Horowitz.

23 A. Jenofsky, "Der icor bay der arbet," *Nailebn-New Life* 16, 12 (December 1942): 18-19; Dr. L. Schatzov, "Farvos shikt der icor mobil eks-ray yunits far der roiter armey?" *Nailebn-New Life* 17, 1 (January 1943): 8. The campaign ended successfully on May 22, 1943, with a luncheon at the Piccadilly Hotel in New York. A. Jenofsky, "Di tsvey naye kampanyes fun icor," *Nailebn-New Life* 17, 6 (June 1943): 15-16; " 'Icor' Briefs," *Nailebn-New Life* 17, 6 (June 1943): 21.

24 Letter from Abraham Jenofsky and Charles Kuntz to Jacob Mestel and Sarah Kindman, New York, Sept. 29, 1942; flyer advertising the ICOR "Kontsert

un fayerung," Dec. 20, 1942, in the Philip Sandler papers, RG420, Box 8, file 17, "ICOR"; Nakhman Meisel, "Abraham Bick," *Vochenblat*, March 18, 1948, 7. Bick "started off as an Orthodox rabbi and ended again as one." Interview, Itche Goldberg, New York, June 12, 1996. Goldberg, the longtime editor of *Yidishe Kultur*, the literary journal published by the YKUF, who died in December 2006, added that during his Communist period, Bick was also a member of the YKUF presidium.

25 Rabbi Abraham Bick, "Der sovyetn-farband—der zayl in kamf gegn fashizm," *Nailebn-New Life* 17, 1 (January 1943): 3-4 [Yiddish section].

26 A. Jenofsky, "Mir fayern fuftsn yor biro-bidzhan," *Nailebn-New Life* 17, 4 (April 1943): 17-18; Moishe Shifres, "Der yontev fun 15 yor biro-bidzhan in new york," *Nailebn-New Life* 17, 5 (May 1943): 5-6; P. Novick, "Di badaytung fun biro-bidzhan," *Nailebn-New Life* 17, 6 (June 1943): 11-12; "Greetings to 15th Anniversary of Biro-Bidjan," *Nailebn-New Life* 17, 6 (June 1943): 23; circular letters from Abraham Jenofsky, national secretary of the ICOR, New York, Feb. 20, April 1, April 15, and May 14, 1943, in the Philip Sandler papers, RG420, Box 8, file 17, "ICOR," YIVO. "Aynlandung tsu der fayerlekher bageygenish fun dem biro-bidzhan yubili komitet mitn icor aktiv;" letter from Khaim Zhitlovsky, Charles Kuntz and Abraham Jenofsky to Kalmen Marmor, New York, Feb. 10, 1943, and undated letter of invitation from Abraham Jenofsky to Kalmen Marmor, all in the Kalmen Marmor papers, 1873-1955, RG205, Microfilm group 495, folder 546 "Icor-korespondents, 1938-1946,"YIVO. Letter from Abraham Jenofsky to Khaim Zhitlovsky, New York, April 19, 1943, in the Abraham Jenofsky papers, RG734, Box 3, folder "Letters by Jenofsky," YIVO.

27 M. L. Olken, "Di biro-bidzhan fayerungen ibern land," *Nailebn-New Life* 17, 5 (May 1943): 12-13.

28 Dr. Khaim Zhiltovsky, *An entfer mayne kritiker* (New York: Cooperative Book League of the Jewish Section, International Workers Order, December 1942), 3-6, 13-16 (emphasis in original).

29 Dr. Khaim Zhitlovsky, "Di problem fun yidisher eynikayt in der itstiker tsayt," *Nailebn-New Life* 16, 12 (December 1942): 3-4 and 17, 1 (January 1943): 9-11 (emphasis in original).

30 Dr. Khaim Zhitlovsky, "Vegn der sovyetisher yidnshaft," in Isaac E. Rontch, ed., *Icor almanakh: 25 yor sovyetn farband 15 yor biro-bidzhan - ICOR Almanac: 25 Years U.S.S.R. 15 Years Biro-Bidjan* (New York: ICOR, May 1943), 17-25 [Yiddish section] (emphasis in original); Dr. Khaim Zhitlovsky, *Di yidn in sovyetn-farband* (New York: ICOR, 1943), 4-10, 12-13, 26-27, 31.

31 Dr. Khaim Zhitlovsky, "Birobidzhan un erets yisroel," in Isaac E. Rontch, ed., *ICOR almanakh – ICOR Almanac*, 38-39 [Yiddish section] (emphasis in original). In the spring of 1943, Zhitlovsky decided to move temporarily from Croton-on-Hudson, NY, to Los Angeles. On his way, he undertook a cross-Canada lecture tour. After a stop in Chicago, he was to speak in Winnipeg, Calgary, Edmonton and Vancouver before arriving in Los Angeles on May

CHAPTER THREE

     15. However, he died on May 6, while lecturing in Calgary. L. Pearlman, "Dr. zhitlovsky's letste teg in calgary," *Kanader Yidishe Vochenblat*, May 13, 1943, 5.

32 P. Novick, "A folk in veytog, a folk in tsorn," *Nailebn-New Life* 17, 1 (January 1943): 12 (emphasis in original).

33 Max Levin and Abraham Jenofsky, *A Call to Jewish Landsmanschaften, Societies, Orders, Auxiliaries, Trade Unions, Synagogues, Congregations, Cultural Institutions, Etc. to Celebrate 15 Years of Biro-Bidjan – A Ruf tsu yidishe landsmanshaftn, sosayties, ordns, okzileris, trayd unyons, shuln, kongregayshons, kultur institutsyes, un farshidine undere organizatsyes tsu der fayerung fun 15 yor biro-bidzhan* (New York: Jubilee Committee to Celebrate 15 Years of Biro-Bijan, n.d.).

34 Benjamin Harshav, *Marc Chagall and his Times: A Documentary Narrative* (Stanford, CA: Stanford University Press, 2004), 470, 522. The Columbia anthropologist Franz Boas was suspected of being a Communist sympathizer and the FBI kept a lengthy file on him over the years. David H. Price, *Threatening Anthropology: McCarthyism and the FBI's Surveillance of Active Anthropologists* (Durham, NC: Duke University Press, 2004), 111, 142, 228-229, 260.

35 Joseph Brainin, born in 1895 in Vienna, died in 1970. He had established the Seven Arts Feature Syndicate and served as its managing director from 1921 to 1938. In the early 1950s, he was chair of the National Committee to Secure Justice in the Rosenberg Case, a Communist-front group that defended Julius and Ethel Rosenberg when they were on trial for espionage. In later life, he became the executive vice-president of the American Committee for the Weizmann Institute of Science in Rehovot, Israel. "Joseph Brainin is Dead at 74; Aide of Weizmann Institute," *New York Times*, Feb. 9, 1970, 39.

36 "Soviet Delegates Urge Unity Here," *New York Times*, July 9, 1943, 5.

37 "In yidishn antifashistishn komitet: unzere shlikhim mikhoels un fefer farfestikn di kemfs-eynikayt fun ale shikhtn yidn in amerike,"*Eynikayt*, Moscow, Sept. 9, 1943, 4. For Philadelphia, see also Philip Rosen et al, "Philadelphia Jewry, the Holocaust, and the Birth of the Jewish State. Section I: Philadelphia Jewry and the Holocaust," in Friedman, ed., *Philadelphia Jewish Life*, 14.

38 Joseph Brainin, "Mission from Moscow," *Soviet Russia Today*12, 4 (August 1943): 10-11, 34.

39 The YKUF journal printed their first two American speeches. "Di ershte reydes fun di yidishe sovyetishe shlikhim," *Yidishe Kultur* 6-7 (June-July 1943): 63-65.

40 "Di yidishe delegatsye fun sovyetn-farband, *Nailebn-New Life* 17, 7 (July 1943): 2, 17; "A historisher khoydesh," *Nailebn-New Life* 17, 8 (August 1943): 2.

41 "Farewell Greetings from the Jewish Soviet Delegation," *Nailebn-New Life* 18, 1 (January 1944): 21; "Di historishe rol fun biro-bidzhan far dem yidishn folk un di oyfgabn fun der icor-organizatsye," *Nailebn-New Life* 17, 9 (September

1943): 2-3; " 'Icor' Briefs," *Nailebn-New Life* 17, 9 (September 1943): 21. The same issue of *Nailebn-New Life*, pp. 21-24, featured an article, translated into English, by the Soviet writer Ilya Ehrenburg, "The Murder of the Jewish People," documenting the mass murders of Jews in Nazi-occupied areas of the USSR.

42 Benjamin Harshav, ed., *Marc Chagall on Art and Culture: Including the First Book on Chagall's Art* by *A. Efros and Ya. Tugendhold (Moscow, 1918),* translations from the French, Russian, Yiddish, and Hebrew by Barbara and Benjamin Harshav (Stanford, CA: Stanford University Press, 2003), 88.

43 Nakhman Meisel, "Der bazukh fun der sovyetish-yidisher delegatsye," *Nailebn-New Life* 17, 10 (October 1943): 9-10.

44 M.L. Olken, "The Importance of the Icor at Present," *Nailebn-New Life* 17, 10 (October 1943): 22-23.

45 Moishe Katz, "Di sovyetish-yidishe delegatsye in amerike – a historishe gesheyenish," *Aynikayt*, Moscow, March 30, 1944, 3.

46 Abraham Jenofsky, "Fuftsn khedushim icor-arbet," *Nailebn-New Life* 18, 3 (March 1944): 13-15 and 18, 4 (April 1944):15-17; circular letter from Charles Kuntz and Abraham Jenofsky, New York, Jan. 7, 1944; in United States Territorial Collection, RG117, Box 57, folder "Icor" 17/16, YIVO; letter from Abraham Jenofsky to Kalmen Marmor, New York, Jan. 28, 1944; in the Kalmen Marmor papers, 1873-1955, RG205, Microfilm group 495, folder 546 "Icor-korespondents, 1938-1946," YIVO.

47 Flyer advertising "Celebration and Concert--10th Anniversary Biro-Bidjan Jewish Autonomous Territory in the U.S.S.R." May 14, 1944; in the Philip Sandler papers, RG420, Box 8, file 17, "ICOR," YIVO; Abraham Jenofsky, "Di badaytung fun di biro-bidzhan fayerung," *Nailebn-New Life* 18, 6 (June 1944): 15.

48 Abraham Jenovsky, "Der Icor un zayne baldike oyfgabn," *Nailebn-New Life* 18, 12 (December 1944): 2-4; Abraham Jenofsky, "Der icor bay der arbet," *Nailebn-New Life* 19, 2 (February 1945): 16-20; FBI report dated Feb. 5, 1945, sent to Hoover on Feb. 28 by Special Agent in Charge E.E. Conroy, originally in NY File 100-14454. File 100-2074, FOIPA Release of Organization for Jewish Colonization.

49 A. Jenofsky, "Biro-Bidzhan hot gemakht groysn forshrit di letste por yor," *Morgn Frayhayt*, July 20, 1945, 3.

50 A. Bakhmutsky, *New Achivements in Birobidjan* (New York: ICOR, 1945), 1-16. Bakhmutsky was purged a few years later.

Shloime Mikhoels (on left) at the gravesite of Sholem Aleichem, New York, 1943 (B.Z. Goldberg's son Mitchell is at the right), Schottenstein-Jesselson Library of the Herbert D. Katz Center for Advanced Judaic Studies at the University of Pennsylvania, Philadelphia

Professor Charles Kuntz, *Nailebn-New Life*, June 1940

Wartime Aid to the Soviet Union: Ambijan

Though a greatly weakened ICOR had managed to soldier on during the two years of the Hitler-Stalin Pact, Ambijan had been forced to cease operations altogether. But both pro-Soviet groups gained a new lease on life in 1941-1945, and Ambijan was renamed the Ambijan Committee for Emergency Aid to the Soviet Union (it would call itself the American Birobidjan Committee after the war). Its main tasks became to promote support for the Soviet Union's war effort and to counter isolationist sentiment, especially during the six-month period between the Nazi invasion of Russia and the Japanese attack on Pearl Harbor.

After seeking advice from Victor A. Fediushine, the Soviet consul general in New York, Edward Aronow, a New York lawyer who served as the secretary-treasurer of Ambijan, called a meeting of the board of directors in early October 1941. They decided to sponsor a dinner at the Hotel Commodore for the consul general, with the proceeds going to Russian War Relief, Inc., a group formed by pro-Soviet elements and headed by Edward C. Carter.[1] In advance of the dinner, Ambijan circulated a lengthy letter to its members emphasizing the urgent need to raise "the immense amounts" required to assist the Russian war effort, and to foster cooperation between the U.S., USSR "and all other peace-loving countries." In order to stimulate the interest and generosity of the American Jewish population, the "deeds of valor" performed by Soviet Jews fighting on the eastern front should be publicized, alongside "a concentrated digest of the systematic campaign of cold-blooded annihilation of helpless Jews by the Hitlerite cohorts of every country which has come under the Nazi heel."[2] The dinner, held on December 3, was attended by Lord Marley and Senator Elbert D. Thomas of Utah, among others, and netted $5,000 towards the purchase of an x-ray unit for the Red Army, announced Samuel DeWitt, the acting chair of Ambijan.[3]

Ambijan began to send out feelers to prominent Americans who had in the past shown interest in its work, including Albert Einstein.[4] Einstein, himself a refugee from Germany, was already a supporter of the Birobidzhan project.[5] In the 1930s, he had approved of the anti-Nazi stance of the CP; and in the 1940s and 1950s, he was distressed by the anti-Communist climate of repression in America that affected the careers of many of his fellow academics and scientists. During World War II, fairly sympathetic to the Soviet Union, he lent his name to Ambijan and other pro-Soviet groups, and he would become honorary president of the pro-Soviet American Committee of Jewish Writers, Artists and Scientists.[6]

Meanwhile, Vilhjalmur Stefansson immediately became active in the numerous CP-led front groups organized to mobilize support for the USSR, lending his support to the American Council on Soviet Relations and Russian War Relief, Inc., among others.[7] He spoke at a major benefit for Russian War Relief, Inc. at Madison Square Garden on October 27, 1941, along with former U.S. ambassador to Moscow Joseph E. Davies, the architect Frank Lloyd Wright, and journalist Walter Duranty of the *New York Times*.[8] He also agreed to speak at the December 3 dinner for Consul General Fediushine. DeWitt thanked Stefansson for agreeing to participate, and Max Levin, chairman of the Board of Directors, later congratulated Stefansson on his "splendid address."[9] Stefansson also participated in the Congress of American-Soviet Friendship held at Madison Square Garden and in various surrounding hotels in New York City on November 7-8, 1942, the 25th anniversary of the Bolshevik Revolution; this gathering was addressed by Ambassador Davies, Vice-President Henry Wallace, Soviet Ambassador Maxim Litvinov, and U.S. Senator Claude Pepper of Florida, among other notables.[10]

Aid to Russia had now become the supreme duty of all Jews, announced Ambijan, because "the fate of Jews the world over is being decided now on the Eastern front." Only with a decisive victory over Germany "will the Jews of Europe find salvation, hope and a future. Even a Russia at war for its existence has been a haven of hope for homeless Jews. A million Jewish refugees from the Baltic countries, Bessarabia, Bukovina, Eastern Galicia, White Russia and the Ukraine... have found a haven in the interior of the Soviet Union." But these Jews "depend entirely upon the relief activities of the Soviet Government." Ambijan noted the formation of the JAFC in Moscow, which had launched an appeal for aid, and asked American Jews "to make the utmost contribution towards providing the greatest possible aid to the Soviet Union in the present emergency....The Russian people are fighting *our* battle. If they lose, *we* lose. If they win, *we* win."[11]

Ambijan chapters threw themselves into the task of collecting and shipping clothing and medical supplies to the Soviet Union. One of their major campaigns involved collecting and sending watches to the Red Army. "Give watches to the Red Army and Help Put a Watch on the Rhine"; "Every Watch Will be a Time Bomb Against Hitler"; and "They give their blood...you give them the Time!" were some of the catchy slogans used in the campaign. Consul General Fediushine had written Max Levin in October 1942 acknowledging the need for watches on the front lines. At a dinner held at the Horizon Club, New York, on December 7, some 2,300 watches were handed over to Fediushine and to M.M. Gousev, who was head of the Amtorg Trading Corp. in New York, the Soviet purchasing and sales agency in the United States for imports and exports to the USSR.[12]

Wartime Aid to the Soviet Union: Ambijan

In 1943 the Industrial Trades Committee of Ambijan was formed, under the leadership of Charles H. Lipsett, the president of Atlas Publishing Company, which published industrial and trade journals; Lipsett was also an advisor to the War Department. It set itself the goal of gathering 10,000 timepieces, new and used. At a dinner held on April 1, Dmitri I. Zaikin, Fediushine's successor in New York, commended Ambijan for its efforts and went on to speak of the "heroism and devotion" displayed by Soviet Jews fighting in the Red Army. The Committee sponsored a concert at Carnegie Hall on April 11, as part of the campaign; major magazines such as the *New Yorker* wrote about the drive. Georgia Gibbs sang Irving Berlin's "Blue Skies" and George Gershwin's "Embraceable You" and Teddy Wilson's band played "I Got Rhythm." At a large public meeting sponsored by the newly-formed Bronx Division of Ambijan, watches were presented to crews of Soviet merchant vessels in the port of New York. These efforts were widely publicized by the National Association of Credit Jewelers and by trade publications such as the *Jewelry News*, *National Jeweler* and the *Jewelers Circular—Keystone*. Receiving centers were set up in communities across America, and many watchmakers and jewelers—who were in the main, not incidentally, Jewish—donated their time to repair and recondition older watches. "Industrialists and businessmen throughout the country are solidly behind the drive to collect watches for the Red Army," proclaimed Ambijan.

Ambijan stepped up the campaign by forming a special American Jewelers Committee to Collect Watches for the Red Army, which included, it claimed, 22 of the nation's leading jewelers. It also announced plans to mobilize 30,000 jewelers across the country in an effort to collect 100,000 watches. Soviet military personnel took part in many of the committee's activities to emphasize the military usefulness of the watches. The Committee delivered watches to Eugene (Evgeny) D. Kisselev, the new Soviet consul general in New York, who on May 10, expressed *"our most sincere and deep gratitude"* for the gifts. Lipsett released a statement of thanks in June from Stalin's top military man, Marshal Grigori Zhukov. "The ready response of the American jewelers throughout the country," stated Lipsett, "supplies fair assurance that this work which now has Marshal Zhukov's best wishes, will be accomplished successfully." On September 20, 100 more watches were presented to the Soviet Consulate in New York. George Gordon Battle, who had assumed the title of acting president of Ambijan following the death of William W. Cohen in 1940, sent out a circular letter on September 29, calling on members to contribute money to the Committee, as the watches being collected required repair and reconditioning. By the end of 1943, 8,000 watches had been shipped to Russia.[13]

CHAPTER FOUR

Another wartime effort by Ambijan, "to show our appreciation and gratitude for the victory at Stalingrad," was to become the official American "sponsor guardian" of Serebryanye Prudy, the Silver Ponds Children's Home and Sanatorium in that city, which by June 1943, although partially destroyed in the battle, housed 500 Jewish war orphans. This venture was undertaken by the Women's Division, headed by Lonnie Levin, and received the support of prominent individuals such as Evelyn Stefansson and New York magistrate Anna M. Kross. Born in Russia in 1891 and brought to the U.S. as a child two years later, Kross had become, in 1933, the first woman judge in the New York City Magistrates Court. Evelyn Stefansson called the idea "irresistible" and hosted a luncheon on behalf of the home on June 5, at which $3,000 was raised. "It is an honor and a privilege to be able to send a message of love and admiration to the children of the heroes and heroines of Stalingrad. The Ambijan is proud of the opportunity accorded to it of cooperating in the loving care of the Stalingrad children," stated the organization. Leading New York pediatricians such as Dr. Bela Schick were also recruited and formed their own committee to advise on the purchase of medicines and vitamins for the orphaned children. Even Hollywood studios got involved, forming a Committee of Famous American Children, chaired by child movie star George Vincent "Skippy" Homeier. Homeier, who had appeared in the anti-Nazi Broadway play and movie *Tomorrow the World*, went on the CBS Radio Network program "We the People" to describe the efforts on behalf of Silver Ponds.

The Women's Division announced that in addition to its efforts to raise $100 per orphan, it would be purchasing a power plant for Silver Ponds. "Our good friends Herman Blum and Sam DeWitt are taking care of getting all the necessary equipment," stated Budish. Ambijan produced *A Letter from Stalingrad*, a film short about Silver Ponds made "with the aid of volunteer experts from the movie industry." It was shown at numerous rallies and concerts, and even in commercial theaters. When the film was shown at Carnegie Hall on December 28, 1943, the program also featured entertainment by Zero Mostel and the cantata "We'll Answer Stalingrad" by Charles Kingsford, sung by Paul Robeson. The magazine *Soviet Russia Today* ran a pictorial feature on the contributions made by Ambijan to the children's home.[14]

During the war years Ambijan also raised money for Jewish war orphans throughout the Soviet Union. By 1943 nine children's camps in New York state were soliciting contributions for the orphans; fundraising events were also held at various summer resorts on Long Island. One such venue was Maud's Summer-Ray, in Sullivan County, New York, which was owned by left-wing artists.[15] Most of the guests at Maud's Summer-Ray were Yiddish-speaking leftists, and charity events were frequent.[16] In all, some $16,000 was raised in 1944 through summer resort activities, reported the *Ambijan Bulletin*.[17]

Ambijan, too, was closely involved with the 1943 visit of Shloime Mikhoels and Itsik Fefer to America. James N. Rosenberg, who by this time wore a number of hats—vice-president and chair of the Board of Directors of the Joint, chair of the Agro-Joint, chair of the advisory committee of the Jewish Council for Russian War Relief, and member of the national committee of Russian War Relief, Inc.—spoke at a reception for Mikhoels and Fefer at the Hotel Astor in New York on July 1. "Schoolbooks will relate how Stalingrad turned the tide and thereby saved the world from Hitler's clutches. To Jews the word will be immortal," he told the audience. Rosenberg described the Soviet Union as a "vast and gallant country" where "anti-Semitism is a crime against the State." This "corner-stone of Soviet policy" helped explain why Hitler had failed to conquer Russia.[18]

The two Soviet guests met with Ambijan at a special gathering of its national committee in the ballroom of the Savoy Plaza Hotel on July 12. The entire leadership was present for what the *Ambijan Bulletin* described as "a truly momentous occasion." Mikhoels and Fefer were welcomed by George Gordon Battle, James N. Rosenberg, Max Levin and J.M. Budish. Rosenberg recalled his 1926 visit to Russia and the early Jewish agricultural settlements; he had heard then "of a possible Jewish Republic or State in Russia." Now, Rosenberg asserted that "Birobidjan may play an important role in the post-war settlement of the Jews victimized by Hitler." He praised the Soviets for having saved some 1.6 million Jews already, and called on American Jewry to express its appreciation for the Soviet war effort

Budish explained for the benefit of Mikhoels and Fefer the work being carried on by Ambijan on behalf of the Soviet Union, "a country where Anti-Semitism has been made as despicable as cannibalism, and equally as impossible." Budish reminded his audience that the pre-war understanding between Ambijan and the Soviets to settle east European Jews in Birobidzhan had never been rescinded and might after the war be resumed. He announced that a special committee of "prominent public men" under the direction of "the eminent scientist Vilhjalmur Stefansson" was being formed to study the role of Ambijan in the post-war reconstruction of Jewish life in the USSR. Budish stated that as of July 1, 1943, Ambijan had raised $150,000 for emergency work. Of course, he continued, "we can never repay our debt of gratitude to the people and armies of the Soviet Union." Max Levin told Mikhoels and Fefer that Ambijan's members were "friends and well-wishers of the Soviet people and government long before the outbreak of war....We have always understood and deeply appreciated the manner in which your country has solved the national minority problem" and "blazed the trail" for others to grant complete freedom to national minorities and ethnic groups.

In their own speeches, Mikhoels and Fefer dwelt upon the creation of a Jewish entity in Birobidzhan as "one of the highest achievements of the Soviet Union's national minorities policy." They also spoke of the participation of Birobidzhan Jews in the war effort "of their motherland, the Soviet Union," and of their contribution "to the common treasure of Jewish culture." Mikhoels told Ambijan's members that the formation of Birobidzhan had been "of great significance to the solution of the Jewish problem....The elements of statehood now enter into the picture of Jewish life in the U.S.S.R. We Jews have now become a people with political rights, a people with state rights, not only a people with the equal rights of Soviet citizenship." Fefer read his poem "A Wedding in Birobidzhan." He also paid tribute to Ambijan's campaign to send watches to the USSR.[19] On September 17, 1,200 New York schoolchildren listened to Mikhoels (speaking in Yiddish) at Town Hall. Skippy Homeier presided over the event, flanked on the platform by Soviet Consul General Kisselev and by Sasha Small, secretary of International Labor Defense. Mikhoels spoke of the friendship and love among the 172 different peoples of the Soviet Union, and of heroic child guerrillas fighting the Nazis.[20]

The U.S. tour by the two emissaries raised $16 million dollars for the Soviet war effort. An editorial in the *Ambijan Bulletin* later recalled how Mikhoels and Fefer had conveyed "the cries of the children, the tragedy in the eyes of the mothers, the appeal of those who died in consecration to their people, their motherland and the freedom of all mankind." It declared that the message brought by the two Soviets had strengthened the bonds of brotherhood between American and Soviet Jews, brought renewed courage to the Jews of America, and "lent wings of inspiration to the members and friends of our own organization, the Ambijan." It wished Mikhoels and Fefer "a happy return to their own gallant land and many, many years of continuous fruitful work."[21]

Ambijan made much of the fact that some 1.6 million European Jews had sought refuge in the USSR. They had been "saved from extermination by the heroism and fortitude of the Soviet people and the Red Army," who had evacuated these Jews, along with their own Jewish communities, in advance of the Nazi onslaught. Birobidzhan itself was "totally mobilized for victory over the blood-stained fascist foe," its factories producing war materiel, its farms food. Tens of thousands had found refuge in Birobidzhan, asserted the organization, and they would play an essential part in the postwar reconstruction: "Ambijan expects that it will again be privileged to cooperate in the settlement of Jews in Birobidjan and elsewhere in the U.S.S.R. as soon as conditions make it possible." Indeed, Ambijan was upset that it was not invited to the American Jewish Conference convened in New York in August 1943, at which more than 500 delegates representing 64 Jewish organizations met to decide what role the American Jewish community would play in representing Jewish demands after the war. "Bearing in mind the overwhelming importance that Birobidjan may assume for the settlement of a great portion of the 1,600,000 Jewish refugees" who had escaped the Nazis, "it would seem essential that the Ambijan should take part."[22]

In November 1943, Ambijan reiterated its position that the postwar resettlement of Europe's Jewish remnant would have to include Birobidzhan. Noting that over three million European Jews had already been murdered by Hitler, Ambijan declared that it was "only due to the gallantry of the Red Army and the policy of the Soviet Union" that some 1.8 million others (it had added 200,000 from its earlier estimate) had found refuge in the USSR. Responding to the increasing influence of the Zionist movement in American Jewish communities, Ambijan argued that "even under the best conditions" Palestine could not alone absorb all the Jews who would have to be resettled. With its natural resources and minerals, rich soil, excellent lumber, fish and fur-bearing animals, and "healthful and invigorating climate," the Jewish Autonomous Region was clearly "one of the most important areas of possible Jewish settlement." Once again, Ambijan reminded the Jewish community of its pre-war agreement with Russia: "We have every reason to expect that, as soon as hostilities cease, Ambijan will again be privileged to cooperate in the settlement of Jews in Birobidjan."[23]

In early January 1944, Budish asked Stefansson to pen an article celebrating the upcoming tenth anniversary of the proclamation of Birobidzhan as a Jewish Autonomous Region.[24] In the article, Stefansson described Birobidzhan's essential role in "the rehabilitation of eastern and central European Jewry...The policy of the Soviet Union, to make all racial and national minorities equal in practice as well as in theory, has given them a unity that has been one of the chief sources of their war strength....On its tenth anniversary, Birobidjan is already a land of fulfilled promise."[25]

The *Ambijan Bulletin* of February 1944 presented itself as a "Salute to the Red Army," praising the Soviets for the victory at Stalingrad. The Soviet Union was the "first great multi-national State in the world," and in Birobidzhan the Jews had been provided with "a State unit of their own."[26] Max Levin provided a history of Ambijan, and wrote about some of its founders and leading lights, including Aaron Lipper; William W. Cohen, with his "unselfish devotion" an inspiration to all; and George Gordon Battle, whose "love for freedom" had been a guiding principle since he replaced Cohen as president.[27]

Chapter Four

By the spring of 1944 Ambijan claimed 6,000 members throughout the country and was recognized by many American Jews as their channel for post-war rehabilitation of European Jews within the USSR; the JAFC, too, had officially recognized Ambijan. The organization moved into new quarters, at 103 Park Avenue, in April. Budish told Stefansson on April 19 that, according to a cable from Moscow, the JAR would begin accepting Jewish refugees from eastern Europe immediately; 3,500 Jewish orphans would be the first to arrive. Ambijan and other pro-Soviet Jewish groups celebrated Birobidzhan's 10th anniversary as a JAR with numerous events, including a dinner at the Hotel Commodore on April 7, 1944 and a gala party at the Waldorf-Astoria on May 16. The party attracted 1,000 guests, who expressed their "deep love and admiration for the heroic people of the Soviet Union." Budish praised retiring president George Gordon Battle. Anna M. Kross "spoke as an ardent Zionist" and expressed her conviction that all Jews should support the Ambijan project. Soviet Consul General Kisselev praised the work of Ambijan, "the oldest among the numerous friends of our country in the United States." He also spoke of the heroic war efforts being made by Soviet Jews, who "occupy an equal and honorable place among the courageous fighters of the Red Army."

Senator Elbert D. Thomas of Utah and Franklin S. Harris, president of Brigham Young University, both long-time supporters of Birobidzhan, were invited to the Waldorf-Astoria party. Harris described the rich natural resources of Birobidzhan and paid homage to the courage and skill of the Jewish pioneers there. Thomas spoke of the Soviet Union as having been the first country to "call out to an unheeding world for unity" against the "common foe" of fascism. He cited Birobidzhan as an "outstanding example" of "the far-sighted policy" of the Soviet Union in regard to national minorities. "The true—the genuine equality which is shared by all the national groups in the Soviet Union has shown the way to all the world. It is the unshakable foundation from which Jewish soldiers in the Red Army were able to strike such heroic blows—strike hard—against the murderers who were exterminating their brother Jews." In the Soviet Union, he noted, anti-Semitism was severely punished as treason against the entire nation. Senator Thomas' remarks were entered into the *Congressional Record* by fellow Utah senator Abe Murdock.

Max Levin also spoke at the dinner, noting that as the war was nearing its end, "the time has come for us to plan to settle non-Russian Jews in Biro-Bidjan." Of those who had been fortunate enough to escape "the Nazi murderers" and find shelter in the Soviet Union, a considerable number, he declared, would want to settle permanently in Birobidzhan, and Ambijan would assist the Soviet government in helping Birobidzhan absorb them. Edward Aronow announced that Ambijan planned to raise $1,000,000 for various relief measures. At the close of the speeches, "Stefansson's call for a standing tribute to Marshal Stalin met with a unanimous response and ovation."[28]

With the war clearly drawing to a close, Ambijan made plans for its first national conference, to be held in New York on November 25-26, 1944. An Advisory Council chaired by Charles H. Lipsett met on October 12 at the Hotel Biltmore to prepare for the conference. With the help of manufacturers such as Isaac Aronoff, already an Ambijan activist, Ambijan enlisted a number of prominent businessmen in its work; they were "welcomed heartily" by Gerson C. Young. Various businesses announced gifts to Birobidzhan, including 50,000 yards of woollen goods, a complete knitting plant, a shoe plant, and two machinery repair shops.[29] Communist theoretician Alexander Bittelman, in a report to the first general conference of the "Morning Freiheit Association" dated September 30, 1944, referred to "special Birobidjan projects undertaken by the Ambijan," in which the ICOR planned to participate.[30]

Max Levin chaired a meeting of the board of directors on October 24 at the Commodore Hotel. Ambijan would face great challenges in the post-war period, he told the 60 people present, and he hoped Ambijan would be able to raise $1,000,000 in cash and even more in merchandise. Budish stated that at the national conference in November, members would discuss the "historic role which may be played" by Birobidzhan in the post-war rehabilitation of the Jewish people: "The needs of the European Jews in the post-war period will be so immense that even the most zealous Zionists could not possibly refuse to lend their co-operation towards the settlement in Birobidjan of those helpless Jews who have found refuge in the U.S.S.R. and who now plead for an opportunity to settle permanently and start life anew" in the Jewish Autonomous Region. "Opportunity has not often knocked at the doors of the long suffering Jewish people. We cannot, we must not, let this opportunity pass by default." Budish declared that the conference would mark "the new era of brotherhood of man that we all crave to develop out of this frightful holocaust."[31]

The November conference was attended by 403 delegates from the U.S., Canada, Mexico, and Cuba, along with an additional 1,000 guests. A "declaration of principles," adopted unanimously, stated that Ambijan had "from the very beginning identified anti-Semitism with fascism." Again tribute was paid to the Soviets, who had opened their doors to some 1.8 million Jews escaping Hitler. The conference pledged to raise $1,000,000 to support refugees in Stalingrad and Birobidzhan and to accelerate the industrial and cultural development of the JAR. In particular, Ambijan agreed to redouble its efforts to resettle 3,500 Jewish orphans in Birobidjan; it would also continue sponsoring Silver Ponds.

Prominent guests and speakers included Senator Elbert D. Thomas, who paid tribute to the national minority policy of the Soviet Union and called Birobidzhan a haven for the Jewish people; James Rosenberg, who spoke of the "beacon lights" of Soviet policy which now "blazed the way for a universal policy of protection of all minorities"; Consul General Kisselev, who praised the "noble contribution to the war effort" being made by Soviet Jews; Soviet ambassador to Washington Andrei Gromyko, who thanked Ambijan for the help it was rendering to the USSR and Birobidzhan in particular; and New York Congressman Emanuel Celler, now a member of Ambijan's national committee. Rabbi Isaac Landman of Temple Beth Elohim in Brooklyn addressed the delegates, reassuring them that many of the Jews who fled Hitler "will be helped to the greatest degree by settlement in Birobidjan." He called it "scandalous" that the U.S. had admitted just 1,000 Jewish refugees during the war, while the USSR had saved 1-½ million.

A public dinner, attended by the delegates plus some 1,000 guests, was hosted by Vilhjalmur and Evelyn Stefansson. The conference elected Lord Marley as honorary president of Ambijan; Stefansson and Lipsett were selected as vice-presidents. Some $96,000 in contributions and pledges was raised. In addition, pledges were made of machinery and equipment, including sewing machines, a shoe manufacturing plant, a needle trades plant, a knitting mill, a machine shop for tractor repairs, and printing machinery and hand tools, with a total value of $100,000.[32]

The national conference had decided that with the help of the new business people who had joined the organization, Ambijan should expand its existing industrial and professional divisions, and create new divisions. There was already an Industrial Trades Committee, under the chairmanship of Charles H. Lipsett. In 1945, the Metal Trades Machinery Division was established, with chapters in New York, Chicago and Cleveland; in this division, 15 major industrialists, including manufacturers such as Milton Heimlich, Herbert Segal and Samuel DeWitt, worked alongside two members of a Communist-controlled union, the United Electrical, Radio and Machine Workers of America (UE), to send to the JAR machine tools, drill presses, sewing machines, and other useful items. Ambijan also formed a Graphic Arts Division, which counted among its members the executives of 26 different printing, publishing, stationary, direct mail, and public relations firms; a Textiles & Wearing Apparel Division, headed by 12 major garment manufacturers along with Jacob S. Potofsky, the general secretary-treasurer of the Amalgamated Clothing Workers of America (ACWA); a Sewing & Knitting Machinery Division, chaired by Nat Minkoff, with seven entrepreneurs and one member from the United

Mechanics Union. The new Agricultural Division was headed by two men who had visited Birobidzhan in 1929: Dr. M.L. Wilson, director of the Extension Service of the U.S. Department of Agriculture, and Franklin S. Harris, president of Brigham Young University. A new Produce Division was led by three fishmongers. There was a new Russian Division, a new Furniture Industry Division, and a new Physicians Division. The new Musicians Division included among its members Sir Thomas Beecham, Leonard Bernstein, Morton Gould, William Morris, and Bruno Walter.[33]

A dinner was held on November 24, 1945 in honor of M.M. Gousev, whose Amtorg Trading Corp. had, in the words of J.M. Budish, "rendered invaluable cooperation to our organization." The guests of honor included James N. Rosenberg, U. S. Senator Harley M. Kilgore of West Virginia, Congressman Celler, and William O'Dwyer, the newly elected mayor of New York. Kilgore said that the development of Birobidzhan was "a credit to the Jewish people"; he described the project as "certainly one answer to some of the immediate and great problems of post-war reconstruction and rehabilitation of the European Jews." Gousev was introduced by the chair, Vilhjalmur Stefansson, who described Gousev's wartime role as the agent in New York for the Soviet government's Purchasing Commission. In his own address, Gousev discussed the need to rebuild the Soviet Union following the devastation of war; rather pointedly, he reminded the audience of business people that the USSR might well become both an important market for American industrial products, and "a valuable source of many raw materials, semi-fabricated and other goods for industrial use and consumer needs in the United States." He hoped that "mutual understanding will be developed on the basis of normal economic relations and mutual interest." Not by coincidence, two of the other speakers were Leo M. Nellis, of College Inn Food Products of Chicago; and Charles H. Lipsett, consultant to the Surplus War Property Board in Washington on the disposal of government surplus commodities. The dinner raised a total of $87,937 in cash and pledges, including $20,000 from Joseph Morgenstern of Cleveland, president of the Electroline Manufacturing Company.[34]

"We Must Lend a Hand!" shouted one Ambijan pamphlet, and on September 6, 1945, Budish announced that supplies worth $100,000 had been shipped to Birobidzhan for the maintenance of the initial 3,500 war orphans.[35] Altogether, the Committee in 1945 shipped a grand total of $456,779.00 in clothing, food, machinery, drugs and surgical supplies, and other miscellaneous items to the USSR.[36]

Endnotes

1. Circular letter from Edward I. Aronow, New York, Oct. 3, 1941; letter from Edward I. Aronow to Vilhjalmur Stefansson, New York, Oct. 23, 1941; Stefansson correspondence, MSS 196, Box 56, 1941--USSR General Folder, Stefansson Collection.
2. "The American Committee for the Settlement of Jews in Birobidjan," circular letter to all members, [late October, 1941]; Stefansson correspondence, MSS 196, Box 56, 1941--USSR General Folder, Stefansson Collection.
3. "Jews Make War Aid Gifts," *New York Times*, Dec. 5, 1941, 2.
4. Letter from the Board of Directors, Ambijan, to Albert Einstein, New York, Oct. 31, 1941; Stefansson correspondence, MSS 196, Box 56, 1941--USSR General Folder, Stefansson Collection.
5. See, for instance, his endorsement on the front cover of the pamphlet *Birobidjan: The Jewish Autonomous Territory in the U.S.S.R.*, in which he spoke of the "generous help" provided by the Soviet government in "the furthering of this colony," which was of "great significance for a part of the Jewish people."
6. See Herbert Romerstein and Eric Breindel, *The Venona Secrets*, 278-279, 397-399; and the full-length study by Fred Jerome, *The Einstein File: J. Edgar Hoover's Secret War Against the World's Most Famous Scientist* (New York: St. Martin's Press, 2002).
7. "Soviet Aid Group Backed," *New York Times*, July 1, 1941, 4; "America Responds to Russia's Needs," *Soviet Russia Today* 11, 2 (June 1942): 17.
8. *New Masses* 41, 4 (Oct. 28, 1941): 25.
9. Letter from Samuel A. DeWitt to Vilhjalmur Stefansson, New York, Nov. 29, 1941; letter from Max Levin to Vilhjalmur Stefansson, New York, Dec. 11, 1941; Stefansson correspondence, MSS 196, Box 56, 1941--USSR General Folder, Stefansson Collection.
10. "Congress of American-Soviet Friendship," *Soviet Russia Today* 11, 7 (November 1942): 6-7, 38; Jessica Smith, "American-Soviet Friendship Congress," *Soviet Russia Today* 11, 8 (December 1942): 8, 11. Litvinov's speech was printed in the 1943 ICOR *Almanac*. "Address of Ambassador Maxim Litvinov," in Isaac E. Rontch, ed., *Icor almanakh—ICOR Almanac*, 5 [English section].
11. "Aid to Russia is the Supreme Duty of All Jews," "Russian Jewish Leaders Appeal to American Jewry," "Our Program and Plans," "Your Destiny is in the Balance," in *A Duty and a Privilege for American Jews: Help to Defend America by Aiding the Soviet Union* (New York: Ambijan Committee for Emergency Aid to the Soviet Union, [1941]), 4-5, 6-7, 10, 12 (emphasis in original).
12. *Give Watches to the Red Army* (New York: Ambijan Committee for Emergency Aid to the Soviet Union, [October 1942]); *Give Watches to the Red Army* (New York: Ambijan Committee for Emergency Aid to the Soviet Union,

[February 1943]); "Watches for the Red Army," *Soviet Russia Today* 11, 10 (February 1943): 6; letter from J.M. Budish to Vilhjalmur Stefansson, New York, Dec. 1, 1942. Stefansson correspondence, MSS 196, Box 60, 1942--USSR General Folder; MSS 196, Box 62, 1943--USSR General Folder, Stefansson Collection.

13 "Marshal Zhukov Thanks American Citizens," press release from Charles H. Lipsett, Industrial Trades Committee, Ambijan, New York, June [19?], 1943, in United States Territorial Collection, RG117, Box 57, folder "Icor" 17/16, YIVO; "Watches Can Shoot," *Birobidjan and the Jews in the Post-War World: A Series of Addresses on the Occasion of the Visit to the U.S.A. of Prof. Mikhoels and Lt.-Col. Feffer of the U.S.S.R.* (New York: American Committee for the Settlement of Jews in Birobidjan (Ambijan), 1943), 17-20; "Ambijan Activities," *Ambijan Bulletin* 2, 3 (April 1943): 7-8, 15-19; "Speech Delivered by Mr. D.I. Zaikin," *Ambijan Bulletin* 2, 3 (April 1943): 18-19; "Program," *Ambijan Bulletin* 2, 3 (April 1943): 16-17; "Red Army Watches Campaign Making Good Progress," *Ambijan Bulletin* 2, 4 (June 1943): 1, 4 (emphasis in original); "Bronx Division has Lively Gathering," *Ambijan Bulletin* 2, 4 (June 1943): 4; "American Jewelers Committee to Collect Watches for the Russian Army Formed by Leaders in the Jewelery Industry," *Ambijan Bulletin* 2, 5 (July 1943): 1, 4; "Ambijan Presents Watches to Red Navy Commander," *Ambijan Bulletin* 2, 6 (October 1943): 1; "Jewelers Launch Watch Drive at Waldorf-Astoria," *Ambijan Bulletin* 2, 6 (October 1943): 4; "Watches Presented to Naval Heroes at Soviet Consulate," *Ambijan Bulletin* 2, 7 (November 1943): 1; "Another 1,000 Watches Shipped to Russian Front," *Ambijan Bulletin* 3, 1 (January 1944): 1; "Summary of Proceedings of the National Conference of the American Birobidjan Committee (Ambijan)," *Ambijan Bulletin* 4, 1 (June 1945): 13-14, 18; "Talk of the Town: Watches for Russia," *New Yorker*, April 10, 1943, 14; circular letter from George Gordon Battle, New York, Sept. 29, 1943, in FBI File 100-99898, Section 1, FOIPA No. 416152, Ambijan.

14 "Ambijan Assumes Sponsorship of Stalingrad Children's Home," *Ambijan Bulletin* 2, 4 (June 1943): 1; "Famous American Children Take Lead in Aid for Children of Silver Ponds," *Ambijan Bulletin* 2, 4 (June 1943): 1; "Silver Ponds," *Ambijan Bulletin* 2, 4 (June 1943): 2; "Women's Division Luncheon Opens Drive for Silver Ponds in New York," *Ambijan Bulletin* 2, 4 (June 1943): 3; "Ambijan to Send Power Plant to Stalingrad Children's Home," *Ambijan Bulletin* 2, 5 (July 1943): 1; "Ambijan—Its Program and Activities," *Ambijan Bulletin* 2, 5 (July 1943): 2; "Cement the Friendship Between Children of the U.S.A. and the U.S.S.R.," *Ambijan Bulletin* 2, 5 (July 1943): 3. "Silver Ponds on the Air," *Ambijan Bulletin* 2, 5 (July 1943): 4.; "Kids Camps Go All Out for Silver Ponds," *Ambijan Bulletin* 2, 5 (July 1943): 4; "Electric Power Plant and Supplies Sailing on their Way to Stalingrad," *Ambijan Bulletin* 2, 6 (October 1943): 5; "Russian Radio Hour on Station WHOM," *Ambijan Bulletin* 2, 6 (October 1943): 6; "American Parents at Summer Resorts Aid Ambijan Drive for Silver Ponds," *Ambijan Bulletin* 2, 6 (October 1943):

6; "Don't Fail to See the New Film: 'A Letter from Stalingrad'," *Ambijan Bulletin* 2, 6 (October 1943): 6; "Children of Stalingrad Festival at Carnegie Hall," *Ambijan Bulletin* 2, 7 (November 1943): 1; "Salute to the Children of Stalingrad a Great Success," *Ambijan Bulletin* 3, 1 (January 1944): 1; "25 Tons of Food and Other Supplies Shipped to Silver Ponds by Ambijan," *Ambijan Bulletin* 3, 3 (April 1944): 1, 4; "A Grand Piano for the Children at Silver Ponds," *Ambijan Bulletin* 3, 7 (November 1944): 7; "Stalingrad's American Children's Home," *Soviet Russia Today* 13, 8 (December 1944): 11; "Young Stage and Screen Stars Aid Home for Stalingrad Orphans," *PM*, New York, June 6, 1943, 26; "Red Guerrilla, 12, is Guest in Absentia Here at 'Salute to the Children of Stalingrad,'" *New York Times*, Dec. 29, 1943, 19; *Our Debt in Stalingrad* (New York: Ambijan Committee, [1944]; pp. 3-6 of the 24-page FBI report of Sept. 19, 1945, submitted by E.E. Conroy, Special Agent in Charge, originally in NY File 100-42538. File 100-99898, Section 1, FOIPA No. 416152, Ambijan. For a review of the movie *Tomorrow the World*, see "Film Reviews," *Variety*, Dec. 20, 1944, 8.

15 See the box advertisement "Stay and Play at Maud's Summer-Ray," which ran during the summers in the *New Masses* throughout World War II; see for instance the *New Masses* 39, 11 (June 3, 1941): 26. The name was a play-on-words transliteration of Maud's Zumeray, or summer place. Maud's was frequented by many left-wing artists, such as Yosl Cutler and Zuni Maud (whose family were the hotel's owners). Cutler and Maud were well known for their Modicut Puppet Theatre in New York, which toured in Europe and the USSR; it sometimes performed at the resort. See Edward Portnoy, "Modicut Puppet Theatre: Modernism, Satire, and Yiddish Culture," *The Drama Review* 43, 3 (Fall 1999): 115-134. Portnoy in his research came across many instances of fund-raising on behalf of the ICOR and Birobidzhan at the hotel. E-mail letter from Edward Portnoy to the author, New York, Nov. 11, 1996. Zuni Maud, originally from Wasilkow, near Bialystok, Poland, died in 1956. For further information on radical summer holiday camps and resorts in the Catskills, see Phil Brown, ed., *In The Catskills: A Century of the Jewish Experience in "The Mountains"* (New York: Columbia University Press, 2002); Esterita "Cissie" Blumberg, *Remember the Catskills: Tales by a Recovering Hotelkeeper* (Fleischmanns, NY: Purple Mountain Press, 1996); and Baila Round Shargel, "Leftist Summer Colonies of Northern Westchester County, New York," *American Jewish History* 83, 3 (September 1995): 337-358.

16 Telephone interview with Edward Cramer, Englewood, NJ, Nov. 5, 1996. His father, Israel Cramer, a clothing manufacturer and member of Ambijan's Advisory Council of businessmen, spent his vacations at Maud's Summer-Ray during the war.

17 "Ambijan Summer Activities," *Ambijan Bulletin* 3, 7 (November 1944): 8. An FBI report quoted an informant describing Far Rockaway as "the center of Pro-Communist mass organization activities." This information is contained on p. 2 of a 13-page report dated April 29-30, 1946, submitted by

E.E. Conroy, Special Agent in Charge, originally in NY File 100-42538. File 100-99898, Section 2, FOIPA No. 416152, Ambijan.

18 James N. Rosenberg, "Soviet Russia and the Jews," *Menorah Journal* 31, 3 (October-December 1943): 296-299.

19 James N. Rosenberg, *On the Steppes: A Russian Diary*, foreword by Louis Marshall (New York: Alfred A. Knopf, 1927), 7; "Prof. Solomon Mikhoels and Itzik Feffer Honored at Special Meeting of the Ambijan National Committee," *Ambijan Bulletin* 2, 5 (July 1943): 1, 3; "Ambijan--Its Program and Activities," *Ambijan Bulletin* 2, 5 (July 1943): 2; " 'Elements of Statehood Enter Picture of Jewish Life' Says Professor Mikhoels," *Ambijan Bulletin* 2, 6 (October 1943): 4; Stefansson cable in *Ambijan Bulletin* 2, 7 (November 1943): 2; Max Levin, "Exponents of Jewish Culture, the Delegation from the USSR," in *Birobidjan and the Jews in the Post-War World*, 3-4; James N. Rosenberg, "Let the World Take Note," *Birobidjan and the Jews in the Post-War World*, 21-22; Charles H. Lipsett, "Jews and Post-War World," *Birobidjan and the Jews in the Post-War World*, 23. See further Bauer, *My Brother's Keeper*, 116; and Thomas A. Kolsky, *Jews Against Zionism: The American Council for Judaism, 1942-1948* (Philadelphia: Temple University Press, 1992), 40-41, for Rosenberg's opposition to a Jewish state in Palestine.

20 "American Children Greet Prof. Mikhoels at Town Hall," *Ambijan Bulletin* 2, 6 (October 1943): 1, 4; "Your Young Eyes Will See the Victory," *Ambijan Bulletin* 2, 6 (October 1943): 3. The speeches by Homeier, Kisselev, and Mikhoels are included in the 16-page booklet *Uncle Vasya is a Hero and Other Stories of the Young Heroes and Heroines of the U.S.S.R.* by Skippy Homeier et al ([New York: Ambijan Committee for Emergency Aid to the Soviet Union, 1943]).

21 "To Professor Solomon Mikhoels and Lt.-Col. Itzik Feffer," *Ambijan Bulletin* 2, 6 (October 1943): 2. This was not to be: Mikhoels was murdered in 1948 and Fefer executed in 1952, during the "Black Years of Soviet Jewry," accused of "Jewish nationalism" precisely because of speeches such as the ones given on their visit to North America.

22 "To the Members and Friends of Ambijan," *Ambijan Bulletin* 2, 3 (April 1943): 5-6; "Food and Birobidjan," *Ambijan Bulletin* 2, 4 (June 1943): 2; "Birobidjan Mobilizes for Victory--A First Hand Report," *Ambijan Bulletin* 2, 4 (June 1943): 3; "Jewish Conference," *Ambijan Bulletin* 2, 4 (June 1943): 2. One report claimed that some 100,000 of these Jews had sought refuge in Birobidzhan. "Birobidjan--A Haven for Jewish Refugees," *Ambijan Bulletin* 2, 4 (June 1943): 2. On the American Jewish Conference, see Aaron Berman, *Nazism, the Jews, and American Zionism, 1933-1948* (Detroit: Wayne State University Press, 1992), 108-112.

23 "Post-War Rehabilitation and Reconstruction of Jewish Life," *Ambijan Bulletin* 2, 7 (November 1943): 2.

24 Letter from J.M. Budish to Vilhjalmur Stefansson, New York, Jan. 13, 1944; Stefansson correspondence, MSS 196, Box 65, 1944--USSR-Ambijan

Committee Folder, Stefansson Collection.

25 Vilhjalmur Stefansson, "10th Anniversary Birobidjan," in *10th Anniversary, Jewish Autonomous Region, May 1944* (New York: 10th Anniversary Committee, May 1944), 1. See also J.M. Budish, *The Jewish Autonomous Region, U.S.S.R.* (New York: Ambijan Committee, [1944]).

26 "We Salute the Red Army!" *Ambijan Bulletin* 3, 2 (February 1944): [4].

27 Max Levin, "American Committee for the Settlement of Jews in Birobidjan (Ambijan)," *Ambijan Bulletin* 3, 2 (February 1944): [5]. For Cohen's obituary, see "W.W. Cohen Dead; Ex-Congressman," *New York Times*, Oct. 13, 1940, Section 1, 49. Although the article listed Cohen's many Jewish and philanthropic endeavours and his membership in a number of clubs and organizations, including the American Jewish Congress, B'nai B'rith and the Masons, no mention was made of Ambijan.

28 "Salute to the Red Army," *Ambijan Bulletin* 3, 3 (April 1944): 4; "Ambijan Celebrates Tenth Anniversary," *Ambijan Bulletin* 3, 7 (November 1944): 4-5; Ambijan circular letter of March 31, 1944; letter from J.M. Budish to Evelyn Stefansson, New York, April 5, 1944; Minutes of the Luncheon Meeting of April 7, 1944; cable from Vilhjalmur Stefansson to Franklin S. Harris, New York, April 12, 1944; letter from J.M. Budish to Vilhjalmur Stefansson, New York, April 19, 1944; letter from J.M. Budish to Vilhjalmur Stefansson, New York, May 17, 1944; Stefansson correspondence, MSS 196, Box 65, 1944--USSR-Ambijan Committee Folder, Stefansson Collection. "Speech to be Delivered by Mr. Max Levin, at Ambijan Dinner, Waldorf-Astoria, on May 16, 1944," ms; United States Territorial Collection, RG251, Box 8, folder "Speech by Max Levin," YIVO; "Senator Thomas Praises Russians," *New York Times*, May 17, 1944, 7. Thomas' speech was reprinted in the *Congressional Record* of May 29, 1944. "Address by Hon. Elbert D. Thomas of Utah, on Tenth Anniversary of the American Birobidjan Committee," *Congressional Record: Proceedings and Debates of the 78th Congress, Second Session*, Appendix, Volume 90--Part 9, March 24, 1944 to June 12, 1944 (Washington: United States Government Printing Office, 1944): A2627-2628. In 1950 Thomas was defeated for reelection by Wallace F. Bennett, after a bitter campaign in which he was accused of being pro-Communist. His liberal voting record, pro-labor policies, and sympathy for the Soviet Union led to his political demise. See also Douglas F. Tobler, "The Jews, the Mormons and the Holocaust," *Journal of Mormon History* 18, 1 (Spring 1992): 59-92.

29 "Advisory Council of Business Men Formed by Ambijan," *Ambijan Bulletin* 3, 7 (November 1944): 1, 8; "Machinery Committee Sends Gifts to Birobidjan and Stalingrad," *Ambijan Bulletin* 3, 7 (November 1944): 7; "Minutes, Luncheon Meeting of Ambijan Advisory Council," Stefansson correspondence, MSS 196, Box 65, 1944--USSR-Ambijan Committee Folder, Stefansson Collection.

30 Alexander Bittelman, *The Jewish People Will Live On!* (New York: Morning Freiheit Association, 1944), 32.

31 J. M. Budish, "Ambijan National Conference Nov. 25-26, New York City," *Ambijan Bulletin* 3, 7 (November 1944): 2.
32 *Ambijan National Conference on Emergency Aid and Reconstruction for the Victims of Fascism* (New York: Ambijan Committee, [November 1944]); J.M. Budish, "Greetings to Jewish Anti-Fascist Committee of USSR and to The Jewish Autonomous Region," *Ambijan Bulletin* 4, 1 (June 1945): 2; James N. Rosenberg, "Minorities in the Postwar World," *Ambijan Bulletin* 4, 1 (June 1945): 11; "Summary of the Proceedings of the National Conference of the American Birobidjan Committee (Ambijan)," *Ambijan Bulletin* 4, 1 (June 1945): 13-27.
33 J.M. Budish, "National Conference Rallies American Jews to Birobidjan," *Ambijan Bulletin* 5, 3 (September 1946): 4-5; Ambijan press release of Feb. 26, 1946 in United States Territorial Collection, RG117, Box 57, folder "Icor" 17/16, YIVO.
34 "Dinner at the Hotel Roosevelt," *Ambijan Bulletin* 5, 1 (February 1946): 4-5; "Potsdam Mandate is Seen Softened," *New York Times*, Nov. 25, 1945, Section 1, 32; report from E.E. Conroy, Special Agent in Charge, to J. Edgar Hoover, New York, Dec. 11, 1945, file 100-99898, Section 1, FOIPA No. 416152, Ambijan. Stefansson had cabled Interior Secretary Harold Ickes to be guest speaker but this did not work out. Letters from J.M. Budish to Vilhjalmur Stefansson, New York, Oct. 24, and Nov. 6, 1945; telegram from Vilhjalmur Stefansson to Harold L. Ickes, New York, Nov. 15, 1945; copy of dinner program and typescript of introduction and speeches; Stefansson correspondence, MSS 196, Box 67, 1945--USSR-Ambijan and American Russian Institute Folder, Stefansson Collection. Charles Lipsett left the pro-Communist movement during the Cold War; he later wrote a number of books about his experiences as a government advisor in wartime. See, for example, Charles H. Lipsett, *The Fabulous Wall Street Scrap Giants* (New York: Atlas Publishing Co., 1969). His obituary can be found in the *New York Times*, Nov. 22, 1978, D19.
35 *We Must Lend a Hand!* (New York: American Birobidjan Committee (Ambijan), [1945]); "Supplies Go to Birobidjan Waifs," *New York Times*, Sept. 7, 1945, 5.
36 "Shipments by American Birobidjan Committee to U.S.S.R. up to December 31, 1945," *Ambijan Bulletin* 5, 1 (February 1946): [16]. The February 1946 *Ambijan Bulletin*, 15, also provides information on the money that had recently been raised by the Graphic Arts Division ($25,000), the Wearing Apparel Division ($10,000) and the Produce Division ($2,000).

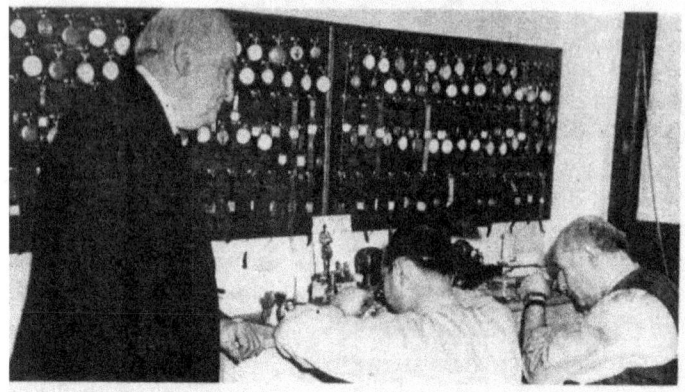

Watches for the Red
Army, *Ambijan Bulletin*,
April 1943

Ad for Maud's Summer-Ray, *New Masses*, June 3, 1941

Ambijan National Conference, Nov. 25-26, 1944. Left to right: J.M. Budish, Vilhjalmur Stefansson, Soviet Ambassador Andrei Gromyko, and Max Levin, *Ambijan Bulletin*, June 1945

The Postwar Orphans' Campaign and the Ambijan-ICOR Merger

Support grew quickly for the campaign on behalf of the resettlement of orphans in Birobidzhan. Charles Kuntz wrote in August 1944 that Birobidzhan, as the only area of concentrated Jewish settlement in the USSR to have escaped the Nazi fury, would play a major part in that country's postwar construction. Many Jews who had sought refuge in central Asia would now gravitate to the JAR; parentless children in particular would find there "a Home without any traces of war to torture their sorely wounded impressionable souls."[1]

A pamphlet distributed in late 1944 announced that "The 'ICOR' is carrying on a Campaign to Help Rehabilitate Jewish Refugee War Orphans in Birobidjan." The back page noted that "$100 will help maintain an orphan for 1 year $50.00 for 6 months $25.00 for 3 months."[2] Another brochure asserted that the problem of rehabilitating the hundreds of thousands of orphans whose parents had been murdered "by the Hitlerite cannibals" was the gravest ever to confront the Jewish people. Birobidzhan was establishing settlements for these orphans that would provide "an ideal Jewish environment" in a "fast growing Jewish homeland, designated to become a Jewish Republic, in a country which has forever solved the so-called 'Jewish Problem.'" The ICOR noted that "Marshal Joseph Stalin expressed to Birobidjan his approval of this project, also his 'fraternal greetings and the thanks of the Government of the U.S.S.R. to the Jewish Autonomous Region'."[3]

In January 1945, an editorial in *Nailebn-New Life* spoke of the "great sums of money that the ICOR will have to find in the near future" to assist in resettling the orphans. These children, described as "[our] dearest treasure," embodied the hope for a better future.[4] A letter sent to ICOR members stated that "Birobidzhan is already accepting 30,000 refugees and housing for children is under construction." The ICOR had resolved to raise the funds necessary to settle 1,000 Jewish refugee children in the region.[5]

Some 70 "top activists" gathered at Rappaport's Restaurant in New York on January 16, 1945, to organize the $100,000 campaign.[6] A conference was convened on February 25 at the Hotel Pennsylvania, New York, "to develop the broadest possible movement for the realization of this noble project in the shortest possible time." The invitation to the conference spoke of the "sacred duty to help provide a haven for the orphaned children of our people." In Birobidzhan, Abraham Jenofsky asserted, "an environment is being created to give the children the education and upbringing which will enable them to grow up healthy citizens in a Jewish homeland." The main burden of the work would be undertaken by the Soviet state, as no non-governmental organization, regardless of its wealth, had the capacity to found cities and settle millions of people. "We should however regard it as a great privilege to support their work."

The main purpose of this conference, announced Jenofsky, was to gain a wide range of support for the new project to settle Jewish refugee war orphans in Birobidzhan. "Can we even comprehend how much effort, money and energy it will take to repair the broken lives of the children, to teach and raise them, to clothe and feed them, to heal them and guard them so that the effects of the horrible catastrophe shall not be carried over from their childhood to adulthood and to the generation that will follow them?" The duty to find orphans a home "is for us Jews especially a traditionally holy task…History demands from us that we… discharge a debt owed to those who have suffered the most, who have given the most precious thing a person possesses—their life."

Jenofsky went on to explain that the national executive had decided to create a fund of $100,000 to help resettle 1,000 Jewish refugee orphans in Birobidzhan. A considerable amount had already been collected since the beginning of the year. He mentioned by name Joseph Morgenstern, of Cleveland, who had donated $3,750 and promised to raise more. The conference ended with a banquet at the Pythian Plaza, where 300 guests donated $7,000. A National Committee of Sponsors to Help Settle Jewish Refugee War Orphans in Birobidjan was formed. Its 200 members included Congressmen Emanuel Celler, Vito Marcantonio, and Adam Clayton Powell Jr., of New York state; John M. Coffee of Washington state; and Samuel A. Weiss of Pennsylvania.[7]

The 11th anniversary of the JAR was commemorated by a joint meeting of the national executives of both Ambijan and the ICOR at Town Hall, New York, on May 19. Anatoly Antonovich Yakovlev, vice consul general of the Soviet Union in New York, addressed the gathering and was presented by the ICOR with a check for $35,000 to sponsor 350 orphans in Birobidzhan.[8] By year's end, the New York ICOR had raised almost $75,000 for the campaign.[9]

Meanwhile, money was flowing in from Jewish communities throughout the country. Charles Kuntz, Abraham Jenofsky, and ICOR national organizer Morris L. Olken undertook visits to Baltimore, Boston, and the Midwest in the spring of 1945 to raise awareness of the campaign. Olken reported that conferences were scheduled for Boston, Chicago, Philadelphia, Washington, Los Angeles, and elsewhere, and that "people everywhere in our great U.S.A. are cheerfully contributing towards the campaign," eager "to help the youngest victims of the

Hitlerite cannibals – the Jewish orphans."[10] From Cleveland, Rabbi David L. Genuth, spiritual leader of the Orthodox synagogue B'nai Jacob Kol Israel, sent $300. In Waukegan, IL, the campaign raised $254.[11] One of the activists involved in Boston was 87-year-old Alice Stone Blackwell, the internationally known women's suffrage leader and daughter of Lucy Stone. At the end of March, the Boston ICOR held a conference which pledged to raise $10,000. Another meeting, on June 24, was addressed by Jenofsky and attended by many members of *landsmanshaftn*. By July 1, the Boston ICOR had collected $9,000.[12] In Baltimore, $10,000 had been donated by the end of 1945.[13] ICOR branches in Los Angeles organized dinners, held concerts and put on plays in order to raise funds. Thanks to the "warm and deep interest" in the war orphans demonstrated by the Jewish masses, reported Nathan Krupin, executive secretary of the Los Angeles ICOR, $30,333 had been donated by July 22. A large number of IWO branches, union locals, *landsmanshaftn*, and societies, had helped raise the money. By the end of the year the Los Angeles branches were able to send approximately $50,000 to the ICOR's headquarters.[14] Yet despite this impressive record of fund-raising, the ICOR was soon to be history, apparently as the result of Soviet pressure to merge the organization with Ambijan.[15]

In March 1946, just prior to the proposed merger, the ICOR held its last national convention, attended by some 200 delegates from over 20 cities. Abraham Jenofsky provided a brief history of the ICOR's activities since 1924, emphasizing the material aid sent to Jewish settlers, first in the Crimea and then in Birobidzhan; the assistance given the Red Army during the war; and the funds now being provided for Jewish orphans. Jenofsky recalled the tens of thousands of books, pamphlets and leaflets the ICOR had published, and the countless mass-meetings, celebrations, conferences, lectures and symposiums it had organized.

Jenofsky reported on the recent interview B.Z. Goldberg had conducted in Moscow with Soviet President Mikhail Kalinin, who had assured the journalist that Birobidzhan would assume great importance in the development of the far east. Plans were now being made to settle 35,000 Jewish war orphans in the region, according to Jenofsky; 3,500 orphans had already arrived. During 1945 the ICOR had expended a great deal of effort to benefit the orphans and had raised $200,000 for the campaign. Jenofsky concluded by telling the delegates they should look forward to uniting with Ambijan in order to build an even broader and more effective organization to assist Birobidzhan.[16]

Ambijan too had made the orphans the focus of its campaigns. "We know that you are ready to make any effort or sacrifice for these children," stated an Ambijan pamphlet published in 1944. It noted that $100 would maintain an orphan for one year. In Birobidzhan, "they can grow up into healthy, normal, proud citizens of a land where there is full equality for all peoples regardless of race, creed, color or nationality."[17] In July 1945 Ambijan, taking advantage of "the dignity and the popularity of the name of Albert Einstein," created an "Einstein Fund for the Settlement Care and Rehabilitation of Jewish Refugee War Orphans in Birobidjan and the Orphans of Heroic Stalingrad." In the first half of the year, Ambijan organized three major concerts in New York to raise money for the Silver Ponds home: On April 13, in Carnegie Hall, there was an evening of Russian music, featuring Leonard Bernstein and the New York Philharmonic Orchestra. On April 22, again at Carnegie Hall, an "All Star Program" was held to celebrate the 11th anniversary of the JAR and to benefit 4,500 orphans. The third concert, on May 13, was advertised as a "Spring Festival of Music for the Benefit of Russian War Orphans." The new Ambijan Brooklyn Division, created in January 1946 with Dr. George Swetlow as chair, was inspired by this event to sponsor annual concerts on behalf of the orphans.[18]

Ambijan was also increasing its presence in the Bronx. A meeting to organize a Bronx chapter had been convened at the Hotel Concourse Plaza on April 28, 1943; Bronx County Court Judge Harry Stackell chaired the gathering of over 200 people. Zina Getmansky, assisted by Fan Groff Bakst, who had become Ambijan's national field organizer in April 1945, worked to recruit more members. That spring, the chapter held the first of its annual Einstein Fund luncheons.[19]

In major cities such as Boston, Chicago, Cleveland and Newark, new Ambijan branches were formed and existing ones enlarged. A meeting of the Newark Division on June 13, 1944 attracted 500 people; more than 500 attended the Division's first annual dinner on February 18, 1945. Radio personality and journalist William S. Gailmor addressed the gathering, which included Vincent J. Murphy, the mayor; Rabbi Joachim Prinz of Temple B'nai Abraham in Newark, who was a leading figure in the American Jewish Congress; and Harry Pine, a "prominent Zionist" who was active in Russian War Relief, Inc. The New Jersey Ambijan Committee held a state conference on June 17-18 in Trenton, with 100 delegates representing 18 communities, to commence a campaign to raise $50,000. Professor Elias A. Lowe, a colleague of Einstein's at the Princeton Institute for Advanced Study, spoke at the event and was elected a member of the state committee. The Agricultural Division of Ambijan organized fund-raising events in various New Jersey farming communities, including Farmingdale, Vineland, and Toms River. U. S. Secretary of Agriculture Clinton P. Anderson spoke at a meeting of the Division on January 27, 1946; Anderson commented on the "great humanitarian significance" of Ambijan's assistance to the orphaned refugees.[20]

The Postwar Orphans' Campaign and the Ambijan-ICOR Merger

In Boston, Dr. Abraham Myerson, a noted neurologist, served as honorary chair of the Division; Abraham Resnick, a past executive director of various Jewish Community Centers in New England, was executive director. Toward the end of 1944, the chapter commenced a campaign, under the direction of Isaac S. Kibrick, to raise $50,000. Kibrick and Resnick also joined Ambijan's national committee. Dr. Joseph G. Brin, editor of the Boston *Jewish Advocate*, was a member of the campaign committee, which sought to include "important and influential" business people; his newspaper provided the group with extensive coverage. On February 1, 1945, Jacob B. Aronoff of the Ambijan Board of Directors, along with some 60 businessmen, attended a dinner at the Hotel Kenmore to kick off the campaign. Aronoff told the audience that even ardent Zionists "have come to recognize the importance of the national minority policy of the Soviet Union" and the "immense contribution" being made by the JAR. On March 22, at a luncheon held at the Cavendish Club, a team of business, trade and professional groups was set up to raise the $50,000. Throughout the winter and spring of 1945-1946, meetings were held in various towns throughout the New England area. On May 19, 1946, 200 delegates attended a New England area conference in Boston; on May 28, a fund-raising dinner attended by 300 people raised $18,000.[21]

The Chicago Division of Ambijan was organized on March 22, 1945, following visits to the city by Jacob B. Aronoff and J.M. Budish. Chicago members of Ambijan were in the mainstream of the community; many were also active in the American Jewish Congress, B'nai B'rith, Hadassah, the Hebrew Immigrant Aid Society, synagogues, and Zionist organizations. The officers were Chicago Municipal Court Judge Harry M. Fisher (honorary chair), Solomon Jesmer (chair), Julia Halperin (vice-chair), Harry Zarbin (treasurer), Harry D. Koenig (secretary), and Ethel Osri (executive director). Osri was a former president of District 6 B'nai B'rith Women and married to Aron Osri, a member of the executive board. Jesmer had been chair of the Chicago Jewish Council for Russian War Relief. Others on the executive included Max Bressler, president of the Chicago Division of the American Jewish Congress; Isadore Isenberg; Aaron Halperin; Dr. George Halperin; Harry Markin; Leo M. Nellis; Dr. Julius Schaffner; Daniel A. Uretz; and Robert Zacharias. Nicholas J. Pritzker, Herman Spertus, and Maurice Spertus were members; so was Rabbi Jacob J. Weinstein of Kehilath Anshe Maariv (universally known as KAM), a past president of Reform Judaism's Central Conference of American Rabbis. The Spertus brothers owned Intercraft Industries and were ardent supporters of the College of Jewish Studies in Chicago, later renamed the Spertus Institute of Jewish Studies. Julia Halperin, Jesmer, Koenig and Zarbin were on the national committee as well.

By September 1946, the *Ambijan Bulletin* would be describing the

CHAPTER FIVE

Chicago Division as "our strongest organization outside New York." At first, the Chicago Ambijan concentrated on raising $100,000 in cash to purchase hospital and dental units for children's homes in Stalingrad and Birobidzhan. A pamphlet, "Life Begins in Birobidjan for 30,000 Jewish Refugee Children," publicized the drive. This won Ambijan the support of Phillip Mitchell, president of Chicago B'nai B'rith Council; and Sidney Hillman, president of the Amalgamated Clothing Workers of America (ACWA), the leading garment union in the country in the men's clothing industry. Hillman called Ambijan's efforts "a great humanitarian undertaking, justifying the support of all enlightened elements in this country. It is a shining example of effective action in taking care of the dispossessed and displaced persons in war-torn Europe."[22]

At the Chicago organization's first executive meeting, held on June 27, 1945, Leo Nellis suggested that the new organization arrange a dinner for people in the machinery business; Jesmer noted that Aaron Halperin and Zacharias had already established contacts with people in that industry and had formed a machinery committee. On October 1, the Division hosted 128 prominent business and communal leaders at a luncheon attended by Pavel Mikhailov, consul general of the USSR; they heard national vice-president Charles H. Lipsett describe the orphans' campaign. Aronoff returned to the city on November 21-22 and spoke at a luncheon of 35 machine tool dealers to solicit support; one man decided to donate an entire machine shop, worth about $25,000, to Birobidzhan.[23]

The first Einstein Fund Dinner, held on December 2, attracted more than 1,000 people and raised some $50,000 in cash and pledges. They were addressed by Senator Harley M. Kilgore of West Virginia, who praised them for their "splendid work" and referred to Birobidzhan as "certainly one answer" to the grave problems facing European Jews. Judge Harry M. Fisher said that as "an ardent Zionist" he considered it his duty to support the movement on behalf of Birobidzhan, which in no way rivalled the Palestine project. He referred to it as "a place of refuge." The FBI, which noted that the Chicago Division had recruited many members of considerable wealth, observed that the judge, who had visited the Soviet Union before the war, had "a long record of activity in left wing groups in Chicago," was a member of the Communist-led National Lawyers Guild, and had spoken at Communist Party gatherings.[24] This did not seem to perturb the Chicago Jewish community, which honored the judge for his 48 years of communal service at a testimonial banquet at the Stevens Hotel on May 2, 1946; the Anglo-Jewish *Sentinel* featured him on its cover.[25]

To launch their campaign to raise $100,000 in cash and $50,000 in machinery to help resettle the first 6,500 war orphans in Birobidzhan, and to celebrate the 18th anniversary of Jewish colonization in Birobidzhan, the Chicago Ambijan organized a city-wide conference and a concert on May 19 at the Palmer House. A circular letter in English and Yiddish sent out to Jewish organizations in the city asserted that "aiding these helpless orphans" was "a sacred obligation for us all which, surely, no conscientious Jewish leader or Jewish organization will refuse to accept....Here is a God-given opportunity for us to demonstrate in terms of practical reality, our humanity, our beneficence, the greatness of our hearts." Alben W. Barkley of Kentucky, the Senate majority leader, addressed the conference, calling support of the project an obligation of the American people.[26]

In advance of the conference, Jack I. Fishbein, editor of the *Sentinel* and a member of the executive committee of the Chicago Ambijan, published a special issue on Birobidzhan; the cover featured Albert Einstein. Fishbein in his own column scolded those still opposed to the campaign on behalf of the orphans: "It would seem that such a humanitarian venture would enjoy the enthusiastic support of every Jew, regardless of class or political ideology. Rescue of children ought not to be a subject for partisan debate." The saving of Jewish lives, whether in Birobidzhan, Palestine, or anywhere else, "is important to all Jews." In the JAR, asserted the editor, "these innocent victims of Hitler's blood-bath will be able to grow up in peace and security with full opportunity to live a happy, useful life," in an atmosphere of "complete equality and freedom from fear." The *Sentinel* "welcomes this opportunity to dedicate this issue to this holy work of Ambijan." Illinois Governor Dwight H. Green sent his best wishes "for the success of your meeting and of your humanitarian program."[27]

On December 1, at the Stevens Hotel, the Division hosted the second Einstein Fund Dinner. In anticipation of the event, the *Sentinel* ran a front page story about the Jewish orphans being resettled in Birobidzhan. The featured speaker was U.S. Senator Claude Pepper of Florida, who considered Ambijan's effort on behalf of the war orphans "one of the noblest deeds of charity." Pepper lauded the Soviet Union for creating in Birobidzhan what amounted to "a Jewish State within the Soviet State." He also stressed the significance of the Jewish Autonomous Region in promoting international understanding. At the dinner, Rabbi G. George Fox of the South Shore Temple delivered the invocation; in his *Sentinel* column the following week, Fox described the audience as being "as fine a crowd of men and women as we ever saw gathered in our city." The rabbi congratulated Sol Jesmer and Ethel Osri, in particular, for their fine work on behalf of Ambijan, which was now "a full-grown philanthropy" accomplishing "untold good." It was announced that Paul Novick, then visiting Moscow, had been told that a new synagogue would be built in the city of Birobidzhan. The 1,200 guests who attended the dinner contributed $47,000.[28]

In Minneapolis, the campaign to help Jewish orphans in the USSR enabled Jewish Communists to make common cause with mainstream Jewish organizations. The Minneapolis Federation for Jewish Service, as it was then known, decided in 1945 to establish a single city-wide United Jewish Appeal (UJA) fundraising drive. But neither the ICOR nor Ambijan adhered to the stricture to curtail their own fundraising. Two of the most prominent Jewish supporters of Ambijan and the ICOR in Minneapolis were Henry Supak and Louis Locketz; each of these men owned a garment manufacturing company in the city.[29]

Locketz wrote to the Federation on April 18, 1945 and explained that the local ICOR branch, of which he was chair, had pledged to raise $10,000 for the campaign for refugee war orphans; $3,000 had already been raised. "But a number of prominent citizens we called on insisted that we approach the Federation for a share to cover our pledge. They thought that the Federation would positively approve our work for the cause and include our pledge in the 1945 campaign." Locketz promised that the ICOR "will do our utmost not to be in your way but we must ask you to give us a prompt reply so that we can arrange our work accordingly and tell our prospective contributors our position." The Minneapolis Federation then allotted $3,500 to Ambijan.[30]

However, in December 1946, Locketz, now chair of the combined ICOR-Ambijan organization in the city, expressed his disappointment that the Federation would in the coming year only allocate $4,000 for the war orphans of Russia. He complained to Federation president I.S. Joseph about "the leadership of our Minneapolis Jewry," who are ideologically "so stale that they cannot conceive of any new currents, irrespective of importance for Jews the world over." Locketz sated that it was essential to give a helping hand to the Jews of devastated Russia, and this would also serve as "a certain measure of appreciation to Russia in saving one and a half million Jews from slaughter by the Nazis." In response, Joseph declared that while he too hoped that American Jews "promote a better feeling of friendship" towards Russia, the Federation could not grant more money to Ambijan until it was able to receive "any authentic information as to the number of Jewish children housed in the Ambijan project [and] how much money is spent there."[31] Still, the Minneapolis Federation remained sympathetic to the Birobidzhan project and allocated Ambijan $4,000 in the 1947 UJA drive, even though, as Charles Cooper, executive secretary of the Federation, wrote to Joseph in November 1947, "when we send money through Ambijan, we are entrusting our funds to an out and out Communist organization."[32]

Los Angeles organized a city-wide Ambijan chapter in 1946,

The Postwar Orphans' Campaign and the Ambijan-ICOR Merger

with Nathan Krupin as executive secretary and Samuel Rosenfeld as president. Krupin, born in 1886 in Visokie Mazovyetsk, now in Poland, had been active in the Wilshire branch of the ICOR and had joined the CPUSA in 1937. Rosenfeld, born in 1885 in Minsk, had been in the Biro-Bidjan Branch of the ICOR in Los Angeles and had been a member of the CP since March 1936. Sam Klapperman, the vice-president, born in Balta, Russia in 1892, had joined the CP in 1937 and was also a former member of the ICOR. Aaron Kertman, the organizer, was, along with his wife Rose, a Communist; he had been active in the ICOR and in the Hollywood Anti-Nazi League before the war. Harry Goldstein, the recording secretary, born in Vitebsk in 1888, had been a member of the City Committee of the ICOR and had joined the CP in 1932. Eva Myers, secretary of the Hollywood chapter, had also belonged to the ICOR, along with many other former ICOR members whose names now appeared on the letterhead of Ambijan branches in Los Angeles.[33]

For the first six months of 1946, the national Ambijan brought in $259,702.58 in various contributions, and disbursed $195,377.00 in relief supplies. At an Ambijan luncheon held at the Waldorf-Astoria Hotel on January 27, Cleveland manufacturer Joseph Morgenstern, president of the Electroline Manufacturing Co. and a major Ambijan supporter, provided $68,040 for the purchase of four diesel generator power units from the Office of Surplus Property of the Reconstruction Finance Corp., a government agency. Obviously, Charles Lipsett had facilitated this purchase, which would provide electric power for new factory and farm units to be built at the new children's settlements in Birobidzhan. Other equipment and supplies worth more than $30,000 were also formally handed over to Vasili A. Kazanyev, the Soviet acting consul general. "The work your organization is doing to aid the Jewish Autonomous Region in rehabilitating the Jewish refugee war orphans is a noble task that commands the sympathy and appreciation of the Soviet people," he told them.[34]

At a National Conference for Birobidjan, held in the Hunter College Assembly Hall in New York on March 9-10, 1946, the ICOR and Ambijan were united under the name American Birobidjan Committee (Ambijan). The conference was attended by 669 delegates representing 272 organizations, including 46 Ambijan and ICOR branches, plus 1,500 guests and members of the public. The delegates included people from four cities in Canada and one in Mexico. The invitation to the conference had called Birobidzhan "a thriving self-governing Jewish state-entity," which was duly represented by five delegates in the Council of Nationalities of the USSR Supreme Soviet. "Richly endowed with natural resources, Birobidjan has become the 'Gem of the Far East.'" It was the "highest expression" of the national minority policy of the Soviet Union, "which has put an end to all forms of national or racial discrimination and has eliminated all vestiges of anti-Semitism," and Jews everywhere "are deeply interested in the methods and policies applied by any state which does away with anti-Semitism." Birobidzhan had contributed to the victory against Nazi Germany by sending 35,000 soldiers to the Red Army. It was providing a home for many of the Jewish war orphans from across Europe who now found themselves in the Soviet Union, and would "undoubtedly extend even greater help for the rehabilitation of many more thousands of Jewish refugees who must start life anew." This task of rehabilitation and reconstruction would require "the mobilization of all the resources of the Jewish people especially in this country which fortunately escaped the immediate ravages of War."[35]

Budish informed the gathering that Birobidzhan "is on its way to become a Jewish Autonomous Republic" and that full union republic status would follow--indeed, he announced that a telegram had just a day earlier arrived from the five Birobidzhan deputies in the Council of Nationalities of the Supreme Soviet, who extended greetings from the "Jewish Republic of the Soviet Union." Birobidzhan had given "enhanced dignity" to the Jewish people, said Budish; he called on all Jews, be they religious or secular, Zionist or non-Zionist, to join in the work of the now-united Ambijan-ICOR, which was "a movement of the Jewish people as a whole" with "no partisan bias."

Budish mentioned some of the "outstanding Americans" and "friends of ethnic democracy" involved with Ambijan: former vice-president and Secretary of Commerce Henry Wallace, Secretary of Agriculture Clinton P. Anderson, U.S. Supreme Court Justice Frank A. Murphy, and U.S. senators Alben W. Barkley, Harley M. Kilgore and Warren Magnuson of Washington State. Magnuson, a guest speaker at the conference, compared Soviet Russia's positive attitude towards Jews in Birobidzhan to that of Britain's negative policy towards Palestinian Jewry. The British would do well to learn from the treatment accorded the Jews in Birobidjan by the Soviet government, "which stands in sharpest contrast to imperialist policy with respect to national minorities and colonial groups within the British Empire." Magnuson emphasized that "Soviet Russia has given the world an example of how to treat minorities. I wish that England could take a page out of that book." He also said that he saw in the Birobidzhan project "a symbol of the larger world encompassing friendship and collaboration between the peoples of America and the Soviet Union."

The "Declaration of Principles and Program" adopted by the conference spoke of the tremendous losses suffered by the Jewish people in World War II, and also noted that 70 per cent of those Jews who had survived the Nazis had been saved by the Soviets. But the survivors, including many war orphans, were in need of rehabilitation. "In these difficult times the Jewish Autonomous Region is a source of encouragement and renewed faith to the long-suffering Jewish people. The story of Birobidjan is the story of the triumph of reason over prejudice; of a far-sighted policy of ethnic democracy over a sad heritage of racial and national oppression and persecution."

The conference elected Albert Einstein as its honorary president; Jacob B. Aronoff, Sholem Levine, Charles H. Lipsett, Elias A. Lowe, Charles Kuntz, and Vilhjalmur Stefansson were elected as vice-presidents. Max Levin was chair of the board of directors, Dr. Lewis Schatzov vice-chair of the board of directors, J.M. Budish the executive vice-president, Abraham Jenofsky the executive secretary, Bernard Parelhoff the secretary, Jack Greenbaum the treasurer, Isaac Aronoff the comptroller, and Morris L. Olken and Joseph M. Bernstein the national organizers.

Some of the ICOR's officers, including Charles Kuntz, Sholem Levine, Dr. Lewis Schatzov, Morris L. Olken, and Abraham Jenofsky, had been elected to the new combined Board of Directors, but many, including such former ICOR activists as Shloime Almazov, were not. The 195-member National Committee comprised people from across the United States, as well as a few from Canada, Cuba and Mexico. Included were artists, entertainers, impresarios and writers, such as Leonard Bernstein, Morris Carnovsky, Marc Chagall, Sol Hurok, Albert Maltz, Samuel Ornitz, Paul Robeson and Menashe Unger; academics like J. Brownlee Davidson, Franklin Harris, Elias A. Lowe, Raphael Mahler, and Jacob Rader Marcus; and a handful of politicians and rabbis, including Emanuel Celler.

Budish hoped that Ambijan would be able to raise $2 million in cash and $1 million in kind for Birobidzhan; the delegates proceeded to adopt a budget of $2.025 million for supplies and $1 million for machinery to be sent to the JAR within the year. Budish praised the ICOR for having been the "initiators, the pioneers in bringing this message of Birobidjan to the Jews of this country and to the entire American people"; Ambijan, on the other hand, had been established "by people who have not felt the same pressures of discrimination as did the broader Jewish masses"--in other words, by Jews who were more affluent and better assimilated.[36] Budish seemed to be intimating that, as a result of their greater wealth and easier access to decision-makers, Ambijan members were now predominant in the pro-Birobidzhan support movement. There were other, additional reasons why the ICOR was now less influential. It had never totally recovered from the 1939 Hitler-Stalin Pact, in large part because its immigrant Yiddish-speaking members, who had been far more fervent in their early commitment to Soviet Russia, and who had consequently experienced a far greater sense of betrayal, were more reluctant than the Ambijan membership to forgive the USSR for its errors and missteps.[37]

CHAPTER FIVE

Ambijan had extensively publicized the Hunter College conference: a half page advertisement, "What is Birobidjan?" appeared in the *New York Times* and the *New York Herald-Tribune* just prior to the meetings. The advertisement referred to Birobidzhan as the "Jewish State unit" in the USSR and provided a brief history of its development. According to the advertisement, the Jewish Autonomous Region was "now on the way to becoming a Jewish Autonomous Republic." The advertisement also emphasized the role the region was playing, "during this period of unprecedented catastrophe suffered by the Jews of Europe," in extending "a helping hand to Jewish refugees from other lands," including orphaned children, so that they "will not be lost to the Jewish people." The ad claimed that of the estimated 175,000 people living in Birobidzhan, Jews comprised 115,000. "This growing Jewish land is entitled to the full material and moral support of all those who believe in ethnic democracy." The ad provided endorsements for the project from Albert Einstein, Soviet ambassador to the U.S. Andrei Gromyko, Senator Alben W. Barkley, Sidney Hillman, William O'Dwyer, James N. Rosenberg, Clinton P. Anderson, and Henry Wallace.[38] *Time* magazine, however, was not impressed: "The Pearl of the Far East," it mocked, "remained embedded in its chilly Siberian oyster."[39]

At a Board of Directors meeting held June 20, Ambijan decided to extend its help to war orphans by also undertaking the sponsorship of a home for Jewish orphans in Poland.[40] As part of its fundraising, Ambijan organized public dinners in San Francisco on September 16, 1946, and in Los Angeles on September 18, honoring Charles H. Lipsett. Senator Magnuson would be a featured speaker at two more dinners in those two cities on October 15 and 16. Concerts and social events were also scheduled for Boston, Baltimore and Miami.[41] Budish and Einstein, in a joint letter dated October 8, asked American Jews to "mobilize our energies and resources" in "this humanitarian endeavor" to rehabilitate the lives of thousands of war orphans being resettled in Birobidzhan and to aid the region in its "great industrial growth, which has made increased settlement possible." The Jewish Autonomous Region was receiving "thousands of applications for admission from Jewish refugees in and outside the USSR."[42]

The Ambijan national dinner, held at the Waldorf-Astoria Hotel in New York on November 11, was attended by 1,000 guests from as far away as Los Angeles, Minneapolis and Chicago. They were told of Ambijan's work in helping 30,000 Jewish war orphans being resettled in Birobidzhan. Ambijan was also assisting 2,500 orphans in the Silver Ponds Children's Home near Stalingrad, and it was providing support for an orphans' home in Poland. B.Z. Goldberg had visited Silver Ponds earlier in the year and had written a glowing report. He remarked that everyone in Stalingrad was "so conscious of Ambijan aid, so appreciative....This work is worth millions for American-Soviet and Jewish-Soviet goodwill." The dinner was addressed by, among others, Vilhjalmur Stefansson and Senator Claude Pepper of Florida. Pepper had visited the Soviet Union a year earlier. He asserted that "Probably nowhere in the world are minorities given more freedom, recognition and respect than in the Soviet Union [and] nowhere in the world is there so little friction, between minority and majority groups, or among minorities." Pepper described Stalin as the greatest man of the times. He lauded the "great work" of Ambijan, which, he hoped, would "arouse all citizens to a better understanding of what Russia is really like." The dinner raised $200,000 in cash and another $75,000 in pledges.[43]

On January 30, 1947, Budish declared that Ambijan would mark the fourth anniversary of the victory at Stalingrad by a campaign to raise a further $100,000 for the relief of orphans housed at the Silver Ponds children's home. He stated that between June and December of 1946 Ambijan had sent $300,000 worth of shipments, including food, clothing, school supplies, machinery and trucks, to Stalingrad and Birobidzhan, for the care of orphans. In both places, people were sincerely touched by the "paternal care" Ambijan was demonstrating toward "these parentless children."[44]

Endnotes

1   Prof. Charles Kuntz, "Biro-Bidjan and Postwar Reconstruction," *Nailebn-New Life* 18, 8 (August 1944): 23-24.

2   "Prof. Charles Kuntz *President* Icor Association, Inc." pamphlet in the Morris Stern papers, RG231, Box 1, unnamed folder, YIVO.

3   "You Can Help Settle Jewish Refugee War Orphans in Birobidjan – 'Icor' helft bazetsn toyznt yidishe flikhtlingen milkhome yesoymim in birobidzhan," undated pamphlet in United States Territorial Collection, RG117, Box 57, folder "Icor" 17/16, YIVO; letter from Charles Kuntz and Abraham Jenofsky to Kalmen Marmor, New York, April 26, 1945, in the Kalmen Marmor papers, 1873-1955, RG205, Microfilm group 495, folder 546 "Icor-korespondents, 1938-1946," YIVO.

4   "30 toyznt yidishe yesoymim in biro-bidzhan," *Nailebn-New Life* 19, 1 (January 1945): 2.

5   Letter from Charles Kuntz and Abraham Jenofsky to Kalmen Marmor,

New York, Jan. 9, 1945, in the Kalmen Marmor papers, 1873-1955, RG205, Microfilm group 495, folder 546 "Icor-korespondents, 1938-1946," YIVO.

6   Abraham Jenofsky, "Der icor bay der arbet," *Nailebn-New Life* 19, 2 (February 1945): 16-20.

7   "'Icor' Association Call to a Conference--Aynladung tsu a konferents," pamphlet in the Morris Stern papers, RG231, Box 1, unnamed folder; A. Jenofsky, "Barikht tsu der konferents," *Nailebn-New Life* 19, 3 (March 1945): 11-15; "Barikht fun der icor-konferents tsu helfn bazetsn yidishe yesoymim," *Nailebn-New Life* 19, 3 (March 1945): 19-20; M.L. Olken, "An Impressive Conference," *Nailebn-New Life* 19, 3 (March 1945): 22-23; Abraham Jenofsky, *Der icor in unzer historisher epokhe: Dergreykhungen un perspektiven* (New York: ICOR, 1945), 3-16.

8   "Far di yesoymim in biro-bidzhan," in the Morris Stern papers, RG231, Box 1, unnamed folder, YIVO.

9   Letter from Abraham Jenofsky to Morris Stern, New York, Nov. 12, 1945; in the Morris Stern papers, RG231, Box 1, unnamed folder, YIVO; A. Jenofsky, "Der icor bay der arbet," *Nailebn-New Life* 19, 12 (December 1945): 18-20.

10 M.L. Olken, "We Are Our Brothers Keepers," *Nailebn-New Life* 19, 4 (April 1945): 23.

11 "ICOR Orphans Campaign," *Nailebn-New Life* 19, 11 (November 1945): 21-22.

12 Sarah Fel-Yellin, "Alice stone blackwell ruft tsu helfn yidishe yesoymim in biro-bidzhan," *Nailebn-New Life* 19, 6 (June 1945): 11; Sarah Fel-Yellin, "Di yesoymim kampanye in boston shtaygt iber dervartungen," *Nailebn-New Life* 19, 7 (July 1945): 16-17.

13 A. Jenofsky, "Der icor bay der arbet," *Nailebn-New Life* 19, 12 (December 1945): 18-20.

14 N. Krupin, "Los angeles komitet hot ibergeshikt $30,333 tsu helfn di yesoymim in biro-bidzhan," *Nailebn-New Life* 19, 8 (August 1945): 14-15; "Barikht far der natsyonaler ekzekutive fun dem 'icor' tsu der spetsyeler konvenshon fun dem 'icor' un tsu der natsyonaler konferents fur birobidzhan, dem 9-10tn marts, 1946," mss; in the Abraham Jenofsky papers, RG734, Box 1, folder 6, YIVO.

15 Interview, Shloime Almazov, New York, July 21, 1971.

16 "Barikht far der natsyonaler ekzekutive fun dem 'icor' tsu der spetsyeler konvenshon fun dem 'icor' un tsu der natsyonaler konferents fur birobidzhan, dem 9-10tn marts, 1946," mss; in the Abraham Jenofsky papers, RG734, Box 1, folder 6, YIVO; Abraham Jenofsky, "Rapid Strides of Birobidjan," *Ambijan Bulletin* 5, 3 (September 1946): 5-6.

17 *4,500 Orphans—Our Debt* (New York: Ambijan Committee, [1944]), [2-4]. This referred to 3,500 Jewish war refugees and another 1,000 Stalingrad orphans that Ambijan planned to support.

18 Advertisements in *New Masses* 55, 4 (April 24, 1945): 27, and 55, 7 (May 15, 1945): 29; "Three Concerts for 'Our Children'," *Ambijan Bulletin* 4, 1 (June

The Postwar Orphans' Campaign and the Ambijan-ICOR Merger

1945): 6; "Brooklyn Division," *Ambijan Bulletin* 5, 1 (February 1946): 13-14. The Brooklyn chapter in 1945 included prominent doctors, judges, lawyers, and professors, according to the FBI. See pp. 20-21 of the 24-page FBI report of Sept. 19, 1945 submitted by E.E. Conroy, Special Agent in Charge, originally in NY File 100-42538. File 100-99898, Section 1, FOIPA No. 416152, Ambijan.

19 "Bronx Division," *Ambijan Bulletin* 5, 1 (February 1946): 13-14. Information on the Bronx chapter is contained on pp. 6-7 of a 33-page report dated Nov. 5, 1944 submitted by E.E. Conroy, Special Agent in Charge, originally in NY File 100-42538. File 100-99898, Section 1, FOIPA No. 416152, Ambijan.

20 "The New Jersey State Conference," *Ambijan Bulletin* 4, 1 (June 1945): 3; "In Our Divisions," *Ambijan Bulletin* 4, 1 (June 1945): 7-8; "Agricultural Division," *Ambijan Bulletin* 5, 1 (February 1946): 8; "Newark Division," *Ambijan Bulletin* 5, 1 (February 1946): 14; letter from J.M. Budish to Vilhjalmur Stefansson, New York, Jan. 27, 1945, inviting Stefansson to the Newark Division dinner on Feb. 18, 1945, in Stefansson correspondence, MSS 196, Box 67, 1945--USSR-Ambijan and American Russian Institute Folder, Stefansson Collection. There is a very complete FBI report on the Newark Ambijan, submitted May 3, 1945, in file 100-99898, Section 1, FOIPA No. 416152, Ambijan. See also for New Jersey pp. 8, 31-32 of a 42-page FBI report dated Feb. 4, 1947, submitted by Edward Scheidt, Special Agent in Charge, originally in NY File 100-42538. File 100-99898, Section 2, FOIPA No. 416152, Ambijan. For more on the community of Jewish immigrant farmers in Farmingdale, NJ, who sent a portion of the money they raised for charities to Birobidzhan, see Gertrude Wishnick Dubrovsky, *The Land Was Theirs: Jewish Farmers in the Garden State* (Tuscaloosa, AL: University of Alabama Press, 1992), 218.

21 "In Our Divisions," *Ambijan Bulletin* 4, 1 (June 1945): 7; "In Our Divisions," *Ambijan Bulletin* 5, 1 (February 1946): 10. There is a very complete FBI report on the Boston Ambijan, submitted June 30, 1945, in file 100-99898, Section 1, FOIPA No. 416152, Ambijan.

22 "New Birobidjan Committee Meets Monday for First Time," *Sentinel*, Chicago, March 22, 1945, 15; "American Birobidjan Committee Opens Chicago Office," *Sentinel*, Chicago, June 28, 1945, 30; "In Our Divisions," *Ambijan Bulletin* 4, 1 (June 1945): 8; "Organizational Activities," *Ambijan Bulletin* 5, 3 (September 1946): 15; letter from Sidney Hillman to Sol Jesmer, Chicago, Nov. 29, 1945; "Life Begins in Birobidjan for 30,000 Jewish Refugee Children" pamphlet, both in Collection No. 20: Chicago Chapter, American Birobidjan Committee, Series B. Papers of Ethel Osri (From Collection No. 82). Folder 11: Einstein Fund Dinners 1945-47, Chicago Jewish Archives.

23 "American Birobidjan Meeting to Hold Dinner," *Sentinel*, Sept. 27, 1945, 8; "$50,000 Goal Set to Aid Orphans," *Chicago Sun*, Oct. 26, 1945, 10; S[olomon] Jesmer, "Ambijan," in J. I. Fishbein, ed., *The Sentinel Presents 100 Years of Chicago Jewry*, 101, 112; Minutes, June 27, 1945; Aug. 15, 1945, Oct. 6, 1945,

CHAPTER FIVE

Nov. 20, 1945; Nov. 27, 1945, in Collection No. 20: Chicago Chapter, American Birobidjan Committee, Series A. Minutes. Folder 2: Minutes, 1945, Chicago Jewish Archives. The executive was told at its first meeting in 1946 that $30,000 had been sent to the national office in New York in 1945. Minutes, Jan. 17, 1946, in Collection No. 20: Chicago Chapter, American Birobidjan Committee, Series A. Minutes. Folder 3: Minutes, 1946, Chicago Jewish Archives.

24 "Kilgore Addresses 1,000 at Ambijan Dinner," *Sentinel*, Chicago, Dec. 13, 1945; "In Our Divisions," *Ambijan Bulletin* 5, 1 (February 1946): 9; "Albert Einstein Fund Dinner" program, in Collection No. 20: Chicago Chapter, American Birobidjan Committee, Series B. Papers of Ethel Osri (From Collection No. 82). Folder 11: Einstein Fund Dinners 1945-47, Chicago Jewish Archives. The FBI files on the Chicago Ambijan, dated Nov. 19, 1946 and Feb. 10, 1947, originally in Chicago file 100-18113, are in File 100-99898, Section 2, FOIPA No. 416152, Ambijan. The *Sentinel*'s motto was "Dedicated to Unity in Jewish life."

25 "'One That Loves His Fellow Men'," *Sentinel*, Chicago, May 2, 1946, 7, 22. See also "The Sentinel Visits Judge Fisher's Testimonial," *Sentinel*, Chicago, May 9, 1946, 31 for an entire page of photos devoted to the event, with Mayor Edward J. Kelly paying tribute to Fisher "on behalf of the entire city of Chicago." The *Sentinel* had a definite left-wing bias in those years. See J. I. Fishbein, ed., *The Sentinel's History of Chicago Jewry, 1911-1986* (Chicago: Sentinel Publishing Co., 1986).

26 "Ambijan to Launch Campaign for Refugee War Orphans," *Sentinel*, Chicago, May 2, 1946, 16; "People in the News," *Sentinel*, Chicago, May 30, 1946, 40; Minutes, June 5, 1946; in Collection No. 20: Chicago Chapter, American Birobidjan Committee, Series A. Minutes. Folder 3: Minutes, 1946, Chicago Jewish Archives. Circular letter of May 4, 1946, in Collection No. 20: Chicago Chapter, American Birobidjan Committee, Series B. Papers of Ethel Osri (From Collection No. 82). Folder 12: Press Releases, Articles, Speeches, Chicago Jewish Archives.

27 J. I. Fishbein, "The Editor Views the News," Sentinel, Chicago, May 16, 1946, 5; "What Leading American Personalities Say of the Ambijan Settlement Project," *Sentinel*, Chicago, May 16, 1946, 10; "Some Outstanding Chicago Leaders Comment on Birobidjan," *Sentinel*, Chicago, May 16, 1946, 13.

28 "Senator Pepper to Address Einstein Fund Dinner," *Sentinel*, Chicago, Nov. 21, 1946, 19; "Birobidjan Haven of Jewish War Orphans," *Sentinel*, Chicago, Nov. 28, 1946, 1, 3; "1,000 Guests at Ambijan's Einstein Fund Dinner," *Sentinel*, Chicago, Nov. 28, 1946, 21; Dr. G. George Fox, "The Watch Tower," *Sentinel*, Chicago, Dec. 12, 1946, 6; "People in the News," *Sentinel*, Chicago, Dec. 12, 1946, 32; "Senator Pepper Lauds Ambijan Work as Aid to World Peace," *Ambijan Bulletin* 6, 1 (February 1947): 6; "Chicago Dinner," *Ambijan Bulletin* 6, 1 (February 1947): 7; "American Birobidjan Committee Chicago Division: Financial Report of the Einstein Fund Campaign and Dinner," in

The Postwar Orphans' Campaign and the Ambijan-ICOR Merger

Collection No. 20: Chicago Chapter, American Birobidjan Committee, Series B. Papers of Ethel Osri (From Collection No. 82). Folder 11: Einstein Fund Dinners 1945-47, Chicago Jewish Archives.

29 E-mail letters from Linda M. Schloff, Director of the Jewish Historical Society of the Upper Midwest, Minneapolis, to the author, Minneapolis, MN, February 24, 2005 and March 11, 2005.

30 Letter from Louis Locketz to Harold Goldenberg, Minneapolis Federation of Jewish Service, Minneapolis, April 18, 1945; letter from Charles I. Cooper to H. Supak, Minneapolis, Oct. 16, 1945; letter from Henry Supak to Charles I. Cooper, Minneapolis, Oct. 18, 1945; archives of the Jewish Historical Society of the Upper Midwest, Minneapolis, MN.

31 Letter from Louis Locketz to I.S. Joseph, Minneapolis, Dec. 4, 1946; letter from I.S. Joseph to Louis Locketz, Minneapolis, Dec. 20, 1946; archives of the Jewish Historical Society of the Upper Midwest, Minneapolis, MN.

32 Letter from Charles I. Cooper to I.S. Joseph, Minneapolis, Nov. 21, 1947; archives of the Jewish Historical Society of the Upper Midwest, Minneapolis, MN. The Minneapolis Federation continued to complain that, though the Ambijan Committee had been admitted as beneficiaries to the Federation, they remained vague as to how the money allocated to them was being spent in Birobidzhan. Cooper in a memo to Joseph in July 1948 remarked that "No Federation in the country has treated this organization so generously. Our action has been used by the Ambijan publicity department extensively." Failure by Locketz and Supak to appreciate this and to "treat the Federation decently this year would make an unfavorable impression upon the Board of the Federation." Letter from Charles I. Cooper to I.S. Joseph, Minneapolis, July 7, 1948; archives of the Jewish Historical Society of the Upper Midwest, Minneapolis, MN. Locketz was now chair of Ambijan in Minneapolis, and Supak the treasurer. Notice from Minneapolis Ambijan in *Nailebn-New Life* 21, 3 (March 1948): 36. Ambijan refused to mend its ways, and so all support from the Minneapolis Federation came to an end.

33 This information is contained on pp. 2, 8 in a 23-page FBI report dated Oct. 22, 1947, and pp. 3-8 in a 22-page FBI report dated April 29, 1948, both submitted by R.B. Hood, Special Agent in Charge, originally in LA File 100-23652. File 100-99898, Section 3, FOIPA No. 416152, Ambijan.

34 Circular letter from J.M. Budish, New York, Jan. 12, 1946; letter from J.M. Budish to Vilhjalmur and Evelyn Stefansson, New York, Jan. 21, 1946; Stefansson correspondence, MSS 196, Box 67, 1946--Ambijan Folder, Stefansson Collection; *Call to the Eastern Regional Conference of the American Birobidjan Committee (Ambijan) for Post War Rehabilitation* (New York: American Birobidjan Committee (Ambijan), 1946); "The Work of Your Organization is a Noble Task," *Ambijan Bulletin* 5, 1 (February 1946): 6-7; "Income and Disbursements," *Ambijan Bulletin* 5, 3 (September 1946): 2; "Electric Power Plant in Birobidjan City," cover page of the *Ambijan Bulletin* 6, 2 (March 1947).

CHAPTER FIVE

35 "Call to National Conference for Birobidjan – Ruf tsu der natsyonaler konferents far birobidzhan," flyer in United States Territorial Collection, RG117, Box 57, folder "Icor" 17/16, YIVO. Letter of invitation from J.M. Budish, New York, Jan. 22, 1946, in the Kalmen Marmor papers, 1873-1955, RG205, Microfilm group 495, folder 585 "Ambidzhan-korespondents, 1946-1950," YIVO.

36 Ambijan press release in United States Territorial Collection, RG117, Box 57, folder "Icor" 17/16, YIVO; "Magnuson Opposes any Anti-Soviet Pact," *New York Times*, March 10, 1946, Section 1: 2; "Birobidjan Groups Merge to Aid Jews," *New York Times*, March 11, 1946: 12; *Call to National Conference for Birobidjan* (New York: American Birobidjan Committee (Ambijan), 1946); "Message from Prof. Einstein," *Ambijan Bulletin* 5, 2 (April 1946): 2; "Proceedings of the National Conference for Birobidjan," *Ambijan Bulletin* 5, 2 (April 1946): 7-10; "Declaration of Principles and Program," *Ambijan Bulletin* 5, 2 (April 1946): 11-12; J.M. Budish, "National Conference Rallies American Jews to Birobidjan," *Ambijan Bulletin* 5, 3 (September 1946): 3-5; FBI report on "National Conference For Ambijan Activities," March 13, 1946, File 100-99898, Section 2, FOIPA No. 416152, Ambijan. See also Marc Chagall's message congratulating Birobidzhan on its 18th anniversary. "Telegrams and Messages of Greeting to the Conference," *Ambijan Bulletin* 5, 2 (April 1946): 4. Einstein replaced Lord Marley, who seems to have terminated his connection to Ambijan by this time. Nicole Taylor, "The Mystery of Lord Marley," 68.

37 For all these reasons, the USSR had clearly come to favor Ambijan over the ICOR prior to the merger. According to an FBI informant, the Soviet embassy in Washington in 1945 had instructed Anotoly Yakovlev, the vice consul general in New York, "to achieve cooperation between AMBIJAN and ICOR. ICOR representatives reported slighted because AMBIJAN had official blessing of USSR. YACOULOV [sic] told representatives of both organizations that each was important in bringing about unity among Jews in United States, ICOR among the Jewish masses and AMBIJAN among richer Jews." See p. 1 of a 9-page report submitted by E.E. Conroy, Special Agent in Charge, dated July 19, 1945, originally in File 100-14454. File 100-2074, FOIPA Release of Organization for Jewish Colonization.

38 "What is Birobidjan?" *New York Times*, March 6, 1946, 19. Ambijan claimed it received $800 in donations in response to the ads. "Response to Newspaper Ads," *Ambijan Bulletin* 5, 2 (April 1946): 4. Of course the actual number of Jews living in Birobidzhan was far less than the ad claimed.

39 "Cultured Pearl," *Time*, March 18, 1946: 34.

40 "Board of Directors Meeting," *Ambijan Bulletin* 5, 3 (September 1946): 14.

41 "Forthcoming Events," *Ambijan Bulletin* 5, 3 (September 1946): 2.

42 Circular letter from Albert Einstein and J.M. Budish, New York, Oct. 8, 1946, in the Kalmen Marmor papers, 1873-1955, RG205, Microfilm group 495, folder 585 "Ambidzhan-korespondents, 1946-1950," YIVO;

43 Circular letter from Albert Einstein and J.M. Budish, New York, Oct. 8, 1946, and letter from J.M. Budish to members of the national committee of Ambijan, New York, Oct. 23, 1946, in the Kalmen Marmor papers, 1873-1955, RG205, Microfilm group 495, folder 585 "Ambidzhan-korespondents, 1946-1950," YIVO; "Bulletin--Organizational Activities," *News from American Birobidjan Committee (Ambijan)*, November 1946: 1-2; B.Z. Goldberg, "Stalingrad Orphans at Silver Ponds," *Ambijan Bulletin* 5, 3 (September 1946): 12-13; "Says Russia Needs Peace," *New York Times*, Nov. 12, 1946, 3; "Senator Pepper Lauds Ambijan Work as Aid to World Peace," *Ambijan Bulletin* 6, 1 (February 1947): 6; "N.Y. Annual Dinner Meeting," *Ambijan Bulletin* 6, 1 (February 1947): 7; "The Jewish Autonomous Region and the American Birobidjan Committee in 1946," *Ambijan Bulletin* 6, 1 (February 1947): 8-10; see also pp. 22-24 of a 42-page FBI report dated Feb. 4, 1947, submitted by Edward Scheidt, Special Agent in Charge, originally in NY File 100-42538. File 100-99898, Section 2, FOIPA No. 416152, Ambijan.

44 "Ambijan to Seek $100,000," *New York Times*, Jan. 31, 1947, 21. A few years after Budish's death in 1966, a committee to commemorate his role in aiding Silver Ponds was organized by the poet David Seltzer and Bernard Roller, who had been chair of the Greater Miami Ambijan in the 1940s. The flyer they circulated spoke of the help provided the children of Silver Ponds as being "one of the most noble acts" undertaken during the war. Their idea of printing a commemorative volume followed the May 1965 visit of a group of American tourists to Volgograd (as Stalingrad had been renamed), where they met some of the people who had been housed in Silver Ponds as children. The book was never published. "Sponsorship Committee to Publish *The Book of Ambijan*: "Uncle Ambijan" and the Stalingrad Children, A Saga of American-Soviet Friendship Dedicated to the Memory of J.M. Budish," flyer in the B.Z. Goldberg papers, Box 70, Soviet Union, folder "American Birobidjan Committee 1948."

Chicago Ambijan Leadership, *Sentinel*, Chicago, May 16, 1946

Senator Claude Pepper on cover of *Sentinel*, Chicago, June 20, 1946

National Conference for Birobidzhan, March 9-10, 1946. . Left to right:
Max Levin, Soviet Consul General Vasili A. Kazanyev, Senator Warren G. Magnuson, Judge Anna M. Kross, Professor Charles Kuntz, and J.M. Budish, *Ambijan Bulletin*, April 1946

The Glory Years, 1946-1948

What should Ambijan emphasize in its work on behalf of Birobidzhan? This was the question Abraham Jenofsky posed to Morris Stern, then vacationing in Miami, in November 1946. Jenofsky told Stern that he had discussed the matter with Gina Medem and they both wondered whether, at this moment, it might not be wiser "to stress the Jewish-national significance of Birobidzhan even more than our actions on behalf of the orphans in Birobidzhan." Medem, who had returned to New York from a lecture tour, said that her audiences had been extremely interested in hearing as much as she could tell them about the Jewish Autonomous Region. "I can tell you that we on the National Committee are considering the question of aiding in the building of the Jewish Autonomous Region in a much more respectful manner than just having the campaign for the orphans."[1] In a follow-up letter, Jenofsky informed Stern of the arrival of pictures from Birobidzhan illustrating the "gigantic industrial and cultural institutions....We are trying to spread this latest news as widely as possible and we hope to produce a Birobidzhan friendship book for the 13th anniversary of the Jewish Autonomous Region."[2] Jenofsky was pleased to note that the American Jewish Committee's *Yearbook* for 1946-1947 had included favorable information on Birobidzhan in its review of the year; Ambijan had reproduced the section as a brochure.[3] In its propaganda, Ambijan increasingly emphasized Birobidzhan. At the same time, the organization continued to publicize the plight of the orphans, especially for fund-raising purposes: most of the concerts, luncheons, and other events stressed Ambijan's part in resettling Jewish children left homeless by the war.

On April 28, 1946, for example, Ambijan sponsored an event at the American Labor Party Hall on Allerton Avenue in the Bronx. The audience was addressed by the historian Raphael Mahler. On May 18, the New York City Committee sponsored a "Concert and Birobidjan Celebration" at Town Hall in Manhattan, featuring Regina Resnick of the Metropolitan Opera Company; Ray Lev, concert pianist; and Misha Mishakoff, concert violinist.[4] The first annual Einstein Fund luncheon for women members of the Bronx Division was hosted by Evelyn Stefansson, on May 8, at the Waldorf-Astoria. An audience of 275 listened as Stella Adler, star of Broadway and Hollywood, recited the poetry of Itzik Fefer; by the end of the evening, $2,500 had been raised.[5]

The Brooklyn Division of Ambijan organized a meeting on March 22, with Jessica Smith, editor of *Soviet Russia Today*, as guest speaker. The Division's second Spring Music Festival, on May 17 at the Brooklyn

Academy of Music, featured Vivian Rivkin at the piano and Dean Dixon conducting the American Youth Orchestra. Albert E. Kahn, a prominent Communist, spoke at the Festival, which netted approximately $6,000. U.S. Senator James E. Murray of Montana addressed a dinner in Newark on April 14; this event raised $4,000.

City-wide conferences were held in Boston, Chicago, Philadelphia and Washington. At a New England area conference convened in Boston on May 19, the 200 delegates decided to initiate a campaign to raise $150,000. On May 28, at a dinner addressed by Senator Alben W. Barkley, $18,000 was contributed. On November 24, B.Z. Goldberg spoke to an audience of 700, raising $2,500. Meanwhile, in Philadelphia, $25,000 was pledged by 75 delegates on April 28; a concert in the Fleischer Auditorium on November 7 brought in more than $2,000 in cash and pledges.[6]

Budish visited the West Coast in April and May, stopping in Los Angeles, Petaluma, Berkeley, Oakland and San Francisco. His itinerary was a busy one. In advance of his trip, Budish had asked Albert Maltz, the author and screenwriter, to organize a gathering of Hollywood people. In his letter to Maltz, dated April 15, 1946, Budish explained, "I would like to enlist the support of additional circles in the community for our movement, especially of some of the people in Hollywood. I must say that until now, we received practically no support from Hollywood though Los Angeles contributed last year some $60,000.00." On May 17, in Hollywood, Budish met with Maltz, who suggested that Edward G. Robinson should be recruited. A provisional Hollywood Ambijan Committee was soon organized.

Three days earlier, Budish had been a guest at a reception, attended by 150 "prominent citizens," at the Soviet Consulate in San Francisco. Later that year in the city, a gala dinner addressed by Senator Warren G. Magnuson and attended by Soviet consul general Constantin Efremov was held at the Fairmont Hotel. Other important guests at the October 15 affair included the authors Thomas Mann and Lion Feuchtwanger, who had come to America as refugees from Nazi Germany. The event raised $11,000.

Senator Magnuson addressed a gathering at the Beverley Hills Hotel a day later; Lion Feuchtwanger, Benno Schneider, Edward G. Robinson, Robert Cummings, Albert Maltz, Paul Henreid and Artie Shaw were among the artists who helped sponsor this event. On October 17 Magnuson spoke at a meeting of more than 1,000 people at the Los Angeles Philharmonic Auditorium; George Jessel, stage and screen star, served as master of ceremonies. Magnuson told the gathering that greater understanding between the U.S. and USSR was the basis for world peace; he warned against "the prophets of doom and the Cassandras of hate" who were enemies to the Soviet Union. Judge Isaac Pacht, chair of the meeting, said he deplored the attempts being made by reactionaries, whom he compared to Nazis, "to whip up anti-Soviet hysteria." The Soviet vice consul, Eugene Tumanzev, also addressed the meeting. Pacht made an appeal for funds, and $20,000 was collected for continued support of the orphans of Birobidzhan and Stalingrad.[7]

The Baltimore Ambijan had been organized in the spring of 1946. Jacob B. Aronoff, a member of Ambijan's Board of Directors, had visited the city and spoke at the Mercantile Club on June 24. According to an FBI informant, Aronoff at first had difficulty "with the wealthy Jews and Zionists there as they did not seem inclined to help the Jews in Russia." Some Jewish organizations in Baltimore, including the Workmen's Circle, were opposed to aiding a pro-Soviet organization such as Ambijan; indeed, the local Young Men's Hebrew Association had refused to rent them space. An official of Associated Jewish Charities said that "any money raised would undoubtedly be used to aid Russia rather than the needy people." But the Ambijan group persisted (with the help of the local CP), and attracted, according to an FBI informant, some "people of integrity" who were "not aware of the true picture with regard to the Communist relationship." A concert held on October 26 brought in more than $1,500 in donations; a banquet held at the Southern Hotel on April 27, 1947 attracted 135 people.[8]

In early 1947, Ambijan counted 20,000 members. There were Ambijan chapters and divisions in 60 cities and towns across the country. Morris L. Olken noted that many Jewish community centers and federations were now taking an interest in Ambijan's work; he was confident that the organization would continue to prosper and grow. Thanks to its thousands of devoted activists, it had raised half a million dollars in 1946.[9] At a meeting of the Board of Directors on February 18, Budish announced that six new branches had been organized since December 12, 1946: three in New York City, a women's auxiliary in Baltimore, a second branch in Miami Beach, and a branch of Jewish farmers in Petaluma, CA.[10] In a meeting with the Chicago Ambijan on March 31, Budish noted that there were 35 cities in the country with active branches.[11]

The pages of the *Ambijan Bulletin* and *Nailebn-New Life* documented the activities of Ambijan branches big and small, from the many chapters in New York City, Boston, Los Angeles, Philadelphia, and other major centers, to those in smaller, outlying communities such as, for instance, Memphis and Omaha. I do not have the space to recount all of their activities, but a few examples will indicate how much work was done even in the smaller communities: A dinner organized by the Wilmington, DE chapter late in 1946 brought in $505. At the beginning of 1947, the Gloversville, NY chapter raised $820 for relief work. In Trenton, NJ, the Sons and Daughters of Israel Home for the Aged collected $50 for displaced orphans; and the Lillian Wald Club of Hartford raised $500 by sponsoring three movie performances, attended by 900 people.[12]

The first Ambijan dinner organized by the Kansas City, MO branch, on January 12, 1947, raised $3,200; it was chaired by Rabbi Samuel Mayerberg of Congregation B'nai Jehudah, the oldest and largest Jewish congregation in the Kansas City metropolitan area. Rabbi Mayerberg, who was well known for his commitment to left-wing causes (he had escaped an assassination attempt in 1932 spurred by his battle against the Tom Pendergast "machine" that then ran the city), expressed his conviction that the people of the United States owed a debt of gratitude to the Soviet government and people for their immense contribution to saving the world from fascism. It was the duty of every Jew, he declared, "to help these innocent victims of Hitler's holocaust with such necessities as food, clothing and shelter to restore them to health and a normal life." A day later, B.Z. Goldberg, recently returned from a visit to Palestine, eastern Europe and the USSR, and Ethel Osri, executive director of the Chicago Division, discussed in detail the various rehabilitation and reconstruction programs to which Ambijan was contributing. The Kansas City chapter pledged itself to raise money to pay for the upkeep of one hundred orphans a year in Birobidzhan, at $100 per child.[13]

The Bronx Ambijan chapter conducted an intensive educational and fund raising campaign to fulfill its commitment to support at least 50 war orphans in 1947. On May 21, the second Einstein Fund luncheon was held at the Waldorf-Astoria. A meeting on June 9 at the Concourse Plaza Hotel was advised that the branch had now raised $7,950 for the year and had a membership of over 100 people. The main speaker was Dr. John Somerville, a specialist on Soviet philosophy at Hunter College. He and his wife Rose Maurer, a well-known Communist, had lived in the Soviet Union in 1935-1937.[14]

Rabbi Abraham Bick spoke to an overflow crowd in Miami on January 15, 1947, on the topic, "The Destiny of the Jews of Europe, Palestine, and Birobidzhan." The new Miami Beach Branch No. 2 held its first public function, a luncheon, at the Roney-Plaza Hotel on April 13. The guest of honor was Yakov M. Lomakin, Soviet consul general in New York; his speech, delivered in Russian, was translated by J. M. Budish. Harold Turk, a former president of a B'nai B'rith lodge, appealed to the 200 people present to help in the rehabilitation work of Ambijan, and $3,000 was donated.[15]

Abraham Jenofsky toured the Midwest between February 8 and 22, visiting six cities. He lectured on Birobidzhan at the Cincinnati Jewish Center on February 9; he was in Chicago from February 11 to 15, speaking at various branches and meeting with the Chicago Division Board of Directors to plan conferences, luncheons, and fundraising drives. On

February 16-18 Jenofsky was in Milwaukee, where he met with the local chapter to describe new developments in the JAR. His speech was reported in the local Anglo-Jewish newspaper; soon afterwards, the paper's editor wrote Jenofsky that he hoped Ambijan "may be instrumental in changing Soviet policy—or at least getting to the ear of our friend 'Uncle Joe.' If there were a change in Soviet policy to allow Jews from outside Russia into Birobidjan, I would be one of the biggest boosters of the project."[16]

The annual Ambijan dinner in Newark, held on February 23, 1947, was attended by 300 guests. Senator Harley M. Kilgore spoke of Ambijan's "splendid work" caring for the Stalingrad orphans and helping them resettle in Birobidzhan. The Jewish Autonomous Region was, he declared, "a successful, living monument, that may well serve as an inspiration for people throughout the world." About $5,000 was raised in cash and pledges. Ambijan was thanked by both Hayden Proctor, acting governor of New Jersey, and Vincent J. Murphy, mayor of Newark, for its "humane efforts in settling refugee war orphans in Birobidjan."[17]

The Cleveland Ambijan was in the midst of an intensive educational campaign. On April 2, Joseph Morgenstern, chair of the Cleveland Division, kicked off a campaign to raise $60,000 for the purchase of 15 prefabricated houses, and equipment for a light manufacturing plant, to be shipped to Birobidzhan. Morgenstern was also helping to organize Ambijan committees in Toledo, Youngstown, Pittsburgh and Detroit.[18]

In Chicago, a campaign to establish a Radio and Electrical Institute in Birobidzhan to train skilled technicians was now under way, and on March 28 the Soviet consul general in New York, Yacov M. Lomakin, travelled to Chicago to help launch the drive to raise $75,000. Budish was in the city in July, and recommended to the executive that they begin to purchase materials for the school; the Chicago Ambijan soon afterwards sent $5,000 to New York for the immediate purchase of equipment.[19]

June 8 was the date set by Chicago Ambijan for a city-wide conference at the Midland Hotel to aid the war orphans. In anticipation of the conference, the *Sentinel*'s editor asserted that helping the refugees in Birobidzhan in no way interfered "with the rebuilding of Eretz Israel." He added, "We should thank God there is a place like Birobidjan where Jewish children can have the opportunity of building a free life for themselves." The conference attracted some 300 delegates from various *landsmanshaftn*, reading circles, cultural groups, professional groups, and unions, who pledged to raise $100,000 in cash and $25,000 in machinery for Birobidzhan. As well, $3,068.30 was donated on the spot. Following the conference, Ethel Osri announced that she was resigning as executive director; "our organization now was on a firm foundation," she told the executive board. She was replaced by *Sentinel* columnist A. Ovrum Tapper.[20]

The always-active Los Angeles division sponsored a conference on February 2 with playwright Albert Maltz as the guest speaker. Birobidzhan's anniversary on March 29 was celebrated at the Embassy Auditorium; the event, chaired by Samuel Rosenfeld and Eva Myers, raised $5,500. Budish, on another western tour, lectured in Los Angeles on July 19; at another meeting two days later, Nathan Krupin, the executive secretary of Ambijan in Los Angeles, and Yitzkhak Levitt, treasurer of the Southern California Ambijan, presented Budish with a check for $5,000 on behalf of the war orphans. In just a few months the Los Angeles region had raised a total of $15,000.

The Los Angeles Soviet consulate hosted a reception for Budish on July 29; the guests were assured that the Soviet Union was doing all it could to build a Jewish entity in Birobidzhan. That same day, the FBI saw a Soviet consular official deliver an envelope to the Ambijan offices; it was later learned that the envelope contained a list of 48 "Jewish and pro-Russian organizations" in the Los Angeles area.[21]

In New York, Ambijan organized its yearly concert, at Town Hall on May 17, to celebrate the establishment of Birobidzhan and to "cement the bonds of friendship between the Jews of this country and the Jewish people in Birobidjan." The Brooklyn chapter held its third annual concert to benefit war orphans in Birobidzhan at the Brooklyn Academy of Music, on May 21; the concert, which featured singer Jan Peerce, netted $4,000. The newly-formed Manhattan branch met at the Waldorf-Astoria on April 23. Fania Chaikin, chair of the branch, who was also active in Hadassah, the women's Zionist organization, gave a summary of the goals of the branch, and Stella Adler recited poetry.[22]

Meanwhile, in response to events in the USSR, Ambijan was intensifying its efforts to fund housing for new settlers in Birobidzhan. Ambijan reported that the Soviet government had described the region as "so dear to the Soviet Jewish working masses" that it "cannot be separated from the Soviet Jewish people—it is their pride, their glory, their future." In the near future "all Birobidjan will be covered with a network of factories, mines and quarries." The Soviet government had also promised that new settlers would be "given all the necessary help."[23]

On January 14, 1947, at a general meeting attended by 150 Ambijan members, J.M. Budish spoke of the need for prefabricated houses in Birobidzhan. Ambijan organized a number of regional conferences to raise awareness of this issue and raise money: in New York, on March 23, with delegates from 200 organizations; in Chicago, on June 9, with 102 organizations represented; in Los Angeles on October 12, with over 200 organizations sending delegates; and in Newark on November 23, with 17 organizations in attendance. Dinners were held in all these cities as well as in Boston, Kansas City, Miami, San Francisco, and Washington, D.C.

Prior to a New York area Birobidjan conference scheduled for March 23, each of the 500 delegates were told that the main topic of discussion would be the latest efforts at resettlement of Jewish war orphans and "tens of thousands" of others, including survivors in displaced persons' (DP) camps. The delegates were promised a slideshow illustrating "gigantic," newly built "industrial, agricultural and cultural institutions." They were told that it was the "manifest duty of American Jews" to help the Jews of the JAR "in their supreme effort" to develop the region, by means of "the same unlimited, self-sacrificing devotion and heroism they put into the war effort."

National organizer Morris L. Olken provided the slideshow, which included images of the children's homes in Birobidzhan City, Bira, Londoko, and Waldheim. Manhattan Councilman Stanley Isaacs congratulated Ambijan on helping "our fellow Jews" in Birobidzhan "in ways that will give them a fuller and a happier life." Jenofsky reported that in the last six months of 1946, Ambijan shipped $317,000 worth of supplies to Birobidzhan and Stalingrad. The delegates voted to raise $500,000 to help in the construction of at least 1,000 prefabricated homes for these new settlers. Budish submitted a detailed report of Ambijan's $2 million budget for 1947. The organization would be sending funds to help care for 3,500 war orphans already in Birobidzhan, and to facilitate the settlement of additional orphans. Ambijan would also assist other refugees and evacuees from the war-torn regions of the USSR, many of whom had found that their former homes were now debris, and all their relatives were dead. At another Ambijan meeting, held at Hunter College on June 3 and attended by 400 people, Budish again announced that many Jews were prevented from moving to Birobidzhan because of the housing shortage. He asked the audience to assist in raising between $750,000 and $1,000,000 to help Ambijan send 200,000 Swedish-built prefabricated houses to the JAR.[24]

On the west coast, too, money was being raised for prefabricated houses; by mid-1947, the Los Angeles Ambijan had raised $85,000 and planned to raise a further $35,000 to purchase 10 prefabricated houses for Birobidzhan. The California state conference, with 51 delegates, was held on October 11-12, 1947. Samuel Rosenfeld, chair of the Los Angeles branch, presided over the gathering; Rabbi Abraham Bick was the guest speaker. The audience contributed $4,000 to the Birobidzhan rehabilitation fund. On December 20, a mass meeting celebrating "Thirty Years of the Soviet Union" was celebrated at the Embassy Auditorium. Nathan Krupin reported that all told, $109,000 was contributed to the fund in 1947. In Petaluma, a "superb" lecture by Rabbi Bick on October

20 "touched every rancher's heart," and by the end of the month the Petaluma chapter had raised $1,200 for Birobidzhan.[25]

Ambijan also addressed appeals to Jewish welfare organizations throughout the country, asking them to allocate money "for the benefit of the Jewish war orphans [who] are looking to you to make possible their complete rehabilitation." Organizer Fan Bakst had attended the national conference of Jewish Federations and Welfare Funds in Atlantic City on January 30-February 2, 1947 and hosted a reception at which Budish spoke about the work of Ambijan. Soliciting funding for Birobidzhan from Jewish Federations had also been part of Jenofsky's Midwestern itinerary in February. Jenofsky had met with the Chicago executive on February 13 and pointed out that the Joint's 1947 budget of $120 million showed no allocation for the Soviet Union. On February 18, in Madison, Jenofsky had urged the Jewish Welfare Fund to assist Ambijan in its rehabilitation program for orphans. He had travelled to St. Paul a day later, where he requested funds for Birobidzhan relief work from the city's United Jewish Fund. On February 20, he had lectured in Minneapolis, a city where Ambijan was at the time a recipient of UJA funding. Ethel Osri returned to Kansas City in late February to help the Ambijan chapter make an appeal for $20,000 in allocations from the city's Jewish Federation. On April 19-20, 1947, New Orleans was the site of the Southeastern Regional Conference of Jewish Federations and Welfare Funds. Ambijan representatives had the opportunity to discuss the organization's program and budget with many of the delegates, who represented 40 Jewish communities.[26] To Budish's regret, however, many communal leaders said they could not give "any allocation to the American Birobidjan Committee." Despite setbacks such as these, which undoubtedly stemmed from the fact that Ambijan was viewed as a pro-Soviet organization, Budish remained confident that many American Jews were beginning to appreciate Ambijan's work and realized that "to continue to discriminate against our organization would be unfair and harmful to the cause of Jewish reconstruction in general."[27]

Local Ambijan chapters also made pleas for funding; the June 8, 1947 Ambijan conference in Chicago passed a resolution calling on the city's Jewish Welfare Fund to make adequate provisions for Ambijan's work for Birobidzhan. Samuel A. Goldsmith, director of the Fund, turned down the request. Budish came to Chicago to make the case for Ambijan at a hearing of the Fund on October 8, but it was to no avail. At a meeting of the Chicago Ambijan executive the next day, Budish suggested that letters be sent out to Ambijan contributors "requesting that they demand of the Jewish Welfare Fund that a fair allocation be made to our organization." Solomon Jesmer was allotted space to pen a full-page guest editorial in the November 6, 1947 *Sentinel* to make the case for Ambijan. He noted that the Jewish Welfare Fund was supposed to represent the entire community, not just segments of it, and pointed out that Ambijan received donations from more than 2,000 individuals and from several hundred Jewish organizations "representing tens of thousands of Chicago Jews." These "repeatedly expressed their desire" that Ambijan be included among the Fund's beneficiaries. The Chicago organization vowed to keep up its campaign at the national conference of Jewish Federations and Welfare Funds, which would be meeting in Chicago on January 24-26, 1948.

Perhaps these complaints were effective: although the Joint steadfastly refused to cooperate, and the Chicago organization again had its request denied by the city's Jewish Welfare Fund, Ambijan was eventually able to announce that 27 Jewish welfare funds had included allocations to the organization in their 1947 budgets, while others intended to do so in 1948. An FBI report of October 27, 1947 noted that the appeal to the Jewish federations was important not only from a financial point of view, but also because any cooperation between the federations and Ambijan would serve to diminish the political prejudice against Ambijan as a "Soviet pro-Communist agency."[28]

In advance of the annual meeting of the national committee scheduled for November 1947, Budish summed up Ambijan's main tasks: to contribute to the rehabilitation of the Jewish war orphans in Birobidzhan; to help new settlers arriving from the European parts of the USSR, especially by funding new homes (at a cost of $3,500 a house); to support the general cultural development of the Jewish Autonomous Region; and to work on behalf of the economic growth that would enable Birobidzhan to receive new migrants.[29]

Held at the Commodore Hotel on November 8-9, the national meeting was attended by delegates from 45 branches in 32 cities. Budish reported to the 150 attendees that the organization now comprised a total of 79 branches in 58 cities. Since March 1946, 20 new branches had been created, including women's branches in New York, Chicago, Boston and San Francisco; branches were currently being organized in 24 more cities. Ambijan publications, including the *Ambijan Bulletin*, *Nailebn-New Life*, and various pamphlets and other literature, had reached a total circulation of 250,000 copies.

Budish also announced that "a full-fledged Yiddish State University" would soon be established in Birobidzhan. The establishment of the university, and the ongoing support to war orphans, would "impose upon us a sacred obligation to redouble our efforts in order that we may do our full share in the historic effort of the Jewish people." There was, he indicated, "growing sympathy and understanding" within the American community of the significance of Ambijan's work.

CHAPTER SIX

Jack Greenbaum, the national treasurer, submitted a financial report: during the period since the last national committee meeting, total income for the organization was $517,413.29. The disbursements for relief amounted to $430,138.33; administrative expenses were $66,259.80. Delegates were told that the organization must continue its efforts to raise $2 million to help the orphans in Birobidzhan and Stalingrad. Max Levin noted that shipments to the Soviet Union in the previous six months had exceeded $100,000.

The annual dinner at the Waldorf-Astoria on November 11 was widely publicized; a quarter-page advertisement appeared in the *New York Times*. The event was attended by 1,000 guests, including Stella Adler, Soviet consul general Yakov M. Lomakin, and Professor Elias A. Lowe. New York City Councilman Stanley M. Isaacs, who presided over the dinner, spoke of the "profound sense of gratitude" owed by Jews to Soviet Russia, which had outlawed anti-Semitism, created the JAR, and provided a haven for 1 ½ million Jewish refugees from German terror during the war. Senator Barkley said that he saw in Birobidzhan "something akin to a divine spark kindled in the hearts of hapless men, women and children when they become self-governing and self-respecting." Birobidzhan, he contended, was a symbol of liberty, equality and democracy. It was "worthy of our support and is indeed only a part of the responsibility mankind must assume" after the devastation of the last world war. The audience contributed $106,000 and pledged an additional $176,000.[30] Jenofsky told Morris Stern that the Ambijan activists who were present had agreed that the 1947 conference and banquet had surpassed all previous ones.[31]

Barkley, who would become President Harry Truman's vice-presidential running mate in 1948, also spoke at the annual dinner of the San Francisco-Oakland District on November 23. More than 500 people attended the San Francisco dinner, and contributions exceeded $8,000. There were many distinguished guests from academia, politics, and religious institutions, including Jesse W. Carter, associate justice of the California Supreme Court, who chaired the event; Lenore Underwood, deputy attorney-general of the state of California; Judge Robert McWilliams, chairman of the San Francisco Conference of Christians and Jews; and Laurence Cross, mayor of Berkeley.[32]

Alben Barkley was also the guest speaker at the Chicago Division's annual Einstein Fund Dinner at the Stevens Hotel on December 6; his photograph graced the cover of the December 4 issue of the *Sentinel*. A circular letter sent out to Ambijan supporters in advance of the dinner asserted that Birobidzhan was offering a home to ever greater numbers of Jewish refugees. "The tempo of settlement and rehabilitation will be much greater, if greater assistance is furnished by us," Solomon Jesmer told the gathering, which included the newly-elected mayor of Chicago, Martin H. Kennelly, that the Division had already sent $15,000 to the national office towards the purchase of equipment for the Radio and Electrical Institute. In his speech, Judge Harry M. Fisher emphasized the urgency of the rehabilitation efforts. More than $33,000 was contributed in cash and pledges at the dinner.[33]

The dream and drama of building a Jewish homeland for the remnants of Jewry in the Soviet Union remained close to the hearts of many ordinary American Jews as well. In Chicago, one rank-and-file member, Sara Lansberg, a nurse at the Mt. Sinai Hospital for 25 years, contributed to the support of several children in Birobidjan. When she died, she left 25 per cent of her estate for work in Birobidzhan, and instructions to have her ashes strewn in the JAR. Harry Herzman, another member, left $500 to Ambijan.[34]

As a new year began, Ambijan continued to highlight progress in Birobidzhan. Budish sent out a letter on January 29, 1948 informing Ambijan supporters that three large contingents, consisting of more than 1,000 Jewish families, and a similar number arriving singly or in small groups, had settled in Birobidzhan in 1947. Many more desired to do so. Given its natural resources, and with the proper tools and facilities, the area "can easily maintain four million people," he wrote.[35] The February 1948 Ambijan newsletter highlighted the new Jewish settlers arriving in Birobidzhan from Yevpatoria (Eupatoria) and elsewhere in the Crimea and from Kherson (Gherson) and Nikolayev in the Ukraine. "The Crimean contingent takes up sixty six railroad cars," the newsletter informed readers, providing detailed information as to their occupations. "The new Jewish settlers going to Birobidjan are eager to perfect their knowledge of the Yiddish language." The Birobidzhan authorities were doing everything in their power to accommodate the new settlers, but more money was needed to overcome shortages of medicine, clothing, and tools and equipment to build housing.[36] The news coming from Birobidzhan "is quite positive," Jenofsky wrote to Morris Stern in March. The JAFC had sent word that 1,100 families from the Nikolayev and Dnepropetrovsk districts in the Ukraine were preparing to move to Birobidzhan. Should immigration continue at this pace in the coming years, "it will not take long for Birobidzhan to bloom even more and raise itself to the next stage of Jewish statehood."[37]

Budish maintained, in the *Ambijan Bulletin* of March-April 1948, that Birobidzhan had been transformed from an "entirely undeveloped territory into a flourishing Jewish Autonomous Region." He described the great progress, agricultural and industrial; the 123,550 acres under cultivation; the beautiful buildings and fine streets in the capital city; and the various schools, cultural institutes, and facilities throughout the region. It was a "self-governing Jewish community," with "all the functions of statehood" and had become in just one generation "one of the most vital centers of Yiddish culture throughout the world." It also had become an important center for post-war Jewish rehabilitation, bringing "hope and encouragement" and "renewed faith" in racial and national equality.[38] In May, Joseph Morgenstern referred to Birobidzhan as "the greatest achievement in Jewish history." At the November 1948 annual meeting of the national committee in New York, Budish noted Morgenstern's exceptional generosity, announcing that Morgenstern and the Cleveland Division had sent a tractor, trailer, two lumber trucks, a car, and some woodworking equipment to Birobidzhan.[39]

Ambijan packaged two articles, "The New Jew in the Soviet Union," by Paul Novick, and "A Jewish State Rises in Birobidzhan," by J.M. Budish, into a 48-page booklet, for wider distribution. Both articles extolled the progress made by Jews in the USSR since 1917, the elimination of anti-Semitism, and the renewed post-war progress in Birobidzhan.[40] Ambijan also published a pictorial album of 20 postcard-sized photos of life in Birobidzhan.[41] The noted Yiddish scholar A.A. Roback published an article on Soviet Yiddish literature in the *Ambijan Bulletin*, in which he asserted that Birobidzhan "has come to occupy an honored position in the Yiddish literature of the USSR."[42]

The name of Soviet Yiddish writer Khayim Melamud was invoked in a pamphlet published by Ambijan that autumn. The pamphlet reprinted from the pro-Communist *New York Star* a two-page pictorial spread highlighting life in Birobidzhan. The cover page declared that Birobidzhan had become "one of the most vital centers of Jewish culture and postwar Jewish rehabilitation in the Soviet Union" and that some 2,000 new Jewish settlers were arriving per month. An article by Melamud, entitled "Building Houses in the Jewish Autonomous Region," appeared in translation on the concluding page of the pamphlet. Melamud, who was then living in Birobidzhan, wrote that Ambijan's gift of a prefabricating plant had made it possible for the JAR to undertake large-scale construction of new housing.[43]

Individual Ambijan branches continued to report a high level of activity. At a meeting held at the Concourse Plaza Hotel on February 19, the Bronx branch celebrated the victory two days earlier of Leo Isacson in a special congressional election. Isacson, a Communist-supported American Labor Party candidate, had won a seat in Congress from the 24th Congressional district in the Bronx, beating the Democratic candidate Karl Propper, following the resignation of the incumbent, Democrat Benjamin J. Rabin. On March 14, at a Bronx Ambijan Conference, those present committed to raise $20,000 for the Orphans Fund and to attract 500 new members. A concert and celebration of the 20th anniversary of

Birobidzhan was held in the Cooperative Colony Auditorium, 2700 Bronx Park East, on April 30, 1948; Abraham Jenofsky was the guest speaker.

The Waldorf-Astoria was the venue for the branch's third annual Einstein Fund luncheon, attended by 200 guests on May 25, held in conjunction with the Manhattan branch. Film actress Kay Medford attended as a special guest. Sam Wanamaker, "star of stage and screen," spoke of the role he hoped to play as a progressive and a Jew. He felt he was no longer "a stateless Jew," thanks to the Soviets, and declared that everything must be done to help Birobidzhan. (He would later move to England as a reaction to McCarthyism.) [44]

When the Brooklyn Division announced that its fourth annual concert for the benefit of the war orphans would take place on May 28, it indicated that 1,500 families had settled in Birobidzhan in the previous six months, including "many children whose parents died in concentration camps. Each has a long history of hardship."[45]

In Gloversville, NY, Evelyn Goldstein arranged a meeting on May 1 to celebrate two decades of Birobidzhan. The meeting was addressed by Olken, who brought along newly arrived photographs from Birobidzhan showing children at play, at school, at work in the fields, and swimming in the Bira River. There were also pictures of factories, schools, libraries, and children's dormitories. In a report published in *Nailebn-New Life*, branch secretary Wolf Broda exclaimed, "Until now we could only imagine in our minds these scenes of Birobidzhan . . . the land which we love and hold dear! And in the hall the voice of the speaker rang out clearly, as he described the new echelons of immigrants who were traveling to settle in Birobidzhan—with songs and joy!" The branch had by now collected $3,300 for the children in Birobidzhan.[46]

On February 7, 300 people attended the annual Newark dinner at the Robert Treat Hotel. They heard speeches by Professor Kuntz; Joel Gross, a Newark attorney; and J. Raymond Walsh, a radio commentator and writer. Baltimore held a meeting March 28 in observance of the 20th anniversary of Birobidzhan, at which Jacob B. Aronoff emphasized that Jewish colonization in the JAR had produced a "growing and vital Jewish state" with a number of important industries. He predicted that a modern steel industry would be in operation by 1952.[47] In Philadelphia, 400 people showed up at the YMHA on May 9 to hear Professor Kuntz, Abraham Jenofsky and Harry Epstein, chair of the Philadelphia Committee, celebrate Birobidzhan. The New England division organized two events in Boston: The first was an assembly at Congregation Mishkan Tefila on March 14, presided over by Isidore Shore, chair of the Roxbury-Dorchester branch. On May 9, 400 people gathered at the New England Mutual Hall to hear Rabbi Abraham Bick and Hunter College professor John Somerville.[48]

CHAPTER SIX

The Detroit division sponsored a city-wide conference on May 23 to decide how the Jewish community might aid in the settlement and maintenance of war orphans and refugees in Birobidzhan. The 62 delegates resolved to launch a campaign to raise $10,000. Isadore Starr and Joseph Schiffer, who had been involved with the local Jewish Council for Russian War Relief and the American Jewish Council to Aid Russian Rehabilitation, were chosen to lead the campaign. Rabbi Mayer Israel Herman of the Brith Sholem Congregation in the Bronx, New York, called upon the Jews of Detroit "to spare no effort in helping settle Jewish orphans and giving aid in the upbuilding of Birobidjan."[49]

Morris L. Olken visited the West Coast from February to April 1948. At one of the events he attended in Los Angeles—a party, on February 22, honoring an Ambijan stalwart—$1,200 was collected for Birobidzhan. When he visited Oakland on February 24, a women's group pledged itself to raise $5,000 for a dental office in Birobidzhan. Two days later Olken spoke to a gathering of students and professors at the University of California campus in Berkeley. A celebration of the 20th anniversary of Birobidzhan's designation as a Jewish national district, held at Embassy Hall, Los Angeles on March 27, featured Hollywood writer and director Herbert Biberman as the guest speaker; the poet Aaron Kurtz recited "Jews of Palestine and Birobidjan are Dancing," which he had written for the occasion. The 1,500 people in attendance, representing scores of Jewish organizations, donated $8,445. In San Francisco, Olken was interviewed on radio station KGO. He attended a Birobidzhan celebration at the Hotel Whitcomb on March 28, addressed by Dr. S.J. Hurwitt, president of the San Francisco Ambijan; this event was also attended by the Soviet consul, Konstantin Efremov.[50]

Olken recounted his trip to California in an article in the May issue of *Nailebn-New Life*. The warmth of the weather was exceeded only by that of the many Ambijan members he had met, Olken wrote. He was impressed by the high levels of participation in the Los Angeles chapters; many people attended, asked questions, and were very involved in all aspects of the work. In addition to asking him to speak at Ambijan events, they arranged for him to lecture to various "folk-organizations," societies and *landsmanshaftn*. His only cause for concern was that most of the membership was Yiddish-speaking: Ambijan was still not attracting English-speaking Jews, in particular the youth. But Olken was pleased to have been able to reach "thousands of Americans" by radio while in San Francisco.[51]

Nathan Krupin reported on a successful "donor banquet" held in Los Angeles on August 1, at the Roosevelt Hotel in Hollywood. Never before, he wrote, had an Ambijan event in Los Angeles been held with such "panache and polish." The guests came from all sectors of the Jewish progressive movement; the well-known "progressive fighter against anti-Semitism and racial discrimination," Carey McWilliams, was a guest speaker. He told the audience that the U.S. had much to learn from the Soviet Union when it came to the treatment of national minorities. The Soviets had solved the question by allowing each of its minorities to attain self-governance. He feared the growing tide of reaction in the U.S., including those who wished to lead America into war against the USSR. A total of $11,000 was raised from the 400-plus people in attendance.

Aaron Kertman sent the national office a letter reporting that Rabbi Bick's recent visit during the annual Southern California conference and dinner on November 13-14, 1948 had been a "huge success," with $4,600 collected. The opening concert was attended by more than 1,500 people, and the conference included 142 delegates from 61 organizations. The conference sent a message to the Soviet Union on its 31st birthday, thanking it for saving millions of Jews during the war, outlawing anti-Semitism, and creating a Jewish entity in Birobidzhan. Altogether, in 1947-1948, a total of $31,505.37 had been collected in Los Angeles, wrote Kertman.[52]

In September 1948, according to J.M. Budish, Ambijan had branches in 24 cities in the U.S.[53] "The members and friends of the American Birobidjan Committee are thrilled to know that the people of Birobidjan think so much of the contribution of Ambijan, and that our cooperation invokes among them a warm-hearted feeling of profound gratitude," wrote Budish to the membership, in advance of the national committee meeting scheduled for November 20-21 at the Hotel Commodore in New York. Jenofsky asked each Ambijan branch and division to send as many members to the annual meeting and banquet as possible. The organization hoped for a minimum of 1,000 people and wanted to raise $200,000 for the Orphans and Rehabilitation Fund. The year 1949, the 15th anniversary of Birobidzhan as a JAR, would be declared a jubilee year, in which Ambijan would redouble its efforts to bring news of Birobidzhan to the Jews of America and attract thousands of new members by organizing lectures, symposia, meetings, concerts and readings, and by the publication and distribution of literature, including the *Ambijan Bulletin* and *Nailebn-New Life*.[54]

The national committee held its annual meeting at the Commodore Hotel on November 20-21. Budish reviewed general developments during the previous 12 months. While reactionaries were attempting to regain control in Germany and elsewhere, there was also bright news: the recovery of the Jewish communities in the east European people's democracies, where "anti-Semitism has been made a crime" and where Jewish culture "is flourishing," and the rapid strides made in Birobidzhan, thanks to "the upsurge of the aspiration of the Jews to achieve full equality

CHAPTER SIX

as a people, to develop Jewish statehood within their multi-national country, and to contribute their own share out of the genius of the Jewish people to the multinational culture of their Soviet motherland." Budish proceeded to provide statistics regarding the agricultural and industrial output of the region and the continued growth of educational facilities. He also provided details about Ambijan's activities in Poland and Birobidzhan, noting that in 1947-1948 Ambijan had contributed $20,000 for the support of a home for war orphans in Poland.

The national committee decided that Ambijan should purchase machinery and equipment for a brick-making plant for Birobidzhan, at a cost of $75,000, to help build homes for the new settlers arriving there. They resolved to supply equipment for a poultry farm, at a cost of $12,000, and to continue to ship consumer goods to Birobidzhan and Stalingrad. The Poultry Farmers' Committee of Lakewood and Vicinity, NJ, which had been organized in the spring of 1947, had already raised $10,000 for the purchase of model poultry farm equipment and was expanding its fund-raising activities into neighboring states.[55]

Senator Claude Pepper addressed those in attendance at the November 21 annual dinner. He predicted that Birobidzhan would soon become an autonomous republic with a Jewish majority, "which will reflect their character, genius, and their dreams." He urged the delegates to "Keep up your great fight; continue your great work; hold on to your old and strong faith." Finally, he praised the Soviet Union as "a nation which has recognized the dignity of all people," as "a nation wherein discrimination against anybody on account of race is a crime," and as a nation "in fundamental sympathy with the progress of mankind." A total of $132,747 was pledged at the banquet.[56] Einstein had written to Budish a few days earlier that, while "poor health prevents me to participate in your celebration," he considered it "of great importance that the principle of mutual assistance should be kept alive regardless of political antagonisms existing in the non-Jewish world. This gives the American Birobidjan Committee at the present time its special significance from the Jewish point of view."[57]

Budish announced in February 1949 that Ambijan had sent a transport of $65,463 worth of goods to the Soviet Union by ship on February 10. The goods were destined for new settlers in Birobidzhan, an orphans' home in Stalingrad, and a hospital in Minsk. The shipment to Birobidzhan, worth $53,604, consisted of 22 crates of clothing and shoes, as well as two trucks for transporting building materials. An earlier delivery to Birobidzhan, worth $29,107, had included a tractor, a trailer, and machinery for excavation. Ambijan had also sent 61 cases of incubators for the poultry farm, worth $9,446, and machinery to produce prefabricated houses from local timber; in the last three months of 1948, 150 houses had been built. The machinery for the brick-making plant that Ambijan had now undertaken to send to the JAR would be making more than bricks, declared Budish; it would also metaphorically be building a bridge of peace and understanding between the people of the two most powerful countries in the world. Altogether, $100,000 was needed to cover the cost of the machinery, transportation and other expenses for the brick-making plant. Ambijan had already paid the suppliers $41,000. In a letter to members asking for more support, Budish quoted Khayim Melamud, who had said that "The contribution by Ambijan invoked warmhearted feeling and profound gratitude among the people of Birobidjan who see in this help an expression of true friendship."[58]

Altogether, according to the historian Robert Weinberg, between 1945 and 1948 Ambijan, the ICOR and kindred groups in the United States sent to the USSR some six million rubles worth of food and supplies intended for the JAR. At the fixed exchange rate of 5.3 rubles to the U.S. dollar, these contributions totalled approximately $1.14 million dollars.[59]

ENDNOTES

1 Letter from Abraham Jenofsky to Morris Stern, New York, Nov. 19, 1946; in the Morris Stern papers, RG231, Box 1, unnamed folder, YIVO.
2 Letter from Abraham Jenofsky to Morris Stern, New York, March 12, 1947; in the Morris Stern papers, RG231, Box 1, unnamed folder, YIVO.
3 Letter from Abraham Jenofsky to Morris Stern, New York, June 19, 1947; in the Morris Stern papers, RG231, Box 1, unnamed folder, YIVO. The pamphlet he referred to was *The Jews in the Soviet Union and Birobidjan* (New York: American Birobidjan Committee (Ambijan), [1946]), written by Henry Frankel of the Foreign Affairs Department of the American Jewish Committee. It was a reprint of part of Frankel's article "Review of the Year 5706--Eastern Europe," in Harry Schneiderman and Julius B. Maller, eds., *American Jewish Year Book 5707 (1946-47).* Vol. 48 (Philadelphia: Jewish Publication Society of America, 1946): 322-334.
4 "3 Artists in Program," *New York Times*, May 19, 1946, 40; Brochures advertising "Biro-bidzhan kontsert" and "Concert and Birobidjan Celebration"; in the Morris Stern papers, RG231, Box 1, unnamed folder, YIVO.
5 "Forthcoming Events," *Ambijan Bulletin* 5, 3 (September 1946): 2; "Organizational Activities," *Ambijan Bulletin* 5, 3 (September 1946): 14.

Altogether the Bronx branch contributed $5,825 in 1946. "Organizational Activities," *Ambijan Bulletin* 6, 5 (October 1947): 15.

6 "Current Events," *Ambijan Bulletin* 5, 2 (April 1946): 2; "Our Program and Immediate Tasks," *Ambijan Bulletin* 5, 2 (April 1946): 3; "Organizational Activities," *Ambijan Bulletin* 5, 3 (September 1946): 14-15; "Organizational Activities," *Ambijan Bulletin* 6, 1 (February 1947): 14. In 1954, Murray, a senator since 1934, narrowly escaped electoral defeat when his opponents circulated a series of advertisements accusing him of being pro-Soviet.

7 "Organizational Activities," *Ambijan Bulletin* 5, 3 (September 1946): 14-15; "From Our Mail Bag," *Nailebn-New Life* 20, 1 (January 1947): 23; "Organizational Activities," *Ambijan Bulletin* 6, 1 (February 1947): 14-15. The Hollywood and Los Angeles information is contained on pp. 2, 5-6, 19 in a 23-page FBI report dated Oct. 22, 1947, submitted by R.B. Hood, Special Agent in Charge, originally in LA File 100-23652. File 100-99898, Section 3, FOIPA No. 416152, Ambijan. Albert E. Kahn had co-authored, with Michael Sayers, *The Great Conspiracy: The Secret War Against Soviet Russia* (Boston: Little, Brown and Co., 1946), which defended Stalin's Moscow purge trials of the 1930s.

8 Organizational Activities," *Ambijan Bulletin* 6, 2 (March 1947): 13-14. See also pp.15-16 of a 42-page FBI report dated Feb. 4, 1947, submitted by Edward Scheidt, Special Agent in Charge, originally in NY File 100-42538, and the 16-page FBI report dated Aug. 29, 1947, submitted by Fred Hallford, Special Agent in Charge, originally in Baltimore File 100-2298, both in File 100-99898, Section 2, FOIPA No. 416152, Ambijan.

9 M.L. Olken, "Der ambidzhan farn folk," *Nailebn-New Life* 20, 1 (January 1947): 16, 21. He hoped that it would continue to grow to the point where "every Jewish home" in the country would be familiar with Birobidzhan.

10 "Review of Activities of American Birobidjan Committee," *Ambijan Bulletin* 6, 2 (March 1947): 7-8. A stronghold of the Jewish pro-Soviet left, Petaluma had been settled by Yiddish-speaking socialist chicken farmers and retained its radical character over many decades. Anna Rosenfield Golden told author Kenneth Kann that "we always sent money to help the Jewish farmers in Birobidzhan." See Kenneth L. Kann, *Comrades and Chicken Ranchers: The Story of a California Jewish Community* (Ithaca, NY: Cornell University Press, 1993), 95-96, 175, 210.

11 Minutes, March 31, 1947, in Collection No. 20: Chicago Chapter, American Birobidjan Committee, Series A. Minutes Folder 4: Minutes, 1947, Chicago Jewish Archives.

12 "From Our Mail Bag," *Nailebn-New Life* 20, 1 (January 1947): 22- 23; "Lillian Wald Club of Hartford Adopts Five Orphans," *Nailebn-New Life* 20, 2 (February 1947): 23.

13 "Organizational Activities," *Ambijan Bulletin* 6, 1 (February 1947): 14; Organizational Activities," *Ambijan Bulletin* 6, 2 (March 1947): 13-14; "Organizational Activities," *Ambijan Bulletin* 6, 4 (May-June 1947): 12; letter from Rae Osadchey to Ethel Osri, Kansas City, MO, January 17, 1947, in

Collection No. 20: Chicago Chapter, American Birobidjan Committee, Series B. Papers of Ethel Osri (From Collection No. 82). Folder 7: Correspondence, 1944-49, Chicago Jewish Archives.

14 The Bronx information is contained on pp. 53-55 of an 82-page FBI report dated Feb. 23, 1949, submitted by Edward Scheidt, Special Agent in Charge, originally in NY File 100-42538. File 100-99898, Section 3, FOIPA No. 416152, Ambijan. A specialist in Soviet philosophy, Somerville had published *Soviet Philosophy, A study of Theory and Practice* (New York: Philosophical Library, 1946). He testified at a number of trials of Communists indicted during the McCarthy period and later wrote *The Communist Trials and the American Tradition: Expert Testimony on Force and Violence, and Democracy* (New York: International Publishers, 1956). He also wrote *The Philosophy of Peace* (New York: Gaer Associates, 1949).

15 Abraham Jenofsky, "Organizatsye un arbet," *Nailebn-New Life* 20, 3 (March 1947): 21; "Organizational Activities," *Ambijan Bulletin* 6, 4 (May-June 1947): 13.

16 Abraham Jenofsky, "Organizatsye un arbet," *Nailebn-New Life* 20, 3 (March 1947): 19-20; "Organizational Activities," *Ambijan Bulletin* 6, 2 (March 1947): 14-15; "Visitor Here Outlines Work of Birobidjan Committee," *Wisconsin Jewish Chronicle*, Milwaukee, Feb. 21, 1947; letter from B.C. Tousman, editor, *Wisconsin Jewish Chronicle*, Milwaukee, March 29, 1947; Jenofsky papers, RG734, Box 3, folder "letters," YIVO.

17 Messages from Acting Governor of New Jersey Hayden Procter and Newark Mayor Vincent J. Murphy, *Nailebn-New Life* 20, 3 (March 1947): 22; "Work of Ambijan Helps Secure World Peace, Says Senator Kilgore," *Ambijan Bulletin* 6, 2 (March 1947): 4; "Organizational Activities," *Ambijan Bulletin* 6, 2 (March 1947): 14-15; "Mayor of City of Newark, N.J. Considers Work of Ambijan Vital Need," *Ambijan Bulletin* 6, 3 (April 1947): 15; "Organization Activities," *Ambijan Bulletin* 6, 5 (October 1947): 14. Kilgore's politics came under fire in later years. See James H. Smith, "Red-baiting Senator Harley Kilgore in the Election of 1952: The Limits of McCarthyism During the Second Red Scare." *West Virginia History* 1, 1 (Spring 2007): 55–74.

18 "Review of Activities of American Birobidjan Committee," *Ambijan Bulletin* 6, 2 (March 1947): 7-8; "Organizational Activities," *Ambijan Bulletin* 6, 3 (April 1947): 13-14; "Organizational Activities," *Ambijan Bulletin* 6, 5 (October 1947): 13.

19 Phineas J. Biron, "Strictly Confidential," *Sentinel*, Chicago, March 27, 1947, 8; "Ambijan Proclaims Chicago-Wide Conference to Aid War Orphans," *Sentinel*, Chicago, May 15, 1947, 16; "Organizational Activities," *Ambijan Bulletin* 6, 2 (March 1947): 13; "Organizational Activities," *Ambijan Bulletin* 6, 3 (April 1947): 12; "Organizational Activities," *Ambijan Bulletin* 6, 4 (May-June 1947): 11-12; Minutes, March 13, 1947; March 17, 1947; May 29, 1947; July 9, 1947; July 31, 1947, in Collection No. 20: Chicago Chapter, American Birobidjan Committee, Series A. Minutes Folder 4: Minutes, 1947, Chicago Jewish Archives.

CHAPTER SIX

20 J.I. Fishbein, "The Editor Views the News," *Sentinel*, Chicago, May 29, 1947, 5; "People in the News," *Sentinel*, Chicago, July 3, 1947, 24; "Ambijan Conference Adopts $100,000 Goal for Birobidjan," *Sentinel*, Chicago, July 10, 1947, 16; Minutes, June 17, 1947; July 17, 1947; Aug. 28, 1947, in Collection No. 20: Chicago Chapter, American Birobidjan Committee, Series A. Minutes Folder 4: Minutes, 1947, Chicago Jewish Archives; "Reminder: American Birobidjan Committee," flyer in Collection No. 20: Chicago Chapter, American Birobidjan Committee, Series B. Papers of Ethel Osri (From Collection No. 82). Folder 10: Programs and Brochures, 1936-48, Chicago Jewish Archives.

21 A.J. [Abraham Jenofsky], "Organizatsye un arbet," *Nailebn-New Life* 20, 4 (April 1947): 18; A.J. [Abraham Jenofsky], "Organizatsye un arbet," *Nailebn-New Life* 20, 8 (September-October 1947): 18-20; "$5,000 More from the Golden State," *Nailebn-New Life* 20, 8 (September-October 1947): 26; "Organizational Activities," *Ambijan Bulletin* 6, 4 (May-June 1947): 12; "Organizational Activities," *Ambijan Bulletin* 6, 5 (October 1947): 13-15. The California information is contained on pp.7-16 in a 23-page FBI report dated Oct. 22, 1947, submitted by R.B. Hood, Special Agent in Charge, originally in LA File 100-23652. File 100-99898, Section 3, FOIPA No. 416152, Ambijan.

22 Circular letter of invitation from J.M. Budish, New York, April 7, 1947; in United States Territorial Collection, RG117, Box 57, folder "Icor" 17/16, YIVO; "Benefit to Aid Children," *New York Times*, May 14, 1947, p. 22; "Organizational Activities," *Ambijan Bulletin* 6,4 (May-June 1947): 14; "Organizational Activities," *Ambijan Bulletin* 6, 5 (October 1947): 14.

23 *The Jewish Autonomous Region: Questions and Answers* (New York: American Birobidjan Committee, March 1948), 5-6, 15. See also Robert Weinberg, "Birobidzhan After the Second World War," *Jews in Russia and Eastern Europe* 3, 49 (Winter 2002): 31-46; B. Z. Goldberg, *The Jewish Problem in the Soviet Union*, 202-205; and Nora Levin, *The Jews in the Soviet Union Since 1917*. Vol. I, 488-492.

24 "Call to New York Area Conference," *Nailebn-New Life* 20, 3 (March 1947): 24; "New York Area Conference," *Ambijan Bulletin* 6, 2 (March 1947): 3; "New York Area Birobidjan Conference," *Ambijan Bulletin* 6, 3 (April 1947): 10-11, 15; Circular letter from Dr. Lewis Schatzov, chairman, and Gussie Walker, secretary, New York Area Conference Arrangement Committee, New York, March 13, 1947, in United States Territorial Collection, RG117, Box 57, folder "Icor" 17/16, YIVO. Memos of June 9, July 23, and Sept. 22, 1947, from Edward Scheidt, Special Agent in Charge, to J. Edgar Hoover; File 100-99898, Section 2, FOIPA No. 416152, Ambijan. See also p. 48 of an 82-page FBI report dated Feb. 23, 1949, submitted by Edward Scheidt, Special Agent in Charge, originally in NY File 100-42538. File 100-99898, Section 3, FOIPA No. 416152, Ambijan.

25 N. Krupin, "Der 'ambidzhan' in los angeles iz a lebediker koyekh in yidishn lebn," *Nailebn-New Life* 20, 7 (July-August 1947): 9-10; A. J. [Abraham Jenofsky],

The Glory Years, 1946-1948

"Organizatsye un arbet," *Nailebn-New Life* 20, 8 (September-October 1947): 18-20; "Organization News," *Nailebn-New Life* 20, 9 (November 1947): 23; "Organizational Activities," *Ambijan Bulletin* 7, 1 (January 1948): 15.

26 Abraham Jenofsky, "Organizatsye un arbet," *Nailebn-New Life* 20, 3 (March 1947): 19-20; "Organizational Activities," *Ambijan Bulletin* 6, 2 (March 1947): 14-15; "To Jewish Welfare Fund Organizations," *Ambijan Bulletin* 6, 2 (March 1947): 2; "Review of Activities of American Birobidjan Committee," *Ambijan Bulletin* 6, 2 (March 1947): 8; "Organizational Activities," *Ambijan Bulletin* 6,4 (May-June 1947): 13; "Visitor Here Outlines Work of Birobidjan Committee," *Wisconsin Jewish Chronicle*, Milwaukee, Feb. 21, 1947, Jenofsky papers, RG734, Box 3, folder "letters," YIVO; Minutes, Feb. 13, 1947; Feb. 20, 1947; Feb. 27, 1947, in Collection No. 20: Chicago Chapter, American Birobidjan Committee, Series A. Minutes Folder 4: Minutes, 1947, Chicago Jewish Archives.

27 J.M. Budish, "American Jews Awaken to Birobidjan," *Ambijan Bulletin* 6, 5 (October 1947): 6-7.

28 S. Jesmer, "The American Birobidjan Committee and the Jewish Welfare Fund," *Sentinel*, Chicago, Nov. 6, 1947, 5; notes from the June 8, 1947 conference; minutes of Sept. 11, 1947; Oct. 2, 1947; Oct. 9, 1947, in Collection No. 20: Chicago Chapter, American Birobidjan Committee, Series A. Minutes Folder 4: Minutes, 1947, Chicago Jewish Archives; FBI report from Edward Scheidt, Special Agent in Charge, New York, to J. Edgar Hoover, FBI director, Oct. 27, 1947, NY File 100-42538. File 100-99898, Section 2, FOIPA No. 416152, Ambijan.

29 Circular letter from Max Levin, New York, May 5, 1947; letter from Vilhjalmur Stefansson to Max Levin, New York, May 7, 1947; Stefansson correspondence, MSS 196, Box 72, 1947--USSR-American Committee for the Settlement of Jews in Birobidjan (Ambijan) Folder, Stefansson Collection; letter from J.M. Budish to members of the national committee of Ambijan, New York, Oct. 7, 1947, in the Kalmen Marmor papers, 1873-1955, RG205, Microfilm group 495, folder 585 "Ambidzhan-korespondents, 1946-1950," YIVO; "The Meeting of the National Committee," *Ambijan Bulletin* 6, 5 (October 1947): 3.

30 Advertisement for the "Annual National Dinner of the American Birobidjan Committee," *New York Times*, Nov. 5, 1947, 24; "Barkley Advocates Admission of DP's," *New York Times*, Nov. 12, 1947, 13; "Report of the Enlarged Meeting of the National Committee November 8 and 9, and the Annual National Dinner, November 11, 1947," *Ambijan Bulletin* 7, 1 (January 1948): 5-8; Alben W. Barkley, "Birobidjan--Symbol of Peace and Equality," *Ambijan Bulletin* 7, 1 (January 1948): 10-11.

31 Letter from Abraham Jenofsky to Morris Stern, New York, Nov. 14, 1947; in the Morris Stern papers, RG231, Box 1, unnamed folder, YIVO.

32 "Organizational Activities," *Ambijan Bulletin* 6, 5 (October 1947): 14; *Ambijan Bulletin* 7, 1 (January 1948): 13-16. Some of the California information

is contained on pp.1-2, 14 of a 22-page FBI report dated April 29, 1948, submitted by R.B. Hood, Special Agent in Charge, originally in LA File 100-23652. File 100-99898, Section 3, FOIPA No. 416152, Ambijan.

33 "Birobidjan Proves Vital in Providing Haven for Many Refugee Jews," *Sentinel*, Chicago, Dec. 18, 1947, 6, 31; Sol Jesmer, "Birobidjan – A Great Jewish Center," *Ambijan Bulletin* 7, 2 (March-April 1948): 6; "Organizational Activities," *Ambijan Bulletin* 7, 1 (January 1948): 13; "Organizational Activities," *Ambijan Bulletin* 7, 2 (March-April 1948): 12-13; circular letter from S. Jesmer, Chicago, Nov. 25, 1947, in Collection No. 20: Chicago Chapter, American Birobidjan Committee, Series B. Papers of Ethel Osri (From Collection No. 82). Folder 11: Einstein Fund Dinners 1945-47, Chicago Jewish Archives.

34 "Organizational Activities," *Ambijan Bulletin* 6, 2 (March 1947): 13; Minutes, Jan. 30, 1947, in Collection No. 20: Chicago Chapter, American Birobidjan Committee, Series A. Minutes Folder 4: Minutes, 1947, Chicago Jewish Archives.

35 Circular letter from J.M. Budish, New York, Jan. 29, 1948, in the Kalmen Marmor papers, 1873-1955, RG205, Microfilm group 495, folder 585 "Ambidzhan-korespondents, 1946-1950," YIVO.

36 "Birobidjan News," *News from American Birobidjan Committee (Ambijan) Organizational Newsletter* 2, 1 (February 1948): 1-3.

37 Letter from Abraham Jenofsky to Morris Stern, New York, March 17, 1948; in the Morris Stern papers, RG231, Box 1, unnamed folder, YIVO.

38 J.M. B[udish], "Twenty Years of Birobidjan," *Ambijan Bulletin* 7, 2 (March-April 1948): 3-5, 8. "In Birobidjan the Jews as a people are given an opportunity to conquer the primitive earth for the first time in recorded history." "Birobidjan--A Contribution to World History," *Ambijan Bulletin* 7, 4 (June-July 1948): 3.

39 "Organizational Activities," *Ambijan Bulletin* 7, 3 (May 1948): 13; J.M. Budish, "Report on the Activities of Ambijan, Nov. 1947 to Nov. 1948," *Ambijan Bulletin* 7, 7 (December 1948): 15.

40 Paul Novick and J.M. Budish, *Jews in the Soviet Union: Citizens and Builders* (New York: New Century Publishers, May 1948).

41 *20th Anniversary of Birobidjan 1928-1948: Second Pictorial Album* (New York: American Birobidjan Committee – Ambijan, 1948).

42 A.A. Roback, "Trends in Soviet-Yiddish Literature," *Ambijan Bulletin* 8, 1 (January-February 1949): 7-10.

43 *Life in the Soviet Far East: Birobidjan* (New York: Ambijan, 1948). The pictorial spread appeared on pp. 12-13 of the Sept. 21, 1948 issue of the short-lived *New York Star*, the successor to another left-wing daily, *PM*, founded in 1940. Melamud's article was also published in Yiddish. Khaim Melamud, "Di hayzer-boyung un der yidisher autonomye gegnt," *Nailebn-New Life* 21, 8 (September-October 1948): 2-3.

44 A.J. [Abraham Jenofsky], "Organizatsye un arbet,' *Nailebn-New Life* 21, 4

The Glory Years, 1946-1948

(April 1948): 20; "Organizational Activities," *Ambijan Bulletin* 7, 3 (May 1948): 14; "A.J. [Abraham Jenofsky], "Organizatsye un arbet," *Nailebn-New Life* 21, 6 (June 1948): 18-19; "Organizational Activities," *Ambijan Bulletin* 7, 4 (June-July 1948): 14-15; pamphlet advertising "Kontsert un fayerung- -Concert and Celebration"; in the Morris Stern papers, RG231, Box 1, unnamed folder, YIVO. The information on the Feb. 19, 1948 Bronx meeting is in FBI reports from Edward Scheidt, Special Agent in Charge, New York, to J. Edgar Hoover, dated Feb. 24, 1948 and March 10, 1948, all originally in NY File 100-42538. File 100-99898, Section 3, FOIPA No. 416152, Ambijan. Information on the May 25, 1948 luncheon is on pp. 58-59, 61 of an 82-page FBI report dated Feb. 23, 1949, submitted by Edward Scheidt, Special Agent in Charge, originally in NY File 100-42538. File 100-99898, Section 3, FOIPA No. 416152, Ambijan.

45 Circular letter advertising the "Erica Morini Concert for the benefit of Jewish Refugee Orphans," sent out by Isidore Shprentz, executive secretary, and Dr. George I. Swetlow, chairman, Brooklyn Division, American Birobidjan Committee, New York, undated; in the Morris Stern papers, RG231, Box 1, unnamed folder, YIVO.

46 A.J. [Abraham Jenofsky], "Organizatsye un arbet," *Nailebn-New Life* 21, 6 (June 1948): 19.

47 "Organizational Activities," *Ambijan Bulletin* 7, 2 (March-April 1948): 14; "Organizational Activities," *Ambijan Bulletin* 7, 3 (May 1948): 14; "Organizational Activities," *Nailebn-New Life* 21, 6 (June 1948): 23. See also for Newark p. 46 of an 82-page FBI report dated Feb. 23, 1949, submitted by Edward Scheidt, Special Agent in Charge, originally in NY File 100-42538. File 100-99898, Section 3, FOIPA No. 416152, Ambijan.

48 A.J. [Abraham Jenofsky], "Organizatsye un arbet," *Nailebn-New Life* 21, 6 (June 1948):19; "Organizational Activities," *Ambijan Bulletin* 7, 3 (May 1948): 14; "Organizational Activities," *Ambijan Bulletin* 7, 4 (June-July 1948): 14.

49 "Organizational Activities," *Ambijan Bulletin* 7, 3 (May 1948): 14-15; "Organizational Activities," *Ambijan Bulletin* 7, 4 (June-July 1948): 13.

50 A.J. [Abraham Jenofsky], "Organizatsye un arbet,' *Nailebn-New Life* 21, 4 (April 1948): 20-21; A.J. [Abraham Jenofsky], "Organizatsye un arbet,' *Nailebn-New Life* 21, 5 (May 1948): 19; "Organizational Activities," *Ambijan Bulletin* 7, 4 (June-July 1948): 13-14. Kertman, who owned a Los Angeles pharmacy, had been a long-time member of the ICOR and had been secretary of the Los Angeles ICOR. See the ads in *ICOR* 8, 1 (January 1935): 20; *ICOR* 8, 3 (March 1935): 30.

51 M.L. Olken, ""Di organizatsyes un fraynt fun birobidzhan ibern land," *Nailebn-New Life* 21, 5 (May 1948): 7-9.

52 A Jenofsky, "Organizatsye un arbet," *Nailebn-New Life* 21, 8 (September- October 1948): 19-21; "From Our Mail Bag," *Nailebn-New Life* 21, 9 (November 1948): 23; A.J. [Abraham Jenofsky] "Organizatsye un arbet," *Nailebn-New Life* 22, 1 (January 1949): 22; A. J. [Abraham Jenofsky], "Oranizatsye un arbet,"

Nailebn-New Life 22, 2 (February 1949): 19-20; "From Our Mail Bag," *Nailebn-New Life* 22, 2 (February 1949): 23; A. J. [Abraham Jenofsky], "Oranizatsye un arbet," *Nailebn-New Life* 22, 4 (April 1949): 20; "Messages of Greetings," *Ambijan Bulletin* 8, 1 (January-February 1949): 6; "Organizational Activities," *Ambijan Bulletin* 8, 1 (January-February 1949): 14. Carey McWilliams published *A Mask for Privilege: Anti-Semitism in America* (Boston: Little, Brown, 1948). From 1955 to 1975 he was editor of the left-wing magazine the *Nation*. See Carey McWilliams, *The Education of Carey McWilliams* (New York: Simon & Schuster, 1978); Peter Richardson, *American Prophet: The Life and Work of Carey McWilliams* (Ann Arbor, MI: University of Michigan Press, 2005).

53 Letter from J. M. Budish, New York, Sept. 28, 1948, to the Advisory Committee of Voluntary Foreign Aid of the U.S. State Department; Case Control No. 200002702, NY File 100-42538; FOIPA No. 416152, Ambijan.

54 Circular letter from J.M. Budish, New York, Sept. 27, 1948; in the Morris Stern papers, RG231, Box 1, folder "ICOR-Birobidzhan," YIVO; A. Jenofsky, "Organizatsye un arbet," *Nailebn-New Life* 21, 8 (September-October 1948): 18; "Welcome, Delegates, to the Meeting of the National Committee," *Ambijan Bulletin* 7, 6 (October-November 1948): 3.

55 "National Committee Maps Extended Program of Cooperation with Jewish Autonomous Region of Birobidjan," *Ambijan Bulletin* 7, 7 (December 1948): 3-5; "Vital Issues Before American Birobidjan Committee," *Ambijan Bulletin* 7, 7 (December 1948): 7; J.M. Budish, "Report on the Activities of Ambijan, Nov. 1947 to Nov. 1948," *Ambijan Bulletin* 7, 7 (December 1948): 8-11, 13-16; "Organizational Activities," *Ambijan Bulletin* 8, 1 (January-February 1949): 15.

56 Herman Morgenshtern, "Sen. Pepper loybt sovyet, zogt foroys sholem mit amerika, bay birobidzhan banket," *Der Tog*, New York, Nov. 23, 1948, reprinted in an undated Ambijan press release, New York, [probably late November 1948]; in United States Territorial Collection, RG117, Box 57, folder "Icor" 17/16, YIVO; "Annual National Dinner," *Ambijan Bulletin* 7, 7 (December 1948): 5; Claude Pepper, "Keep up Your Great Fight--Continue Your Great Work," *Ambijan Bulletin* 7, 7 (December 1948): 6-7.

57 Letter from Albert Einstein to J.M. Budish, Princeton, NJ, Nov. 15, 1948; B.Z. Goldberg papers, Box 70, Soviet Union, folder "American Birobidjan Committee 1948."

58 Circular letter from J.M. Budish, New York, January [no day], 1949; Morris Stern papers, RG231, Box 1, folder "ICOR-Birobidzhan," YIVO. "New Jersey Poultry Farmers Present Machinery," *Nailebn-New Life* 22, 3 (March 1949): 24; "A Brickmaking Plant for Birobidjan," *Ambijan Bulletin* 8, 3 (July-August 1949): 3-4; "Organizational Activities," *Ambijan Bulletin* 8, 3 (July-August 1949): 13; J.M. Budish, "Birobidzhan un ambidzhan," *Nailebn-New Life* 22, 8 (September-October 1949): 1-2.

59 Weinberg, *Stalin's Forgotten Zion*, 78-80.

Ad for Einstein Fund Dinner, *Sentinel*, Chicago, Dec. 4, 1947

Flyer advertising Bronx Ambijan Concert for 20th Anniversary of Birobidzhan, April 1948, YIVO Institute for Jewish Research, New York

Flyer advertising concert for Birobidzhan, Town Hall, New York, May 1947, YIVO Institute for Jewish Research, New York

Ambijan and the Birth of Israel

Even ardent Zionists had come to recognize the immense contribution made by the Jewish Autonomous Region to Jewish life, declared the November 1944 national conference of Ambijan; in turn, Ambijan members were "equally concerned with the welfare, prosperity, and unhindered progress of the Jewish community in Palestine." Ambijan took pains to emphasize that Birobidzhan was not to be seen as "competition" for Palestine.[1] Morris L. Olken asserted in June 1944 that the two Jewish communities were not antagonistic towards each other: "Quite the contrary. The great Yishuv in Palestine and Biro-Bidjan can go on building up a Jewish life, each one helping the other. This mutual assistance has been going on without interruption, particularly since Hitler's treacherous invasion of the U.S.S.R. Jews in Palestine as well as Jews in the Soviet Union understand that Hitlerism is the implacable enemy of all Jews."[2]

Though Communists were no longer completely hostile to Jewish settlement in Palestine, given the condition of Holocaust survivors languishing in displaced persons' camps in Europe, they still could not openly ally themselves with Zionism. Many pro-Soviet Jews found it expedient to concentrate on attacking British policy in Palestine. The ICOR, for example, passed a resolution at its January, 1944 plenum denouncing the British government's "White Paper" of May 1939, which had severely curtailed Jewish immigration to Palestine.[3]

At the National Conference for Birobidjan held in March 1946, at which Ambijan and the ICOR merged into the American Birobidjan Committee, guest speaker Warren Magnuson, the U.S. senator from Washington state, asserted that the treatment accorded the Jews in Birobidjan by the Soviet government "stands in sharpest contrast to imperialist policy with respect to national minorities and colonial groups within the British Empire." The conference as a whole declared itself "deeply concerned with the welfare and prosperity of the Jewish community in Palestine, and *we emphatically join in the demand for the abrogation of the White Paper.*" Another Ambijan supporter, Senator Barkley, speaking to a United Jewish Appeal conference in New Haven on March 10, stated that the plight of the Jews in post-war Europe should concern "all civilization," and that Palestine should be opened to the "hungry, unwanted and homeless Jews of Europe."[4]

In a pamphlet entitled *Crisis in Palestine*, published in September 1946, Moses Miller, who had been president of the Jewish Peoples Committee Against Fascism and Anti-Semitism before World War II, attacked the new British Labour government for its handling of the Palestine issue. Britain, Miller explained, had never intended to fulfill its commitments to the Jewish people but was instead motivated by the desire to maintain its control over the Middle East. Britain wanted to turn the Middle East into a base for anti-Soviet intrigue and a "possible jumping off point for a war against the Soviet Union." The Communist position favored an independent Palestine "based upon Arab-Jewish unity," asserted Miller. Partition would result in a Jewish state that would rely "on imperialism and its military" to survive. "Is this the utopia for which Jews fled from Europe? What role could such a puppet state play in the affairs of nations?" Such a state would in fact be "a mockery of statehood and a betrayal of the Jewish people." The aspiration of the *yishuv*, Miller declared, "cannot be achieved by ignoring the just and legitimate aspirations of the Arabs." Both peoples in Palestine needed freedom; both must struggle together against imperialism, in alliance with the "labor and democratic forces throughout the world." Miller suggested that an international trusteeship under the UN be established to assist Palestine's progress towards full independence; the Soviet Union would participate fully in these arrangements.[5]

Alexander Bittelman, the prominent Communist theoretician and an editor of the CPUSA journal *Political Affairs*, successor to the *Communist*, also opposed partition in 1946. He argued that partition would mean the splitting up of the homeland of Arabs and Jews by foreign imperialist powers into "an arbitrary number of parts." Palestine must become independent and free, on the basis of Arab-Jewish unity.[6] At a national Communist Party conference held in New York on November 29, 1946, Bittelman outlined the Communist position on Palestine. He called on Jewish Communists to "support fully the building of a national Jewish homeland in Palestine." But, "we believe that both peoples," Arabs and Jews, "have equal rights to develop a free national existence in their common country." The *yishuv* was a "vital part of our people, which is developing as a nationality." Communists, he asserted, believed the best solution would be achieved by transferring Palestine to the UN and working for Jewish-Arab unity to create "an independent state of the two peoples."[7]

Local Ambijan branches, though, were by 1946 already favorable to the cause of the Jews in Palestine. For instance, when the Chicago Zionist Emergency Council on July 3 asked other Jewish organizations in the city to condemn the British arrest of Jewish Agency leaders in Palestine, and to demand that Britain permit the entry of 100,000 displaced persons from Europe into the Mandate, Solomon Jesmer, president of the Chicago Ambijan, responded immediately, sending out more than 1,000 letters to members requesting that they "give every possible assistance to the recommendations contained in the telegram." Carl Bromberg, chair of the Landsmanshaftn Division, suggested at an executive meeting that efforts should be made to get together with local Zionist leaders "for a more sympathetic understanding of our program."[8]

In any case, a year later Soviet policy had changed course: now Moscow supported partition in Palestine. Andrei Gromyko, the Soviet representative at the United Nations, made an impassioned speech on behalf of Jewish statehood at a special session of the world organization on May 14, 1947: Gromyko said the war had demonstrated "that not one state of Western Europe has been in a position to give proper help to the Jewish people and to defend its interests, or even its existence, against the violence that was directed against it from the Hitlerites and their Allies. The fact that not a single Western European State has been in a position to guarantee the defense of the elementary rights of the Jewish people, or compensate them for the violence they have suffered at the hands of the Fascist hangmen, explains the aspiration of the Jews for the creation of a state of their own." It would be unjust, Gromyko argued, to deny the right of the Jewish people to realize this aspiration.

The speech, reported the *New York Times*, had "caused elation in Zionist circles," especially since Gromyko had linked the plight of Jewish refugees in Europe with the settlement of the Palestine issue. The *Ambijan Bulletin* published the speech in its entirety, calling attention to the Soviet representative's "warm sympathy towards the Jewish people," and proclaiming his performance to be "the outstanding event of the session." But then, remarked the *Bulletin*, it was "natural, indeed inevitable," that the Soviet Union, having already provided Jews with the opportunity to develop their own statehood in Birobidzhan, should apply the same principles to the international problem of Palestine.[9]

Alfred D. Low has remarked that Moscow's post-war Soviet propaganda on behalf of Birobidzhan "virtually coincided with its vigorous though short-lived defense of Zionist aspirations in the U.N."[10] As a result, the pro-Soviet groups found mainstream Jewish organizations more receptive to their work. For example, when Ambijan sponsored a concert on August 3, 1946, in Saratoga Springs, New York, the event was publicized by Hadassah, the Women's Zionist Organization of America; and B'nai B'rith.[11]

In October 1946, B.Z. Goldberg, who had spent two weeks in Palestine, advised readers of *Der Tog* that the Jewish fighters there were not "bandits" or "terrorists," but rather, "partisans" fighting for Jewish liberty. He extended this definition to the right-wing Revisionist Zionist *Irgun* and "Stern Gang" (*Lehi*) as well as to the mainstream *Haganah*.[12] In November 1947, Budish wondered why the Jewish people, instead of receiving reparations for their destruction during the war, were instead still subject to discrimination and attacks. He complained about the "brutalities against the refugees on the Exodus and the dilatory attitude of the U.S. on the proposed democratic solution of the Palestine problem."[13]

In December, Gina Medem asserted in *Nailebn-New Life* that the creation of a sovereign Jewish state in Palestine would complete the victory over Hitler that had begun with the Soviet triumph at Stalingrad. She lauded the Soviet leadership for its support for a partition of Palestine. Medem's narrative was that of the Zionist movement itself: The 2,000-year saga of Jews wandering through countless countries "in which they were unwelcome guests" was coming to an end. She recounted the stories of the Jewish *khalutzim* [pioneers], who had reclaimed the dusty soil and created fields of crops and vineyards where there had been little but empty fields. She described the *yishuv*'s 30-year struggle against the British overseers; she dismissed the Arab states opposing Jewish sovereignty as being nothing more than British satellites. The article concluded by again noting that the Soviet victories from Stalingrad to Berlin had paved the way for the creation of a Jewish state on the banks of the Jordan.[14]

Joseph Brainin's American Committee of Jewish Writers, Artists and Scientists now supported the new line on Palestine. Brainin had plans to expand the Committee's activities, including the establishment of an international English-language periodical and a proposed international conference. "Needless to say," he wrote to B.Z. Goldberg in May of 1947, "the attitude of the USSR to Palestine has clarified the atmosphere and should make these projects realizable on a broader basis than previously anticipated."[15] Goldberg wrote to Mikheols and Fefer a few days later, ecstatic that the Gromyko speech had defused some of the "anti-Soviet hysteria that is now dominating the American scene." The Committee was trying hard "to counteract this trend in the Jewish world," and Goldberg was convinced that Gromyko "has done wonders in this respect. It took the wind out of the sails" of those who tried to make the Soviet Union appear as the enemy of the Jewish hopes in Palestine: "Now, at least the Zionist dogs must keep their tongues." The Jewish masses, Goldberg asserted, saw in the speech "a confirmation of their faith in the Soviet Union as the friend of the Jews and of all just causes. We are now mobilizing for greater activity, and we wish you to know about it and cooperate with us."[16]

In a memorandum to Einstein, Brainin asked the honorary president of Ambijan to take note of a large gathering in the Manhattan Center that had celebrated the 30th anniversary of the Bolshevik Revolution on November 12, 1947. Chaired by Brainin, it had been attended by some 3,500 people. The speakers included Nahum Goldmann, the prominent

Zionist and president of the World Jewish Congress, alongside Communists such as Shloime Almazov and Ben Gold of the International Fur and Leather Workers Union. The meeting "expressed gratitude to the Soviet Union for its granting of equal rights to its Jewish population, its outlawing of anti-Semitism, its establishment of an autonomous region in Biro-Bidjan and for its championing of a Jewish state in Palestine." The meeting, Brainin asserted, "unquestionably strengthened the prospects of friendly relations between American, Palestinian, and Soviet Jewries." On November 28 Ambijan sponsored a luncheon for representatives of "progressive Jewish organizations in Palestine."

That very week, the UN General Assembly debated the partition of Palestine. On November 26, Andrei Gromyko stood up again to support the creation of a Jewish state in the Middle East; three days later, the USSR and its allies all voted in favor of a Jewish state. Resolution 181 passed with 33 votes in favor, 13 against, 10 abstentions and one absent.

Brainin lost no time securing Gromyko as the guest of honor at the American-Soviet-Palestine Friendship Dinner to be held at the Hotel Commodore in New York on December 30, and Gromyko's photo appeared on the cover of a brochure publicizing the event. The brochure declared, "We hail with joy and special satisfaction the decision of the United Nations approving the creation of an independent Jewish state in Palestine. The fulfillment of the national aspirations of the Jewish people is an event of far-reaching significance, not only for the Jews, but for the whole of mankind." Other speakers at the dinner included Dr. Emanuel Neumann, president of the Zionist Organization of America; playwright Arthur Miller; and Max Levin of Ambijan. Brainin wrote to Einstein that the Soviet ambassador's speech, along with Neumann's, contributed to strengthening relations between the American, Palestinian and Soviet Jewish communities.[17]

Meanwhile, on December 12, 1947, Alexander Bittelman told the National Jewish Commission of the CPUSA, which had been formed in 1946, that in order to secure Jewish rights, Communists must support a third party candidacy under Henry Wallace in the 1948 presidential election. The UN resolution to establish Arab and Jewish democratic states in Palestine, "a historic step toward the realization of a dream of centuries," was due primarily to the efforts of the Soviet Union, which was promoting the national aspirations of the Jewish people. President Truman, on the other hand, could not be trusted to help implement the resolution. American imperialism would try "to make the Jewish state its puppet" and, in the interests of "Wall Street," would prolong friction between the Arabs and Jews to "obstruct the economic unity and the political co-operation of the two states." In this it would be aided both by pro-fascist Arabs and by reactionary Zionists. Bittelman spent considerable time trying to demonstrate that Communist support of a Jewish state in Palestine was not a capitulation to "the bourgeois nationalist and chauvinist ideology and official policies of Zionism" but was entirely compatible with Marxist theory. The "erroneous identification of Jewish statehood with Zionism was responsible for many past errors of American Jewish Communists" and had been rectified by the party in 1946, when it had formed the Commission.[18]

When Leo Isacson won the 24th Congressional district in the Bronx in a special election held on February 17, 1948, his victory was in large part due to perceived Soviet support for a Jewish state. Isacson, a member of Bronx Lodge 746 of the JPFO, was a member of the ALP from the time of its inception in 1936. He had served in the New York state assembly in 1945-1946. The prominent New York Communist Lillian Gates wrote in *Political Affairs* that Isacson had won the election because Jewish Communists and Zionists had joined hands."[19] His victory "symbolized the fighting policy of the third party and the Communist Party for the establishment of Israel, and was an important factor for launching the Progressive Party."[20]

Congressman Isacson would soon travel to the newly founded state of Israel. "As a Zionist since boyhood," he declared upon his return, he had for more than 30 years wished to make the journey. Isacson spoke in Yiddish to Holocaust survivors who had sought a new life "in the long-promised Jewish national homeland" and whose "jubilation knew no bounds" when the new state was proclaimed. He observed that many people in the new state were angry at President Truman's continuing arms embargo, in effect since November 1947; they considered Henry Wallace, the Progressive Party candidate in the forthcoming November 1948 presidential election, to be a friend of Israel. Isacson compared the defense of Jerusalem to the Battle of Stalingrad and was convinced that "the Jewish people will emerge victorious in their heroic defense of Israel." He called upon the U.S. to end its "betrayal" of Israel and grant immediate de jure recognition to the new state.

The new Progressive Party called for the admission of Israel to the United Nations, the extension to Israel of financial assistance, and American help to transport displaced persons who wished to emigrate from Europe to Israel. It also appealed to Arabs to accept the UN decision to create two states in Palestine. Arabs should refuse "to be used as tools in a war against Israel on behalf of British and American monopolies, for the latter are the enemies of both Arabs and Jews."[21]

But the Isacson victory had served as a warning to Truman. By May he had become decidedly more pro-Zionist. He extended de facto recognition to the new state of Israel almost immediately following its proclamation on May 14 (though de jure recognition was delayed until

January 31, 1949).²² In the November 1948 general election, when the ALP served as the New York state arm of Wallace's Progressive Party, Isacson lost his district seat to a Democrat. Other ALP candidates in the Bronx in November 1948 included Albert E. Kahn, a member of the CPUSA and president of the JPFO, and Leon Straus of the Communist-run Furrier's Union; neither was victorious.²³

Henry Wallace remained a supporter of the pro-Soviet Jewish left after his loss. On February 21, 1949, at the annual Ambijan dinner in Newark, he expressed his belief that "God has given the Jewish people a sacred mission—the mission of building world peace and understanding." Israel and Birobidzhan were "mighty monuments" to this vision: while both were of great symbolic value to the Jews of the world, each was "a bridge between different types of civilizations." The Jewish people, in Birobidzhan and in Israel, were destined "to contribute enormously to an understanding between the Anglo-Saxon and the Slavic worlds."²⁴

Ambijan had sent a telegram of congratulations to David Ben-Gurion, chair of the executive committee of the Jewish Agency for Palestine in Tel Aviv, after the historic November 1947 vote in the UN General Assembly calling for the partition of Palestine: "the age-old dream of the Jewish people is about to be realized," it said, thanks to the united leadership of the U.S. and Soviet Union. "We wish for the Jewish State of Palestine enduring peace, prosperity and serenity."²⁵

J.M. Budish explained the Soviet decision to support a Jewish state in Palestine as the logical outcome of its policy of allowing each national group a right to self-determination, which had already been demonstrated internally by the creation of a Jewish region in Birobidzhan.²⁶ Budish declared that "The cooperation of American Jews with both Palestine and Birobidjan will make an invaluable contribution to the rehabilitation of the Jewish people and the preservation and development of Jewish culture."²⁷

In January 1948, Jenofsky noted that Ambijan would be making plans to celebrate the 20th anniversary of the initial proclamation making Birobidzhan a Jewish area of settlement. But, he added in a letter to Morris Stern, "1948 will also be the year in which a Jewish country will be established in Palestine, or, to put it better...in *erets yisroel*."²⁸ When Budish sent out invitations for a grand celebratory concert to be held at Carnegie Hall on April 17, marking the 20th anniversary of Birobidzhan, he reassured recipients that "The warm support given by the Delegation of the Soviet Union to the decision of the United Nations for the establishment of an independent Jewish state in Palestine is conclusive proof that there is no competition between Palestine and Birobidjan." An Ambijan pamphlet remarked that "The peaceful development of the Jewish statehood in Birobidjan with the friendly cooperation of all the peoples of the Soviet Union, encourages and stimulates the implementation of the U.N. decision in favor of the state of Israel."[29] Budish wrote in an editorial in the *Ambijan Bulletin* that "The fact that the Jews have gained all the attributes of a nation in Birobidjan contributed enormously to bringing about the United Nations decision in favor of an independent Jewish state in Palestine." For if Jews had the inherent right to build a state within the Soviet Union, there was no reason to deny that same right to the Jews of Palestine.[30] Another editorial stated that "the bonds between the people of Israel on the one hand and the Jews of the U.S.S.R. and the United States are growing stronger." It was "this spirit of unity" that should animate the entire Jewish community.[31]

Throughout 1948, then, despite worsening east-west tensions, Ambijan still appeared to retain its organizational cohesiveness. It could still attract the goodwill and cooperation of national politicians, thanks in large measure to its support for the new Jewish state. It had branches in 24 cities; its organizers anticipated further expansion. No doubt the group's vitality depended more on its support for a Jewish state in Palestine than on its work in Birobidzhan. In any event, local Ambijan branches were full of enthusiasm for both these Jewish polities.

On March 9, 1948, at a meeting of the Bronx Branch, Zina Getmansky, the chair, expressed her doubt concerning the prospects of a Jewish state in Palestine; she believed that Birobidzhan would emerge as the sole Jewish state in the world. Abraham Jenofsky emphatically disagreed, stating that no one should ever doubt that a Jewish state would also be established in Palestine. By May 25, when the Bronx branch, in conjunction with the Manhattan branch, held its third annual Einstein Fund luncheon at the Waldorf-Astoria, Getmansky seemed to be more in agreement with Jenofsky: she spoke of the importance, for the survival of the entire Jewish people, of the "two Jewish states in the far and the near east."[32]

On March 14, Isacson's victory was celebrated at a conference of the Bronx Ambijan. The audience of 150, representing 32 organizations, were told by the chair, Jacob Levenson, that Isacson's election demonstrated that the electorate was opposed to the administration's policy on Palestine. Levenson emphasized that the Soviet Union was the only country that advocated a Jewish state in Palestine. J.M. Budish denounced those elements in the U.S. for whom "oil is more important than a Jewish State in Palestine"; he called on the Jews of the Bronx to aid in the building of a Jewish republic within the USSR, which, he claimed, would also help in the promotion of a Jewish state in Palestine.[33]

On May 2, the Bronx Ambijan scheduled a symposium featuring rabbis Abraham Bick and Mayer Israel Herman of the Brith Sholem

Congregation; the rabbis were to address the question, "Is There a Common Bond of Mutual Interest and Aspirations between the Jewish States—Palestine and Birobidjan." The event attracted 400 people, who commenced the proceedings by singing both the "Star-Spangled Banner" and "Hatikvah," the new Israeli national anthem. Rabbi Herman, the secretary of the Bronx board of rabbis, asserted that "support for Birobidjan will also help to strengthen the Jewish state in Palestine." Rabbi Bick agreed. The audience adopted a resolution urging President Truman to lift immediately the U.S. embargo on arms to the new Jewish state in Palestine, and to grant it full diplomatic recognition.[34]

At the Einstein Fund luncheon held at the Waldorf-Astoria Hotel in New York on May 25 by the Bronx and Manhattan branches of Ambijan, Jacob B. Aronoff stated that "Our sisters and brothers are fighting heroically to strengthen the newly-born state of Israel. Israel is fighting not only for its Jewish homeland, it is today in the forefront of the struggle for democracy." The struggle for Jewish rights was world-wide. "We must get used to the idea of two Jewish states. There are five Anglo-Saxon states; seven Arab states; seven Slav states; and three Scandinavian states. With the dispersion of Jews all over the world, one state cannot meet all the needs of all the Jews everywhere," he told them. At a later meeting of the two branches, he declared that Birobidzhan would preserve and develop the cultural values created in Yiddish, while Israel would preserve and develop those values created in Hebrew.[35]

Morris Olken, while on a western trip, spoke to a gathering of professors and students at the University of California campus at Berkeley on February 26, 1948 on the topic "Birobidzhan—Eretz Israel: Two Countries, One People."[36] On June 5, the Los Angeles Ambijan heard Zishe Weinper, the Yiddish poet, essayist and editor, general secretary of the YKUF and a contributor to its journal *Yidishe Kultur*, tell them that they were celebrating not just the 14th anniversary of the JAR, but also "the birth of a Jewish nation in *erets yisroel*." He said that "a two-thousand-year old dream was becoming a reality in front of our eyes," and reminded them that, had the Nazis not been defeated at Stalingrad, none of this would have come to pass. The annual conference on November 13-14 sent a message of solidarity to Israel.[37] In Berkeley, Aronoff spoke to the Ambijan East Bay Branch on August 10 on "Jewish Statehood in the Near East (Israel) and in the Far East (Birobidjan)."[38] The September-October 1948 *Nailebn-New Life* included a poem, entitled "Birobidzhan un yisroel," which began with the line, "From the Jordan to the Bira, From the Negev to Bidzhan." The author was Sarah Fel-Yellin, a member of the recently formed Esther Levitt Women's Club in Los Angeles and a vice-president of the Southern California Ambijan. Fel-Yellin may not have been a great poet, but her sentiments were clear: There were two Jewish states in the world, and Ambijan supported both.[39]

The Chicago Ambijan drafted a cable on May 12 to David Ben-Gurion, extending congratulations upon the impending declaration of the new Jewish state. "On this day when the Jewish state of Eretz Israel is coming into being we extend to the newly formed government of the Jewish state and to the Jewish people of Palestine our heartfelt greetings and best wishes for the stabilization and continued progress and prosperity and for peace and security of the Jewish state." The telegram was signed by Solomon Jesmer, the president, and 19 other members of the executive committee.[40] "The world will be enriched by the two Jewish States...Palestine and Birobidjan should and will maintain close cultural ties with each other and with the rest of the world," Jesmer asserted. "We in the United States must see the historical significance of the co-existence of these two Jewish States and cooperate with both of them."[41]

The Chicago Ambijan celebrated these two "historic events" at a concert on June 19, 1948, in a "striking demonstration of the unity of the Jewish people at this decisive moment." Judge Harry M. Fisher spoke of the importance of Birobidzhan and Israel. "For the Jewish people badly need *both*," he stated. Indeed, it was because of his lifelong devotion to the cause of Zionism that he so appreciated the significance of Jewish statehood in Birobidzhan. "These two Jewish States must and should live in peace and friendly cooperation with each other," said Jesmer, when the Chicago committee presented an ambulance to Max Swiren, Chicago president of Americans for Haganah. "We are certain that close cultural ties will develop between them. Friends of Birobidjan are friends of Israel....May Israel live and prosper!" Swiren responded that this gesture proved that almost all American Jews were united in their support and defense of Israel. In Cincinnati, a lawn party held on July 25 on the grounds of the Bureau of Jewish Federations raised $500 both for the settlement of war orphans in Birobidzhan and for a fund for Israel, reported the secretary, Mollie Tenenholtz.[42]

Jenofsky announced that the November 1948 national committee meeting of Ambijan would celebrate both the 20th anniversary of Birobidzhan and the creation of the new state of Israel—the two Jewish states in the near and far east.[43] Budish's letter of invitation for the annual national dinner, to be held at the Hotel Commodore on November 21, noted that Ambijan would be marking "the general recognition of the right of the Jews to nationhood. This right was first given the Jews by the Soviet Union. At present, the Soviet Union is the most consistent and warm supporter of the independence and territorial integrity of Israel." Budish was adamant that Ambijan's program "on behalf of

Birobidjan, peace, and the independence of Israel" would be "forcefully advanced." The national committee "found equal inspiration" in both Jewish states.[44]

The meeting included a session devoted to "Birobidjan and Israel." There were reports and addresses from Max Levin, B.Z. Goldberg, Joseph Morgenstern, Rubin Saltzman, general secretary of the JPFO, and others. Levin outlined the attitude of Ambijan to Birobidzhan and Israel; both states, he declared, were "marking triumphs in the struggle of the Jewish people for the achievement of full equality." He referred to the decisive part played by the Soviet Union in the establishment of the Jewish state and in the defense of its independence and territorial integrity. This was why, Levin reminded his audience, "May 7th, 1934 will forever remain a red calendar day in the history of the Jewish people." Senator Claude Pepper spoke of the "Jewish heroes" fighting to gain the Negev for the new state of Israel. A resolution was passed asserting that "the elevation of Birobidjan to the status of a Jewish Autonomous Region has equally made effective [the Jewish] right to statehood." Soviet recognition of this right "has opened new vistas for the Jewish people everywhere and it was one of the most important factors that enabled the Jewish people to secure the recognition of their right to statehood from the United Nations, when the U.N. decided in favor of the establishment of the independent state of Israel."

Budish lauded the establishment of Israel, and noted that its fight against aggression was aided by "invaluable allies among the new-born peoples' democracies." He announced at the meeting that Ambijan would now support a children's home in Tel Aviv and finance a book-binding training workshop in Haifa for the reorientation of refugee girls.[45] The workshop was located at the Haifa Home maintained by the Women's League for Palestine, and the League issued a statement expressing the hope that this cooperation with Ambijan "will mark a significant advance in world Jewish unity in behalf of constructive action for the state of Israel." Arline Meyer, executive secretary of the League, sent a letter to Budish on December 6 thanking Ambijan for a check for $3,000 for the maintenance of the workshop.[46]

Ambijan organized a New York Area Conference on March 5-6, 1949, at the New School for Social Research. Jenofsky stated that Gromyko's speech had opened "a new stage in the history of the Jewish people." On the other hand, Jenofsky remarked, the American and British governments had tried to prevent the creation of the Jewish state or, at the very least, to reduce its territory after it had declared its independence. When the first session of the Israeli Knesset convened in February 1949, the Soviet emissary to Israel attended as a guest; the ambassadors of Britain and the U.S., in contrast, declined to attend. The Soviet Union and the new democracies had in many ways "strengthened the hands of the heroic fighters of Israel who have achieved such colossal victories." The Soviet policy in regards to Israel was not based on political calculation, stated Jenofsky; rather, it was the result of the Soviet determination to solve the national question for minority peoples. The Soviets, he continued, had already solved such problems within their own borders. By establishing Birobidzhan as a Jewish national region, the Soviets had provided Jews with the means to become a full-fledged nation. Ambijan was now supporting various projects in the new Jewish state of Israel.[47]

Moishe Katz summed up the first months of Israel's existence in the January 1949 issue of *Nailebn-New Life*. The emergence of the state, and its heroic struggle against the enemies that tried to choke it at birth, had captured the attention of Jews all over the world. It had come into being over the opposition of the mandatory power, Great Britain; even the U.S. had been having second thoughts just a few months after the UN resolution, in November 1947, to partition Palestine. After Washington placed an arms embargo on the new Jewish state, only the valiant effort of the Soviet Union and its east European allies had enabled Israel to prevail.[48]

In an editorial celebrating Israel's first anniversary in May 1949, Jenofsky again remarked on the help the fledgling state had received from the Soviet Union. This timely assistance had enabled the state to achieve military victory over its enemies, which included not just Arab states, but Britain itself. Indeed, Jenofsky asserted, even the U.S. State Department "placed stones on the road" through various machinations and manoeuvres, to prevent Israel from achieving a convincing and historic victory. And when Israel had applied to join the United Nations, only the Soviet Union had come out strongly in its favor in the Security Council; the other great powers had been more tentative.[49]

Budish met with left-wing Israeli delegates at the first Soviet-sponsored World Peace Congress in Paris in the spring of 1949. He discussed with them the support Ambijan would be providing for the children's home in Tel Aviv; they presented him with pictures of the home. Budish described his three meetings with the Israelis at a Hunter College celebration in New York on May 8 and again at a conference held at the Palmer House in Chicago on May 15. The Chicago conference, reported A.M. Margolis, heard how "the great Jewish community in Israel was building and developing our Jewish country guided by the ideology of collective creativity."[50] Fan Bakst visited Israel in the autumn of 1949. She spoke of her trip at a meeting of the Bronx Ambijan on October 6 and at the Sea Gate, Brooklyn branch on November 15.[51]

At its December 1949 national conference, J.M. Budish reported that expenditures in Israel had amounted to $11,000 for the year. He recommended that Ambijan greatly increase its assistance to "progressive institutions" in Israel, including those that operated children's homes and schools. Ambijan responded to appeals from Israel for aid "with the full understanding that there is only one general sound foundation for Jewish reconstruction and the achievement of full Jewish equality everywhere, namely the development and strengthening of international friendship, and especially friendship with the Soviet Union, as an indispensable basis for world peace."

Paul Novick linked the two Jewish centers. The Soviets had created a precedent by establishing a Jewish polity in Birobidzhan, a polity recognizing the need for national equality and self-determination, and the need to help oppressed peoples—values which would later enable the Jews in Palestine to create their own state. The USSR played an historic role in the birth of Israel because it was committed to the self-determination and the equality of all nations. It was because the Soviet Union based its foreign policy on such fundamental principles that it was so steadfast and reliable. In contrast, Novick remarked, Britain had acquiesced in the annexation by King Abdullah of Jordan of east Jerusalem and the part of Palestine held by the Arab Legion. Novick concluded by stating that Ambijan must continue to support the progressive elements in the Jewish state, as opposed to those who would move the country into the imperialist camp.[52]

In order that Ambijan might become "a more significant factor in the fight for freedom and friendship," wrote Jenofsky, "the work for rehabilitation was being broadened to include not just Birobidzhan but also the progressive elements in Israel."[53] Ambijan was now raising funds for a children's home and school in Tel Aviv; a bookbinding training shop for refugee girls in Haifa; dental clinics for two kibbutzim; and paper supplies for the League for Israel-Soviet Friendship. In 1950, just before its demise, it sent a delegation to Israel to arrange for further rehabilitation efforts, including extension of its support for children's homes and help in establishing a cooperative to produce electrical supplies for the building industry.[54]

Local chapters remained enthusiastic. The New Jersey Ambijan dinner, held in Newark on February 21, 1950, was addressed by Budish, who would soon be travelling to Israel on a mission for Ambijan. Nathan Mack, a prominent member in Newark, left for Israel in mid-May 1950, taking with him a $500 check for the children's home Ambijan now supported in Tel Aviv. On March 12, the Atlanta Ambijan Mothers Club hosted a dinner at which national organizer Morris L. Olken "gave a most inspiring talk" about the projects Ambijan was supporting in Israel. Pat Paul, the secretary, wrote that the club "was glad to hear of the further undertaking of even greater projects in Israel in the near

CHAPTER SEVEN

future."⁵⁵ At a dinner celebration for Birobidzhan and Israel on April 30 at the Golden Slipper Restaurant in Philadelphia, Harry Epstein, chair of the branch, introduced Budish, who spoke about his visit to Israel. The event brought in $500 in contributions. The Bronx and Manhattan chapters held their fifth annual luncheon at the Waldorf-Astoria on May 17; the audience heard from various Ambijan officials and from Stella Adler. Jacob B. Aronoff and Budish appealed for them to provide maximum support for Ambijan's projects in Israel; these, they said, were an essential part of Ambijan's philosophy and program. The audience heeded their message, donating $560 for the children's home in Tel Aviv.⁵⁶

Over 1,000 people gathered at the Embassy Auditorium in Los Angeles on March 25 to hear Albert Kahn, who had returned from a session of the executive committee of the Soviet-sponsored World Peace Council held in Stockholm. The meeting was chaired by Aaron Kertman, chair of the Southern California Division. Samuel Rosenfeld of the Los Angeles Ambijan made an appeal for Ambijan projects in Israel, which netted about $4,000. Ambijan had assumed additional obligations in Israel, by becoming partners with the educational and social network *Agudath Tarbut La'am* (Association for Popular Culture). Budish and Gina Medem spoke on August 5 at a celebration for Birobidzhan and Israel in Los Angeles, attended by 1,200 people; $1,000 was collected for Ambijan. As late as May 5, 1951 the Southern California Division, now known as the Southern California Committee for Jewish Rehabilitation, held a meeting to raise money for *Agudath Tarbut La'am*. In Petaluma, too, money was being raised for *Agudath Tarbut La'am* by supporters of Ambijan, including some people in the local Poale Zion group. The Ambijan chapter raised $400 at a March 10 party. However, this activity caused a rift in the community, when the local Labor Zionists contacted the Israeli Embassy in Washington to ask for more information about *Agudath Tarbut La'am*. An official told them that the money would be used by the Israeli Communist Party. The local Ambijan supporters in turn called this a "smear campaign" that would only result in hardship for needy children's homes. In the resulting battle, the left-wingers were ousted from the Jewish Community Center.⁵⁷

One of Ambijan's last projects was the convening, together with the American Committee of Jewish Writers, Artists and Scientists, of a New York Area Conference for International Friendship and Peace at the Barbizon-Plaza Hotel in New York on May 6-7, 1950. The conference, attended by 456 delegates, concluded with a concert at Town Hall. Budish and Dr. Lewis Schatzov, vice-chairman of the Board of Directors of Ambijan, who had been part of an Ambijan delegation to a peace conference in Tel Aviv on March 10-11, reported on conditions in Israel, as did Joseph Morgenstern, who had just returned from spending 2 ½ months in the new Jewish state. They complained about the rightward drift of the "right-Socialist-clerical regime" in Israel and expressed their hope that the "progressive creative forces" would overcome these tendencies, to prevent Israel from becoming an American pawn in the Cold War. The conference extended greetings to both Birobidjan and Israel on the occasion of their 16th and second anniversaries, respectively. After an appeal from Abraham Jenofsky, $7,000 in cash and pledges was collected.[58]

On May 8, Ambijan's board of directors met to discuss the activities of the organization. They decided that support for the "progressive" movement in Israel was more important than aid to Birobidzhan and that from now on very little would go to the JAR. Many Ambijan members were now visiting Israel; three had recently travelled to Israel from New York, as had Joseph Morgenstern from Cleveland.[59] From January 1 through June 1, 1950, Ambijan spent $20,747 on goods to Israel, Birobidzhan, Stalingrad, Poland, France and Belgium.[60] The U.S. Embassy in Tel Aviv asked the FBI to look into Ambijan's links in Israel; it was determined that the organization was "working in complete cooperation with the Communist Party of Israel." As well, the FBI discovered that Cleveland businessman "Jay" Morgenstern, while in Israel on behalf of Ambijan, had signed an agreement with an Israeli cooperative, dated April 19, 1950, to establish a corporation to produce electrical fittings. A further memo noted that "Jay" was in fact Joseph Morgenstern. [61] By 1951, Ambijan had effectively become a support group for the pro-Soviet Israeli left.

Endnotes

1. "Summary of the Proceedings of the National Conference of the American Birobidjan Committee (Ambijan)," *Ambijan Bulletin* 4, 1 (June 1945): 13, 22.
2. M.L. Olken, "The significance of Biro-Bidjan," *Nailebn-New Life* 18, 6 (June 1944): 23-24.
3. "Rezolutsyes ongenumen bay dem natsyonaln plenum fun icor," *Nailebn-New Life* 18, 4 (May 1944): 17.
4. "Barkley Backs Appeal," *New York Times*, March 11, 1946: 12; Ambijan press release in United States Territorial Collection, RG117, Box 57, folder "Icor" 17/16, YIVO; "Declaration of Principles and Program," *Ambijan Bulletin* 5, 2 (April 1946): 11 (emphasis in original).
5. Moses Miller, *Crisis in Palestine* (New York: New Century Publishers, September 1946): 3, 6, 11, 14-32.
6. Alexander Bittelman, *Palestine: What is the Solution?* (New York: Morning Freiheit Association, 1946), 4-7.
7. Alexander Bittelman, *Program for Survival: The Communist Position on the Jewish Question* (New York: New Century Publishers, January 1947): 19-23, 34. Bittelman was born in 1890 and died in 1982.
8. "Ambijan Aids Zionist Cause," *Sentinel*, Chicago, July 25, 1946, 22; Minutes, July 12, 1946; Aug. 26, 1946, in Collection No. 20: Chicago Chapter, American Birobidjan Committee, Series A. Minutes. Folder 3: Minutes, 1946, Chicago Jewish Archives.
9. For Gromyko's speech, see Thomas J. Hamilton, "Russia Urges U.N. to Split Palestine, Failing Dual State," *New York Times*, May 15, 1947, 1, 9; J. M. B[udish], "Soviet Delegation to the United Nations on the Palestine Problem," *Ambijan Bulletin* 6, 4 (May-June 1947): 3; "Andrei Gromyko's Statement on Palestine," *Ambijan Bulletin* 6, 4 (May-June 1947): 6-9. "Excerpts of Speeches of Gromyko, el-Khouri," *New York Times*, May 15, 1947, 8; United Nations General Assembly, First Special Session, May 14, 1947, UN Document A/PV77. Much has been written about the Soviet position on Palestine at this time. See, for instance, Arnold Krammer, *The Forgotten Friendship: Israel and the Soviet Bloc, 1947-53* (Urbana, IL: University of Illinois Press, 1974); Yaakov Ro'i, *Soviet Decision Making in Practice: the USSR and Israel, 1947-1954* (New Brunswick, NJ: Transaction Books, 1980); and Laurent Rucker, *Moscow's Surprise: The Soviet-Israeli Alliance of 1947-1949*. Cold War International History Project Working Paper Series #46 (Washington, DC: Woodrow Wilson International Center for Scholars, 2005). See also the two-volume collection of *Documents on Israeli-Soviet Relations, 1941-1953* (London: Frank Cass, 2000), jointly produced by the Israeli and Russian Foreign Ministries and the Israeli and Russian State Archives and edited by Eytan Bentsur and B.L. Kolokolov. Most of the Arab world had possessed a sympathetic attitude towards Nazi Germany, a fact which also earned them the enmity of the USSR.

10 Alfred D. Low, *Soviet Jewry and Soviet Policy* (New York: Columbia University Press, 1990), 212.
11 The audience of approximately 300 people listened to Yiddish singer Isa Kremer and donated $950. They also heard a speech by Rabbi Abraham J. Bick, who was becoming an increasingly prominent member of Ambijan; at this time, he was already a member of the national committee. This information is contained on pp. 17-18 of a 42-page FBI report dated Feb. 4, 1947, submitted by Edward Scheidt, Special Agent in Charge, originally in NY File 100-42538. File 100-99898, Section 2, FOIPA No. 416152, Ambijan.
12 B.Z. Goldberg, "Ikh kum fun yidisher front in erets yisroel," *Der Tog*, Oct. 12, 1946, p 5; B.Z. Goldberg, "Der yidisher vidershtand in erets yisroel," *Der Tog*, Oct. 13, 1946, 1.
13 J.M. Budish, "This Anniversary and the Jewish People," *Soviet Russia Today* 16, 7 (November 1947): 25.
14 Gina Medem, "Tsum geburt fun a yidisher melikhe," *Nailebn-New Life* 20, 10 (December 1947): 1-4. See also historian Raphael Mahler's article "Di arabishe feudale reyaktsye in atake oyf medines yisroel," *Nailebn-New Life* 21, 6 (June 1948): 1-5.
15 Letter from Joseph Brainin to B.Z. Goldberg, Niantic, CT, May 20, 1947; B. Z. Goldberg papers, Box 69, Jewish Antifascist Committee in the USSR; American Committee of Jewish Writers, Artists, and Scientists, Inc., folder "American Committee of Jewish Writers, Artists and Scientists."
16 Letter from B.Z. Goldberg to Itsik Fefer and Shloime Mikhoels, New York, May, 28, 1947; B.Z. Goldberg papers, Box 69, Jewish Antifascist Committee in the USSR; American Committee of Jewish Writers, Artists, and Scientists, Inc., folder "American Committee of Jewish Writers, Artists and Scientists."
17 Memorandum to Albert Einstein from Joseph Brainin, [early 1948]; microfilm ZP-*PBM n.c. Reel 122, No. 28, Jewish Division, New York Public Library, New York; "American-Soviet-Palestine Friendship Dinner," brochure in the B.Z. Goldberg papers, Box 79, A-Antonovsky, folder "American Committee of Jewish Writers, Artists."
18 Alexander Bittelman, *To Secure Jewish Rights: The Communist Position* (New York: New Century Publishers, March 1948): 16-22, 28-36. For CP support of Wallace in 1948, see Thomas W. Devine, "The Communists, Henry Wallace, and the Progressive Party of 1948," *Continuity: A Journal of History* 26 (Spring 2003): 33-79.
19 Paul Buhle, *Marxism in the United States*, 193. Jews made up at least 35 per cent of the district's electorate—some estimates went as high as 55 per cent—and were by far the largest single ethnic group in it. David J. Saposs, *Communism in American Politics* (Washington: Public Affairs Press, 1960), 82.
20 Lillian Gates, "New York's 1949 Elections," *Political Affairs* 28, 12 (December 1949): 52. However, she noted, the vote for the ALP had dropped considerably

in the 1949 New York City municipal elections because of "serious failure to dispel the confusion created by the concerted and false charges of anti-Semitism in the Soviet Union."

21 Leo Isacson, *Journey to Israel* (New York: Progressive Party, [1948]): 2-3, 5-8, 10, 14-16. See also I.F. Stone, *This is Israel* (New York: Boni and Gaer, 1948), which also was meant to help the Progressive cause among Jews. It received a favorable review in the *Ambijan Bulletin* 7, 6 (October-November 1948): 15.

22 There is a wealth of material on this period. See, for example, Michael Joseph Cohen, *Truman and Israel* (Berkeley, CA: University of California Press, 1990) and Ronald Radosh and Allis Radosh, *A Safe Haven: Harry S Truman and the Founding of Israel* (New York: Harper/Collins 2009).

23 Isacson died in 1996 at the age of 86. See his obituary in *Jewish Currents* 50, 10 (November 1996): 40.

24 Henry A. Wallace, "American Support of Birobidjan Hopeful Sign Toward Peace," *Ambijan Bulletin* 8, 2 (March-April 1949): 7-9; "Henry Wallace Guest Speaker at Newark Anniversary Dinner," *Nailebn-New Life* 22, 4 (April 1949): 23.

25 Ambijan press release of Dec. 3, 1947, in the Kalmen Marmor papers, 1873-1955, RG205, Microfilm group 495, folder 585 "Ambidzhan-korespondents, 1946-1950," YIVO; "Ambijan Cables Congratulations to Jewish Agency in Palestine," *Ambijan Bulletin* 7, 1 (January 1948): 2.

26 J.M. B[udish], "Palestine and Birobidjan," *Ambijan Bulletin* 7, 1 (January 1948): 3-4, 11.

27 Circular letter from J.M. Budish, New York, Jan. 29, 1948, in the Kalmen Marmor papers, 1873-1955, RG205, Microfilm group 495, folder 585 "Ambidzhan-korespondents, 1946-1950," YIVO.

28 Letter from Abraham Jenofsky to Morris Stern, Jan. 7, 1948; in the Morris Stern papers, RG231, Box 1, unnamed folder, YIVO.

29 Letter of invitation from J.M. Budish, New York, March 15, 1948, in United States Territorial Collection, RG117, Box 57, folder "Icor" 17/16, YIVO; *In Behalf of Jewish War Orphans and New Jewish Settlers in Birobidjan* (New York: American Birobidjan Committee (Ambijan), [1948].

30 J.M. B[udish], "Twenty Years of Birobidjan," *Ambijan Bulletin* 7, 2 (March-April 1948): 5.

31 "Jewish Unity on a World Scale," *Ambijan Bulletin* 7, 4 (June-July 1948): 3.

32 "Organizational Activities," *Ambijan Bulletin* 7, 4 (June-July 1948): 14-15. Information on the March 9, 1948 Bronx meeting is on p. 58 of an 82-page FBI report dated Feb. 23, 1949, submitted by Edward Scheidt, Special Agent in Charge, originally in NY File 100-42538. File 100-99898, Section 3, FOIPA No. 416152, Ambijan.

33 The information on the March 14, 1948 Bronx meeting is in FBI reports from Edward Scheidt, Special Agent in Charge, New York, to J. Edgar Hoover, dated April 8, 1948, and April 17, 1948, all originally in NY File 100-42538.

File 100-99898, Section 3, FOIPA No. 416152, Ambijan. See also the 4-page bilingual pamphlet *Call to Bronx Ambijan Conference – Ruf tsu der bronx ambijan konferents* (New York: Bronx Ambijan and Bronx Jewish Council, 1948).

34 "Organizational Activities," *Ambijan Bulletin* 7, 3 (May 1948): 14; A.J. [Abraham Jenofsky], "Organizatsye un arbet," *Nailebn-New Life* 21, 6 (June 1948): 18-19.

35 "Organizational Activities," *Ambijan Bulletin* 7, 4 (June-July 1948): 15; "Organizational Activities," *Ambijan Bulletin* 7, 6 (October-November 1948): 13.

36 M.L. Olken, ""Di organizatsyes un fraynt fun birobidzhan ibern land," *Nailebn-New Life* 21, 5 (May 1948): 8.

37 A Jenofsky, "Organizatsye un arbet," *Nailebn-New Life* 21, 8 (September-October 1948): 20; A. J. [Abraham Jenofsky], "Oranizatsye un arbet," *Nailebn-New Life* 22, 2 (February 1949): 19-20. Weinper, born in Trisk, Ukraine in 1892, came to New York in 1920. He published *Birobidzhan* (New York: Kultur tsvayg baym ICOR, 1935). He was a leader of the YKUF, which published *Dos z. vaynper-bukh* (New York: YKUF Farlag, 1962) in his honor.

38 "From Our Mail Bag," *Nailebn-New Life* 21, 8 (September-October 1948): 25

39 At a Bay Cities branch Purim gathering on March 12, 1949, she referred to Birobidzhan and Israel as "sister republics." Sarah Fel-Yellin, "Birobidzhan un yisroel," *Nailebn-New Life* 21, 8 (September-October 1948): 9; A.J. [Abraham Jenofsky], "Organizatsye un arbet," *Nailebn-New Life* 22, 4 (April 1949): 20-21. A few years later Sarah Fel-Yellin published *Tsu zun un freyd* (Los Angeles: Sore Fel-Yelin Bukh-Komitet, 1957).

40 Minutes, May 12, 1948; May 19, 1948, in Collection No. 20: Chicago Chapter, American Birobidjan Committee, Series A. Minutes. Folder 5: Minutes, 1948, Chicago Jewish Archives; photostat of the telegram, in Collection No. 20: Chicago Chapter, American Birobidjan Committee, Series D. Miscellaneous. Folder 21: Telegram to David Ben-Gurion, Chicago Jewish Archives.

41 Sol Jesmer, "Birobidjan—A Great Jewish Center," *Ambijan Bulletin* 7, 2 (March-April 1948): 6.

42 S. Jesmer, "Two Historic Events," *Ambijan Bulletin* 7, 5 (August-September 1948): 9; "Organizational Activities," *Ambijan Bulletin* 7, 5 (August-September 1948): 12-14 (emphasis in original); A. Jenofsky, "Organizatsye un arbet," *Nailebn-New Life* 21, 8 (September-October 1948): 21.

43 A Jenofsky, "Organizatsye un arbet," *Nailebn-New Life* 21, 8 (September-October 1948): 18.

44 Circular letter from J.M. Budish, New York, Sept. 27, 1948; in the Morris Stern papers, RG231, Box 1, folder "ICOR-Birobidzhan," YIVO.

45 "National Committee Maps Extended Program of Cooperation With Jewish Autonomous Region of Birobidjan," *Ambijan Bulletin* 7, 7 (December 1948): 3-5; Claude Pepper, "Keep up Your Great Fight—Continue Your Great

Work," *Ambijan Bulletin* 7, 7 (December 1948): 6-7; "Meeting of the National Committee," schedule, in the Kalmen Marmor papers, 1873-1955, RG205, Microfilm group 495, folder 585 "Ambidzhan-korespondents, 1946-1950," YIVO; "Resolution #2 Adopted at the Enlarged Meeting of the National Committee of Ambijan, November 20th and 21st, 1948—Commodore Hotel, New York, N.Y.", in United States Territorial Collection, RG117, Box 57, folder "Icor" 17/16, YIVO.

46 Undated Ambijan press release, New York, [probably late November1948]; in United States Territorial Collection, RG117, Box 57, folder "Icor" 17/16, YIVO. The League statement was published in an article, "Birobidjan Group to Give Workshop in Palestine," *New York Herald-Tribune,* Nov. 21, 1948, reprinted in the press release; letter from Arline Meyer to J.M. Budish, New York, Dec. 6, 1948, reprinted in "Organizational Activities," *Ambijan Bulletin* 8, 2 (March-April 1949): 15. See also "To Support Haifa Workshop," *New York Times*, Nov. 18, 1948, 6.

47 "Call to New York Area Conference marking the 15th Anniversary of the Jewish Autonomous Region—Birobidjan; Ruf tsu ale yidishe organizatsyes, landsmanshaftn, sosayties, fraternale ordn, froyen-okzileris, kongregayshons, trayd-unyons, un kultur-institutsyes tsu der konferents in new york un umgegnt tsum 15tn yubili fun birobidzhan alts yidishe autonomye gegnt"; brochure in the Morris Stern papers, RG231, Box 1, folder "ICOR-Birobidzhan," YIVO; "Barikht tsu der ambidzhan konferents," New York, March 5-6, 1949, mss; in the Abraham Jenofsky papers, RG734, Box 1, folder 5, YIVO.

48 Moishe Katz, "Der ershte yor fun der melikhe yisroel," *Nailebn-New Life* 22, 1 (January 1949): 1-3.

49 A. J. [Abraham Jenofsky], "Leyt artiklen," *Nailebn-New Life* 22, 5 (May 1949): 1. In the fall of 1948, Israel had applied for membership in the United Nations but failed to win the necessary majority in the Security Council. In the spring of 1949, the application was renewed, and Israel was admitted by the General Assembly on May 11, with 37 votes in favor, 12 against, and nine abstentions.

50 Circular letter from Bernard Parelhoff, secretary, Board of Directors, Ambijan, New York, May 25, 1949; Morris Stern papers, RG231, Box 1, unnamed folder, YIVO; "Organizational Activities," *Ambijan Bulletin* 8, 3 (July-August 1949): 13-14.

51 "Sea Gate Luncheon," *Ambijan Bulletin* 8, 4 (December 1949):13; Fan Bakst, "A Glimpse of the Children of Israel," *Ambijan Bulletin* 8, 4 (December 1949): 14.

52 A. Jenofsky, "Der baytrog fun ambidzhan in di letste tsvey yor," *Nailebn-New Life* 22, 10 (December 1949): 16-21; P. Novick, "Birobidzhan, yisroel un di sovyetishe politik," *Nailebn-New Life* 22, 9 (November 1949): 9-12 (emphasis in original); "Birobidjan, Israel, and World Peace," *Ambijan*

Bulletin 8, 4 (December 1949): 4; "Birobidjan and the Struggle for National Equality, International Friendship and Peace," *Ambijan Bulletin* 9, 1 (January-February 1950): 12; "Ambijan National Conference," *Ambijan Bulletin* 9, 1 (January-February 1950): 15; "Barikht tsu der natsyonaler konferents fun dem ambidzhan komitet," New York, Dec. 10-11, 1949, mss; in the Abraham Jenofsky papers, RG734, Box 1, folder 5, YIVO.

53 Letter from Abraham Jenofsky to Joshua Gershman, New York, Nov. 25, 1949; in the Joshua Gershman papers, F1412-1, Box 2, File 19, Archives of Ontario, Toronto. Gershman was a prominent Canadian Communist who edited the weekly bilingual Yiddish-English language *Vochenblat* and was a prominent leader of the Canadian Birobidjan Committee.

54 "Ambijan National Conference," *Ambijan Bulletin* 9, 1 (January-February 1950): 15; "Jewish Rehabilitation and World Peace," *Ambijan Bulletin*, 9, 2 (July-August 1950): 3. See the letter of thanks for the $5,000 Ambijan sent to support the Tel Aviv home in "Organizational Activities," *Ambijan Bulletin* 8, 2 (March-April 1949): 15.

55 "Newark Bids 'Bon Voyage' to Mr. & Mrs. Nathan Mack," *Ambijan Bulletin* 9, 2 (July-August 1950): 15; "New Jersey Ambijan Dinner Outstanding Success," *Nailebn-New Life* 23, 3 (March-April 1950): 23; "A fine Evening in Atlanta, Georgia," *Nailebn-New Life* 23, 3 (March-April 1950): 23. See also p. 12 of a 42-page report dated Oct. 27, 1950, submitted by Edward Scheidt, Special Agent in Charge, originally in NY File 100-42538. File 100-99898, Section 6, FOIPA No. 416152, Ambijan.

56 "Fifth Annual Waldorf Astoria Luncheon Held May 17, 1950," *Ambijan Bulletin* 9, 2 (July-August 1950): 14; "Dinner Celebration," *Nailebn-New Life* 23, 3 (March-April 1950): 21.

57 "Los Angeles" and "Petaluma, California," *Ambijan Bulletin* 9, 2 (July-August 1950): 15. The Southern California information is also on pp. 5-7 of the 46-page FBI report of R.B. Hood, Special Agent in Charge, May 9, 1950, originally in LA File 100-23652. File 100-99898, Section 5, FOIPA No. 416152, Ambijan; and FBI Memo from SAC, San Francisco, to Director, FBI, Jan. 29, 1952, originally in SF File 100-26751. File 100-99898, Section 6, FOIPA No. 416152, Ambijan.

58 "New York Area Conference Demands Outlawing of Atom Bomb," *Ambijan Bulletin* 9, 2 (July-August 1950): 6-7; J.M. Budish, "The Peace Movement in Israel," *Ambijan Bulletin* 9, 2 (July-August 1950): 8-9; "New York Area Conference Extends Greetings to Birobidjan and Israel," *Ambijan Bulletin* 9, 2 (July-August 1950): 16. This was the last *Ambijan Bulletin* published. See also pp. 1-7 of the FBI report from Special Agent in Charge, New York, to Director, FBI, June 7, 1950, originally in NY File 100-42538. File 100-99898, Section 5, FOIPA No. 416152, Ambijan. Joseph Morgenstern was born in 1889 in Russia and came to the U.S. in 1903. He became president of the Cleveland branch of the ICOR at its formation. See his letter to Reuben

Brainin, Cleveland, Jan. 2, 1929, inviting Brainin to speak in Cleveland, in Group III, Box a., folder "ICOR—Correspondence," Reuben Brainin Collection, JPL. He reminisced about his early life in America in his article "Cleveland Fifty Years Ago," *Jewish Life* 12, 1 (January 1958): 19-21, 46.

59 FBI report from Special Agent in Charge, New York, to Director, FBI, June 8 1950, originally in NY File 100-42538. File 100-99898, Section 5, FOIPA No. 416152, Ambijan.

60 This information is contained on p. 6 of a 42-page report dated Oct. 27, 1950, submitted by Edward Scheidt, Special Agent in Charge, originally in NY File 100-42538. File 100-99898, Section 6, FOIPA No. 416152, Ambijan.

61 Telegram from Los Angeles FBI Office to FBI Director, May 7, 1951; Department Memos from Special Agent in Charge in Los Angeles to FBI Director, Sept. 19, 1951, Oct. 6, 1951, and Nov. 1, 1951, originally in LA File 100-23652. File 100-99898, Section 6, FOIPA No. 416152, Ambijan.

Gina Medem, from *A Lebnsveg*

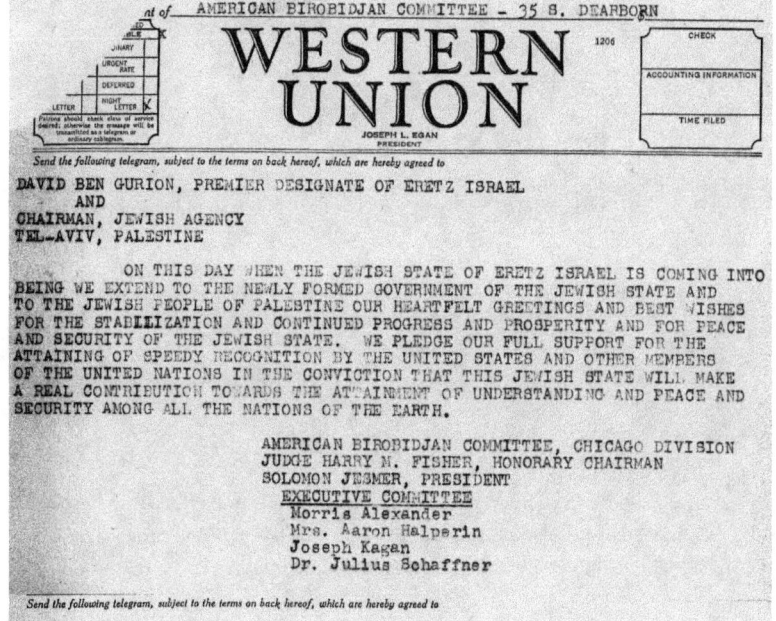

Chicago Ambijan telegram to David Ben-Gurion, May 12, 1948, Chicago Jewish Archives, Spertus Institute of Jewish Studies, Chicago

Andrei Gromyko on cover of flyer for American-Soviet-Palestine Friendship Dinner, Dec. 30, 1947, Schottenstein-Jesselson Library of the Herbert D. Katz Center for Advanced Judaic Studies at the University of Pennsylvania, Philadelphia

The Gathering Storm: McCarthyism, Cold War, and Decline

Despite their support for Israel, the post-war climate would prove fatal to Ambijan and other Jewish groups sympathetic to the USSR. The onset of the Cold War led to anti-Communist hysteria and the excesses of McCarthyism. Jewish "progressives" were open to charges of being dupes, if not indeed agents, of the Soviet Union.[1] Ambijan became increasingly marginalized in the American Jewish community; much of its work now consisted of trying to discredit the accounts of Soviet anti-Semitism that appeared with increasing frequency in the media.

When news of Shloime Mikhoels' death in January 1948, ostensibly as a result of a traffic accident, reached the United States, Ambijan meetings were held in his memory. At one memorial evening held in Chicago on February 14, Solomon Jesmer said that this "sudden and untimely loss" would be keenly felt; a recording of the speech Mikhoels had made when in Chicago in 1943 was played at the service. In Seattle, Harry Horowitz wrote that at a meeting of the branch held on February 2, they joined in mourning Mikhoels' "untimely death." At the national committee meeting in New York held later that year, Budish spoke of the "grief and distress" the members felt upon hearing the news of this "serious loss."[2] Paul Novick, in the *Morgn Frayhayt*, in an article entitled "Mikhoels is no More...," tried to reassure the readership: "If he were still able to tell us something he would say: the [Jewish] people must live!"[3] But if Novick suspected something was wrong, he did not elaborate. B.Z. Goldberg received a letter from the JAFC a month after Mikhoels' death that ended with the plea, "Do not forget about us."[4] He too said nothing. The pro-Soviet movements would for years be unable or unwilling to admit that Mikhoels' death was a murder engineered by Stalin to signal the start of a major anti-Jewish campaign in the USSR, one that would usher in the "black years" of Soviet Jewry.

Others were not so easily fooled. Typical of the increased scrutiny of events in the USSR were two reports on growing anti-Semitism in that country and the deteriorating situation in Birobidzhan, by Drew Middleton and C.L. Sulzberger, respectively, in the *New York Times* of February 13 and 15, 1948. Middleton reported that little was now being written about Birobidzhan in the general Soviet press. Sulzberger stated that Jews in actual fact comprised less than one-quarter the total population of 100,000 people in Birobidzhan and that the numbers of new settlers were very limited. One of the primary functions of the secret police in Birobidzhan was "to prevent disillusioned pioneers from departing."[5]

"The American people will not be misled by such flimsy fabrications," responded J.M. Budish in the Ambijan newsletter of March 1948. He refuted allegations that the region had "fallen into decay" and that Moscow had "lost interest in the area" with seven pages of predictably impressive statistics concerning population growth and economic development. The city of Birobidzhan, he insisted, had "many fine buildings, paved streets, asphalt sidewalks, substantial industries, producers' cooperatives, nurseries, kindergartens, schools, colleges, theaters, radio broadcasting stations, libraries, bookstore, a beautiful Park of Culture and Rest, a modern railroad station, an airport, two hotels, electric street lights, modern hospital, department stores, mechanized bakery, etc." The alleged "dilapidation" described in the *Times* had "no relationship whatever to the actual condition of the thriving and beautiful city," Budish reassured Ambijan supporters. As for the Soviet government having lost interest in Birobidzhan, Budish asserted that, on the contrary, the USSR "has devoted every effort" to the area's development. From the beginning, this "very realistic project" was intended to enable the Soviet Jews to develop a state of their own within the "multi-national structure of the Soviet Union." Budish insisted that the development of Birobidzhan had been carried out "with a greater measure of success than history records for any similar colonization project."

Budish rejected the possibility that in European areas of the USSR, "the anti-Semitism engendered during the war has not died out," which the Sulzberger article had offered as perhaps the main reason some Jews might wish to move to the far east. There was no anti-Semitism in the USSR, Budish asserted, as could be demonstrated by the fact that Ambijan members "receive hundreds of letters from their relatives and friends in the Soviet Union" and there was no reference in such letters "to any anti-Semitism whatever."

Budish also noted that B.Z. Goldberg had spent several months in the Soviet Union in 1946, visiting most of the centers of Jewish population, and had concluded that there was no anti-Semitism in the country. Clearly, the *Times* articles were "products of a biased and malicious imagination" designed to "mislead public opinion" and "sow enmity between this country and the U.S.S.R."[6] Goldberg was himself quoted in the *Times* as saying that the Soviet Union was "the only country on earth where the Jew does feel really free and equal, on a par with all other people in his country." As for Birobidzhan, it was "a growing land, resembling in many respects the American Northwest during the days of our pioneers."[7]

Goldberg told an interviewer from the National Council of American-

The Gathering Storm: McCarthyism, Cold War, and Decline

Soviet Friendship that he had travelled throughout the Soviet Union, meeting with members of Jewish communities, and had heard no complaints of anti-Semitism "or of discrimination against Jews in any field whatever," including the military and diplomatic services. He had also met, in Moscow, with Moishe Silberstein and Alexander Bakhmutsky, respectively chair of the executive committee of the Birobidzhan Soviet and secretary of the region's Communist Party, who discussed conditions in the JAR. The population of the region, they said, was approximately 160,000, of which about 45-50 per cent was Jewish. Increased Jewish immigration would soon make Jews a majority. Goldberg also was told that a Yiddish state university would soon be established there. And he denied that the secret police prevented disillusioned settlers from leaving. The region was "going through a process of development and civilization similar to that of our northwestern regions before they became states, or that of Alaska today. Pioneers come and go, but the bulk of them remain to develop their new country." Goldberg added that the *Times* correspondents had clearly "swallowed whole some of the very stale anti-Soviet propaganda which has been discredited many years ago."[8]

Yet while in the Soviet Union in 1946, he had been unable to obtain permission to visit the JAR, which he had last seen 12 years earlier. Upon his return to the U.S., Goldberg had privately written to Fefer and Mikhoels, informing them that this had proved "a handicap" to Ambijan: "No sooner did I arrive when I began to get telephone calls from important leaders of the Ambijan," worried about the "true situation" in Birobidzhan. "It seems that many of the people around Ambijan do not have the faith in the project that sustained them the years before. I naturally reassured them," by explaining that there was a ban on travel in the far east for correspondents, "and I expressed my confidence that by next spring or summer...when the general situation will be more cheerful," it would be possible for an American delegation to visit Birobidzhan.[9] This never materialized, but Goldberg kept any disappointment he may have felt to himself when defending the Soviets in 1948.

Moishe Katz also rejected stories of Soviet anti-Semitism; they were, he asserted in *Nailebn-New Life*, part of a campaign of lies by right-wing organizations against the USSR, a "trick" being used to prepare Jews for war against the Soviet Union. This was nothing new, he suggested: "in the 32 years since the October Revolution, they had tried out every form of libel," in order to "besmirch the Soviet revolution in the eyes of the world, isolate the Soviet Union and scare away any potential friends." A common tactic of the right-wingers was to describe the country as a "decaying hell on earth."

But there was one thing the enemies of the Soviet Union had been unable to besmirch: its nationality policy, which had liberated all of the peoples in the country and given them equality. "Even those Jews who were prepared to believe the worst things that its enemies said about the Soviet Union, were absolutely certain about one thing: that in the Soviet Union there was no anti-Semitism, and none was possible, as it had been torn out by its roots," Katz wrote. When it came to protecting the Jewish people, Jews the world over had acknowledged that "the Soviet Union has earned their complete trust." It was this very Jewish confidence in the USSR that anti-Soviet elements in the community were now trying to undermine.[10]

Rabbi Bick weighed in as well, focusing on the attacks against the new people's democracies. At first, these "naysayers" had declared that it would be impossible for Jews to rebuild their lives and communities in the lands where millions had been killed. But they were now being proven wrong: in Poland, Romania, and elsewhere, a healthy and productive Jewish life had re-emerged. The reactionaries then switched to a different argument, insisting that, despite any evidence to the contrary, Jewish life in these countries would inevitably eventually expire. Bick countered their allegations by providing statistics on Jewish life in Romania and Poland—the numbers of Yiddish theaters, schools, periodicals, choirs, libraries, radio programs, and synagogues—as indicated in the Yiddish press in those countries. He also described his own visit to Poland the previous December; he had found a vibrant community in the process of regeneration. "Today's Poland, like today's Hungary and Romania, is a people's democracy; the government and the organs of communication are in the hands of the working masses of the cities and countryside."[11]

Jack Greenbaum had also visited Poland to disburse funds from Ambijan. He contended, in the *Ambijan Bulletin*, that in Poland, "the ugly practices of antisemitism are being systematically eradicated." As a result, the Jews of Poland had succeeded "in such a short period of time" in reestablishing themselves economically and culturally. Greenbaum described the new Jewish cooperatives, especially in the "Recovered Territories" (former German areas incorporated into Poland after the war), and the new cultural organizations, such as the Jewish Cultural Society and the Jewish Historical Institute. A Jewish theater had been established in Lodz, and another was soon to be opened in Wroclaw. There were now Jewish professors in the universities, and the work of Jewish artists was being exhibited in galleries and museums. "The overall picture of the Jew in Poland is reassuring....For the first time in the history of Poland, the Jew is an equal."[12]

The *Ambijan Bulletin* of July-August 1949 included as well a six-page article deploring the appearance in the American press of stories filled with "trickery and distortion," designed to alienate American Jews from any sympathy with the USSR. Ambijan denied reports that the Soviets had embarked on a campaign to eliminate Jewish intellectuals from public life, and that Jewish publishing houses and newspapers had been shut down and writers arrested. Readers were reminded that article 123 of the Soviet constitution forbade anti-Semitism and that many recent winners of Stalin prizes were Jewish. The campaign against the Soviet Union was actually in itself an "extraordinary anti-Semitic hoax, certainly as absurd and perhaps in the long run as damaging as any fabrication since the Protocols of the Learned Elders of Zion."[13]

In addition to problems arising from the intensifying Cold War and increasing domestic suspicion, Ambijan was weakened by internal scrutiny and turmoil. Edward Aronow had been secretary-treasurer of Ambijan since its founding; indeed, for the first few years of its existence, he had financed the Committee out of his own pocket. But in January 1946 Aronow resigned in protest over "transactions connected with purchases made by the Committee in a manner which, to put it mildly, I consider violative of the best interests of the Committee and the intended beneficiaries, namely, the orphans of Stalingrad and Birobidjan." At a meeting of the Board of Directors held on February 9, Aronow described financial irregularities that "may one day bring shame upon each of us." He and Samuel Getmansky, chair of the purchasing committee, had attended a meeting on January 17 where Budish had announced that 150 reconditioned sewing machines, to be sent to Birobidzhan, had been purchased for $4,350 from Milton Heimlich, chair of the Metal Trades Machinery Division. However, the mechanic who inspected the machines told Getmansky they were worthless "junk," and Getmansky refused to authorize the payment to Heimlich. Aronow was disgusted that just ten days later, at an Ambijan luncheon held at the Waldorf-Astoria Hotel, Budish had praised Heimlich, the man "who sold these inadequate machines to Ambijan for use in the Soviet Union." Instead of responding to the accusations against Heimlich, continued Aronow, Budish had engaged in *ad hominem* attacks against Heimlich's critics. Aronow also informed the Directors that in a conversation on February 8, Judge Anna Kross had told him that she believed the Budishes had too much power within the organization: three members of the Budish family served on the administrative committee in charge of day-to-day operations. She wanted to "throw Budish out," along with various other "crooks," prior to the March national conference. Aronow asked the Board to investigate the situation and prevent any repetition of such incidents in the future.[14] But it was Budish who stayed on after the 1946 national conference as the executive vice-president, while Heimlich remained chair of the division. Aronow was replaced as treasurer by

CHAPTER EIGHT

Jack Greenbaum. Getmansky and Kross left soon afterwards.

In 1947, an FBI informant reported complaints from one member of the Ambijan national committee (the name is blacked out in the confidential report) that the national office was spending 35 per cent of the incoming funds on itself; printing costs alone consumed $35,000 a year. Salaries of the national officers were also too high.[15] In 1949, the FBI reported that a member of the national committee and the Bronx Ambijan Division had resigned from the organization (and also the Communist Party) on March 21, protesting against the high salaries and expense accounts of "[name marked out; probably J.M. Budish] and his gang," who were spending thousands of dollars on trips to California, Florida, Cuba, and elsewhere. The departing member said he had given thousands of dollars to Ambijan but would no longer be "a sucker."[16]

Another informant, who had been a Comintern agent between 1928 and 1938, was interviewed by the FBI in Paris in January 1951. He said that "if the Birobidjan Committee is presently operating in the United States, it is being run as a racket by some individuals as this relief organization cannot send anything to Siberia as the Soviet policy of developing this area has terminated."[17] In September 1954, Herschel Weinrauch, an émigré from the Soviet Union who had worked on the Birobidzhan newspaper, testified before the U.S. House of Representatives Select Committee on Communist Aggression. Weinrauch described the entire Birobidzhan project as a "fake" used to defraud American donors. Ambijan, he stated, had collected millions of dollars but most of the money remained in the hands of the CPUSA. "When I came to the United States six years ago," he testified, "I was astonished to see that money was still being given for Birobidzhan," as the region had ceased being Jewish years earlier.[18]

Of the money and supplies that Ambijan did manage to send to the Soviet Union, very little appears to have reached its intended destination. Machinery earmarked for Birobidzhan would routinely be sent elsewhere in the country. In a letter dated August 28, 1945, Shloime Mikhoels and Itzik Fefer, the leaders of the JAFC in Moscow, informed Georgy M. Malenkov, Soviet deputy prime minister and a secretary of the Communist Party Central Committee, that the electric power plant and various others goods for Silver Ponds, sent over by Ambijan in 1943, had never reached the orphanage. Mikhoels and Fefer pointed out that the ICOR and Ambijan, "headed by the well-known polar explorer Stevenson [sic] and the prominent lawyer George Gordon Battle," wished to help in the reconstruction of Jewish life in the USSR. These organizations also served as "a kind of rallying point for broad masses of foreign Jews to express their social and political sympathy towards the Soviet Union." If only they could be allowed to send their assistance directly to the designated recipients, rather than to a "depersonalized"

194

central Soviet aid agency, their efforts would certainly intensify. But Mikhoels and Fefer reasoned in vain: their request was rejected.[19]

Ambijan had officially kept its distance from the Communist Party. According to an FBI informant who spoke to the Bureau in 1944, Ambijan, whose offices were located first on Madison Avenue and then on Park Avenue, "caters to the better class Jews." According to the informant, however, although the organization was officially headed by non-Communists, the actual behind-the-scenes leader of Ambijan was a Communist Party functionary assigned by the CP: "she makes the decisions and outlines the program and policies of the organization, but she remains in the background and is not publically known as the leader." Her connection to the CP was known to the officers of the organization and "they undoubtedly condone her relationship with the Party by sponsoring her directives." The woman in question, I have deduced from a close reading of the material, was Sasha Small, who was also the secretary of International Labor Defense. FBI Special Agent E.E. Conroy referred to Small in 1945 as "a paid functionary of the Communist Party."[20] In addition, now that the secret Soviet spy cables known as the *Venona* documents have been declassified by the FBI, Joseph Milton Bernstein, one of Ambijan's national organizers, has been identified as a contact through which the Soviet military intelligence agency, the GRU, communicated with Soviet agents employed by the U.S. government.[21]

An FBI informant told another Bureau agent on May 15, 1946 that he had overheard a member of the national committee remark that Ambijan was very careful "not to give them a chance to call us a Communist Front"; this person was angry that someone "had made a slip," by including the name of the organization on tickets being sold by the New York State CP for an event to raise money for the *Daily Worker*. The national committee member worried that tickets might fall into the hands of government officials (as indeed they did). An informant's report dated August 28 provided the FBI with more evidence of the close ties between the CP and Ambijan: it noted that a special conference of Jewish Communists called by the New York State CP for August 31 included on the agenda "the strengthening of the work of such mass organizations as the AMBIJAN COMMITTEE." Ambijan was to be encouraged to "concentrate more on propaganda of friendship to the Soviet Union." The increased tension between the U.S. and USSR had weakened Ambijan, which now needed to organize mass meetings to counteract anti-Soviet propaganda.[22]

At the end of March 1947 Budish reassured the Chicago membership that Ambijan was recognized by the U.S. government "as a legitimate organization. None of the officers have ever been called for investigation, or have been questioned or harassed, in any manner. This places a legal sanction on our work. We are also recognized by Jewish and non-

Jewish people as a relief organization, and not as a so-called 'Russian organization.'"[23] But in actual fact, the FBI was now tracking Ambijan's activities closely. Director J. Edgar Hoover sent a memo to Attorney General Tom Clark on April 15, 1947, attesting to the Communist connections of the Ambijan leadership. Budish had been employed by the Amtorg Trading Corp., Hoover wrote, and was "a most active Communist Party member." Jacob B. Aronoff had been "determined by physical surveillance" to be a close associate of "a known Soviet espionage agent." The Chicago chair, attorney Solomon Jesmer, a member of the Communist-dominated National Lawyers Guild, "has described himself as the unofficial Soviet Consul in Chicago" and "is known as the leading fund-raiser in Chicago for pro-Soviet groups." Sasha Small, a member of the Sunnyside Club, Queens County, New York CP, was the actual leader of Ambijan, but "she remains in the background."[24] The FBI also knew that Small worked for TASS, the Soviet news agency. However, Small had lied when asked on April 29, 1949 if she belonged to any clubs, societies or other organizations. Alexander M. Campbell, the Assistant Attorney General of the Criminal Division, Department of Justice, wrote to Hoover that Small's lie constituted a "willful omission"; under the terms of the Foreign Agents Registration Act, she was required to register as the agent of a foreign government.[25]

In December 1947, Attorney General Clark published a list of 90 "subversive" organizations; within a few years it had grown to almost 200. Even the IWO, which had 184,398 members organized into 15 different ethnic sections in 1946, lost its tax exemption status as a fraternal benefit organization in 1948; its charter was revoked by the State of New York in 1951. After unsuccessful appeals, IWO was disbanded in 1953, although the JPFO--some 30 per cent of overall IWO membership--lived on as the Jewish Cultural Clubs and Societies and the Emma Lazarus Federation of Jewish Women's Clubs. (Rubin Saltzman, a vice-president of the IWO, was general secretary of the JPFO at this time.) Ambijan had already been forced under the Foreign Agents Registration Act to register as the agent of a foreign government and would soon be declared a "subversive" organization, under the provisions of Executive Order 9835 of March 21, 1947, "Prescribing Procedures for the Administration of an Employees Loyalty Program in the Executive Branch of the Government," which was designed to search out any "infiltration of disloyal persons" in the U.S. government.[26]

The FBI was also discouraging businesses from dealing with Ambijan. For example, a Jewish businessman in Cleveland in the machinery export business received an order from Ambijan on July 21, 1947, for some equipment for Birobidzhan. He contacted local FBI officials on July 24, and was told that Ambijan was a Communist front. "It seems best to decline their inquiry, although it is an interesting selection of easily procurable items," he wrote to FBI headquarters in Washington on September 11. On the same day he informed the Ambijan office in New York that "Your inquiry was greatly appreciated but we regret to have to inform you that we are no longer in position to furnish machinery of the types you require." The Cleveland businessman received a letter one week later from Hoover, telling him that the information he had furnished "is appreciated."[27] Ambijan members, too, were being targeted. Nathan Krupin of Los Angeles, for example, applied for a passport for himself and his wife on September 22, 1947. Both had been members of the Communist Party since 1934 and he was known to have been in contact with Soviet consular officials in Los Angeles. Krupin said they would be visiting France and Palestine but withheld the fact that they planned to travel also to the Soviet Union. The local FBI office suggested that the State Department be informed and, presumably, would deny the application.[28]

As the government's relentless campaign against the pro-Soviet movements began to take its toll, Ambijan was increasingly ostracized. One example: Ambijan, as was its custom, organized a concert at Carnegie Hall for April 17, 1948, to celebrate yet another Birobidzhan anniversary, the 20th. The new Soviet ambassador, Alexander S. Panyushkin, agreed to be the guest speaker; the music was to be provided by violinist George Enesco and by Richard Tucker, leading tenor of the Metropolitan Opera Company. Ambijan's invitation called on its supporters to turn out and reminded them that more money was needed to help settle incoming Jewish immigrants to Birobidzhan. But at the last moment, both Enesco and Tucker backed out, despite the threat of legal action by Ambijan, citing the "political implications" of the concert. Tucker stated, "I do not approve of confusing humanitarian causes with political issues." Ambijan did manage to find substitute performers, pianist Ray Lev and violinist Mischa Mischakoff of the NBC Symphony Orchestra.

The Soviet ambassador, unruffled, spoke of the "Lenin-Stalin national policy of equality and friendship of peoples" which had allowed the Jews to freely develop their culture and participate on an equal basis with all other nationalities in the country. He praised the patriotism of the Jews of Birobidzhan, remarking that 2,000 of them had been decorated for heroism during the war, and he thanked Ambijan for its "fruitful work." The audience gave Panyushkin "a standing ovation" for his address. A total of $20,000 in cash and over $14,000 in pledges was collected.[29]

As the Cold War intensified, Communists and their allies found themselves increasingly vulnerable within the Jewish community. J.M. Budish attempted to reassure members of the Chicago Ambijan on September 30, 1948; after he spoke, Board member Samuel Cheifetz stated that "we must drive the fear out of ourselves, then we will be able to continue on with our work."[30] At Ambijan's National Committee meeting held on November 20-21, Budish referred to the "contemptible attempts made by some divisive elements in our community who have become the betrayers of the Jewish people to the forces of fascism."[31] Isaac Aronoff, the national comptroller, informed the delegates that during the 12-month period ending September 30, the total income of the organization was $268,225.66, down from the $302,060.70 it had collected the previous year. Aronoff attempted to explain away the dwindling levels of support by referring to the "emergency situation" in Israel, which taxed the resources of American Jewry. He also speculated that Ambijan members had been "preoccupied" with Henry Wallace's quixotic campaign as standard-bearer for the Progressive Party, a campaign endorsed by those on the pro-Communist left.

Some supporters began to rethink their ties to Ambijan: Budish had invited Stefansson by phone and followed up with a long letter requesting his presence at the meeting, but Stefansson, still listed as a vice-president, sent word that "Doctor forbids going out. Sorry to miss seeing you and other friends and to miss Senator Pepper's talk." Councilman Stanley M. Isaacs wrote that he was unable to attend due to a "prior engagement."[32]

Henry Wallace himself was the guest speaker at the dinner of the New Jersey Division of Ambijan, in Newark, on February 21, 1949. He spoke of the "excess of fear" that was sweeping through America. He said that many friends had tried to dissuade him from speaking, warning that "anything having to do with Russia is too hot. One of them was actually praying that I might get ill so I couldn't come, but I'm glad I have come," he stated. "To me, understanding and peace with Russia is business number one today."[33] Wallace would not be dissuaded from his support of Ambijan; indeed, on March 7 he presented Max Levin, J.M. Budish and Nathan Frankel, chair of the National Administrative Committee of Ambijan, with a gift of hybrid Golden Bantam sweet corn seed for an agricultural experimental station in Birobidzhan.[34]

Ambijan sent Fan Bakst, Morris L. Olken, and Nathan Frankel, chair of the national administrative committee, as delegates to the 17th annual meeting of the Council of Jewish Federations and Welfare Funds, in Philadelphia on January 14-16, 1949. They chastised the CJF for not including Ambijan as one of the recipient organizations for funds collected through the United Jewish Appeal for use in Jewish rehabilitation and resettlement in Europe, especially in the Soviet Union.[35] The California Ambijan state conference that met in San Francisco on April 9-10 passed a resolution demanding that the leadership of the United Jewish Appeal not discriminate against Soviet Jewry when distributing relief funds. It asked that a percentage of these funds go towards aiding Jewish war victims and towards Birobidzhan.[36] Later that year, Ambijan again complained that the practice of centralizing fund raising and distribution for Israel through the UJA was "non-democratic" and discriminatory.[37] Budish on October 5 declared at an Ambijan luncheon that the UJA was now "in the hands of the most reactionary Jewish capitalists"; he recommended that Jews should donate money to "progressive" Jewish forces in Israel.[38] Thus, despite its support, albeit limited, for various Israeli projects, Ambijan was fast becoming a black sheep in the mainstream Jewish community.

Ambijan was now facing financial difficulties as well. Early in 1949 it had signed contracts with the W.A. Riddell Corp. of Bucyrus, Ohio; Towmotor Corp. of Cleveland; and Columbia Exporters Inc. of Portland, Oregon, to supply Birobidzhan with $75,000 worth of machinery for a plant capable of producing 22 million bricks a year – sufficient for the building of 1,150 three-room dwellings. The Riddell Corp., from which Ambijan purchased most of the machinery for the brick-making plant, had informed the organization that it would be ready to ship on August 15, 1949, but that Ambijan would have to provide the final payment of $41,000 still owed before the machinery could be sent to the USSR. The Chicago organization at a conference held on May 15 voted to loan the national office $10,000.[39] On June 8, J.M. Budish spoke to the Bronx Ambijan. He proclaimed that "members could not afford to take a vacation from their work": Ambijan needed more money to pay for the machinery.[40] The organization managed to come up with the rest of the money only after pleading with its members, in a letter dated August 3, to send contributions immediately.[41] "It was a hard task to raise the necessary funds during the summer season," reported *Nailebn-New Life* in September, thanking "all who responded to our urgent appeal with special contributions to cover the cost of this important project."[42] An FBI memo of November 2, 1949, noted that Ambijan now had "trouble raising funds because of Israel."[43]

Speeches by Abraham Jenofsky and Moishe Katz at the New York Area Conference to mark the 15th anniversary of the JAR on March 5-6 indicated that Ambijan was now fully aware of its increasingly precarious political position. Jenofsky spoke to the gathering about the worsening world situation which, he warned, made a third world war an increasing possibility. There were many organizations in the country agitating for war with the Soviet Union in order to eliminate the people's republics that had been established in eastern Europe. Every day, newspapers were filled with lies and false information about the Soviet Union and the new democracies. Every hour, radio reports were broadcast designed to frighten millions of listeners. Some of the

Jewish press was equally bad, he added, second to none in their libels. Katz's speech addressed the same issue. "We are living in a twilight time between war and peace," he warned; the world could easily be plunged into an atomic war that would wipe out all of humanity. Katz stated that the "Anglo-American imperialist bloc" was far stronger than the Axis powers had been a decade earlier, and that the anti-Communist hysteria now being unleashed was reminiscent of the aggressive anti-Soviet propaganda back then. The fight for peace now had to become the most pressing task for Ambijan.[44]

In Detroit, James Waterman Wise on March 6 warned listeners at an Ambijan meeting against those reactionaries in Washington who were trying to incite war between the U.S. and the Soviet Union. A new war would obliterate humanity and end civilization, he said. If being a proponent of peace meant being called a "traitor," he declared, then he'd be proud to assume that title. His words were greeted with "stormy ovations" and some 40 people stayed on until 8 o'clock the next morning discussing the world situation.[45] At a Chicago conference held on May 15, Ethel Osri decried the timidity that had overtaken Chicago Jewish leaders who had only a few years earlier sung the praises of the Soviet Union; now, in the face of reaction and red-baiting, they had deserted Ambijan. Harry Koenig and Sol Jesmer feared that the Einstein Fund Dinner scheduled for November 26 might become "a fiasco," as no one seemed to be working on it. "It is very essential that all of our loyal friends support the dinner this year," read a letter sent out by the Committee. "You are fully aware of the many pressures that are being brought to bear on people to refrain from supporting organizations such as ours."[46]

In his report on the April 1949 California state conference, Nathan Krupin observed that it had been held at a very grave moment, when "a wild reactionary movement is brewing in the country, the imperialist powers are getting ready for a new, third world war, aimed at the Soviet Union and the new people's democracies."[47] The Ambijan Board of Directors met in New York on June 9 in a special session in order to "discuss the urgent problems of our organization. The present vicious campaign against the Soviet Union by spurious charges of anti-Semitism, and its real purpose, will be discussed on the basis of documented facts that will be submitted at the meeting."[48]

As part of its focus on preventing an American-Soviet war, Ambijan participated in the First World Peace Congress held in Paris in April 1949 and in an American Intercontinental Peace Congress in Mexico City in September 1949. These were part of a Soviet-inspired international peace campaign, which included major conferences in Asia, Canada and Israel as well. Nathan Frankel, chair of Ambijan's Administrative Committee, addressed the Mexico City conference on September 8, stating that "if there will be no peace in the world, then the future of Jews is not assured." He warned the delegates about the anti-Communist "witch-hunters" in the U.S., whose hysteria had made them "completely crazy." Frankel reported on his trip to the Administrative Committee at a meeting on October 5 held at the Woodstock Hotel in New York. Representatives of other organizations, including B.Z. Goldberg, who had become chair of the American Committee of Jewish Writers, Artists and Scientists, also attended, as did members of a number of *landsmanshaftn*.[49]

Nathan Krupin of Los Angeles and Bernard Roller, chair of the Greater Miami Ambijan, came to New York and met with the Ambijan leadership on October 25 to discuss issues that would be debated at the upcoming national conference to be held that December. Among those taking part were Budish, Jenofsky, Sholem Levine, Gina Medem, Morris L. Olken, Dr. Lewis Schatzov, and another 50 or so activists from the New York City Committee and its various branches. The two guests described the mood in their cities. It was, as Moishe Katz had said a week earlier in a speech to a New York Ambijan branch banquet, "a very hard time that we are living through right now."[50]

In Boston, the Ambijan held a city-wide conference and concert on November 20. The president of the New England District, Abraham Resnick, opened the proceedings by mentioning the stories attacking Birobidzhan printed recently in the Boston *Globe*. In response, the conference agreed to raise $10,000 in order to mount a series of events in 1950 which would create a positive image of Birobidzhan.[51] The Ambijan Committee in Chicago organized a number of luncheons in the fall of 1949; Dr. John B. Thompson, Dean of the Rockefeller Chapel at the University of Chicago, on November 2 spoke about the need for world peace.[52] The New York City Committee at a meeting two months later optimistically urged its branches to help publicize Birobidzhan, and attract new members, during 1950 by sponsoring cultural events at least once a month.[53] In fact, there was little the branches could do to forestall the imminent disintegration of the parent organization.

Ambijan, with Albert Einstein still its honorary president, held its final national conference at the Commodore Hotel in New York on December 10-11, 1949. The conference was attended by 248 delegates representing 120 organizations, and by Vasily Zonov, a counselor at the Soviet Embassy in Washington. Ambijan claimed to still have some 15,000 members in 65 branches (including 15 branches in New York, seven in Los Angeles, and two in Chicago) in 26 states, but by now it was no longer able to attract a prominent politician as a keynote speaker at the annual dinner, and had to make do with Hunter College professor John Somerville, who addressed "American-Soviet Relations—Key to World Peace."

It was the duty of the members of Ambijan to help mobilize the American Jewish community to oppose those who had created the Cold War climate and who desired to instigate war between America and the USSR, said Jenofsky. American Jews, in order to safeguard their own lives and security, must ally themselves with the progressive forces in the country and around the world, in order to stave off those who were plotting a new world war that would obliterate entire nations and peoples.

As for Birobidzhan, the more it progressed, the more its enemies tried to detract from its achievements by parading so-called "experts" who spread lies about the region. Before the war, they had stated that Birobidzhan was being settled to serve as a bulwark against Japanese expansion; they were certain that the Jewish Autonomous Region would be the first victim of any invasion in the far east. After the war, they warned that Birobidzhan was vulnerable to an invasion by China. But the armies of Chiang Kai-shek (Jiang Jieshi) had been defeated, and the new, democratic China on the other side of the Amur posed no threat to Birobidzhan. "If only we could say the same about Israel's neighbors!" Jenofsky concluded his speech by describing Ambijan's rehabilitation campaigns on behalf of Birobidzhan, Stalingrad, and, more recently, Israel and Poland. True, the amounts sent were not enormous, but they were sent as fraternal aid, in a spirit of friendship, "with no strings attached."

B.Z. Goldberg brought greetings from the American Committee of Jewish Writers, Artists, and Scientists, which, he stated, continued to "foster close relations between the Jews of this country and the Jews of the Soviet Union, and naturally with Birobidjan Jewry," in the common struggle against fascism "in all its forms everywhere." He called on "all progressive people" to stick together….The forces of reaction have the money on their side. But we have the people, and between people and money, I am sure the people will win."

Budish again denounced the attempts being made to "slander" the Soviet Union through "fabrications which are no less absurd and damaging than the notorious Protocols of the Learned Elders of Zion." Hoping to rally the troops, he warned against the "defeatism" that had taken hold of many Jews. The success of Birobidzhan effectively and conclusively disposed of the false theories of "despair and submission to anti-Semitism"; it gave proof that a nation that resolved to do away with discrimination and oppression "can do so in the shortest period of time." Budish did admit that, due to the strained nature of Soviet-American relations, Ambijan was unable to send a delegation to Birobidzhan. Nonetheless, he maintained, "we have…authentic information concerning developments in Birobidjan." Official reports "supply adequate information concerning the Jewish Autonomous Region." He went on to produce statistics regarding the "rapid strides" made in the postwar years, resulting in a "relatively high standard of living" that made the region a great center of attraction for Jewish settlers.

Budish announced that Ambijan's total expenditure on projects in the Soviet Union, Israel and Poland was down to $162,518.00. In 1949, the brick-making plant and the poultry farm, with a total worth of $140,518, had been sent to Birobidzhan. As well, shipments to children in Stalingrad amounted to $12,000. Budish suggested that for its next project, Ambijan should undertake to send medical instruments and laboratory equipment to the hospitals in Birobidzhan. A total of $44,000 was collected from delegates during the conference.

In Stefansson's case, Budish's plea made little impact. "Regretting that an indisposition" made it impossible for him and his wife to attend, he instead sent his "warmest greetings and best wishes." Clearly the "famous Arctic explorer," as he was invariably called, by now served as little more than a ceremonial icon for the organization. He was nonetheless again duly elected as one of 10 vice-presidents, along with Isaac Aronoff, Jacob B. Aronoff, B.Z. Goldberg, Jack Greenbaum, Charles Kuntz, Sholem Levine, Princeton professor Elias A. Lowe, Joseph Morgenstern, and Rubin Saltzman. Nathan Frankel, formerly chair of the administrative committee, was elected chair of the national Board of Directors, replacing Max Levin. Dr. Lewis Schatzov replaced Isaac Aronoff as comptroller, and Israel Cramer replaced Jack Greenbaum as treasurer. J.M. Budish remained as executive vice-president, Abraham Jenofsky as executive secretary, Morris L. Olken as national organizer, Bernard Parelhoff as secretary, and Fan Bakst as field organizer. Max Levin, introducing his successor, spoke of Frankel's "outstanding career of public and communal activities" (he had been executive secretary of New York Mayor Fiorello La Guardia's City Industrial Relations Board in the 1930s) and his "unexcelled leadership."[54] A telegram from Albert Einstein, regretting his inability to attend, alongside his photograph, graced the front and back covers of the *Ambijan Bulletin* of January-February 1950. The *Bulletin* proclaimed that Ambijan's endeavours were helping "to keep alive the principle of mutual assistance in a world subject to so much antagonism and conflict; and by the same token, they are contributing to the cementing of international understanding and friendship, and the furthering of world peace."[55]

Ambijan and the American Committee of Jewish Writers, Artists and Scientists jointly hosted a New York Area Conference for International Friendship and Peace at the Barbizon-Plaza Hotel in New York on May 6-7, 1950. The Cold War was causing a revival of fascism, anti-Semitism and discrimination at home, while Nazism was resurgent in West Germany, they wrote in their call to participants. The atmosphere in the U.S. was intended to intimidate and frighten the Jewish community into joining the reactionary, pro-forces. At the conference, Nathan Frankel, noting the defeat of Senator Claude Pepper, a major supporter of Ambijan, in the Florida Democratic primary, said that "McCarthyism is on the march in our country." Joseph Brainin, too, worried about McCarthy's attacks, which were now "the most infamous in the history of America." Moishe Katz feared that "In a new war the American Fascists will make a better job on the Jews than Hitler did."[56]

The various western Communist parties, including the American one, had now returned to an ultra-leftist sectarianism reminiscent of the pre-war, 1928-1935 "Third Period." Fearing that the United States was on the verge of fascism, the CPUSA entered a period of political isolation and internal paranoia, ordering most of its top leaders and cadres to go "underground." But this was not a viable option for groups such as Ambijan, which had tried to be inclusive in its outreach. Ambijan's situation became even more untenable when the Korean War broke out in June 1950, intensifying American feelings of enmity toward the Soviet Union.[57] On September 28, 1950, Nathan Frankel met with representatives of the Foreign Agents Registration Section of the Department of Justice. Frankel stated that Ambijan had not sent any shipments to Birobidzhan since November 1949; since then, it had concentrated on assisting Israel.[58]

In May 1950, *Nailebn-New Life* had become *Di Velt*, publishing in Yiddish only, with Rabbi Bick as editor. It ceased publication entirely in June 1951. The *Ambijan Bulletin* had ceased with the issue dated July-August 1950. In November 1950, a message sent to Ambijan, purportedly by the leadership of the Jewish Autonomous Region, declared that Birobidzhan no longer required nor wanted any outside help. By the end of the month, Ambijan vacated its offices at 103 Park Avenue, New York. There would be no more public meetings, no more appeals for contributions. Despite an attempt by some in the group to keep it alive under the name "Jewish Committee for Rehabilitation in Israel, France, and Belgium," Ambijan ceased operations entirely in 1951, at the height of the Korean War. A certificate of dissolution was filed on March 28 with Thomas J. Curran, Secretary of State of New York.[59] At a meeting of the American Friends of Stalingrad (formerly the Russian Division of Ambijan), held in New York on February 4, 1951, Budish had declared that the organization was officially dissolving "because the Jews of Birobidjan did not need any more outside help and because the Soviet Government was helping in the building of Birobidjan." In fact, the Treasury Department was pursuing Ambijan for failure to pay back taxes, citing it as a subversive, rather than philanthropic, organization.[60]

New World Review (the former *Soviet Russia Today*) in September 1951 denied that the dissolution of Ambijan was proof that the Soviets had abandoned the plan to make Birobidzhan a Jewish homeland; rather, Ambijan's assistance had become unnecessary because Birobidzhan was receiving ample budgetary support from the Soviet government: "The Committee ceased functioning not because Birobidzhan was given up, but on the contrary, because Birobidzhan is growing and prospering."[61]

Endnotes

1. There is an enormous literature concerning espionage by American Communists on behalf of the Soviet Union during the Cold War period. John Earl Haynes and Harvey Klehr document some of the early post-war cases in *Early Cold War Spies: The Espionage Trials that Shaped American Politics* (New York: Cambridge University Press, 2006). See also Harvey Klehr, John Earl Haynes and Fridrikh Igorevich Firsov, *The Secret World of American Communism* (New Haven: Yale University Press, 1995); Harvey Klehr, Kyrill M. Anderson and John Earl Haynes, *The Soviet World of American Communism* (New Haven: Yale University Press, 1998); and John Earl Haynes, Harvey Klehr, and Alexander Vassiliev, *Spies: The Rise and Fall of the KGB in America* (New Haven: Yale University Press, 2009).
2. A. Ovrum Tapper, "Unreasonable Prices for Kosher Meat Create Critical Problem," *Sentinel*, Chicago, Feb. 5, 1948, 27; "Organizational Activities," *Ambijan Bulletin* 7, 2 (March-April 1948): 12, 14; J.M. Budish, "Report on the Activities of Ambijan, Nov. 1947 to Nov. 1948," *Ambijan Bulletin* 7, 7 (December 1948): 13.
3. Paul Novick, "Nito Mikhoels…," *Morgn Frayhayt*, Jan. 15, 1948, 3.
4. Letter from Itzik Fefer and Grigori Kheyfets to B.Z. Goldberg, Moscow, Feb. 11, 1948; B.Z. Goldberg papers, Box 69, Jewish Antifascist Committee in the USSR; American Committee of Jewish Writers, Artists, and Scientists, Inc., folder "World Jewish Congress: Jewish Anti-Fascist Committee." Kheyfets, who had served as Soviet consul general in San Francisco from 1941 to 1944, was at the time the acting general secretary of the JAFC. He would be arrested soon afterwards and sentenced to a gulag. For a complete list of all the members of the JAFC between 1941 and 1948, see Shimon Redlich, *Propaganda and Nationalism in Wartime Russia*, 175-178.

5   Drew Middleton, "Anti-Semitism Seen Mounting in Russia," *New York Times*, Feb. 13, 1948, 13; C.L. Sulzberger, "Soviet Jews' Area Reported in Decay," *New York Times*, Feb. 15, 1948, Section 1, 5. The U.S. Embassy in Moscow transmitted to the State Department a memo dated May 29, 1946, reporting on a traveler who had passed through Birobidzhan on April 19 and May 9. He described the region as austere, remarking that the homes in the cities "looked rather like barracks." No Yiddish books or newspapers seemed to be available. The population looked "shabby." He saw neither paved streets nor much in the way of construction, other than the building of a factory by prison labor in Birakan. The prisoners "appeared to be Russians." Memorandum, May 29, 1946, dispatch 124, Embassy, Moscow. Case control No. 200102944; File 100-2074-81, FOIPA No. 416152, Ambijan.

6   J.M. Budish, "The Truth About Actual Conditions in Birobidjan," *News from American Birobidjan Committee (Ambijan) Organizational Newsletter* 2, 2 (March 1948): 1-7.

7   "Anti-Semitism's Rise in Russia is Disputed," *New York Times*, Feb. 26, 1948, 10; "Birobidjan Group Here Denies Area Lags; Challenges Report on Soviet Jewish Colony," *New York Times*, March 28, 1948, Section 1, 12. Goldberg was in the Soviet Union between January 11 and June 8, 1946.

8   "Prominent Jewish Leader Contradicts New York Times," National Council of American-Soviet Friendship *Report on the News*, New York, Feb. 22, 1948, 1-5; "Refuting the 'Times' on Anti-Semitism," *Soviet Russia Today* 16, 12 (April 1948): 32. In a book Goldberg had published a year earlier, he commended the USSR for its treatment of national minorities, whose rights were guaranteed under the 1936 Stalinist constitution. He cautioned readers not to believe all the anti-Soviet propaganda that filled their daily newspapers; even the *New York Times* misrepresented Soviet policies and printed falsehoods. Behind those who were whipping up anti-Soviet feelings stood "international capital," which hoped to establish "dollar-imperialism throughout the world." B. Z. Goldberg, *Sovyetn-farband: Faynt oder fraynt?* (New York: Amerikaner Komitet fun Yidishe Shrayber, Kinstler un Visinshaftlekher, 1947), 22-26, 48.

9   Two follow up letters to the JAFC stressed that, given the increasingly hostile attitudes to the Soviet Union in many quarters, "it is very necessary to increase the activities of the pro-Soviet Jewish organizations in America." Yet many of the leaders in these groups "are complaining that that they were being ignored in the Soviet Union," and were not receiving replies to inquiries or acknowledgement of relief shipments. Goldberg also pleaded with Mikhoels and Fefer to send Ambijan articles about Jewish schools in the JAR, including photos. "You have no idea what a stink they are making here about the lack of Jewish schools in the Soviet Union," and such materials "are urgently necessary for the morale of the workers in the Ambijan movement here." Letters from B.Z. Goldberg to Itsik Fefer and Shloime Mikoels, New York, Oct. 17, Oct. 25, and Nov. 6, 1946; in the B.Z. Goldberg papers, Box 69,

Jewish Antifascist Committee in the USSR; American Committee of Jewish Writers, Artists, and Scientists, Inc., folder "American Committee of Jewish Writers, Artists and Scientists."

10   Moishe Katz, "Der 'antisemitisher' lign-kampayn gegn sovyetn-farband," *Nailebn-New Life* 22, 6 (June 1949): 1-3. Katz died in 1960. "Moishe Katz, Editor for a Jewish Paper," *New York Times*, June 6, 1960, 29. Dr. Lewis Schatzov published a similar article, recounting "the new slanders against the Soviet Union." These were lies so fantastic, he wrote, that they were the equivalent of insisting that "water burns—and fire extinguishes." To state that anti-Semitism existed in the USSR was the same as saying it was still ruled by the tsar. Anti-Semitism and reaction had been "bosom brothers" under the old regime. But the Soviets, by eliminating the old order, had put an end to the conditions that had produced anti-Semitism. Dr. L. Schatzov, "Der nayer bilbul oyfn sovyetn-farband," *Nailebn-New Life* 22, 7 (July-August 1949): 8-9. Schatzov died at age 72 in 1963. "Dr. Lewis Schatzov, Dentist Here for 40 Years," *New York Times*, Aug. 24, 1963, 15.

11   Rabbi Abraham Bick, "Di moyreh far fuler frayhayt," *Nailebn-New Life* 22, 7 (July-August 1949): 10-11.

12   Jack Greenbaum, "Jewish Life in Poland Four Years After Liberation," *Ambijan Bulletin* 8, 2 (March-April 1949): 5-6.

13   Tom O'Connor, "The Big Lie of 'Soviet Anti-Semitism'," *Ambijan Bulletin* 8, 3 (July-August 1949): 5-11. O'Connor was a journalist with the pro-Soviet *Daily Compass*, another successor to the *PM*. His pamphlet *The Truth About Anti-Semitism in the Soviet Union* was published at the same time by the American Committee of Jewish Writers, Artists and Scientists.

14   Letter from Edward I. Aronow to J.M. Budish and Max Levin, New York, Jan. 31, 1946; transcript of conversation between Edward Aronow and Anna Kross, Feb. 8, 1946; transcript of address by Edward Aronow to Ambijan Board of Directors, Feb. 9, 1946; Stefansson correspondence, MSS 196, Box 67, 1946—Ambijan Folder, Stefansson Collection.

15   Memo of July 23, 1947, from Edward Scheidt, Special Agent in Charge, to J. Edgar Hoover; File 100-99898, Section 2, FOIPA No. 416152, Ambijan.

16   This information is contained on p. 28 of a 78-page FBI report dated Nov. 2, 1949, submitted by Edward Scheidt, Special Agent in Charge, originally in NY File 100-42538. File 100-99898, Section 4, FOIPA No. 416152, Ambijan.

17   FBI report from Edward Scheidt, Special Agent in Charge, New York, to Director, FBI, March 1, 1951, originally in NY File 100-42538. File 100-99898, Section 6, FOIPA No. 416152, Ambijan.

18   "Birobidzhan Help Called Diverted," *New York Times*, Sept. 23, 1954, 5. See Weinrauch's book *Blut oyf der zun (yidn in sovyet-rusland)* (New York: Farlag "Mensh un Yid", 1950).

19   Shimon Redlich, *War, Holocaust and Stalinism: A Documented History of the Jewish Anti-Fascist Committee in the USSR* (Luxembourg: Harwood Academic Publishers, 1995), Document 57, 255-257; Document 58, 258-259. Ironically,

CHAPTER EIGHT

such advice would later become the basis for charges that the JAFC's leaders were traitors who wished to allow foreign agents to enter the country on behalf of its capitalist and Zionist enemies.

20   This information is contained on p. 12 of a 33-page report dated Nov. 5, 1944 submitted by E.E. Conroy, Special Agent in Charge, and on p. 9 of an 11-page memo to J. Edgar Hoover of March 21, 1945. Both memos are originally in NY File 100-42538. File 100-99898, Section 1, FOIPA No. 416152, Ambijan. Small also occasionally wrote for ICOR publications. See "Where Women Are Really Free," *ICOR* 8, 4 (April 1935): 35. "All over the vast expanse of the Workers Fatherland women are taking their place in every phase of Socialist Construction. They have won their freedom in the emancipation of the whole working class from the system of profit and exploitation."

21   John Earl Haynes and Harvey Klehr, *Venona: Decoding Soviet Espionage in America* (New Haven, CT: Yale University Press, 2000), 176-180, 236, 242; Romerstein and Breindel, *The Venona Secrets*, 169, 397. Bernstein was never prosecuted.

22   The affair brought in $212 for the *Daily Worker*. This information is contained on pp.14-15, 18-19 of a 42-page FBI report dated Feb. 4, 1947, submitted by Edward Scheidt, Special Agent in Charge, originally in NY File 100-42538. File 100-99898, Section 2, FOIPA No. 416152, Ambijan (capitalization in original).

23   Minutes, March 31, 1947, in Collection No. 20: Chicago Chapter, American Birobidjan Committee, Series A. Minutes. Folder 4: Minutes, 1947, Chicago Jewish Archives.

24   Memo from John Edgar Hoover, Director, FBI, to Attorney General Tom Clark, April 15, 1947, see pages 4-10. File 100-99898, Section 2, FOIPA No. 416152, Ambijan. (The names Budish and Small are blacked out on my declassified copy but it clearly refers to them.) Hoover even suspected Jacob B. Aronoff of having been a Comintern agent. FBI memo of March 15, 1945. File 100-99898, Section 1, FOIPA No. 416152, Ambijan. In 1949, FBI New York Special Agent in Charge Edward Scheidt considered Aronoff a leader of the National Council of Jewish Communists [actually, the National Jewish Commission], second only to Alexander Bittelman. This information is contained on p. 44 of a 78-page FBI report dated Nov. 2, 1949, submitted by Edward Scheidt, Special Agent in Charge, originally in NY File 100-42538. File 100-99898, Section 4, FOIPA No. 416152, Ambijan. Aronoff died in 1952, see his obituary in the *New York Times*, Nov. 18, 1952, 31. Another FBI report from G.R. McSwain, Special Agent in Charge, had stated that Sol Jesmer was considered by some to be the most prominent Communist in Chicago. FBI file dated Nov. 19, 1946, originally in Chicago file 100-18113. File 100-99898, Section 2, FOIPA No. 416152, Ambijan.

25   Memos from Alexander M. Campbell, Assistant Attorney General, Criminal Division, Department of Justice, to J. Edgar Hoover, Director, FBI, July 7 and Oct. 10, 1949. File 100-99898, Section 4, FOIPA No. 416152, Ambijan.

26 For a general overview of the period, see Kenneth O'Reilly, *Hoover and the Un-Americans: The FBI, HUAC, and the Red Menace* (Philadelphia: Temple University Press, 1983); Richard M. Fried, *Nightmare in Red: The McCarthy Era in Perspective* (New York: Oxford University Press, 1990); Ted Morgan, *Reds: McCarthyism in Twentieth-Century America* (New York: Random House, 2003); and Robert Justin Goldstein, *American Blacklist: The Attorney General's List of Subversive Organizations* (Lawrence, KS: University Press of Kansas, 2008). Sabin relates the destruction of the IWO in his book *Red Scare in Court*. See also David A. Shannon, *The Decline of American Communism: A History of the Communist Party of the United States Since 1945* (New York: Harcourt, Brace, 1959), 84-85; Peter L. Steinberg, *The Great "Red Menace": United States Prosecution of American Communists, 1947-1952* (Westport, CT: Greenwood Press, 1984), 27-31; and Caute, *The Great Fear*, 173-174, 188.

27 FBI memo from E.C. Fitch to D.M. Ladd, Sept. 18, 1947; letter from unidentified Cleveland exporter to FBI in Washington, Sept. 11, 1947; letter from unidentified Cleveland exporter to Ambijan office in New York, Sept. 11, 1947; letter from John Edgar Hoover to unidentified Cleveland exporter, Sept. 18, 1947. File 100-99898, Section 2, FOIPA No. 416152, Ambijan.

28 Memo from R.B. Hood, Special Agent in Charge, to FBI director, Sept. 25, 1947. File 100-99898, Section 2, FOIPA No. 416152, Ambijan. Hood was also aware that Krupin was trying to obtain a visa to visit Birobidzhan. See the information contained on pp.12-13 in a 23-page FBI report dated Oct. 22, 1947, submitted by R.B. Hood, Special Agent in Charge, originally in LA File 100-23652. File 100-99898, Section 3, FOIPA No. 416152, Ambijan. Krupin did on Sept. 30, 1947 receive a passport for travel to Britain, France and Palestine. See the information contained on pp.2-3 in a 5-page FBI report dated Sept. 16, 1948, submitted by R.B. Hood, Special Agent in Charge, originally in LA File 100-23652. File 100-99898, Section 3, FOIPA No. 416152, Ambijan. For more on FBI activities during this period, see Katherine A.S. Sibley, *Red Spies in America: Stolen Secrets and the Dawn of the Cold War* (Lawrence, KS: University Press of Kansas, 2004).

29 Letter of invitation from J.M. Budish, New York, March 15, 1948, in United States Territorial Collection, RG117, Box 57, folder "Icor" 17/16, YIVO; flyer advertising the concert, Stefansson correspondence, MSS 196, Box 75, 1948—USSR Folder, Stefansson Collection; invitation to the reception for Honorable Alexander S. Panyushkin, in the Kalmen Marmor papers, 1873-1955, RG205, Microfilm group 495, folder 585 "Ambidzhan-korespondents, 1946-1950," YIVO; "Enesco Boycotts Benefit Concert," *New York Times*, April 17, 1948, 13; "Concert Audience Hails Soviet Envoy," *New York Times*, April 18, 1948, Section 1, 60; A.J. [Abraham Jenofsky], "Organizatsye un arbet," *Nailebn-New Life* 21, 4 (April 1948): 20; "Continued Development of Jewish Autonomous Region Assured," *Ambijan Bulletin* 7, 3 (May 1948): 6, 12; "Organizational Activities," *Ambijan Bulletin* 7, 3 (May 1948): 13; *News from American Birobidjan Committee (Ambijan) Organizational Newsletter* 2, 4 (May

1948). The *Times* gave the figure of 2,000 as being in attendance; Ambijan said 3,000 had come.

30 Minutes, Sept. 30, 1948, in Collection No. 20: Chicago Chapter, American Birobidjan Committee, Series A. Minutes. Folder 5: Minutes, 1948, Chicago Jewish Archives.

31 J.M. Budish, "Report on the Activities of Ambijan, Nov. 1947 to Nov. 1948," *Ambijan Bulletin* 7, 7 (December 1948): 14.

32 "National Committee Maps Extended Program of Cooperation with Jewish Autonomous Region of Birobidjan," *Ambijan Bulletin* 7, 7 (December 1948): 3; "Messages of Greetings," *Ambijan Bulletin* 8, 1 (January-February 1949): 5. Stefansson had already begun harboring doubts much earlier. Max Levin found it necessary to write to him in October 1947 to reassure him about conditions in the Soviet Union and Birobidzhan. Letter from Max Levin to Vilhjalmur Stefansson, New York, Oct. 7, 1947; Stefansson correspondence, MSS 196, Box 72, 1947—USSR-American Committee for the Settlement of Jews in Birobidjan (Ambijan) Folder, Stefansson Collection. Levin also sent Stefansson an article by Professor Henry Pratt Fairchild, "The Bogy of Soviet Slave Labor," *Soviet Russia Today* 16, 5 (September 1947): 11-12, 24-25, as an "antidote."

33 Henry A. Wallace, "American Support of Birobidjan Hopeful Sign Toward Peace," *Ambijan Bulletin* 8, 2 (March-April 1949): 7-9; "Organizational Activities," *Ambijan Bulletin* 8, 2 (March-April 1949): 13; "Henry Wallace Guest Speaker at Newark Anniversary Dinner," *Nailebn-New Life* 22, 4 (April 1949): 23.

34 "Henry A. Wallace Sends Gift of Hybrid Corn to Birobidjan," *Ambijan Bulletin* 8, 3 (July-August 1949): 12.

35 "American Cooperation in Post-War Jewish Rehabilitation," *Ambijan Bulletin* 8, 1 (January-February 1949): 3; "Organizational Activities," *Ambijan Bulletin* 8, 1 (January-February 1949): 13.

36 N. Krupin, "A derfolgraykhe ambidzhan shtat-konferents in California," *Nailebn-New Life* 22, 5 (May 1949): 12-13.

37 "Reds Here Persist in Berating Israel," *New York Times*, April 20, 1949, 15.

38 "Ambijan National Conference," *News from American Birobidjan Committee (Ambijan)*, December 1949: 3-4. Some money from Jewish federations did still trickle in. The Shreveport, LA federation sent Ambijan $100 in the spring of 1950. "Honor Roll," *Nailebn-New Life* 23, 3 (March-April 1950): 25. See also p. 27 of a 42-page report dated Oct. 27, 1950, submitted by Edward Scheidt, Special Agent in Charge, originally in NY File 100-42538. File 100-99898, Section 6, FOIPA No. 416152, Ambijan.

39 Minutes, June 15, 1949, in Collection No. 20: Chicago Chapter, American Birobidjan Committee, Series A. Minutes. Folder 6: Minutes, 1949-50, Chicago Jewish Archives.

40 "Organizational Activities," *Ambijan Bulletin* 8, 3 (July-August 1949): 15; Memo of June 23, 1949, from Edward Scheidt, Special Agent in Charge, to J.

The Gathering Storm: McCarthyism, Cold War, and Decline

Edgar Hoover; File 100-99898, Section 4, FOIPA No. 416152, Ambijan.
41 This information is contained on p. 25 of a 78-page FBI report dated Nov. 2, 1949, submitted by Edward Scheidt, Special Agent in Charge, originally in NY File 100-42538. File 100-99898, Section 4, FOIPA No. 416152, Ambijan. Budish sent a letter to Vilhalmur Stefansson appealing for a contribution. He told Stefansson that Ambijan was having great difficulty raising money and this was creating "a real emergency situation." Letter from J.M. Budish to Vilhjalmur Stefansson, New York, July 5, 1949; Stefansson correspondence, MSS 196, Box 78, 1949—USSR Folder, Stefansson Collection.
42 "Brickmaking Plant for Birobidjan," *Nailebn-New Life* 22, 8 (September-October 1949): 23. See also the November issue of the magazine, for letters from people who had sent in checks in response to the appeal for funds. *Nailebn-New Life* 22, 9 (November 1949): 23. The Cincinnati Ambijan contributed $500 to the brick-making plant campaign at its July 17 lawn fete on the grounds of the Bureau of Jewish Education. "Cincinnati Contributes $500 for the Brick Plant," *Ambijan Bulletin* 8, 4 (December 1949): 2.
43 FBI memo, New York, Nov. 2, 1949, Case Control No. 200002702, NY File 100-42538; FOIPA No. 416152, Ambijan.
44 "New York Ambijan Conference," *Ambijan Bulletin* 8, 2 (March-April 1949): 6-7; Moishe Katz, "Der ambidzhan un der kamf far sholem," *Nailebn-New Life* 22, 4 (April 1949): 5-7; Moishe Katz, "Dos yidishe lebn oyfn shvel fun yor 5710," *Nailebn-New Life* 22, 8 (September-October 1949): 2-5.
45 A.J. [Abraham Jenofsky], "Organizatsye un arbet," *Nailebn-New Life* 22, 4 (April 1949): 21-22.
46 "Organizational Activities," *Ambijan Bulletin* 8, 3 (July-August 1949): 14; letter from Sol Jesmer to J.M. Budish, Chicago, Oct. 25, 1949; letter from A. Ovrum Tapper, executive director, H.B. Ritman, chairman, Einstein Fund Dinner, and Daniel A. Uretz, president, to Ethel Osri, Chicago, Nov. 8, 1949, in Collection No. 20: Chicago Chapter, American Birobidjan Committee, Series B. Papers of Ethel Osri (From Collection No. 82). Folder 9: Fundraising Letters, Chicago Jewish Archives.
47 N. Krupin, "A derfolgraykhe ambidzhan shtat-konferents in California," *Nailebn-New Life* 22, 5 (May 1949): 12-13.
48 Circular letter from Bernard Parelhoff, secretary, Board of Directors, Ambijan, New York, May 25, 1949; Morris Stern papers, RG231, Box 1, unnamed folder, YIVO; "Organizational Activities," *Ambijan Bulletin* 8, 3 (July-August 1949): 13.
49 Nathan Frankel, "Will Cooperate in Fight for Peace," *Ambijan Bulletin* 8, 4 (December 1949): 8; A.J. [Abraham Jenofsky], "Organizatsye un arbet," *Nailebn-New Life* 22, 8 (September-October 1949): 22. Albert Kahn organized the American delegations to the pro-Soviet "world peace congresses" held in Paris in April 1949 and in Warsaw in November 1950, and attended the meeting of the World Peace Council in Stockholm in March 1950 that launched the "Stockholm Appeal" calling for an absolute ban on nuclear

weapons. Kahn died in 1979, at age 67. Eleanor Blau, "Albert E. Kahn, A Writer Critical of Government in McCarthy Era; An Unaffiliated Marxist," *New York Times*, Sept. 19, 1979, D21. For more on the Soviet-inspired postwar "peace movement," see Robbie Lieberman, *The Strangest Dream: Communism, Anti-Communism, and the U.S. Peace Movement, 1945-1963* (Syracuse, NY: Syracuse University Press, 2000).

50 A.J. [Abraham Jenofsky], "Organizatsye un arbet," *Nailebn-New Life* 22, 9 (November 1949): 21-22.

51 A.J. [Abraham Jenofsky], "Organizatsye un arbet," *Nailebn-New Life* 22, 10 (December 1949): 22-23.

52 A. Ovrum Tapper, "Rockefeller Chapel Dean Calls for Return to 'Peace' at Ambijan Meet," *Sentinel*, Chicago, Nov. 10, 1949, 28.

53 A.J. [Abraham Jenofsky], "Organizatsye un arbet," *Nailebn-New Life* 23, 1 (January 1950): 20.

54 A. Jenofsky, "Der baytrog fun ambidzhan in di letste tsvey yor," *Nailebn-New Life* 22, 10 (December 1949): 16-21; "Ambijan National Conference," *News from American Birobidjan Committee (Ambijan)*, December 1949: 2-3; "The Ambijan Annual National Dinner," *Ambijan Bulletin* 9, 1 (January-February 1950): 13. "Let Us Redouble our Efforts," *Ambijan Bulletin* 9, 1 (January-February 1950): 3; "Birobidjan and the Struggle for National Equality, International Friendship and Peace," *Ambijan Bulletin* 9, 1 (January-February 1950): 9-13. Circular letter from J.M. Budish, New York, Dec. 6, 1949; Stefansson correspondence, MSS 196, Box 78, 1949—USSR Folder, Stefansson Collection; "Barikht tsu der natsyonaler konferents fun dem ambidzhan komitet," New York, Dec. 10-11, 1949, mss; in the Abraham Jenofsky papers, RG734, Box 1, folder 5, YIVO; typed mss. of B.Z. Goldberg's speech in the B.Z. Goldberg papers, Box 94, Letters: Nachman-Outlook, folder "National Ambijan Dinner (1949)." There is a full list of all the members of the new Board of Directors elected in 1949 in "National Officers Installed at Meeting of Board of Directors, Dec. 20, 1949," *Ambijan Bulletin* 9, 1 (January-February 1950): 4.

55 Front cover of *Ambijan Bulletin* 9, 1 (January-February 1950).

56 "Ruf tsu ale yidishe organizatsyes," *Nailebn-New Life* 23, 3 (March-April 1950): 1; "New York Area Conference Demands Outlawing of Atom Bomb," *Ambijan Bulletin* 9, 2 (July-August 1950): 6-7. These were the last issues of the *Ambijan Bulletin* and *Nailebn-New Life* published. See also pp. 1-7 of the FBI report from Special Agent in Charge, New York, to Director, FBI, June 7, 1950, originally in NY File 100-42538. File 100-99898, Section 5, FOIPA No. 416152, Ambijan. Pepper lost the Democratic primary in Florida in 1950 to George Smathers, who labeled him a pro-Soviet extremist. See Alex Lichtenstein, "In the Shade of the Lenin Oak: 'Colonel' Raymond Robins, Senator Claude Pepper, and the Cold War," *American Communist History* 3, 2 (December 2004): 185-214. See also Claude Denson Pepper and Hays Gorey, *Pepper: Eyewitness to a Century* (San Diego, CA: Harcourt Brace Jovanovich,

1987) for Pepper's own view. For more on the dilemmas faced by many Jewish organizations during this period, see Aviva Weingarten, *Jewish Organizations' Response to Communism and to Senator McCarthy* (London: Vallentine Mitchell, 2008).

57 Steinberg, *The Great "Red Menace,"* 120-121, 192-193, 212-213, 230-232, 262-263, 268. See also on the destruction of the party in the post-war period Michal R. Belknap, *Cold War Political Justice: The Smith Act, the Communist Party, and American Civil Liberties* (Westport, CT: Greenwood Press, 1977), especially 185-206; and Griffin Fariello, *Red Scare: Memories of the American Inquisition. An Oral History* (New York: W.W. Norton, 1995), 199-204. For the contentious and continuing debate between various schools of historians over the role and place of the party in American life and its relationship to the Soviet Union, see John Earl Haynes and Harvey Klehr, *In Denial: Historians, Communism and Espionage* (San Francisco: Encounter Books, 2003); John Earl Haynes, "The Cold War Debate Continues: A Traditionalist View of Historical Writing on Domestic Communism and Anti-Communism," *Journal of Cold War Studies* 2, 1 (Winter 2000): 76-115; and John Earl Haynes and Harvey Klehr, "The Historiography of American Communism: An Unsettled Field," *Labour History Review* 68, 1 (April 2003): 61-78.

58 Memoranda from James M. McInerney, Assistant Attorney General, Criminal Division, Department of Justice, to J. Edgar Hoover, Director, FBI, Washington, Sept. 13, 1950 and Oct. 2, 1950. Files 100-99898-146 and 100-99898-149, FOIPA No. 416152, Ambijan.

59 Harry Schwartz, "Soviet Abandoning 'Jewish Homeland'," *New York Times*, April 22, 1951, Section 1, 20. See also pp. 5-6 of a 20-page FBI report dated March 29, 1951, and pp. 7 of a 10-page FBI report dated Nov. 29, 1951, both submitted by Edward Scheidt, Special Agent in Charge, both originally in NY File 100-42538. File 100-99898, Section 6, FOIPA No. 416152, Ambijan.

60 Memo from F.J. Baumgardner to A.H. Belmont, Washington, May 29, 1953. File 100-99898, Section 6, FOIPA No. 416152, Ambijan.

61 "Question Box: Birobidzhan," *New World Review* 19, 7 (September 1951): 55-56.

Paul Novick, courtesy *Jewish Currents*

Albert Einstein on cover of *Ambijan Bulletin*, January February 1950

Islands of Resistance, 1949-1950

Henry Wallace and the Progressive Party had failed, in the 1948 presidential campaign, to reverse the Cold War climate of domestic anti-Communism, and many of Ambijan's liberal fair-weather friends had abandoned the movement. Yet, as late as 1949-1950, Ambijan still retained a modicum of support, particularly in the Jewish left's historic heartland—the older Jewish neighborhoods of Boston, Chicago, Cleveland, Detroit, Los Angeles, Newark, New York, and Philadelphia, where the ICOR had flourished in the 1920s and 1930s.

The national organization continued to soldier on. At Ambijan's New York Area Conference on March 5-6, 1949, Abraham Jenofsky asserted that in its 15 years as an autonomous region, Birobidzhan could already boast a "rich history of colossal achievements." The settlers had built a "new, modern and progressive land, where there had previously been taiga, desert." The early pioneers had endured tremendous hardships, and even now much labor was still required to extract the natural riches of the region, which included coal and gold. Yet, the effort still remaining was "an entirely different level of battle against the taiga as opposed to 15 years ago." Large areas were now under cultivation in a modern and highly mechanized way. The region now included 66 collective farms, five state farms, an agricultural experimental station, and nine machine tractor stations. The old libel spread about Jews being unsuitable for agricultural pursuits had been totally debunked: "A new type of Jew has been created in Birobidzhan." Jews there were farmers, beekeepers, fishermen, and lumberjacks, remarked Jenofsky. They were also active in industry: Birobidzhan now had 64 major plants, manufacturing paper, cement, textiles and furniture. Their products were marketed throughout the country: Some of the marble found in the Moscow metro stations had come from Birobidzhan.

Yiddish was the JAR's official language: signs in railway stations, public buildings, street signs, all appeared in Yiddish alongside Russian. As a result of new immigration since the war's end, the number of children in Yiddish schools had increased dramatically—in 1948, there were 17,600 pupils in elementary schools alone. The region had five institutions of higher learning and a number of trade schools, not to mention specialized academies for art, music, dance, and sports. There was a state theater, and 24 movie theaters. The Birobidzhan National Library, named after Sholem Aleichem, housed more than 200,000 books; the region had 29 other libraries and 44 reading rooms. Every community had a club. A cultural center named for the recently deceased

Shloime Mikhoels had been built in the capital. Apart from two main newspapers, one in Yiddish and one in Russian, there were a number of smaller, trade papers devoted to agricultural and industrial topics, as well as a literary and artistic journal, the *Birobidzhaner Almanakh*. Books and brochures by writers, poets and scientists were being published. The region had also developed the facilities necessary to care for the physical health of its population, including 17 hospitals, 55 medical centers, and 32 polyclinics.

The war had of course taken a terrible toll, but Jenofsky predicted that Birobidzhan, "a land twice as big as Holland and three times the size of Denmark," with enormous natural resources, would continue to develop economically and culturally. The American Birobidzhan Committee could play an important part in helping Birobidzhan, he continued, not just by sending aid, but also by continuing to bring its accomplishments to the attention of the American Jewish community. The intent of Ambijan was to ensure the future of both Jewish states and "the survival of our people throughout the world," by fostering friendship between the U.S. and the Soviet Union.[1]

The New York branches remained active. At the Concourse Plaza Hotel on February 2, Olken told the Bronx Ambijan that "The Soviet Union is spending huge sums of money on Birobidjan. The Soviet government is building in Birobidjan all kinds of factories, theaters, schools and many other things which go into the making of a new state." On March 19, Bronx members held a jamboree at Pilgrim Hall on the Grand Concourse. Nathan Frankel was there to defend the foreign policy of the Soviet Union.[2] The Coops were also the venue for a concert celebrating the 15th anniversary of the JAR on March 27; the performers included folk singer Martha Shlamme and pianist Israel Schlein.[3] The Bronx Division's fourth annual Einstein Fund luncheon was held at the Waldorf-Astoria on May 26. Charlotte Rosewald spoke to 130 people about the recent World Peace Congress in Paris and described the work being done by Ambijan in the cause of peace.[4]

On May 8, there was a concert at the Hunter College Auditorium, where Budish described his recent trip to France and Poland, including a visit to the Warsaw Ghetto monument, and his attendance at the World Peace Congress in Paris. He gave special prominence to the role played at the Paris Congress by the actor and singer Paul Robeson.[5] Then pianist Irene Rosenberg, soprano Maria Kurenko, and the Jewish People's Philharmonic Chorus, directed by Dr. Leo Kopf, performed songs from Birobidzhan intended to "reflect the great strides made by the development of Jewish culture in this self-governing Jewish community." One of the pieces performed was an oratorio entitled "Birobidjan." The concert drew an audience of 2000 people.[6]

Henry Wallace spoke to the fifth annual dinner of the New Jersey Division, in Newark, on February 21; the dinner was attended by approximately 400 people and raised $4,000. Wallace stated that although he had travelled through Siberia in June 1944, he was unable to go to Birobidzhan because the Soviets feared that a visit from him might provoke an incident leading to premature war with Japan. He had been able to visit areas near Birobidzhan, and he had been told that Birobidzhan's natural resources could support a population of more than a million people: "After traveling all over Southern Siberia, I can say that it is my considered opinion that the pioneering opportunities in the Amur River country are probably better than any place in the Soviet Union...I know of no other place with as good a climate and with as good a soil which is not occupied." He was certain that Birobidzhan would within 15 years develop a prosperous industry and a thriving agriculture. Wallace expressed admiration for the "ethnic democracy" practiced in the Soviet Union, which enabled minority groups to develop their own cultures. As a result, "Birobidjan in my opinion has a significance in the life of world Jewry second only to that of Israel itself." Indeed, Wallace asserted, Birobidzhan could play an even more important role than Israel in solving the problems between East and West.[7]

Morris Olken had written in *Nailebn-New Life* that the 15th anniversary of Birobidzhan as a JAR was "a great holiday" which should be "celebrated everywhere," and indeed it was observed in several other American cities.[8] James Waterman Wise spoke on March 6 to a gathering of more than 800 people at the Eastern Congregation Hall in Detroit. He made an eloquent appeal to Detroit Jews to give their wholehearted support to both Israel and Birobidzhan: to help one was also to help the other. Waterman Wise also spoke at the Broadwood Hotel in Philadelphia on May 8. The celebration in Milwaukee on March 8, with entertainment by Maxim Brodin and Zelda Zlatin, attracted 200 people and raised $800. The celebration in Miami on March 27 was chaired by Charles Resnick, a prominent businessman; he was introduced by Bernard Roller, chair of the Greater Miami Ambijan. The Miami event was attended by 300 people and brought in $1,351. There were also gatherings in Atlanta and Kansas City; the Atlanta Ambijan Mothers Club had by September contributed $900 to the war orphans fund, reported Gertie Merlin, the secretary.[9]

Jenofsky travelled to Chicago to help organize their May 15 conference to celebrate 15 years of autonomy in Birobidzhan.[10] J.M. Budish reported on his trip to France and Poland; although he felt pain when he viewed the remains of the Warsaw ghetto, he was uplifted by the signs of a new Jewish life in Poland. He had visited 43 professional, industrial and cultural Jewish enterprises; he toured factory cooperatives, sports clubs, children's homes, schools, museums, theaters, and book publishing houses; and he saw "thousands of Jewish farmers and miners at work in fields and factories." Budish said he had been amazed "by the magnitude of their achievements" over the past three years. He told his Chicago audience that he could find no signs of anti-Semitism in Poland. "There is no desire to leave that country on the part of the Jews. They want to remain there and help rebuild it." Of course, they would be pleased to receive technical and financial help from Ambijan. Incoming president Daniel A. Uretz said that the new settlers in Birobidzhan would become "a productive new generation building the Jewish Autonomous Region," which, Budish assured the conference, would soon become a Jewish republic.[11]

At a banquet held in Cincinnati on April 3, the guest of honor was Professor Jacob Raider Marcus, president of the Hebrew Union College; he spoke on the role of Birobidzhan in Jewish life. In Washington, DC, a concert at the National Press Club Auditorium on November 13 was attended by 800 people and raised $1,061.00. The Roxbury-Dorchester branch in Boston, too, remained very active, under the leadership of Isidore Shore, a vice-president of the New England Division of Ambijan. Olken spoke to the branch on September 8; he emphasized the need to meet the increased demands from Israel, Poland and Birobidzhan for help in rehabilitating children. The branch pledged to organize a special committee to facilitate its work in these areas. All this activity was, wrote Jenofsky, "an expression of the desire for peace and in opposition to the Cold War being waged against the Soviet Union."[12]

California remained a relative stronghold of Ambijan. The Southern California Division of Ambijan, headquartered at 1058 North Western Avenue, Los Angeles, had nine chapters in 1949: Bay Cities, City Terrace, two in Eastside, Hollywood, Long Beach and San Pedro, Ontario, Fairfax and the Esther Levitt Women's Club. These chapters would remain a going concern until the final demise of the organization. Ambijan sponsors in Los Angeles included entertainment industry people such as Harold Arlen, Morris Carnovsky, Robert Cummings, Albert Maltz, Edward G. Robinson, Paul Henreid, Samuel Ornitz and Artie Shaw. During the war, movie studios, run mostly by Jews, in large part had been sympathetic to the USSR and to domestic "progressives."[13]

At a meeting of the City Terrace branch on February 4, 1949, the secretary, Dora Levy, reported that $1,300 had been raised in the previous few months. On March 26, 1,400 people celebrated 21 years of Jewish colonization in Birobidzhan, with Albert Maltz as guest speaker and Sarah Fel-Yellin as chair. The audience applauded all of Maltz's references to Stalin. A total of $8,000 was raised through donations and sales of a souvenir booklet.

Representatives of Ambijan chapters met at the Jewish Community Center in San Francisco on April 9-10 for a California Ambijan state conference. Again, the speakers were Albert Maltz and Sarah Fel-Yellin. Some 400 guests attended Maltz's speech on the first evening and $2,000 was collected. On the next day, Fel-Yellin recounted the history of Birobidzhan and the help the JAR had received from American Jewry over the years. Samuel Rosenfeld spoke of the work of the California Ambijan; he was pleased with the Los Angeles branches, and hoped they might help bolster the branches in northern California, which were smaller and less active. The conference decided to organize annual donors' dinners in Los Angeles and San Francisco.[14]

The Los Angeles donors' dinner on August 14 was held at the Roosevelt Hotel in Hollywood. John Somerville, the Hunter College professor who was a visiting professor at Stanford University and a specialist in "Soviet philosophy," was a guest speaker, along with "the beloved and colorful" Hollywood director Herbert Biberman, who attended the dinner with his wife, the actress Gale Sondergaard. Biberman said he had come in order to demonstrate his personal respect and love for Ambijan, which was working on behalf of peace and cooperation with the Soviet Union. "In a world of hate," he maintained, "it was an honor and a pleasure to be present at such a festive occasion." Biberman criticized the leaders of American Jewry, who refused to believe that the Jews of the Soviet Union were living in security and absolute equality. Nearly 400 people attended the banquet, filling the hall to capacity and donating over $12,000. Nathan Krupin praised the large turnout, declaring it proof of the desire of the Jewish community to contribute to the building of Birobidzhan.

On November 26-27, Samuel Rosenfeld provided a report of activities in the Los Angeles area to 176 delegates representing 61 organizations at the annual Southern California conference. During the first nine months of 1949, Southern California had sent $12,000 to New York headquarters. The Southern California Ambijan elected Aaron Kertman as chair, Samuel Rosenfeld as executive secretary, Harry Goldstein as organizer, and Eva Myers as treasurer. Nathan Krupin became cultural and press director; Mendel Yellin became the recording secretary; and Sarah Fel-Yellin became a vice president.[15]

As the Jewish new year 5710 arrived in the autumn of 1949, Jenofsky sent greetings to the membership and noted that Ambijan's efforts at rehabilitation were now concentrated on three areas: Birobidzhan, Israel and Poland. He told them that because the United Jewish Appeal and the Joint were discriminating against "progressive" Jewish institutions by allocating very few funds to them, Ambijan had assumed additional obligations. It had become partners with the educational and social network of *Agudath Tarbut La'am* in Israel, and with the Central Committee of Jews in Poland, and would be donating money to their children's homes; donations to children's homes in Birobidzhan and Stalingrad would continue as before. Jenofsky remarked that "the aggravated international situation, and the serious problems it creates for the Jewish people, impose upon us greater responsibilities and obligations."[16]

At Ambijan's final national conference in December 1949, Jenofsky reminded his listeners that it had been a quarter century since the ICOR had been created to inform American Jews about the Soviet Union's solution of the national question in general and the "Jewish question" in particular. In the ensuing 25 years there had been momentous events in Jewish life: the catastrophic murder of six million Jews by the Nazis and fascists, and the creation of two national Jewish states—Birobidzhan in the far east and Israel in the near east. Now, he added, Jewish cultural and communal life was being rebuilt in the new democracies of eastern Europe.

Since the end of the war, Birobidzhan had been making tremendous strides, with the construction of new factories, workers' homes, schools, hospitals, and stadiums. Currently the Jewish Autonomous Region was producing ten times as many products as in 1936. Jenofsky claimed that some 25,000 children attended 144 schools in which Yiddish was the language of instruction. A pedagogical institute, a medical school, a school for cultural workers, a music school, a graphics school, and a railway training school had been established in the JAR. The war orphans had been absorbed and many were distinguishing themselves in music, dance, and teaching. The economic and cultural advances in the JAR, based on socialist principles, were creating "a new epoch in the history of the Jewish people." Within the next few years the region would become an important center of both heavy and light industry, producing building materials, prefabricated housing, locomotives, paper, textiles, footwear, clothing, and many other items. It was essential that Ambijan's publications continue to disseminate the truth about the building of Jewish life in Israel, in the new democracies, in Birobidzhan, and throughout the Soviet Union.[17]

Writing in *Nailebn-New Life*, Lewis Schatzov declared that the story of the ICOR constituted "a wonderful chapter in the history of the Jewish masses in America." Schatzov recounted the ICOR's early projects in the agricultural colonies in Belarus, Ukraine and the Crimea, and, after 1928, its ideological and material help for Birobidzhan. The ICOR had even sent a commission of experts to Birobidzhan in 1929 to study the feasibility of Jewish immigration to the region. Meanwhile, Schatzov wrote, Ambijan was founded to help settle foreign Jews, especially those from Poland, in the JAR. For a time, due to international tensions, this goal seemed unattainable, and Ambijan had come close to winding up its affairs. But the leaders of Ambijan, "men of vision," cultured people prominent in politics, business, and the professions, understood that the promise of Birobidzhan could still be realized in a world of peace, and they decided to work towards establishing friendship between the United States and the Soviet Union. "In this they proved to be very successful. They drew into their work people who were very influential in American life. Many mayors, Congressmen, senators, church leaders and heads of other institutions supported the excellent work of Ambijan." Now Ambijan and the ICOR were united. Schatzov was confident that the unified organization would strengthen the progressive forces in Jewish life and continue its work, not just on behalf of Birobidzhan, but also on behalf of Israel and Poland.[18]

Schatzov was wrong, of course. But even in 1950, the last full year of Ambijan's existence, the national organization, and its branches, continued to hold meetings, sponsor galas, and solicit donations. Between January and July, Ambijan sent a total of $20,747 in rehabilitation gifts for children in Israel, France, Poland, Belgium and Lithuania.[19]

The Bronx and Manhattan chapters sponsored a number of events in February and March, including a lecture by Israel Epstein on "China Today." Born in Warsaw in 1915, Epstein had grown up in China and worked there as a journalist before coming to the U.S in 1945. In 1951 he would return to the new People's Republic to become a supporter of Mao Zedong's revolutionary regime and editor of the English-language *China Reconstructs* (later *China Today*). The Manhattan branch held a grand bazaar on March 10-12 in Greenwich Village, with refreshments and entertainment, and organized a concert at Town Hall on May 7, to celebrate the 16th anniversary of the JAR and the second anniversary of Israel. On February 1, the Brooklyn Ambijan held a forum featuring Eslanda Robeson, wife of Paul Robeson; a Sephardic Jew who wrote and lectured on African affairs, she had just returned from a visit to China and the USSR. The Brownsville chapter in Brooklyn held its annual banquet and dance on February 4 and raised $400; together with the Eastern Parkway branch, it held a forum on February 21, at which Eslanda Robeson spoke.[20]

In Trenton, NJ, on February 12, Morris L. Olken spoke about Soviet-American relations as the key to peace; the Trenton chapter presented $145 to the state Ambijan at the annual dinner in Newark, which took place on February 21. Charles Kuntz, J.M. Budish, Nathan Frankel and Professor John Somerville spoke; Somerville's lecture on world peace and friendship among nations was "received with great acclaim." Fred Allen, "prominent Newark attorney and educator," was the host for the event, which brought in $1,600 from the 150 guests.[21] In Philadelphia, the annual concert was held on January 6, at the Sylvania Hotel. Guest speaker William Mandel discussed the need for friendship between America and the USSR. A call for contributions to Ambijan's rehabilitation efforts netted $500. Mandel, a regular contributor to the American publication *Soviet Russia Today* who spoke Russian, was a close friend of Vilhjalmur Stefansson and was collaborating with him on a 20-volume *Encyclopedia Arctica*. Boston's "progressive people" heard Olken lecture on January 29 at a "Victory Folks Forum," on "Soviet-American Relations—Key to World Peace."[22] In Miami, close to 300 people celebrated both the 25th anniversary of the ICOR-Ambijan organization and the 16th year of the JAR on March 2 at the Miamian Restaurant. The speaker was Moishe Katz, now foreign editor of the *Morgn Frayhayt*; $830 was collected. Two days later, Morris L. Olken lectured on "The Path to Peace."[23]

William Mandel lectured on "Soviet Policy in the Far East" in Los Angeles on February 8. He noted that the formation of the People's Republic of China gave the Soviet Union a powerful new ally in Asia. Mandel, who was also selling copies of his 1946 book, *A Guide to the Soviet Union*, went on to lecture in San Francisco on February 17. A day later he was in Petaluma, where, according to Dora Wronsky, the secretary, he delivered "a brilliant analysis of the present world situation, the forces working for peace and understanding among nations."[24]

The national leaders struggled to keep Ambijan alive. That summer, in an attempt to mobilize the membership, Budish visited chapters in Washington, DC, Chicago, Philadelphia, Baltimore, Cincinnati, Minneapolis, Detroit, Newark, Seattle, Portland, OR, San Francisco and Los Angeles. But the end was near. The Chicago Ambijan held a conference at the Palmer House on June 11, 1950; this seems to have been their last official function. On June 22, Daniel Uretz called a special meeting of the Ambijan Committee, and reported that Budish had advised him that the national organization could no longer afford the expense of operating the Chicago office. The committee voted that the office be liquidated. Budish travelled to Chicago in July and spoke to the committee at a meeting held on July 27. He informed them that the organization "does not now furnish any further assistance to Birobidjan, since it is no longer required there." The Chicago Ambijan closed their offices on November 9, 1950.[25]

As late as May 5, 1951, the Southern California Division, now known as the Southern California Committee for Jewish Rehabilitation, held a meeting at which Rabbi Bick spoke about "The Sixth World Power—the Peace Movement." Bick related his recent experiences as a delegate to the Second World Peace Congress held in Warsaw in November 1950. He criticized Israel for supporting the U.S. in the Korean War. But the Southern California Committee ceased to exist soon afterwards.[26]

ENDNOTES

1 "The Importance of Ambijan Activities," *Nailebn-New Life* 22, 4 (April 1949): 24; "Barikht tsu der ambidzhan konferents," New York, March 5-6, 1949, mss; in the Abraham Jenofsky papers, RG734, Box 1, folder 5, YIVO.

2 "Organizational Activities," *Ambijan Bulletin* 8, 2 (March-April 1949): 15. See also p. 75 of a 78-page FBI report dated Nov. 2, 1949, submitted by Edward Scheidt, Special Agent in Charge, originally in NY File 100-42538. File 100-99898, Section 4, FOIPA No. 416152, Ambijan.

3 Letter from Abraham Jenofsky to Morris Stern, New York, March 11, 1949; brochure advertising "Kontsert un fayerung"; in the Morris Stern papers, RG231, Box 1, unnamed folder, YIVO.

4 "Bronx, N.Y. Branch Fourth Annual Luncheon," *Nailebn-New Life* 22, 6 (June 1949): 23.

5 Letter from Abraham Jenofsky to Morris Stern, New York, April 9, 1949; Morris Stern papers, RG231, Box 1, unnamed folder, YIVO; "Organizational Activities," *Ambijan Bulletin* 8, 3 (July-August 1949): 13.

6 Letter from Abraham Jenofsky to Morris Stern, New York, April 9, 1949; Morris Stern papers, RG231, Box 1, unnamed folder, YIVO; Circular letter from J.M. Budish, executive vice-president, Ambijan, New York, April 18, 1949; Morris Stern papers, RG231, Box 1, unnamed folder; YIVO; ad for the concert, *Ambijan Bulletin* 8, 2 (March-April 1949): 16; "Organizational Activities," *Ambijan Bulletin* 8, 3 (July-August 1949): 13.

7 "Organizational News Items," *Nailebn-New Life* 22, 3 (March 1949): 23; "Henry Wallace Guest Speaker at Newark Anniversary Dinner," *Nailebn-New Life* 22, 4 (April 1949): 23; Henry A. Wallace, "American Support of Birobidjan Hopeful Sign Toward Peace," *Ambijan Bulletin* 8, 2 (March-April 1949): 7-9 and *Nailebn-New Life* 22, 6 (June 1949): 23-24. For Wallace's trip through the Soviet Far East in 1944, and his incredible naiveté at not realizing the truth about some of the places he was shown—they were in fact gulag slave labor camps run by the secret police—see Tim Tzouliadis, *The Forsaken: An American Tragedy in Stalin's Russia* (New York: Penguin Press, 2008), 218-226.

8 M.L. Olken, "Aktuayleh oyfgabn fun dem ambidzhan," *Nailebn-New Life* 22, 5 (May 1949): 10-11.

9 "Organizational Activities," *Ambijan Bulletin* 8, 2 (March-April 1949): 14-15; "Organizational Activities," *Ambijan Bulletin* 8, 3 (July-August 1949): 15; A.J. [Abraham Jenofsky], "Organizatsye un arbet," *Nailebn-New Life* 22, 5 (May 1949): 19-20; "Atlanta Continues its Good Work," *Nailebn-New Life* 22, 8 (September-October 1949): 23.

10 Letter from Abraham Jenofsky to Morris Stern, New York, April 28, 1949; Morris Stern papers, RG231, Box 2, "Correspondence" folder, YIVO.

11 A.M. Margolis, "Barikht fun der 15ter yubili-konferents fun chicagoer ambidzhan," *Nailebn-New Life* 22, 6 (June 1949): 15-16; "Organizational

Activities," *Ambijan Bulletin* 8, 3 (July-August 1949): 14. The annual Einstein Fund Dinner, held on November 26, featured Keith Wheeler, a journalist with the *Chicago Sun-Times*, as guest speaker. Henry Wallace, Paul Robeson, and Franklin D. Roosevelt Jr., were among the names suggested for guest speaker at the Einstein Dinner, but there is no evidence they were ever contacted. Minutes, July 13, 1949, in Collection No. 20: Chicago Chapter, American Birobidjan Committee, Series A. Minutes. Folder 6: Minutes, 1949-50, Chicago Jewish Archives.

12 "Ambijan Evening in Washington Huge Success," *Ambijan Bulletin* 8, 4 (December 1949): 2; "Organizational Activities," *Ambijan Bulletin* 8, 4 (December 1949): 15; A.J. [Abraham Jenofsky], "Organizatsye un arbet," *Nailebn-New Life* 22, 5 (May 1949): 20; A.J. [Abraham Jenofsky], "Organizatsye un arbet," *Nailebn-New Life* 22, 8 (September-October 1949): 20-21; A.J. [Abraham Jenofsky], "Organizatsye un arbet," *Nailebn-New Life* 22, 9 (November 1949): 22; A.J. [Abraham Jenofsky], "Organizatsye un arbet," *Nailebn-New Life* 23, 1 (January 1950): 21.

13 See the full-page advertisement placed by eight major Hollywood movie studios in the *Ambijan Bulletin* 2, 3 (April 1943): 1. Below a picture of the Statue of Liberty holding aloft her torch in the evening, it reads, "The motion picture industry salutes the greatest star of all!" Ornitz was one of ten screenwriters who on November 24, 1947, were cited for contempt of Congress. They became known as the "Hollywood Ten." See Arthur Eckstein, "The Hollywood Ten in History and Memory," *Film History* 16, 4 (2004): 424-436. There is an extremely large body of literature on blacklisting in the movie industry during the McCarthy era. For a sympathetic Communist view written at the time, see Gordon Kahn, *Hollywood on Trial: The Story of the 10 Who Were Indicted* (New York, Boni & Gaer, 1948). For a more complete history of Communist activity in the film industry, see Gerald Horne, *Class Struggle in Hollywood 1930-1950: Moguls, Mobsters, Stars, Reds, and Trade Unionists* (Austin, TX: University of Texas Press, 2001); Larry Ceplair and Steven Englund, *The Inquisition in Hollywood: Politics in the Film Community, 1930-60* (Urbana, IL: University of Illinois Press, 2003); and Ronald Radosh and Allis Radosh, *Red Star over Hollywood: The Film Colony's Long Romance With the Left* (San Francisco: Encounter Books, 2005).

14 A.J. [Abraham Jenofsky], "Organizatsye un arbet," *Nailebn-New Life* 22, 4 (April 1949): 20-21; N. Krupin, "A derfolgraykhe ambidzhan shtatkonferents in California," *Nailebn-New Life* 22, 5 (May 1949): 12-13. See also pp. 1-2 of the seven-page FBI Report of R.B. Hood, Special Agent in Charge, Sept. 28, 1949, originally in LA File 100-23652. File 100-99898, Section 4, FOIPA No. 416152, Ambijan. Maltz, an author, short-story writer, playwright and screenwriter, was blacklisted in Hollywood after 1947 for refusing to testify about Communist affiliations to the House Un-American Activities Committee. He was fined and sentenced to a year's imprisonment in 1950. He moved to Mexico after his release following nine months in jail and

remained there until 1962. His book *A Long Day in a Short Life* (New York: International Publishers, 1957) is based on his experiences.

15 A.J. [Abraham Jenofsky], "Organizatsye un arbet," *Nailebn-New Life* 22, 7 (July-August 1949): 20-21; "Organizational Activities," *Ambijan Bulletin* 8, 3 (July-August 1949): 15; N. Krupin, "Der 'donor-diner' in los angeles – a prekhtike aktsye far birobidzhan in far sholem," *Nailebn-New Life* 22, 8 (September-October 1949): 17-18; "American-Russian Relations Key to World Peace," *Nailebn-New Life* 22, 8 (September-October 1949): 23-24; "Organizational Activities," *Ambijan Bulletin* 8, 4 (December 1949): 15. The Yellins were an important couple in the California Ambijan; both were in the Communist Party. Mendel was born in Bialystok, Poland in 1894, Sarah in nearby Krynki, in 1895. A rising star, Sarah had given a series of lectures on Ambijan in New York and New Jersey in June of 1949; at a meeting of the East Bronx Ambijan on June 15, she was introduced by Gina Medem. On June 20, an evening was organized in her honor at Rappaport's Restaurant in Manhattan, with most of the national executive present.

16 "Ambijan National Conference Sunday, Dec. 11, 1949," *Nailebn-New Life* 22, 8 (September-October 1949): 24; A.J. [Abraham Jenofsky], "Organizatsye un arbet," *Nailebn-New Life* 22, 8 (September-October 1949): 20. *Agudath Tarbut La'am* was a movement tied to MAKI, the Israeli Communist Party.

17 A. Jenofsky, "Der baytrog fun ambidzhan in di letste tsvey yor," *Nailebn-New Life* 22, 10 (December 1949): 16-21; "Barikht tsu der natsyonaler konferents fun dem ambidzhan komitet," New York, Dec. 10-11, 1949, mss; in the Abraham Jenofsky papers, RG734, Box 1, folder 5, YIVO.

18 Dr. L. Schatzov, "A fertl yorhundert fun hilf un oyfklerung," *Nailebn-New Life* 22, 10 (December 1949): 14-16.

19 A.J. [Abraham Jenofsky], "Organizatsye un arbet," *Nailebn-New Life* 23, 2 (February 1950): 21-22; "Shipments of Rehabilitation Gifts by Ambijan Committee," *Ambijan Bulletin* 9, 2 (July-August 1950): 4.

20 A.J. [Abraham Jenofsky], "Organizatsye un arbet," *Nailebn-New Life* 23, 1 (January 1950): 21; A.J. [Abraham Jenofsky], "Organizatsye un arbet," *Nailebn-New Life* 23, 2 (February 1950): 20-21; A.J. [Abraham Jenofsky], "Organizatsye un arbet," *Nailebn-New Life* 23, 3 (March-April 1950): 20; ad for "Grand Bazaar," *Nailebn-New Life* 23, 2 (February 1950): 23. The information on the Town Hall concert is contained on pp.12-13 of a 42-page report dated Oct. 27, 1950, submitted by Edward Scheidt, Special Agent in Charge, originally in NY File 100-42538. File 100-99898, Section 6, FOIPA No. 416152, Ambijan. Israel Epstein had written a number of books about the Chinese Communist revolution, including *The People's War* (London: Victor Gollanz, 1939); *I Visit Yenan: Eye Witness Account of the Communist-led Liberated Areas in North-West China* (Bombay: People's Publishing House, 1945); and *The Unfinished Revolution in China* (Boston: Little, Brown and Co., 1947). Epstein died in Beijing May 26, 2005. See his autobiography, *My China Eye: Memoirs of a Jew and a Journalist* (San Francisco: Long River Press, 2005).

CHAPTER NINE

21 "Trenton Ambijan Active," *Nailebn-New Life* 23, 3 (March-April 1950): 23; "New Jersey Ambijan Dinner Outstanding Success," *Ambijan Bulletin* 9, 2 (July-August 1950): 15.
22 A.J. [Abraham Jenofsky], "Organizatsye un arbet," *Nailebn-New Life* 23, 1 (January 1950): 21; "Boston Ambijan Lecture Successful," *Nailebn-New Life* 23, 3 (March-April 1950): 23.
23 A.J. [Abraham Jenofsky], "Organizatsye un arbet," *Nailebn-New Life* 23, 3 (March-April 1950): 20; "Miami, Florida," *Ambijan Bulletin* 9, 2 (July-August 1950): 2.
24 A.J. [Abraham Jenofsky], "Organizatsye un arbet," *Nailebn-New Life* 23, 1 (January 1950): 21; A.J. [Abraham Jenofsky], "Organizatsye un arbet," *Nailebn-New Life* 23, 2 (February 1950): 21-22; A.J. [Abraham Jenofsky], "Organizatsye un arbet," *Nailebn-New Life* 23, 3 (March-April 1950): 20-21; "Petaluma Pleased with Mandel's Lecture," *Nailebn-New Life* 23, 3 (March-April 1950): 23; "Los Angeles," "San Francisco, California," *Ambijan Bulletin* 9, 2 (July-August 1950): 15. The Southern California information is also on pp. 5-7 of the 46-page FBI report of R.B. Hood, Special Agent in Charge, May 9, 1950, originally in LA File 100-23652. File 100-99898, Section 5, FOIPA No. 416152, Ambijan.
25 A.J. [Abraham Jenofsky], "Organizatsye un arbet," *Nailebn-New Life* 23, 2 (February 1950): 21; "Executive Vice-President J.M. Budish on Organizational Tour of West Coast," *Ambijan Bulletin* 9, 2 (July-August 1950): 4; Minutes, June 22, 1950; July 27, 1950, in Collection No. 20: Chicago Chapter, American Birobidjan Committee, Series A. Minutes. Folder 6: Minutes, 1949-50, Chicago Jewish Archives. Chicago information is in the 4-page FBI Report of G.R. McSwain, Special Agent in Charge, Jan. 6, 1951, originally in File 100-18113. File 100-99898, Section 6, FOIPA No. 416152, Ambijan.
26 FBI Memo from SAC, San Francisco, to Director, FBI, Jan. 29, 1952, originally in SF File 100-26751. File 100-99898, Section 6, FOIPA No. 416152, Ambijan.

Flyer advertising Ambijan conference celebrating 15th anniversary of Birobidzhan as a Jewish Autonomous Region, 1949 (English side), YIVO Institute for Jewish Research, New York

רוף

צו אַלע אידישע אָרגאַניזאַציעס, לאַנדסמאַנשאַפֿטן, סאָסייעטיס, פֿראַטערנאַלע אָרדנס,
פֿרויען־אָקזיליערים, קאָנגרעגיישאַנס, טרייד־יוניאָנס און קולטור־אינסטיטוטעס

צו דער

קאָנפֿערענץ
אין ניו־יאָרק און אָמגעגנט

צום 15טן יוביליי פֿון ביראָבידזשאַן
אַלס אידישע אויטאָנאָמע געגנט

פּראָגראַם:	פֿייערלעכע דערעפֿענונג:
וויוויען ריפֿקין	שבת, דעם 5טן מערץ, 1949, 8:30 אָוונט
קאָנצערט־פּיאַניסטין	אין אָדיטאָריום פֿון דער
נאָרמאַן אַטקינס	ניו־סקול פֿאַר סאָשיעל ריסוירטש
באַריטאָן	66 וועסט 12טע גאַס. ניו־יאָרק.
באַגריסונגען: פֿאָרשטייער פֿון אָרגאַניזאַציעס	

	זיצונגען — זונטאָג, דעם 6טן מערץ:
אײער אָרגאַניזאַציע איז געבעטן צו דערװײלן צװײ	1טע זיצונג — 10:30 אינדערפֿרי.
דעלעגאַטן צו דער קאָנפֿערענץ. שיקט אײער קרעדענשל	2טע זיצונג — פֿון 2 ביימאָג ביז 5 פֿאַרנאַכט
אין אָפֿיס פֿון אַמבידזשאַן.	אין קאָמאָדאָר האָטעל
New York Area Conference	42טע גאַס בײַ לעקסינגטאָן עווענין. ניו־יאָרק.
American Birobidjan Committee (Ambijan)	
103 Park Avenue, New York 17, N. Y. • MU 3-8895-6-7	

פֿון דער באַגריסונג פֿון
פּראָפֿעסאָר אַלבערט איינשטיין,
ערן־פּרעזידענט פֿון דעם
אַמעריקאַנער ביראָבידזשאַן קאָמיטעט:

„עס איז פֿון גרויס וויכטיקייט פֿאַר אידן, אַז דער פּרינציפּ פֿון נעגנזייטיקער הילף זאָל אָנגעהאַלטן
ווערן, טראָצן די פֿאַלישיסטישע מיספֿאַרשטעדענעניש וואָס עקסיסטירט אין דער נים־אידישער וועלט. דאָס גיט צום דעם
אַמעריקאַנער ביראָבידזשאַן קאָמיטעטן הײנטו צו מאָג אַ ספּעציעלע באַדיטונג. באַדיטונג פֿונעם אידישן שמאַנדפּונקט. נאָך
מער: אַם די אויפֿגאַבע קאָן בײטראָגן צום פֿאַרליכטערן די אָנגעציגענע שפּאַנונג, וועלכע עקזיסטירט צום
באַדוירן צווישן דעם מזרח און מערב, און צום דערגרייכן אַ בעסערע נעגנזייטיקע פֿאַרשטענדיקונג."

רעגיסטראַציע־אַפּצאָל: 1 דאָלער פֿון אַ דעלעגאַט. פֿאַר װעלכן ער קריגט אױך אַ בילעט צום קאָנצערט.

Flyer advertising Ambijan conference celebrating 15th anniversary of Birobidzhan as a Jewish Autonomous Region, 1949 (Yiddish side), YIVO Institute for Jewish Research, New York

Conclusion: From Hope to Hoax

In 1946, when Ambijan incorporated with the ICOR, veteran ICOR activists such as Abraham Jenofsky and Morris Stern feared that the more anglicized elements in Ambijan would dominate the pro-Birobidzhan movement. Even in the Jewish Communist movement, with its mainly immigrant base, there were ever fewer Yiddish speakers after World War II. The official Communist position was that, while Yiddish would continue to play a major role "in the struggle for a progressive mass Jewish culture in America," English would eventually come to dominate in Jewish economic and cultural life.[1]

Jenofsky shared Stern's belief that "Ambijan ought to concern itself more with Yiddish and with Yiddish literature." In a letter dated December 20, 1946, Jenofsky wrote Stern that Ambijan had recently published two brochures in Yiddish and would be paying greater heed to the *landsmanshaftn*. As for making use of the language at meetings, "there is no policy of discriminating against Yiddish." In New York, where the city committee was comprised almost entirely of former ICOR branches, the official language of business was Yiddish. At a recent meeting of the city committee, for example, Dr. Lewis Schatzov and Morris L. Olken had made presentations in Yiddish while Professor Kuntz spoke in English. Yiddish was still routinely spoken in the other big cities where there were many branches. "But I don't want to hide the fact that nationally…the dominant language is English. Even those who have to strain to make themselves understood in English speak it," Jenofsky wrote.[2] If Ambijan did not take this into account, "we will be the losers."[3]

Clearly Jenofsky feared that the more assimilated (and more affluent) Jews in Ambijan would become hegemonic, marginalizing those who had spent more than two decades working within the ICOR. This would not turn out to be the case. In fact, as the Cold War intensified, the old-guard Yiddish speakers, mainly doctrinaire ICOR veterans, would assume greater roles in the amalgamated organization. A number of founders and early "stars," such as William Cohen, Lord Marley, and James N. Rosenberg, had died, drifted away, or moved on to other endeavors.[4] Many of the more moderate Ambijan members, liberals who had felt comfortable belonging to Ambijan between 1934 and 1945, when the battle waged was against foreign fascism and Nazism, jumped ship once the "enemy" became America itself. While these fair-weather friends departed, the tried and true ICOR people—activists such as Jenofsky, Stern, Gina Medem, Moishe Katz, Charles Kuntz, and Lewis Schatzov—

stayed on. Their dominance in the new, combined organization was reflected in its publications: although the ICOR had stopped publishing *Nailebn-New Life* in December 1945, in January 1947 Ambijan resuscitated the dual-language periodical. Many articles in the later issues of *Nailebn-New Life* even referred to "the ICOR-Ambijan."[5]

The May 1949 issue of *Nailebn-New Life* carried an article on Khaim Zhitlovsky, on the sixth anniversary of his death. The March-April 1950 number printed a speech delivered by Jenofsky at a memorial meeting held on February 25, 1950 at the New School for Social Research in New York for Reuben Brainin, who had died in November 1939. The meeting commemorating the noted ICOR activist had been sponsored jointly by Ambijan and the American Committee of Jewish Writers, Artists and Scientists.[6] The Ambijan of the 1930s would scarcely have noticed these stalwarts of Yiddishist diaspora nationalism and territorialism.

Perhaps the old-timers, who had invested so much psychological capital in the movement, were the only ones still able to sustain their faith in the USSR. Indeed, Rabbi Bick wrote an article in praise of Stalin on the occasion of his 70th birthday in December 1949. Quoting liberally from Stalin's own writings, Bick described how "the man who had himself suffered from oppression took it upon himself to figure out a way to liberate all oppressed peoples." Stalin's policies had also completely altered the Soviet Jewish community, he asserted: The Soviet Jews had become workers, farmers, intellectuals, and heroes. The most wonderful result of Stalin's nationality policy was the creation of the Jewish Autonomous Region: "Jews in the Soviet Union, in the new democracies, and the progressive Jewish masses in Israel and throughout the world, recognize the great assistance given by the Soviet state towards the proclamation, and military victory, of the state of Israel, a consequence of Stalin's desire for the self-determination for all peoples."[7]

The true situation in the USSR was of course very different. As the Cold War intensified, Stalin became increasingly paranoid and the USSR more xenophobic. Beginning in November 1948, anti-Jewish purges wracked the Soviet Union. The Jewish Anti-Fascist Committee, which had been created during World War II to encourage Western Jewish support for the alliance with the Soviet Union, was dissolved, along with most other Jewish institutions, including those in Birobidzhan. The last Jewish school in Birobidzhan was shut down in 1948; in 1950, all remaining Jewish schools in the USSR were closed. Not a single Yiddish publication would be published from 1948 until 1959. Jews were dismissed, under various pretexts, from all important political, diplomatic and military positions. The number of Jews in the Supreme Soviet declined precipitously. Israel was increasingly described as an American "colony" and satellite of western imperialism, especially after it sided with the U.S. in the Korean War. In 1953, Moscow broke off diplomatic relations with Israel following the explosion of a bomb near the Soviet embassy in Tel Aviv. Relations were resumed after Stalin's death, but deteriorated further in 1955 when the Soviets began to sell arms to Egypt and to cultivate closer relations with other Arab states.

In the last years of Stalin's rule, most high-profile Soviet Jewish intellectuals who had been involved with western Jewish movements were executed after trials in which they were accused of plotting on behalf of "Zionism" and "imperialism." Jewish officials now stood accused of counter-revolutionary nationalism and of conspiring with American imperialism against the Soviet Union; specifically, they were charged with plotting to turn the Crimea into a Jewish republic that would serve as a "bridgehead" for Zionism and U.S. imperialism. The JAFC had sought support from Soviet officials for this project, especially after most of the Tatar population of the peninsula was deported by Stalin in May 1944 for having allegedly collaborated with the Nazis during the occupation. While in New York in 1943, Mikhoels and Fefer had also discussed, with James N. Rosenberg, chair of the Board of Directors of the Joint, the possibility of having the Joint finance new Jewish settlements in the Crimea. These conversations were now examined through a more sinister lens. Ironically, evidence of this anti-Soviet treachery even included past contacts with Jewish pro-Communist organizations such as the ICOR and Ambijan, and with individuals such as B.Z. Goldberg, who travelled widely in the Ukraine, Belarus, and the Baltic states in 1946, and Paul Novick, who visited the Soviet Union from September 1946 to the spring of 1947. The two Americans had both been watched carefully by Soviet intelligence as they made contact with Soviet Jewish leaders. Mikhoels and Fefer would later stand accused of having been given instructions by the two Americans, on behalf of the Joint, to "tear the Crimea away from the Soviet Union."[8]

Former ICOR national secretaries Dr. Elias (Elye) Wattenberg and Leon Talmy, who had both immigrated to the USSR in the 1930s and who had become members of the JAFC in Moscow during the war, were arrested, along with their wives, in the late 1940s. Wattenberg, originally a Left Poale Zionist, was the first secretary of the ICOR and had attended the GEZERD Congress held in Moscow in November 1926. He and his wife Chaika Ostrovskaya left for the USSR in March 1933. During the Second World War the Wattenbergs served as editors and translators for the JAFC. Talmy, Wattenberg's successor as the ICOR's national secretary, had already immigrated to the USSR along with wife Sonya and their son Vladimir in October 1932.[9] In the 1930s Talmy became a translator and head of the English section of the Foreign Languages Publishing House in Moscow, where Chaika Ostrovskaya Wattenberg was an assistant editor. Talmy's wartime dispatches from Kuibyshev (now Samara), the city to which the Soviet government and the JAFC moved when Moscow was threatened by the Nazis in 1941, were published in various Yiddish-language Communist newspapers. By that time, Sonya Talmy was an English teacher at the Moscow Institute of Foreign Languages

Although Talmy had been a founder of the American CP, and had written pro-Soviet articles for the *Nation*, while Wattenberg had represented Soviet commercial interests in New York, this did them more harm than good: their years in America had made them vulnerable to charges of espionage. Stalin put Talmy and Wattenberg on trial with others connected in various ways to the JAFC, including the renowned Yiddish writers and intellectuals Peretz Markish, Leyb Kvitko, David Hofshteyn, Itsik Fefer and David Bergelson.[10]

The fifteen accused were all charged with a range of capital offenses, from treason and espionage to bourgeois nationalism. Talmy and Wattenberg, along with 11 others (including Chaika Wattenberg), were convicted and executed on August 12, 1952.[11] After Talmy's death, Sonya was briefly exiled to Siberia in 1952-1953. Son Vladimir, born in New York in 1924, had been arrested on charges of "betraying the Motherland" in 1947 while serving with the Soviet Army in Berlin. Sentenced to 25 years in a Siberian labor camp, he was released in 1955.[12]

The so-called "Doctors' Plot" signalled the beginning of yet more repression. On January 13, 1953, the Soviets announced that a conspiracy had been unmasked among Jewish doctors in the USSR to murder Kremlin leaders. Mass arrests quickly followed. A new wave of persecution was halted only as a result of Stalin's death on March 5, 1953.[13]

Meanwhile, in all the east European countries under Soviet domination, Jews were regarded as traitors and aliens. In Czechoslovakia in 1952, 14 Communist leaders were arrested for treason and espionage, including the deputy premier and secretary of the Communist Party, Rudolph Slansky. Eleven of the 14 were Jewish; they were accused of being Titoist and Zionist agents in a conspiracy organized by an Anglo-American network. Nine of the Jews were executed, in a flurry of anti-Semitic propaganda. Similar show trials took place in East Germany, Hungary, Romania and other Soviet satellite states.[14] The slightest deviation from the Soviet pattern was declared treasonable and tens of thousands of people were sent to slave labor camps. Foreign and international Jewish welfare agencies were expelled.

Abraham Bick defended the trials, rejecting as "ill-intentioned lies" those "rumors which claim that these enemies of the people, these spies, were tried because they were Jews."[15] On the other hand, James Waterman Wise admitted that he had been wrong "in a conviction earnestly held":

"I refer, of course, to the status of the Jews in the Soviet Union, and to Russia's adoption of anti-Semitism as a political instrument."[16]

When the Moscow bureau chief of the *New York Times*, Harrison Salisbury, was permitted to visit Birobidzhan in June 1954, he was constantly shadowed by Soviet MVD (later KGB) secret police agents: "Never, in my stay in Russia, had I experienced such surveillance." Nonetheless, he managed to learn a great deal about the JAR, which seemed to have no particular Jewish character. "Established originally as a Jewish settlement colony in an obvious move to provide a counterweight to Palestine in the early thirties," he concluded, "it was plain that Birobidjan had lost its significance as a Jewish center a long time ago." It was now part of the Soviet gulag, "MVD-land."[17] In one factory he was shown "excellent" American-made cloth-cutting machines, presumably sent through Ambijan. He was told by Lev Yevfremovich Vinkevich, the head of the regional government, that the Jews in Birobidzhan all preferred to use Russian rather than Yiddish. A full-page feature article in the *New York Times*, with many photographs, noted that the importance of Birobidzhan as a "Jewish homeland" was in decline.[18] Salisbury's dispatches, editorialized the newspaper, "testify eloquently to the failure of the once much publicized Soviet effort to build a 'Jewish homeland' at Birobidzhan in eastern Siberia." Most of the settlers left because "they could not stand the climate or the primitive conditions of life." While Birobidzhan had all of the hardships associated with frontier areas, it lacked "the attractions of a free life or prospective riches to draw the adventurous."[19]

It was now apparent that Birobidzhan would in all likelihood remain marginal to the future of Soviet Jewry. Most Jews who had survived the Nazi invasion chose to remain in the large cities of western Russia, Ukraine, Belarus and the Baltic states. Jewish immigration to Birobidzhan had long since ceased, though the Jewish Autonomous Region continued to exist as a legal entity.

Stalin and his successor, Nikita Khrushchev, tried to blame the Jews themselves for the stagnation of Birobidzhan. Stalin "is supposed to have noted privately [at the Yalta Conference during the war] that he was displeased with the Jews, who had failed to build up their own territory—Biro-Bidzhan."[20] In 1958, Khrushchev told a correspondent for the French newspaper *Le Figaro* that Soviet Jews "do not like collective work, group discipline. They have always preferred to be dispersed. They are individualists."[21] As one American Jewish social democrat noted in a Bundist journal in 1959, "at the 25th anniversary of the great Bolshevik Birobidzhan project, we can only speak of a great fiction." The Birobidzhan project, like so much else, had been exposed as largely fraudulent and a complete failure.[22]

Michael Stanislawski has suggested that the Soviet government encouraged the Birobidzhan venture for a combination of reasons: "Far Eastern foreign policy, the hope of winning support among Western Jewry, and the need to ameliorate the economic crisis of the Jews in the Soviet Union." Certainly the project was initiated, not by the Jews themselves, but by the Soviet leadership.[23] Apart from the inhospitable climate, "Jews felt no attachment to a territory that was utterly alien to them, and had no roots in their tradition or consciousness."[24] After all, the Soviet notion of a culture that was national only in form denuded Jewish culture of all its traditional folkways and historical values. Even when schools taught in Yiddish, there was nothing particularly "Jewish" about their curriculum. So why make sacrifices to settle in Birobidzhan?[25]

Yet Jewish Communists had feared that if too much stress was placed on the Jewishness of the region rather than on "building socialism," the ever-dangerous virus of "Jewish nationalism" might gain the upper hand. For that and many other reasons, Chimen Abramsky has concluded, the Birobidzhan venture, "born of contradictory trends in policy, executed haphazardly, and without due consideration for Jewish feelings and sentiments, was doomed to failure and tragic collapse."[26]

The Jewish Communists had grieved Stalin's death in 1953. But much worse was to come: in February 1956, at the 20th Congress of the CPSU, Nikita Khrushchev exposed the murderous deeds of Stalin and his henchmen. Detailed revelations of anti-Semitic repression in the Soviet Union after 1948 were published in the Polish press and elsewhere. Jessica Smith, editor of *New World Review* (formerly *Soviet Russia Today*) was forced to admit, "I owe our readers an explanation of our editorial position on many matters now revealed in quite a different light than we formerly presented them....I can only express the deepest regret that through my own too unquestioning faith I have misled so many others in certain respects."[27]

Nowhere was the crisis of faith more profound than among the Jewish Communists. For most, it was now apparent that the ideals they had taken so seriously had been used by the Soviets as a cynical camouflage for despotism. "The defining feature of the history of the Soviet Union," as Tim Tzouliadis and so many others have noted, "beyond which all else pales into insignificance, was the murder of millions of innocent citizens by the state."[28] The Jewish Communists now realized that, in their aspirations to build a democratic future without war and oppression, they had committed themselves to a social system that proved, in every sense, the negation of that vision, a system where capricious arrests, often for trifling and seemingly absurd reasons, were followed by sentences to slave labor camps where cold, starvation and punishing work crushed inmates physically and spiritually. To have lived as a Communist had meant lying about, or at least living a lie in regards to, the main events in their own lives and in the history of their times.

Rabbi Bick remained faithful until the Arab-Israeli War of June 1967. He left the editorial board of the *Morgn Frayhayt* in February 1968 because, as he wrote to his friend B.Z. Goldberg, the Soviets, in their uncritical support of the Arab cause and in their vicious anti-Israeli statements, had become anti-Semites. "I want to remain faithful to my own ideals and to the highest interests of the Jewish people—the state of Israel." Soon Bick was writing for *Der Tog* about the anti-Semitic books being produced in the Soviet Union. *Morgn Frayhayt* editor Paul Novick wrote to Bick to recall that even in 1956, Bick had remained faithful to the ideals that inspired the Soviet revolution, because he had known that that the road to a better world is not an easy one. Now, however, Bick had been caught up in the anti-Soviet hysteria fomented by religious and chauvinistic elements in Israel. "A shame, and hurtful," concluded Novick.[29]

In fact, Novick himself would soon become as disillusioned as Bick. Novick had begun to steer the *Morgn Frayhayt* away from uncritical loyalty to Moscow as early as 1956, when he was deeply disturbed by the revelation that in 1952, Stalin had executed many Yiddish writers, including some who had been *Morgn Frayhayt* contributors. He realized that Jewish Communists had been all too ready to take Soviet party officials at their word when they had defended Stalin. But leaving the Communist movement was no easy task, and Novick was among the last to go. By the late 1960s, he was critical of Soviet Jewish policy and disturbed by the anti-Semitic outbursts in Poland.[30] As a result, he was expelled from the CP's central committee after the 1967 Middle East war; in 1972, accused of serving "Jewish nationalism and Zionism," he was expelled from the party as a whole.[31]

After Ambijan's demise, Jenofsky was for a time unemployed. But he devoted himself to the YKUF and by 1970 had become its general secretary. Jenofsky died in 1976 at age 75. He was survived by his wife, Freida Barash Jenofsky, who had come to the U.S. in 1920 and who worked until 1950 for the Soviet Purchasing Commission in New York; and by his daughter, Lillian (Lenna).[32] At a memorial service held that April 1, Paul Novick spoke of the energy Jenofsky had exerted on behalf of the ICOR, Ambijan, and the YKUF. He had been a "faithful worker" for the progressive Jewish movement until his last days, fighting against both religious "obscurantism" and bourgeois "assimilationism."[33]

In 1979, Shloime Almazov died at age 90. At the unveiling of Almazov's tombstone a year later, Novick spoke of Almazov's life: he "threw himself into numerous progressive activities. He was the leader of the ICOR movement, which was an important one among the Jewish masses in the United States and Canada." Novick recalled the creation of Birobidzhan and its impact. "This was a period when anti-Semitism was, without mercy, conquered in the Soviet Union, when Jewish culture bloomed like never before in the history of the Jewish people." Almazov's role at that time, "as a mobilizer of the broad masses, with the help of such personalities in Jewish life as Reuben Brainin, Jacob Milch, Professor Charles Kuntz, was a wonderful high point in his work as a communal activist. [He] used to recall that period with nostalgia and with pain, because of its sharp collapse." For the last decades of his life, Almazov worked on the *Morgn Frayhayt*, and "the paper was his life," said Novick. "We remember him as a fellow fighter."[34]

As late as 1947, the *Morgn Frayhayt* had enjoyed a circulation of more than 20,000. But as its readership began literally to die, the paper experienced financial difficulties. Novick, who continued as its editor after leaving the CPUSA, admitted to Paul Buhle that the *Morgn Frayhayt* "discovered its unique identity and mission within the Left too late."[35] It became a weekly in 1981 and ceased publication entirely on September 11, 1988. Novick, who died a year later, remained a Marxist; in the words of Morris Schappes, the longtime editor of *Jewish Currents*, "He shed his illusions, but not his principles…Novick learned from his blunders, and taught us to learn too."[36]

What are we to make of the non-Jewish fellow-travelers in Ambijan? Lord Marley died in 1952, so did not live to see his hopes for Birobidzhan and Soviet Jewry totally dashed. In her essay on Marley, Nicole Taylor describes him as "enigmatic." How, she asks, can we reconcile his apparently genuine commitment to improving the situation of European Jews with his membership in Communist fronts that were in the end little more than a "cynical charade"? Was his commitment to Birobidzhan simply a by-product of his pro-Soviet sympathies, or did he genuinely believe that the JAR could help solve the crisis facing European Jewry in the 1930s? Were the idealistic accounts of his visits motivated by naive enthusiasm, or deliberate misrepresentation? "Marley the myth-maker or Marley the true believer? Communist stooge or friend of the Jews? We may never know for certain," she concludes.[37] By the late 1940s, Marley had nothing more to do with the Birobidzhan project. His obituary in the *Times* of London speaks rather cryptically of the "advanced views" expressed in his writings on "Siberia, the Far East, Fascism, and the Jewish refugees." The *Times* made no mention of his Communist activities, perhaps because he always denied being an actual member of the Party.[38]

Vilhjalmur Stefansson, on the other hand, lived long enough to learn the truth about Birobidzhan and, unlike Marley, did suffer some of the consequences of his pro-Soviet politics during the McCarthy period.

After the war, Stefansson had been retained by the U.S. Office of Naval Research in 1946 to compile and publish a 20-volume *Encyclopedia Arctica*, which would have demonstrated Soviet superiority in the development of the Arctic. "In Stefansson's view, scholarship was too important to give way to Cold War hysteria, and he rightly felt that the Soviet Union's information about the North would have to be included if the encyclopedia were to be useful."[39] However, though Stefansson "had little concern for the paranoia and posturing of the Cold War," its realities caused him a major setback.[40] In August 1951, he was denounced as a Communist before a Senate Internal Security subcommittee by Louis Budenz, a Communist-turned-Catholic who had served as managing editor of the *Daily Worker* until 1945 and who had gained notoriety as a McCarthyist enemy of all things pro-Soviet. Stefansson denied the charge, joking that "I would hate to be called a Communist by almost anyone else, but I don't mind it much from Budenz."[41]

A year later, however, Stefansson's work on the encyclopedia was terminated without explanation. No doubt the Navy had become uneasy about a man who continued to hold membership in CP front organizations and who spoke to their members about Soviet progress in polar development; he had even been known, on occasion, to contact the Soviet embassy. It certainly did not help his cause that William Mandel, a longtime member of the CPUSA, was involved with the work.[42]

In 1955, both Stefanssons were grilled about their alleged Communist associations by New Hampshire Attorney General Louis C. Wyman. (The Stefanssons had moved to Hanover, NH in December 1951, following the termination of the encyclopedia project. They transferred their ever-growing library on the Arctic to Dartmouth College.) Stefansson admitted in his autobiography, written just before his death in 1962, that he found the rivalry between capitalism and communism "depressing." At first he did not take McCarthyism seriously, even when an attempt was made by some newspapers to "tar me with the pink brush." But his and Evelyn's later experiences with investigators such as Wyman taught him that McCarthyism "is a sinister poison that affects the innocent perhaps more than the guilty."[43] Stefansson did admit that he had been a member of some organizations that had been declared subversive, including some involved in pro-Soviet Jewish work, "but he denied having played any role in a group such as Americans Concerned for the Settlement of Jews [sic] other than in activities that were connected with its stated purpose."[44] Perhaps by then he had had second thoughts concerning Ambijan. At any rate, in his autobiography he made no mention of his work on their behalf or on behalf of any other pro-Soviet group. Nor, for that matter, did his otherwise very complete obituary in the *New York Times*.[45]

Conclusion

How shall we explain Stefansson's pro-Communist activities? He seems to have been an archetype of the "front man" who served the Communist movement as "a useful idiot," in the cynical phrase often uttered by true Communists about fellow-travelers. Clearly, he was no fanatic or ideologue. In order to retain his name on letterheads, in order to publish his statements in pro-Soviet press releases and publications, in order to secure his presence on the dais at Ambijan-sponsored events, he was constantly flattered and coaxed by apparatchiks such as Budish. We can assume, then, that Stefansson maintained feelings of goodwill for the Soviet Union, based on his acceptance, at face value, of Soviet claims regarding just about everything and anything from advances in science and Arctic development to the elimination of anti-Semitism and exploitation. We may conclude that to some extent Stefansson's relationship with the pro-Soviet left was a bargain of mutual self-interest: each party needed and made use of the other. Yet it is also true that Stefansson obviously believed in the superiority of the Soviet system. In any case, his own professional career was intertwined with the fortunes of the USSR. He needed their good will; his post-war encyclopedia project, for example, depended on access to Soviet sources and data unavailable to others not in their favor. This in turn meant keeping himself in the good graces of American Communists, even as he grew busier with his own work and had less time, and perhaps less interest, in theirs.[46] During the confrontation between Aronow and Budish in 1946, for instance, the first question that came to Stefansson's mind was whether their quarrel might adversely affect his and Evelyn's own work.[47] As Evelyn Stefansson put it so tactfully in a 1947 letter to Fan Bakst, Ambijan's field organizer, the Stefanssons had found "less and less time for pleasurable things" as work on the *Encyclopedia Arctica* progressed.[48]

By the late 1940s, many Jewish Communists had begun to seriously doubt the politics of the Soviet Union. Some even found themselves developing pro-Israel feelings. They had "attempted to balance political internationalism with a secular concept of ethnic identity and wound up Jewish-conscious."[49] A top CPUSA official and member of the National Committee, John Williamson, delivered a report on May 3, 1950, castigating many of the party's Jewish members and organizations for not being sufficiently sound in their defense of the USSR. He suggested a "systematic ideological campaign in the Morning Freiheit popularizing the Soviet Union, its tremendous achievements in the socialist solution of the Jewish question."[50]

Williamson had cause for concern. As the Jewish Communists became more enamored of Israel, they grew less interested in Birobidzhan—after all, how could the JAR compete with the "real thing," even for pro-Soviet

Jews? This did not go unnoticed in Moscow. According to Binyamin Pinkus, the Soviets decided in late 1948 that Ambijan had links to Zionist groups.[51] Increasingly wary of any contacts with American groups, even on the pro-Communist left, the Soviets seemed indifferent to Ambijan's demise, implied Shloime Almazov.[52] Abraham Jenofsky in an interview with the author confirmed that Moscow wanted no more aid of any kind from sources in the United States.[53] Organizations such as Ambijan had become more of a hindrance than a help. Indeed, officials in the JAR who were arrested after 1948 were accused of having betrayed the interests of the Soviet Union, because ties to, and acceptance of aid from, Ambijan "facilitated the dissemination of pro-American sentiments," by giving the impression "that the United States and not the Soviet people" were responsible for Birobidzhan's achievements.[54] After 1950 or so, for those remaining in what was left of the pro-Soviet Jewish movement, it had become a case of political "unrequited love." Further blows would be delivered in 1956, 1967, and 1973.

Yet even at the height of left-wing support for Jewish statehood in Israel, Ambijan hewed to the classical Marxist-Leninist line that the "solution to the Jewish question" would come only with the abolition of capitalism and the assimilation of the Jewish people into a socialist world that transcended nationality. While Ambijan supported Israel and would defend its territorial integrity, the organization did not consider Israel—or Birobidzhan, for that matter—to be a solution of the Jewish problem, for Jews in any other country.[55] So in the end, not only were Jewish Communists not Zionists, they were not even genuine territorialists.

Many writers have been all too ready to blame the destruction of the "old left" movements on McCarthyism. McCarthyism definitely took its toll, intimidating many people who were members of front organizations. This book itself provides evidence of FBI surveillance of the top leadership of Ambijan. But I would argue that the collapse of Communist front groups was not solely or even primarily due to McCarthyism. Most of the rank-and-file members were too insignificant, economically and politically, to be targeted. If someone owned a small grocery or worked in a garment shop, what, really, could the FBI do to him or her? Such persecution as there was affected academics, teachers, civil servants, and the entertainment industry in Hollywood—people employed by non-Jewish institutions, or people in the "public eye" who depended for their livelihood on its goodwill.

Even as late as 1950, Ambijan publications were filled with photos taken at Ambijan events; everyone in the pictures was prominently identified in the captions. Each number of *Nailebn-New Life* included an "Honor Roll" of donors. These people did not go underground or use pseudonyms. Few were actual Communist Party members. They did not fear losing their livelihoods or being arrested.

So how are we to understand the demise of Ambijan and similar groups? I maintain that the movement died a natural death, primarily as a result of its focus on Europe and on immigrants from Europe. Originally, this focus was a source of strength. But few members of these groups went on to become full-fledged Communists. And although the idea of Yiddish as an official language in Birobidzhan was dear to the hearts of the immigrant left-wingers, their own ambivalent attitude toward the whole issue of assimilationism (or at least acculturationalism) in American Jewish life was never adequately resolved. External events, especially the Holocaust, the establishment of Israel and the evidence of anti-Semitism in the USSR and Communist eastern Europe, impacted powerfully on the movement. The underlying contradictions led to disillusionment or disinterest and a decline in membership. McCarthyism was just the last blow.

American Jews were disillusioned by the failure of Jewish colonization efforts in the Soviet far east. Even more to the point, by the 1950s most American Jews were aware that in Russia, the Jewish alliance with communism had ended in the destruction not only of traditional Jewish life, "but in the destruction of nearly all aspects of autonomous Jewish life."[56] Revelations of anti-Semitism in the highest ranks of the Soviet Communist hierarchy also led to defections on the part of fellow-travelers. Despite the heady propaganda produced by the ICOR and Ambijan in the 1930s, the "Jewish problem" in the Soviet Union had proven to be deep-rooted. Perhaps the *coup de grâce* was the creation of the state of Israel, to which most overseas Jewish efforts were henceforth directed. The deaths of six million Jews made it more difficult to sustain a faith in Internationalism. Despite the Allied victory, it had become apparent that European Jewry had been the true losers of the war. Many Jews drew the conclusion that the catastrophe was due to statelessness and lack of sovereignty, a condition that could at least partially be rectified in Israel, but not in Birobidzhan.

An entire era of Jewish life had come to an end; Ambijan was just one of the casualties. As the state of Israel became the central and most important feature of post-war Jewish life, Birobidzhan receded into the mists of memory. The Jewish Communists, for all of their ideals, their cleverness, and their efforts, were never able to prove that a Soviet Jewish republic had actually emerged in the far east. As Israel's star rose, so did groups like Ambijan ossify and wither away. The members of Ambijan, and the rest of the Jewish Communist movement, had become caught in the ambiguity, indeed contradictions, of their own ideology: a pro-Soviet internationalism combined with an interest in Jewish national regeneration; support for a Zionist-style enterprise in far-off Siberia, coupled with opposition to Zionism itself.

In any case, the Jewish community in the immediate post-war world was a very different place than it had been in the 1930s and 1940s. Jews were moving out of the old downtown neighborhoods and into the suburbs; they were leaving unionized work in the garment factories to enter business and the professions. Jewish Communists found it difficult to re-establish their institutions and gain a hearing for their ideas in these newer areas of settlement. The increasingly bourgeois socio-economic position of Ambijan's own membership, which had prospered greatly during World War II, made it difficult for the organization to retain the loyalty even of those already in the movement.

Finally, there was the large influx of Holocaust survivors into the country after World War II. Most of these immigrants were more traditionalist in culture and religion. Certainly they harboured few illusions about the USSR and the new people's democracies, which many knew firsthand. More recent Jewish immigration from the Soviet Union and its successor states brought further waves of people who were living proof of the failure of the Bolshevik experiment. As a result of the new immigration, the Jewish community as a whole shifted away from the politics of the far left: "The older Yiddish-socialist subculture could not survive this constellation of forces, nor...could Communists and other radicals find effective ways of challenging it."[57] By the 1960s, American Jews focused their hopes on Israel; most had come to see the USSR as an enemy of the Jewish people and its state.

Given how important the pro-Birobidzhan movement had been in American Jewish life, it is surprising to realize how quickly it was forgotten. Students for a Democratic Society (SDS) was formed in 1960, and the "Port Huron Statement" was drafted just eleven years after the demise of Ambijan. Yet the university-centered New Left, including its many members who were Jewish "red diaper babies," and who must have heard about Birobidzhan in their homes, had no interest in revisiting this history, which already seemed "old." Indeed, the New Left tended to regard the CPUSA and its front organizations as impediments to socialist transformation.

Yet the YKUF, the *Morgn Frayhayt*, and a few other remnants survived the 1950s, as some of those Jewish Communists who had been involved with the Birobidzhan support movements, continued their pro-Soviet activities in a much-diminished Communist world.[58] Irving Howe has remarked that many Jewish Communists were "marked by a deep ambivalence toward everything Jewish.... They declared themselves internationalist, even cosmopolitan, in outlook and concerned mostly with raising the class consciousness of all workers, yet they could not escape the impulse common to many immigrant Jews of building a hermetic community of their own."[59] Such "aging immigrants could not give up a lifetime of psychological investment," observed Arthur Hertzberg. As Paul Lyons wrote about Jewish Communists in Philadelphia, they were "reluctant to abandon [their] protective if shrinking subculture."[60] The Communist Party was their life; in time it became, as Maurice Isserman put it, "a comfortable retirement home."[61] They belonged to a party that was stronger than any religion.

To be fair, for some, Communist thought retained an ethical core, and Communism remained, ideally, a noble search for social justice. They realized that in the Soviet Union it had been transformed into a barbarous totalitarianism, but they blamed this on the Soviet leadership, in particular Stalin. A few began to look at other "models," especially China and Cuba. But these countries were of little interest to those who had become Communists or pro-Communists specifically because they valued their Jewish culture, and had believed that the USSR had "solved the Jewish question." As an "ethno-political" movement, after 1956 "Jewish Communism" had virtually ceased to exist.

In the summer of 1947, Harry Zarbin had stated at an Ambijan meeting in Chicago that it would be most helpful for a delegation from America to visit Birobidzhan and report their findings upon their return. "Until this can be arranged, we will have to work on faith."[62] It was, unfortunately, a faith misplaced.

Endnotes

1   Even so, Communists maintained, Yiddish would still retain its importance, because the development of closer cultural relations with Soviet Jews and with the Jews of the new east European democracies, "greatly strengthens the position of Yiddish in the American Jewish nationality group." "Communist Work Among the American Jewish Masses," *Political Affairs* 25, 11 (November 1946): 1044-1045.

2   Letter from Abraham Jenofsky to Morris Stern, New York, Dec. 20, 1946; in the Morris Stern papers, RG231, Box 1, unnamed folder, YIVO.

3   Letter from Abraham Jenofsky to Morris Stern, New York, April 8, 1947; in the Morris Stern papers, RG231, Box 1, unnamed folder, YIVO.

4   After World War II, James N. Rosenberg, who died in 1970 at the age of 96, led a United States committee for the passage of the Genocide Convention

at the United Nations. He retired from his law practice in 1947 to devote himself to the arts, as a painter, printmaker, poet, and patron. "James N. Rosenberg, a Lawyer-Painter, is Dead; Philanthropist Aided Hoover in Relief Work in '21," *New York Times*, July 22, 1970, 40.

5 Dr. L. Schatzov, "A fertl yorhundert fun hilf un oyfklerung," *Nailebn-New Life* 22, 10 (December 1949): 14-16. Charles Kuntz was referred to as "a pioneer in the Icor-Ambijan movement" in a story about the February 1949 annual New Jersey state Ambijan dinner in Newark. "New Jersey Ambijan Dinner Outstanding Success," *Nailebn-New Life* 23, 3 (March-April 1950): 23.

6 "Dr. khaim zhitlovsky," *Nailebn-New Life* 22, 5 (May 1949): 13; A. Jenofsky, "Tsum tsentn yortsayt fun reuben brainin," *Nailebn-New Life* 23, 3 (March-April 1950): 15-16. A Reuben Brainin Children's Clinic was established in his name in Tel Aviv.

7 Abraham Bick, "Y. stalin – der vegvayzer fun felker-frayntshaft," *Nailebn-New Life* 22, 10 (December 1949): 3-4.

8 B.Z. Goldberg, "Ten Years Later," *Israel Horizons* 10, 8 (October 1962): 19. See Gennady Estraikh, *Yiddish in the Cold War*, 40; Shimon Redlich, *Propaganda and Nationalism in Wartime Russia*, 53-57, 130-131; Arno Lustiger, *Stalin and the Jews: The Red Book. The Tragedy of the Jewish Anti-Fascist Committee and the Soviet Jews*, translated from the German by Mary Beth Friedrich and Todd Bludeau (New York: Enigma Books, 2003), 336-337.

9 Telephone interview with Vladimir Talmy, Silver Spring, MD, Aug. 17, 1996;Yankl Stillman, "Surviving Stalinism: An Interview with Vladimir Talmy," *Jewish Currents* 57, 4 (July-August 2003): 18-19. Talmy was born in Lachowicze, Poland, in 1893 and came to the U.S. in 1912. Wattenberg was born in 1887 in Stanilawow, Poland, and arrived in the U.S. in 1920. See their telegram of greetings to the 1935 ICOR convention calling on the delegates to "Carry on your splendid work with still more vigor and determination." "Greetings to Convention: Watenberg [sic] and Talmy Cable from Moscow," *ICOR* 8, 3 (March 1935): 30.

10 At an event in Miami on March 27, 1949, celebrating Birobidzhan, the famous poem "Ikh bin a yid" by Itzik Fefer was read by Max Azar to the audience. A.J. [Abraham Jenofsky], "Organizatsye un arbet," *Nailebn-New Life* 22, 5 (May 1949): 19. Unbeknownst to the Ambijan members, Fefer was already languishing in prison.

11 Vaksberg, *Stalin Against the Jews*, 152-153, 226-237. The full transcript of the trials, translated into English, has been made available in Joshua Rubenstein and Vladimir P. Naumov, eds., *Stalin's Secret Pogrom: The Postwar Inquisition of the Jewish Anti-Fascist Committee* (New Haven: Yale University Press, 2001).

12 He, his mother, and his Russian-born wife came to the United States in 1980, where Talmy obtained work as a translator for the U.S. government in Washington. Telephone interview with Vladimir Talmy, Silver Spring, MD, Aug. 17, 1996;Yankl Stillman, "Surviving Stalinism," 20-21.

13 See Jonathan Brent and Vladimir P. Naumov, *Stalin's Last Crime: The Plot Against the Jewish Doctors, 1948-1953* (New York: HarperCollins, 2003) and Simon Sebag-Montefiore, *Stalin: The Court of the Red Tsar* (New York: Alfred A. Knopf, 2004) for portraits of Stalin and his entourage of sycophants and murderers, who nourished a culture of sadism, ruthlessness and dread that fueled a regime that murdered tens of millions of people. For more on the campaign against "rootless cosmopolitans" and other Jewish enemies of the Soviet state, see also Konstantin Azadovskii and Boris Egorov, "From Anti-Westernism to Anti-Semitism," *Journal of Cold War Studies*, 4, 1 (Winter 2002): 66-80.

14 See further Paul Lendvai, *Anti-Semitism Without Jews: Communist Eastern Europe* (Garden City, NY: Doubleday, 1971).

15 Abraham Bick, "A Letter from Prague," *Jewish Life* 7, 4 (February 1953): 7. See also Louis Harap, *The Truth About the Prague Trial* (New York: Jewish Life, 1953).

16 Quoted in Lucy Dawidowicz, "American Reaction to Soviet Anti-Semitism," in Morris Fine, ed., *American Jewish Year Book 1954*. Vol. 55 (New York: American Jewish Committee, 1954): 152-153. Waterman Wise quit the Communist Party after the signing of the Hitler-Stalin Pact in 1939 but resumed his pro-Soviet activities with Ambijan after 1941. He moved to France in 1950 and became an art dealer. He died in 1983. "James W. Wise, 81; Author and Lecturer Warned of the Nazis," *New York Times*, Nov. 30, 1983, B6.

17 Harrison E. Salisbury, *American in Russia* (New York: Harper & Brothers, 1955), 279-285.

18 Harrison E. Salisbury, "Jewish Province in Soviet Depicted," *New York Times*, June 21, 1954, 9; Harrison E. Salisbury, "Birobidzhan Jews Drop Yiddish, Prefer Russian, Visitor is Told," *New York Times*, June 22, 1954, 6; "Importance of Birobidzhan as Soviet's 'Jewish Homeland' is Found to be on Decline," *New York Times*, June 28, 1954, 7.

19 "Siberian Journey," *New York Times*, June 25, 1954, 20.

20 Bernard D. Weinryb, "Antisemitism in Soviet Russia," in Lionel Kochan, ed., *The Jews in Soviet Russia Since 1917*, 321.

21 Quoted in Amir Weiner, "Nature and Nurture in a Socialist Utopia: Delineating the Soviet Socio-Ethnic Body in the Age of Socialism," in David L. Hoffman, *Stalinism: The Essential Readings* (Oxford: Blackwell Publishers, 2003), 268.

22 Isor Goldberg, "A yubl vos vert nisht gefayert: 25 or fun der birobidzhaner autonomer gegnt," *Unzer Tsayt* 10 (October 1959): 30.

23 Michael Stanislawski, "Introduction" to Israel Emiot, *The Birobidzhan Affair: A Yiddish Writer in Siberia*, translated from the Yiddish by Max Rosenfeld (Philadelphia: Jewish Publication Society of America, 1981), xiv-xv.

24 Chimen Abramsky, "Russian Jews—A Bird's Eye View," *Midstream* 24, 10 (December 1978): 38.

25   See David Shneer, "The Weakness of the Birobidzhan Idea," *Jews in Russia and Eastern Europe* 3, 49 (Winter 2002): 5-30.
26   Abramsky, "The Biro-Bidzhan Project, 1927-1959," 76-77.
27   Jessica Smith, "A Statement to Our Readers," *New World Review* 24, 5 (May 1956): 46-49; Jessica Smith, "The Khrushchev Report," *New World Review* 24, 7 (July 1956): 49-52. Smith, who was married to the well-known Communist lawyer John Abt, worked at the Soviet embassy for many years.
28   Tzouliadis, *The Forsaken*, 358.
29   Undated [probably April1968] letter from Rabbi Abraham Bick to B.Z. Goldberg; "A. Bick's avekgeyn fun der 'morgn-frayhayt.' A deklaratsye fun p. novick," undated typewritten ms.; letter from Paul Novick to Abraham Bick, New York, Feb. 21, 1968; all in file RG1247, Box 2, folder 15 "A. Bick," in the Paul Novick papers, YIVO. Indeed, in June of 1956 Bick had invoked his Fifth Amendment right against self-incrimination in hearings before the House Un-American Activities Committee. "2 Silent at Inquiry into Foreign Travel," *New York Times*, June 15, 1956, 25.
30   See Paul Novick, *The Jewish Problem in Poland* (New York: Morning Freiheit, 1969) and *Di natsyonale un yidishe frage in itstiken moment* (New York: Morgn Freiheit, 1970).
31   Gennady Estraikh, *Yiddish in the Cold War*, 119-124; Sid Resnick, "Pesekh novick: redakter fun der 'morgn-frayhayt'," 1-5, 8; Paul Buhle, "Paul Novick: A Radical Life," *Radical America* 17, 5 (September-October 1983): 74-75; Peter B. Flint, "Paul Novick is Dead," *New York Times*, Aug. 22, 1989, D3.
32   Nathan-David Korman, "A kultur-boyer un a folks-mentsh: gedanken vegn abraham jenofsky," *Morgn Frayhayt*, April 13, 1976, 6; and Gedaliah Landman, "Gelebt un gekemft far a velt fun sholem," *Morgn Frayhayt*, April 18, 1976, 12. Jenofsky was also for a time a vice-president of Rabbi Bick's Union of American Jews of Ukrainian Descent. See a letter from Rabbi Abraham Bick, president, and Joseph Rapoport, executive chairman, New York, Dec. 19, 1946, informing Jenofsky that at its Nov. 24, 1946 convention, he had been re-elected as a vice-president; Abraham Jenofsky papers, RG734, Box 3, folder "Letters by Jenofsky," YIVO.
33   "Rayde Jenofsky memorial, April 1, 1976," typescript in the Paul Novick papers, RG1247, Box 10, folder 111 "Jenofsky", YIVO. Jenofsky's daughter, Lillian Jarvis, born in 1931, in a letter to me indicated that she was not close to her father when he was alive. He was considered "the family red sheep, albeit honored, when he was alive," though "he was definitely overworked and most definitely underpaid." Letter from Lillian B. Jarvis to the author, San Francisco, Oct. 2, 1996. Jenofsky's wife Freida, who died in 1993, wrote an unpublished 36-page typed manuscript, now deposited at the YIVO, in which she recalled that her husband earned $25 a week as national secretary of the ICOR, and later $75 a week with Ambijan. She also remembered that Itzik Fefer conversed with her daughter in Yiddish at the July 8, 1943 rally at the Polo Grounds in New York and autographed her program with the

phrase "To the little girl that speaks such beautiful Yiddish."
34 "Sol A. Pearl, Wrote Under Name S. Almazov for Morning Freiheit," *New York Times*, April 24, 1979, section 4, 17; P. Novick, "A nomen tsu gedenken," *Morgn Frayhayt*, New York, June 26, 1980, 3, 6.
35 Paul Buhle, *Marxism in the United States*, 1.
36 "*Morgn Freiheit*, April 2, 1922—Sept. 11, 1988," *Jewish Currents* 42, 11 (November 1988): 3; Morris U. Schappes, "Paul Novick: In Sorrow and Pride," 5.
37 Nicole Taylor, "The Mystery of Lord Marley," 69.
38 "Obituary: Lord Marley," *Times*, London, March 3, 1952, 6. The Labour MP Morgan Philips Price remembered Marley as someone whose "logic would sometimes carry him into waters deeper than he intended to go." "Lord Marley," *Times*, London, March 29, 1952, 9.
39 William R. Hunt, *Stef: A Biography of Vilhjalmur Stefansson, Canadian Arctic Explorer* (Vancouver: University of British Columbia Press, 1986), 257.
40 David H. Price, *Threatening Anthropology*, 287.
41 "Stefansson Denies Charge," *New York Times* Aug. 24, 1951: 8; Price, *Threatening Anthropology*, 292. Budenz had claimed that he had been given the names of 400 "hidden" Communist Party members by Jack Stachel, a CP national organizer. Robert M. Lichtman, "Louis Budenz, the FBI, and the 'List of 400 Concealed Communists': An Extended Tale of McCarthy-Era Informing," *American Communist History* 3, 1 (June 2004): 31. See also Louis Budenz, *Men without Faces: The Communist Conspiracy in the USA* (New York: Harper and Brothers, 1950). A confidential 1944 FBI report termed Stefansson "an extreme left winger and Communist Fellow Traveler." This information is contained on p. 26 of a 33-page report dated Nov. 5, 1944 submitted by E.E. Conroy, Special Agent in Charge, originally in NY File 100-42538. File 100-99898, Section 1, FOIPA No. 416152, Ambijan.
42 William Marx Mandel, born in New York in 1917, had lived in the USSR as a child in 1931-1932. He joined the CPUSA in 1935. Mandel was the author of *The Soviet Far East and Central Asia* (New York: Dial Press, 1944), which contained information about Birobidzhan, and *A Guide to the Soviet Union* (New York: Dial Press, 1946). Though Mandel was denounced as a Communist by Senator McCarthy in March 1953, he had actually been expelled from the party a year earlier. Victor S. Navasky, *Naming Names* (New York: Viking Press, 1980), 118. See also William Mandel, *Saying No to Power: Autobiography of a 20th Century Activist and Thinker* (Berkeley, CA: Creative Arts Book Co., 1999)
43 Vilhjalmur Stefansson, *Discovery: The Autobiography of Vilhjalmur Stefansson* (New York: McGraw-Hill, 1964), 297, 359-374; Hunt, 260.
44 Hunt, *Stef*, 262-263. While Hunt devotes a chapter to Stefansson's marriage and politics, he makes light of Stefansson's Communist affiliations, taking at face value Stefansson's claims that he was merely interested in Soviet achievements in Arctic exploration and settlement. Price, too, considers

Stefansson to be merely a "liberal" who never belonged to any "Communist or Socialist political organizations" (xiv, 237-238, 305); Price asserts that "Vague reports of supposed Communist-related activities led the FBI to maintain long-term investigations of anthropologists like…Viljalmur Stefansson" (348). Other biographers gloss over Stefansson's politics completely: "He does not seem to have taken politics seriously," wrote Erick Berry, in *Mr. Arctic: An Account of Vilhjalmur Stefansson* (New York: David McKay, 1966), 175. See also Diubaldo, *Stefansson and the Canadian Arctic*, for another work in which Stefansson's politics go almost unmentioned. Diubaldo does, however, refer to a Russian book, *Vilhjalmur Stefansson: 1879-1962*, by Evgenia Aleksandrovna Olkhina, published in Moscow in 1970 by the Academy of Sciences of the U.S.S.R., which lauds Stefansson's accomplishments and praises him as a friend of the Soviet people (Diubaldo, 2). Stefansson did belong to many CP fronts, and although it is difficult to determine just how pro-Soviet he actually was, I find it impossible to believe that he was entirely unaware of the political allegiances of these groups and their members.

45   "Vilhjalmur Stefansson, 82, Dies; Led Many Expeditions in Arctic," *New York Times*, Aug. 27, 1962: 1, 23.
46   See also Henry Srebrnik, "An Idiosyncratic Fellow-Traveller: Vilhjalmur Stefansson and the American Committee for the Settlement of Jews in Birobidzhan," *East European Jewish Affairs* 28, 1 (Summer 1998): 37-53.
47   Handwritten note from Vilhjalmur Stefansson to Evelyn Stefansson, New York, Feb. 4, 1946; Stefansson correspondence, MSS 196, Box 67, 1946—Ambijan Folder, Stefansson Collection.
48   Letter from Evelyn Stefansson to Fan Bakst, San Francisco, Dec. 1, 1947; Stefansson correspondence, MSS 196, Box 72, 1947—USSR-American Committee for the Settlement of Jews in Birobidjan (Ambijan) Folder, Stefansson Collection.
49   Leviatin, *Followers of the Trail*, 210.
50   John Williamson, "For a United-Front Policy Among the Jewish People—Sharpen the Struggle Against Bourgeois Nationalism," *Political Affairs* 29, 6 (July 1950): 63, 69-70. Williamson later served a term in jail and was then deported to his native Britain.
51   Binyamin Pinkus, "Change and Continuity in Soviet Policy Towards Soviet Jewry and Israel, May-December 1948," *Israel Studies* 10, 1 (Spring 2005): 115.
52   Interview with Shloime Almazov, New York, July 21, 1971. Almazov was not very forthcoming, but he seemed to me to be a bitter man. My guess was that he never reconciled himself to the 1946 merger of the ICOR and Ambijan, which he had seen as a takeover by more affluent and well-connected Jews of an organization to which he had devoted himself for decades.
53   Interview with Abraham Jenofsky, New York, July 19, 1971.
54   Weinberg, *Stalin's Forgotten Zion*, 82. Alexander Bakhmutsky, the secretary

of the Birobidzhan CP, received a 25 year prison sentence.
55 "Ambijan National Conference," *News from American Birobidjan Committee (Ambijan)*, December 1949: 4
56 Mendelsohn, *On Modern Jewish Politics*, 119.
57 Paul Lyons, "Philadelphia Jews and Radicalism," in Friedman, ed., *Philadelphia Jewish Life*, 61.
58 "It's very painful for us, the leftovers," lamented Shirley Novick, widow of Paul and herself a former activist. She compared their faith in Communism as being similar to the unquestioning religious fervor of Khasidim. Interview, Shirley Novick, New York, June 13, 1996.
59 Irving Howe, *World of Our Fathers: The Journey of the East European Jews to America and the Life They Found and Made* (New York: Simon and Schuster, 1976), 330.
60 Arthur Hertzberg, *The Jews in America: Four Centuries of an Uneasy Encounter: A History* (New York: Simon and Schuster, 1989), 265; Paul Lyons, *Philadelphia Communists*, 165.
61 Maurice Isserman, *If I Had a Hammer ...: The Death of the Old Left and the Birth of the New Left* (New York: Basic Books, 1987), 24.
62 Minutes, Aug. 28, 1947, in Collection No. 20: Chicago Chapter, American Birobidjan Committee, Series A. Minutes. Folder 4: Minutes, 1947, Chicago Jewish Archives.

Appendix:
Paul Novick's 1936 Visit to the Jewish Autonomous Region

Paul Novick visited Birobidzhan between July 25 and September 25, 1936, and published a book describing his experiences. He traveled on trains, boats, and horse-drawn wagons, visiting cities and towns, collective farms, and endless miles of taiga and forest. Birobidzhan, he remarked in the very first sentence of his book, was "a word ... now on the lips of Jews the world over." The region was the manifestation of the "complete solution of the Jewish question through workers' power." It provided hope to millions of Jews, particularly in Poland, "who are prepared to go, and wait impatiently for that joyful moment."

Perhaps unconsciously, the atheist and Communist Novick used Biblical imagery throughout the book: "Yes, she is beautiful and rich," he wrote. "This is an outstanding land, containing everything required to sustain a great industry and a rich agriculture." In its "tremendously fruitful soil," crops "grow and ripen ... if ever there was a land where honey flowed it is—the Jewish Autonomous Region." But this near-empty space had fewer than two people per square kilometer: "A land one and one half times the size of Belgium...contains about sixty thousand people. It needs many millions—of Jews." Thousands of acres of productive land awaited the people who would till it, Novick wrote. He had travelled by boat along the Amur River and had not seen a single soul for many kilometers. The countryside cried out for people. There was much to do in Birobidzhan, which was becoming "the Jewish socialist autonomous republic, the national home for the Jewish people."

Novick spent 15 days in the city of Birobidzhan, which was growing so fast it would soon be a world center. Though it had a population of only 28,000, Novick reported that it felt like a much larger city, with its wide avenues and sidewalks, its parks, theaters and technical schools. Wherever one looked, one saw new buildings under construction; one heard the "music of saw and hammer." Novick visited children's schools and buildings housing the local Communist Party and Soviet. Birobidzhan was becoming home to many writers, teachers and cultural workers: It was "a new country, a new life" for the "old Jewish people," who were now "becoming younger."

Novick next visited the Birofeld and Frayland collective farms. His guide, one of the earliest Jewish pioneers in Birobidzhan, said to him, as they ascended a hill and saw before them a green and sunny countryside, with fresh and soft colors: "Well, look at this promised (and delivered) land!" They inspected an apiary belonging to Birofeld,

Appendix I

with 1,500 beehives and fields of wheat and soy. There would be many human and natural obstacles still to overcome but, Novick felt, "things were moving forward."

His next outing took Novick south to Blucherovo on the Amur River across from Manchuria. Here, too, officials told Novick that settlers were needed, to cultivate 2,000 hectares of land. Novick boarded a boat upriver to Stalinsk and then Amurzet, marveling at the scenery en route, but also aware of the Japanese on the other side of the river.[1] "I have seen the Mississippi, the Rhine, the Nile and the Thames," he wrote, "and this river can certainly compare." Wild flowers grew along the banks of the river, and the forests spread out in every direction. "The air was fragrant and fresh." He was overwhelmed by the beauty of the area. A fellow passenger, a Russian, told Novick he was impatient with the pace of Jewish settlement. "Take a look at what we own!...Gold and coal and iron! Endless forests! And did you see the empty tracts of level land? Everything is available here!"

Novick recalled that in the northern part of Birobidzhan, in the resort of Kaldur, a spa famous for its mineral waters, "A feeling of joy overcame me, that the Jewish Autonomous Region possessed such a treasure." He urged that Kaldur—"one of the most beautiful pearls in the Jewish Autonomous Region"—be developed quickly, "to bring health and life and joy for the masses of working people."

When Novick returned to the capital city of Birobidzhan, he was greeted by much activity: the paving of various streets; the demolition of old buildings to construct new hotels, restaurants, and a library; and the laying of a foundation for a new electricity station which would be able to supply power for a projected population of 120,000. The pace of construction and activity was amazing, and for this he credited the Communist activists. A plenum of the local Communist Party was in session, and "One could feel how quickly the road was being taken to reach the coming Jewish Soviet-republic!" The Communist plenum was making "grandiose plans" for 1937: there were to be 25 new collective farms, a new knitting mill, a wagon plant, electricity plants, a shoe factory, and a sock and rope factory. Plans called for 10,000 new settlers in 1937. As its socialist prosperity increased, the USSR would be even more eager to assist in developing Jewish statehood in Birobidzhan "with a generous, freely extended Soviet hand." Novick was particularly impressed at how hard Russians and other non-Jews were working together to build the Jewish Autonomous Region: "Birobidzhan is making a new leap forward. Birobidzhan is racing forward towards true development."

Novick also reported on his meetings with the local Jewish commanders of the Red Army that protected Birobidzhan against the Japanese on the other side of the Amur. Speaking Yiddish, they asked him to inform the Jews of America that in Birobidzhan, the Leninist-Stalinist national policy was being carried out: "All of us, Jews and non-Jews, we are building the Jewish region!" Birobidzhan was an example of the fraternal relations between nationality and nationality in the Soviet Union. Novick was reminded that on August 29, the Jewish Autonomous Region had been declared the center of Jewish national culture for the entire Jewish working people. Novick marveled at the fact that Russian children were attending Yiddish language schools and becoming familiar with Yiddish literature. This was indeed an example of the "new civilization, the Soviet one, and proof of how it had solved the national question."

Novick's train trip back to Moscow took eight days. His thoughts remained with Birobidzhan as he travelled westwards, for the first six hours, from one station to another within the Jewish Autonomous Region: "One becomes drawn in by the rapid pace of construction in this beautiful land…One feels at home as soon as one enters. You meet so many familiar people, even if meeting them for the first time…So it hurt to leave. Hard to say one's goodbyes. In one's mind there were so many memories." Novick admitted it would take very hard work to make Birobidzhan a success: "The road to the Jewish Soviet-republic is not through flowers and music." It was not easy to deal with "virgin earth." People and materials had to be brought from far away. "But behind Birobidzhan stood the vigor of the great Soviet nation, of the great Communist Party." Every nationality in the Soviet Union, including the Jews, was worthy of self-determination, of a healthy national culture, and a healthy economic life.[2]

Upon Novick's return to Moscow, he was interviewed by the *Moscow News*. "Foreign Jews, carefully selected, are being invited to settle in Biro-Bidjan as rapidly as housing accommodations can be prepared for them," he told the newspaper.[3]

Reading Novick's book, one can sense the tremendous longing for a Jewish "place of our own," a piece of the globe where Jews would be in the majority and run their own affairs, even if that place, rather than being totally sovereign, was merely a "national home." His loving descriptions bring to mind the chronicles of Jewish travelers to the land of Israel. To Novick, Birobidzhan seemed a place where Jews were building a homeland, helped by socially progressive, non-Jewish but philosemitic friends. Novick's account served almost as a fantasy counterpart to the real world his readers inhabited. In that real world, American Jews daily encountered animosity and anti-Semitism; European Jews suffered and died at the hands of fascists; while in Palestine, Jews struggled to achieve statehood in opposition both to the British imperial authorities and the indigenous Arabs. Little wonder, then, that reportage such as Novick's was used by Ambijan and the ICOR to attract enthusiastic new members.[4]

Appendix I

Endnotes

1 Blucherovo later became known as Leninskoye. Stalinsk was previously called Stalinfeld, and later Oktyabrskoye; it no longer exists.
2 Paul Novick, *Yidn in biro-bidzhan*, 9-12, 15-22, 27-32, 36-37, 46-60, 73, 81-91.
3 The article was reprinted by the ICOR. See Julia Older, "Biro-Bidjan as it Grows," *Nailebn-New Life* 10, 12 (December 1936): 9-11 [English section].
4 The fantasy of Birobidzhan as a Soviet "promised land" for Jews extended to outright falsehoods. The September 1936 issue of *Nailebn-New Life*, on p. 12 [English section] ran a photo entitled "A Spot in Biro-Bidjan" showing a grove of palm trees!

Appendix: George Koval

At the March 26, 1933 ICOR national executive plenum held in New York, national secretary Shloime Almazov admitted that some of the Americans who had emigrated to Birobidzhan had returned home, unprepared for pioneer work. But others, remarked Almazov, such as the Koval family, had adjusted and were doing very well.[1] The ICOR in June 1935 printed a letter that George Koval had written to relatives in the U.S. Born in Sioux City, IA, in 1913, he had migrated to Birobidzhan with his parents Abraham and Ethel, themselves originally immigrants from Telekhani in Belarus, in tsarist Russia, and two brothers, Isiah (Shiye) and Gabriel. At the time of writing he was studying engineering at the Mendeleev Institute of Chemical Technology in Moscow. Abraham Koval had been secretary of the Sioux City branch of the ICOR.[2] Two years later, Arkady Rovner wrote in *Nailebn-New Life* that the Kovals had been well-to-do and had owned a spacious home in Sioux City. Yet they gave up their "well-established" life so that their three sons would have in Birobidzhan those opportunities that they could no longer expect in the crisis-ridden United States. The Kovals were said to "bless the day" that they decided to emigrate. They were now distinguished citizens and patriots of the "great Soviet Fatherland." In the summer of 1936 the family was visited by Abraham Koval's sister and her husband, also ICOR members, who returned to Sioux City "overbrimming with enthusiasm for what they saw in the Soviet Union generally, and in Biro-Bidjan in particular." The Kovals, Rovner declared, were participating in "the rejuvenation of a nation, the building of a new Jewish nation in the Jewish Autonomous Territory."[3]

Also in the summer of 1936, while on a visit to Birobidzhan, Paul Novick met Shiye Koval, who was now one of the best tractor drivers on the Icor commune. Shiye's two brothers were studying chemistry in Moscow, their mother told Novick, and she had much *nakhes* [satisfaction] from them. Novick thought to himself that the Kovals had exchanged the uncertainty of life as small storekeepers in Sioux City for a worry-free existence for themselves and their children.[4]

George Koval, who died in Moscow on January 31, 2006, went on to have a most unusual career. In November 2007, Russian Federation President Vladimir Putin posthumously honored him with the "Gold Star and Hero of Russia" medal. It was revealed that Koval, under the code name "Delmar," was a GRU (Main Intelligence Directorate of the General Staff of the Soviet Armed Forces) "mole" working on the Manhattan Project during World War II. Speaking at the award ceremony,

Appendix II

Putin stressed that Koval's work had strengthened Russia's defense capabilities considerably and had drastically reduced the amount of time it took for Russia to develop its nuclear weapons. Upon graduating with honors from the Mendeleev Institute, Koval had been recruited and trained by Soviet military intelligence, and was sent back to the United States for nearly a decade of scientific espionage, from roughly 1940 to 1948. He initially gathered information about new toxins that might find use in chemical arms.

After America entered World War II in December 1941, Koval was drafted into the U.S. Army, and by chance found himself moving toward the bomb project, then in its infancy. The Army in 1943 sent him for special wartime training at City College in Manhattan. There, Koval and a dozen or so of his Army peers studied electrical engineering. Meanwhile, the Manhattan Project asked the Army for technically adept recruits, and in 1944, Koval headed to Oak Ridge, TN, where the main job was to make bomb fuel, considered the hardest part of the atomic endeavor. Koval gained wide access to the complex, and in June 1945, his duties expanded to include top-secret plants near Dayton. In 1948, Koval fled the United States when American counterintelligence agents found Soviet literature hailing the Koval family as happy immigrants from the United States. A year later, Moscow detonated its first bomb, surprising Washington at the quick loss of what had been an atomic monopoly.[5]

Endnotes

[1] "Barikht fun general-sekretar tsu dem icor plenum, gehaltn in new york, 26tn marts, 1933," *ICOR* 6, 4 (April 1933): 13; "In der icor baveygung," *ICOR* 6, 5 (May 1933): 18.

[2] "Letters from the Soviet Union Tell of New Happy Life," *Nailebn-New Life* 9, 2 (June 1935): 45. There is a picture of the Koval family taken before they left for Birobidzhan in the *ICOR* 5, 7 (July 1932): 14. In November 1928 Abraham Koval had arranged a great reception in Sioux City for Reuben Brainin, who was on a speaking tour, and $600 was collected for the ICOR. "In der 'icor' baveygung," *ICOR* 1, 4 (December 1928): 14.

[3] A. Rovner, "Pen Portraits of American Jews in Biro-Bidjan," *Nailebn-New Life* 11, 4 (April 1937): 14-15 [English section].

[4] Paul Novick, *Yidn in biro-bidzhan*, 73, 81-84.

[5] William J. Broad, "A Spy's Path: Iowa to A-Bomb to Kremlin Honor," *New York Times*, November 12, 2007, A1, A19; Michael Walsh, "Iowa-Born, Soviet-Trained," *Smithsonian* 40, 2 (May 2009): 40-47.

Selected Bibliography

Primary Sources
Manuscript Collections

Archives of Ontario, Toronto
    Joshua Gershman papers
        F1412-1, Box 2, File 19
Asher Library, Spertus Institute of Jewish Studies, Chicago
Chicago Jewish Archives
    Collection No. 20: Chicago Chapter, American Birobidjan Committee
        Series A. Minutes
        1. Chicago Committee Minutes 1936-1939
        2. Minutes, 1945
        3. Minutes, 1946
        4. Minutes, 1947
        5. Minutes, 1948
        6. Minutes, 1949-50
        Series B. Papers of Ethel Osri (From Collection No. 82)
        7. Correspondence, 1944-49
        8. Misc. Committee Correspondence
        9. Fundraising Letters
        10. Programs and Brochures, 1936-48
        11. Einstein Fund Dinners, 1945-47
        12. Press Releases, Articles, Speeches
        13. Notes, Reports, etc.
        Series C. Other Organizational Records
        14. Files of Harry Koenig
        Series D. Secondary Material
        21. Telegram to David Ben-Gurion
Baker Memorial Library, Dartmouth College, Hanover, New Hampshire
    Vilhjalmur Stefansson Collection
        Stefansson Correspondence, MSS 196, Box 38, 1935--USSR Folder
        Stefansson correspondence, MSS 196, Box 40, 1936--USSR Folder
        Stefansson correspondence, MSS 196, Box 43, 1937--USSR A-B Folder
        Stefansson correspondence, MSS 196, Box 44, 1938--H General Folder
        Stefansson correspondence, MSS 196, Box 46, 1938--USSR Folder
        Stefansson correspondence, MSS 196, Box 56, 1941--USSR General Folder
        Stefansson correspondence, MSS 196, Box 60, 1942--USSR General Folder
        Stefansson correspondence, MSS 196, Box 62, 1943--USSR General Folder
        Stefansson correspondence, MSS 196, Box 65, 1944--USSR-Ambijan
            Committee Folder
        Stefansson correspondence, MSS 196, Box 67, 1945--USSR-Ambijan

and American Russian Institute Folder
        Stefansson correspondence, MSS 196, Box 67, 1946--Ambijan Folder
        Stefansson correspondence, MSS 196, Box 72, 1947--USSR-American
                Committee for the Settlement of Jews in Birobidjan (Ambijan) Folder
        Stefansson correspondence, MSS 196, Box 75, 1948--USSR Folder
        Stefansson correspondence, MSS 196, Box 78, 1949--USSR Folder
Jewish Historical Society of the Upper Midwest Archives, Barry Family Campus, Minneapolis
    Ambijan and ICOR files
Jewish Public Library Archives, Montreal
    Reuben Brainin Collection
    Group II, Box b., folder 26, "Brainin and the USSR – ICOR – Announcements & Flyers"
    Group II, Box b., folder 27, "Brainin & the USSR – ICOR – Reports, Minutes"
    Group II, Box b., folder 28, "Reuben Brainin ICOR of Jamaica Branch (Long Island) – Flyers"
    Group III, Box a., folder "ICOR – Correspondence"
    Group III, Box x., folder "Wise, James Waterman"
New York Public Library, Jewish Division
    microfilm ZP-*PBM n.c. Reel 122, No. 28, Memorandum to Albert Einstein from Joseph Brainin, [1948]
Schottenstein-Jesselson Library at the Herbert D. Katz Center for Advanced Judaic Studies, University of Pennsylvania, Philadelphia
    Ben-Zion Goldberg (Benjamin Waife) Papers
    Box 61, Articles on the Soviet Union
        Folder "The Jews Go Back to the Wilderness"
    Box 69, Jewish Antifascist Committee in the USSR; American Committee of Jewish Writers, Artists, and Scientists, Inc.
        Folder "American Committee of Jewish Writers, Artists and Scientists"
        Folder "Jewish Anti-Fascist Committee"
        Folder "World Jewish Congress: Jewish Anti-Fascist Committee"
    Box 70, Soviet Union
        Folder "Ambijan"
        Folder "American Birobidjan Committee 1948"
        Folder "1946 – BZG Trip to Europe and Palestine"
    Box 72, Personal Matters
        Folder "Biography – BZG"
    Box 79, Letters: A-Antonovsky
        Folder "American Committee of Jewish Writers, Artists"
    Box 94, Letters: Nachman-Outlook
        Folder "National Ambijan Dinner (1949)"
    Box 97, Letters: Sadovski-Schocat
        Folder "Misc. S"

Tamiment Institute Library, Archival and Manuscript Collections, New York University, New York
   International Workers Order Collection
      Box 1, folder 5, "Jewish People's Fraternal Order of the International Workers Order, November, 1950," typed mss. written by Lucy Dawidowicz.
      Box 1, Folder 10, Jewish People's Fraternal Order--Statements, Plans, etc.
      Box 1, Folder 19, Jewish People's Fraternal Order--Correspondence
United States National Archives, College Park, MD
   Federal Bureau of Investigation surveillance files on Ambijan and the ICOR, accessed via the Freedom of Information/Privacy Acts
      No. 416152, Ambijan
      File 100-2074-81
      File 100-42538
      File 100-99898-146
      File 100-99898-149
      File 100-99898, Section 1
      File 100-99898, Section 2
      File 100-99898, Section 3
      File 100-99898, Section 4
      File 100-99898, Section 5
      File 100-99898, Section 6
   Organization for Jewish Colonization
      File 100-2074
Yeshiva University Archives, New York
   Russian Relief Collection
      Box 2, Birobidzhan folder
YIVO Institute for Jewish Research, New York
   Abraham Jenofsky papers
      RG734, Box 1, folder 4
      RG734, Box 1, folder 5
      RG734, Box 1, folder 6
      RG734, Box 3, folder "Letters by Jenofsky"
   Kalmen Marmor papers, 1873-1955
      RG205, Microfilm group 495, folder 544 "Icor-korespondents, 1925-1929"
      RG205, Microfilm group 495, folder 545 "Icor-korespondents, 1930-1937"
      RG205, Microfilm group 495, folder 546 "Icor-korespondents, 1938-1946"
      RG205, Microfilm group 495, folder 585 "Ambidzhan-korespondents, 1946-1950"
   Paul Novick papers
      RG1079, Box 1, folder "Correspondence, Reports, 1940s, letters"
      RG1247, Box 2, folder 15 "A. Bick"
      RG1247, Box 10, folder 111 "Jenofsky"

Bibliography

Philip Sandler papers
    RG420, Box 4, "Materyaln vegn der ICOR kampanye far a folks-delegatsye"
    RG420, Box 8, file 17, "ICOR"
Morris Stern papers
    RG231, Box 1, folder "ICOR-Birobidzhan"
    RG231, Box 1, unnamed folder
    RG231, Box 2, "Correspondence" folder
United States Territorial Collection
    RG117, Box 57, folder "Birobidzhan,"
    RG117, Box 57, folder "Icor" 17/16
    RG251, Box 8, folder "Speech by Max Levin"
    RG251, Box 8, folder 82 "Letter from Icor"

Interviews and Correspondence

Shloime Almazov, New York, July 21, 1971
Svetlana Chervonnaya, Moscow, August 16, 2005
Edward Cramer, Englewood, NJ, Nov. 5, 1996
Itche Goldberg, New York, June 12, 1996
Lillian B. Jarvis, San Francisco, Oct. 2, 1996
Abraham Jenofsky, New York, July 19, 1971
Jack Mazow, Houston, TX, Sept. 25, 1996
Shirley Novick, New York, June 13, 1996
Edward Portnoy, New York, November 11, 1996
Daniel Rosenberg, Eugene, OR, March 8, 2004
Linda M. Schloff, Minneapolis, February 24, 2005 and March 11, 2005
David Seltzer, New York, July 19, 1971
Amy Swerdlow, New York, May 21, 1996
Vladimir Talmy, Silver Spring, MD, Aug. 17, 1996
Dia Winograd, Santa Fe, NM, Nov. 1, 1995

Published Articles, Pamphlets and Books

The major periodicals I examined were the *Ambijan Bulletin* (New York) 1943-1950; *ICOR* (New York) 1925-1935; and *Nailebn-New Life* (New York) 1935-1950, as well as occasional issues of *Jewish Life*, *New Masses* and *Soviet Russia Today*. I have not included separately in the bibliography the numerous articles appearing in these, or elsewhere in the Communist and pro-Communist press. I have also not listed the news stories about Birobidzhan and its support organizations that were published in American newspapers and news weeklies. They are all cited in the endnotes.

"Abraham Olkin," *Jewish Life* 7, 9 (July 1953): 19.

"Address by Hon. Elbert D. Thomas of Utah, on Tenth Anniversary of the American Birobidjan Committee," *Congressional Record: Proceedings and Debates of the 78th Congress, Second Session*, Appendix, Volume 90--Part 9, March 24, 1944 to June 12, 1944. Washington: United States Government Printing Office 1944: A2627-2628.

"Address of Ambassador Maxim Litvinov," in Isaac E. Rontch, ed. *Icor almanakh: 25 yor sovyetn farband 15 yor biro-bidzhan - ICOR Almanac: 25 Years U.S.S.R. 15 Years Biro-Bidjan*. New York: ICOR May 1943: 5 [English section].

Almazov, Shloime. *Der sovyetish-daytsher opmakh: vos meynt er?* New York: Icor 1939.

-- "Di yidishe masn in Amerike in 1932 un der icor," *Icor yor-bukh - ICOR Year Book 1932*. New York: National Executive Committee of the ICOR 1932: 5-8 [Yiddish section].

-- *Mit dem vort tsum folk: Derfarunger fun a lector*. New York: YKUF Farlag 1947.

-- *The Soviet Union and the World Crisis*. New York: ICOR 1939.

-- *Ten Years of Biro-Bidjan 1928-1938*, translated from the Yiddish by Nathan Farber. New York: ICOR May 1938.

-- "To the Artists' Committee Arranging the Collection for the Birobidjan Museum," in *Biro-Bidjan: Exhibition of Works of Art Presented by American Artists to the State Museum of Biro-Bidjan*. New York: Art Committee of ICOR 1936: 3.

-- *Tsen yor biro-bidzhan 1928-1938*. New York: ICOR May1938.

Aman, Dudley Leigh, First Baron Marley. *Biro Bidjan as I Saw It*. New York: ICOR 1934.

Ambijan National Conference on Emergency Aid and Reconstruction for the Victims of Fascism. New York: Ambijan Committee [November 1944].

Aronsberg, S.J. *Soviet Jews – A New Way of Life*. New York: ICOR 1941.

Arnold, John. *The Jewish People Today*. New York: Workers Library Publishers 1940.

Astour, Michael C. *Geshikhte fun der frayland-lige un funem teritorialistishn gedank*. Buenos Aires: Freeland League, 2 vols. 1967.

Baidukov, George. *Over the Pole*, translated from the Russian by Jessica Smith. New York: Harcourt Brace 1938.

Bailin, I. B. "Gina birenzweig un gina medem (eynike kharakter-shtriken)," in Gina Medem, *A Lebnsveg: Oytobyografishe notitsn*. New York: Gina Medem Bukh-komitet 1950: 7-12.

Barikht fun der amerikaner icor ekspertn-komisye. New York: ICOR 1930.

Bakhmutsky, Aleksander. *New Achivements in Birobidjan*. New York: ICOR 1945.

Bick, Abraham. *Doyres dervakhen: biografishe novella*. New York: YKUF Farlag 1957.

-- *Morris winchevsky: Der troymer un kemfer*. New York: YKUF Farlag 1955.

-- *Moyshe hess: a kronik*. New York: YKUF Farlag 1949.

Bibliography

-- *R'Ya'akov emdin*. New York: YKUF Farlag 1946.

Biro-Bidjan and You. New York: Astoria Press 1929.

Birobidjan: The Jewish Autonomous Territory. New York: American Committee for the Settlement of Jews in Birobidjan (Ambijan) 1936.

Birobidjan: The Jewish Autonomous Territory in the U.S.S.R. New York: American Committee for the Settlement of Jews in Birobidjan [1936].

Bittelman, Alexander. *The Jewish People Will Live On!* New York: Morning Freiheit Association 1944.

-- *Palestine: What is the Solution?* New York: Morning Freiheit Association 1946.

-- *Program for Survival: The Communist Position on the Jewish Question*. New York: New Century Publishers January 1947.

-- *To Secure Jewish Rights: The Communist Position*. New York: New Century Publishers March 1948.

Brainin, Joseph. "The 'Crime' of Reuben Brainin," *Jewish Life* 4, 4 (February 1950): 7-9.

-- "Pierre van Paassen: A Memoir," *Midstream* 14, 2 (February 1968): 61-66.

Brainin, Reuben. "Bagrisung fun khaver brainin bay der natsyonaler konvenshon fun icor in marts, 1935," in Reuben Brainin, *Umshterblekhe reyd: vegn birobidzhan un vegn der sovyetisher layzung fun der natsyonaler frage*. New York: ICOR 1940: 13-14.

Budenz, Louis. *Men without Faces: The Communist Conspiracy in the USA*. New York: Harper and Brothers 1950.

Budish, J.M. "The American Birobidjan Committee," in *Birobidjan: A New Hope for Oppressed European Jews. Year Book of the American Committee for the Settlement of Jews in Birobidjan, Published on the Occasion of the Farewell Dinner Rendered to the Right Honorable Lord Marley at the Hotel Commodore*. New York: Ambijan Dec. 22, 1936: 14-19.

-- "Di rizige sotsyalishtishe boyung inm sovyetn farband," *Icor yor-bukh - ICOR Year Book 1932*. New York: National Executive Committee of the ICOR 1932: 19-23 [Yiddish section].

-- *The Jewish Autonomous Region, U.S.S.R.* New York: Ambijan Committee [1944].

"A Call for a People's Delegation to Biro-Bidjan," *Icor Yor-bukh - ICOR Year Book 1936*. New York: National Executive Committee of the ICOR 1936: 4 [English section].

Call to Bronx Ambijan Conference – Ruf tsu der bronx ambijan konferents. New York: Bronx Ambijan and Bronx Jewish Council 1948.

Call to the Eastern Regional Conference of the American Birobidjan Committee (Ambijan) for Post War Rehabilitation. New York: American Birobidjan Committee (Ambijan) 1946.

Call to National Conference for Birobidjan. New York: American Birobidjan Committee (Ambijan) 1946.

Cohen, William W. "Foreword," in *Birobidjan: A New Hope for Oppressed European Jews. Year Book of the American Committee for the Settlement of Jews in Birobidjan, Published on the Occasion of the Farewell Dinner Rendered to the Right Honorable Lord Marley at the Hotel Commodore.* New York: Ambijan Dec. 22, 1936: 1.

Davies, Raymond Arthur and Andrew J. Steiger. *Soviet Asia: Democracy's First Line of Defense.* New York: Dial Press 1942.
Dawidowicz, Lucy. "American Reaction to Soviet Anti-Semitism," in Morris Fine, ed. *American Jewish Year Book 1954.* Vol. 55. New York: American Jewish Committee 1954: 152-153.
Degras, Jane, ed. *The Communist International 1919-1943 Documents.* Vol. III: *1929-1943.* London: Oxford University Press 1965.
Dennen, Leon. *Where the Ghetto Ends: Jews in Soviet Russia.* New York: Alfred H. King 1934.
Di ershte trit fun biro-bidzhan. New York: ICOR 1929.
Di Lage fun di yidishe masn, biro-bidzhan un icor / *The Jewish Masses, Biro-Bidjan, and the ICOR.* New York: ICOR [1931]).
A Duty and a Privilege for American Jews: Help to Defend America by Aiding the Soviet Union. New York: Ambijan Committee for Emergency Aid to the Soviet Union [1941].

Epstein, Ab. *Gezen in biro-bidzhan.* New York: ICOR 1931.
Epstein, Israel. *I Visit Yenan: Eye Witness Account of the Communist-led Liberated Areas in North-West China.* Bombay: People's Publishing House 1945.
-- *The People's War.* London: Victor Gollanz 1939.
-- *The Unfinished Revolution in China.* Boston: Little, Brown and Co. 1947.
-- *My China Eye: Memoirs of a Jew and a Journalist.* San Francisco: Long River Press 2005.
Epstein, Melech. *The Jew and Communism: The Story of Early Communist Victories and Ultimate Defeats in the Jewish Community, U.S.A. 1919-1941.* New York: Trade Union Sponsoring Committee 1959.
-- *Jewish Labor in U.S.A.: An Industrial, Political and Cultural History of the Jewish Labor Movement, 1882-1914.* New York: Ktav 1969.
-- *Pages from a Colorful Life: An Autobiographical Sketch.* Miami Beach: Block Publishing 1971.

Fel-Yellin, Sarah. *Tsu zun un freyd.* Los Angeles: Sore Fel-Yelin Bukh-Komitet 1957.
Fischer, Louis. "Forward to the Soil!" *Menorah Journal* 11, 2 (April 1925): 172-177.
-- "The Jews and the Five-Year Plan," the *Nation* 134, No. 3490 (1932): 597-599.
-- "On the Land," *Menorah Journal* 14, 4 (April 1928): 388-394.

-- "Progress in the Colonies," *Menorah Journal* 15, 4 (October 1928): 343-349.

4,500 Orphans—Our Debt. New York: Ambijan Committee [1944].

Founding a New Life for Suffering Thousands: Report of Dr. Joseph A. Rosen on Jewish Colonization Work in Russia. New York: United Jewish Campaign 1925.

Frankel, Henry. *The Jews in the Soviet Union and Birobidjan.* New York: American Birobidjan Commitee (Ambijan) [1946].

-- "Review of the Year 5706--Eastern Europe," in Harry Schneiderman and Julius B. Maller, eds. *American Jewish Year Book 5707 (1946-47).* Vol. 48. Philadelphia: Jewish Publication Society of America, 1946: 322-334.

"From the American Angle," in Isaac E. Rontch, ed. *Icor almanakh: 25 yor sovyetn farband 15 yor biro-bidzhan - ICOR Almanac: 25 Years U.S.S.R. 15 Years Biro-Bidjan.* New York: ICOR May 1943: 12-14 [English section].

Give Watches to the Red Army. New York: Ambijan Committee for Emergency Aid to the Soviet Union [October 1942].

Give Watches to the Red Army. New York: Ambijan Committee for Emergency Aid to the Soviet Union [February 1943].

Goldberg, B.Z. *The Jewish Problem in the Soviet Union: Analysis and Solution.* New York: Crown 1961.

-- *Sovyetn-farband: Faynt oder fraynt?* New York: Amerikaner Komite fun Yidishe Shrayber, Kinstler un Visinshaftlekher 1947.

-- "Ten Years Later," *Israel Horizons* 10, 8 (October 1962): 14-20.

Goldberg, David. *Sussman Sees it Through: A Reappraisal of the Jewish Position Under the Soviets.* New York: Bloch Publishing Co. 1935.

Goldberg, Isor. "A yubl vos vert nisht gefayert: 25 yor fun der birobidzhaner autonomer gegnt," *Unzer Tsayt* 10 (October 1959): 27-30.

Greenberg, Hayim. "Why Not Biro-Bidjan?" in [Hayim Greenberg, ed.] *Jewish Frontier Anthology 1934-1944.* New York: Jewish Frontier Association 1945: 26-33.

Harap, Louis. *The Truth About the Prague Trial.* New York: Jewish Life 1953.

Hindus, Maurice G. "The New Spirit in Russia," *Menorah Journal* 13, 1 (February 1927): 70-76.

-- *Russia Fights On.* London: Collins 1942.

-- *House Without a Roof: Russia After Forty-Three Years of Revolution.* New York: Doubleday 1961.

Homeier, Skippy et al, *Uncle Vasya is a Hero and Other Stories of the Young Heroes and Heroines of the U.S.S.R.* [New York: Ambijan Committee for Emergency Aid to the Soviet Union 1943].

Hope. New York: American Birobidjan Committee (Ambijan) [1946].

In Behalf of Jewish War Orphans and New Jewish Settlers in Birobidjan. New York: American Birobidjan Committee (Ambijan) [1948].

Isacson, Leo. *Journey to Israel*. New York: Progressive Party [1948].

Jaffee, Yaacov S. "Vos far a land iz biro-bidzhan?" *Yidisher Kemfer*, March 22, 1946: 4-6.

The Jewish Autonomous Region: Questions and Answers. New York: American Birobidjan Committee March 1948.

Jewish Colonization in Soviet Russia. New York: ICOR [1927].

Kahn, Albert E. and Michael Sayers. *The Great Conspiracy: The Secret War Against Soviet Russia*. Boston: Little, Brown and Co. 1946.

Kahn, Gordon. *Hollywood on Trial: The Story of the 10 Who Were Indicted*. New York: Boni & Gaer 1948.

Koenig, Harry D. "Birobidjan Over Chicago," in *Birobidjan: A New Hope for Oppressed European Jews. Year Book of the American Committee for the Settlement of Jews in Birobidjan, Published on the Occasion of the Farewell Dinner Rendered to the Right Honorable Lord Marley at the Hotel Commodore*. New York: Ambijan Dec. 22, 1936: 21, 37.

Jenofsky, Abraham. *Der icor in unzer historisher epokhe: Dergreykhungen un perspektiven*. New York: ICOR 1945.

Jesmer, Solomon. "Ambijan," in J. I. Fishbein, ed. *The Sentinel Presents 100 Years of Chicago Jewry*. Chicago: Sentinel Publishing Co. 1948: 101, 122.

"Jewish National Organizations," in Harry Schneiderman, ed. *American Jewish Year Book 5700 (September 14, 1939 to October 2, 1940)*. Vol. 41. Philadelphia: Jewish Publication Society of America 1939: 450, 471-472.

"Jewish National Organizations," in Harry Schneiderman, ed. *American Jewish Year Book 5706 (1945-46)*. Vol. 47. Philadelphia: Jewish Publication Society of America 1945: 563.

Kuntz, Charles. "Birobidjan and Culture," in *Biro-Bidjan: Exhibition of Works of Art Presented by American Artists to the State Museum of Biro-Bidjan*. New York: Art Committee of ICOR 1936: 3.

-- "Biro-Bidjan in Socialist Reconstruction," *Icor yor-bukh - ICOR Year Book 1932*. New York: National Executive Committee of the ICOR 1932: iii-xi [English section].

-- "Birobidjan Story," *Icor Yor-bukh - ICOR Year Book 1933*. New York: National Executive Committee of the ICOR 1933: 14-31 [English section].

Levin, Max. "Birobidjan--A Positive Force in Jewish Life," in *Birobidjan: A New Hope for Oppressed European Jews. Year Book of the American Committee for the Settlement of Jews in Birobidjan, Published on the Occasion of the Farewell*

Dinner Rendered to the Right Honorable Lord Marley at the Hotel Commodore. New York: Ambijan Dec. 22, 1936: 4-5.

-- "Exponents of Jewish Culture, the Delegation from the USSR," in *Birobidjan and the Jews in the Post-War World: A Series of Addresses on the Occasion of the Visit to the U.S.A. of Prof. Mikhoels and Lt.-Col. Feffer of the U.S.S.R.* New York: American Committee for the Settlement of Jews in Birobidjan (Ambijan) 1943: 3-4.

Levin, Max and Abraham Jenofsky. *A Call to Jewish Landsmanschaften, Societies, Orders, Auxiliaries, Trade Unions, Synagogues, Congregations, Cultural Institutions, Etc. to Celebrate 15 Years of Biro-Bidjan – A Ruf tsu yidishe landsmanshaftn, sosayties, ordns, okzileris, trayd unyons, shuln, kongregayshons, kultur institutyes, un farshidine undere organizatsyes tsu der fayerung fun 15 yor biro-bidzhan.* New York: Jubilee Committee to Celebrate 15 Years of Biro-Bijan n.d.

Life in the Soviet Far East: Birobidjan. New York: Ambijan 1948.

Lipsett, Charles H. *The Fabulous Wall Street Scrap Giants.* New York: Atlas Publishing Co. 1969.

-- "Jews and Post-War World," in *Birobidjan and the Jews in the Post-War World: A Series of Addresses on the Occasion of the Visit to the U.S.A. of Prof. Mikhoels and Lt.-Col. Feffer of the U.S.S.R.* New York: American Committee for the Settlement of Jews in Birobidjan (Ambijan) 1943: 23.

"Lord Marley," in *Birobidjan: A New Hope for Oppressed European Jews. Year Book of the American Committee for the Settlement of Jews in Birobidjan, Published on the Occasion of the Farewell Dinner Rendered to the Right Honorable Lord Marley at the Hotel Commodore.* New York: Ambijan Dec. 22, 1936: 3.

Lost zikh mer nit narn!! Bakent zikh mit di emest'e faktn! Entfert di felsher! New York: National Executive of the ICOR December 1936.

Maltz, Albert. *A Long Day in a Short Life.* New York: International Publishers 1957.

Mandel, William. *A Guide to the Soviet Union.* New York: Dial Press 1946.

-- *Saying No to Power: Autobiography of a 20th Century Activist and Thinker.* Berkeley, CA: Creative Arts Book Co. 1999.

-- *The Soviet Far East and Central Asia.* New York: Dial Press 1944.

Marmor, Kalmen. *Mayn lebns-geshikhte*, 2 vols. New York: YKUF Farlag, 1959.

McConnell, Francis J. "Birobidjan and the Spirit of Social Service," in *Birobidjan: A New Hope for Oppressed European Jews. Year Book of the American Committee for the Settlement of Jews in Birobidjan, Published on the Occasion of the Farewell Dinner Rendered to the Right Honorable Lord Marley at the Hotel Commodore.* New York: Ambijan Dec. 22, 1936: 7-8.

McWilliams, Carey. *The Education of Carey McWilliams.* New York: Simon & Schuster 1978.

-- *A Mask for Privilege: Anti-Semitism in America.* Boston: Little, Brown 1948.

Medem, Gina. *A lebnsveg: Oytobyografishe notitsn*. New York: Gina Medem Bukh-komitet 1950.

-- *Lender, felker, kamfn*. New York: Gina Medem Bukh-komitet 1963.

-- "Nokh amol birobidzhan," *Icor yor-bukh - ICOR Year Book 1932*. New York: National Executive Committee of the ICOR 1932: 66-69 [Yiddish section].

-- "A yubiley fun natsyonaln shtolts," in Isaac E. Rontch, ed. *Icor almanakh: 25 yor sovyetn farband 15 yor biro-bidzhan - ICOR Almanac: 25 Years U.S.S.R 15 Years Biro-Bidjan*. New York: ICOR May 1943: 41-42 [Yiddish section].

Meisel, Nakhman. "Reuben brainin," introduction to Reuben Brainin, *Fun mayn lebns-bukh*. New York: YKUF Farlag 1946: 7-16.

-- "Reuben brainin un dr. khaim zhitlovsky," in Nakhman Meisel, ed. *Tsum hundertstn geborntog fun reuben brainin: Zamlung*. New York: YKUF Farlag 1962: 136-152.

-- "Reuben brainin (zikhroynes)," in Nakhman Meisel, ed. *Tsum hundertstn geborntog fun reuben brainin: Zamlung*. New York: YKUF Farlag 1962: 93-97.

Miller, Moses. *A Jew Looks at the War*. New York: Jewish Peoples Committee June 1940.

-- *Crisis in Palestine*. New York: New Century Publishers September 1946.

-- *Soviet Anti-Semitism — the Big Lie*. New York: Jewish Life 1949.

Murray, James E. "A Quarter Century of Progress," in Isaac E. Rontch, ed. *Icor almanakh: 25 yor sovyetn farband 15 yor biro-bidzhan - ICOR Almanac: 25 Years U.S.S.R. 15 Years Biro-Bidjan*. New York: ICOR May 1943: 3-4 [English section].

Novick, Paul. *Di natsyonale un yidishe frage in itstiken moment*. New York: Morgn Freiheit 1970.

-- *The Jewish Problem in Poland*. New York: Morning Freiheit 1969.

-- *Yidn in biro-bidzhan: A bazukh in der yidisher autonomye gegnt*. New York: ICOR 1937.

Novick, Paul and J.M. Budish, *Jews in the Soviet Union: Citizens and Builders*. New York: New Century Publishers May 1948.

O'Connor, Tom. *The Truth About Anti-Semitism in the Soviet Union*. New York: American Committee of Jewish Writers, Artists and Scientists 1949.

Olgin, Moissaye J. "The Splendid Example of the American Artists," in *Biro-Bidjan: Exhibition of Works of Art Presented by American Artists to the State Museum of Biro-Bidjan*. New York: Art Committee of ICOR 1936: 4.

"Our Co-Workers Say," in *Birobidjan: A New Hope for Oppressed European Jews. Year Book of the American Committee for the Settlement of Jews in Birobidjan, Published on the Occasion of the Farewell Dinner Rendered to the Right Honorable Lord Marley at the Hotel Commodore*. New York: Ambijan Dec. 22, 1936: 20.

Our Debt in Stalingrad. New York: Ambijan Committee [1944].

Pepper, Claude Denson and Hays Gorey. *Pepper: Eyewitness to a Century*. San Diego, CA: Harcourt Brace Jovanovich 1987.

"Prominent Leaders Appraise Birobidjan," in *Birobidjan: A New Hope for Oppressed European Jews. Year Book of the American Committee for the Settlement of Jews in Birobidjan, Published on the Occasion of the Farewell Dinner Rendered to the Right Honorable Lord Marley at the Hotel Commodore*. New York: Ambijan Dec. 22, 1936: 34-36.

The Promise of Birobidjan: Summary of Proceedings of Meeting of Board of Governors, Directors, Chairmen of Divisions, and Sponsors of the American Committee for the Settlement of Jews in Birobidjan Held at the Aldine Club, New York City, August 4, 193. New York: American Committee for the Settlement of Jews in Birobidjan 1937.

Recht, Charles. "The Jewish Question Answered," in *Birobidjan: A New Hope for Oppressed European Jews. Year Book of the American Committee for the Settlement of Jews in Birobidjan, Published on the Occasion of the Farewell Dinner Rendered to the Right Honorable Lord Marley at the Hotel Commodore*. New York: Ambijan Dec. 22, 1936: 12-13.

Report of the American Icor Commission for the Study of Biro-Bidjan and its Colonization. New York: ICOR 1930.

"Review of the Year 5697," in Harry Schneiderman, ed. *American Jewish Year Book 5698 (September 6, 1937 to September 25, 1938)*. Vol. 39. Philadelphia: Jewish Publication Society of America 1937: 246-247.

Revutsky, Abraham. "Bira-Bidzhan: A Jewish Eldorado?" *Menorah Journal* 16, No. 2 (1929): 158-168.

Reynolds, Louis G. *The Pact and the Jew: How it Has Affected the Destiny of 5,000,000 Jews*. Los Angeles: City Committee ICOR [1939].

Rosenberg, James N. *How the Back-to-the-Soil Movement Began: Two Years of Blazing the New Jewish "Covered Wagon" Trail Across the Russian Prairies*. Philadelphia: United Jewish Campaign 1925.

-- "Let the World Take Note," in *Birobidjan and the Jews in the Post-War World: A Series of Addresses on the Occasion of the Visit to the U.S.A. of Prof. Mikhoels and Lt.-Col. Feffer of the U.S.S.R.* New York: American Committee for the Settlement of Jews in Birobidjan (Ambijan) 1943: 21-22.

-- *On the Steppes: A Russian Diary*. New York: Alfred A. Knopf 1927.

-- "Soviet Russia and the Jews," *Menorah Journal* 31, 3 (October-December 1943): 296-299.

Rukhadze, Avtandil. *Jews in the USSR: Figures Facts Comment*. Moscow: Novosti Press Agency 1984.

Shipman, Samuel S. "The Story of the Jewish Territory," in *Birobidjan: A New Hope for Oppressed European Jews. Year Book of the American Committee for the Settlement of Jews in Birobidjan, Published on the Occasion of the Farewell Dinner Rendered to the Right Honorable Lord Marley at the Hotel Commodore.* New York: Ambijan Dec. 22, 1936: 25-28.

Somerville, John. *The Communist Trials and the American Tradition: Expert Testimony on Force and Violence, and Democracy.* New York: International Publishers 1956.

-- *The Philosophy of Peace.* New York: Gaer Associates 1949.

-- *Soviet Philosophy, A study of Theory and Practice.* New York: Philosophical Library 1946.

"Sponsors of the People's Delegation to Biro-Bidjan," *Icor Yor-bukh - ICOR Year Book 1936.* New York: National Executive Committee of the ICOR 1936: 5 [English section].

"A Soviet Jewish Republic in the Making," *Literary Digest* 116, 6 (August 5, 1933): 13.

"Soviet Viewpoints," in *Birobidjan: A New Hope for Oppressed European Jews. Year Book of the American Committee for the Settlement of Jews in Birobidjan, Published on the Occasion of the Farewell Dinner Rendered to the Right Honorable Lord Marley at the Hotel Commodore.* New York: Ambijan Dec. 22, 1936: 22-23.

Stefansson, Evelyn. *Here is Alaska.* New York: Scribner's 1943.

-- *Within the Circle: Portrait of the Arctic.* New York: Scribner's 1944.

Stefansson, Vilhjalmur. *The Adventure of Wrangel Island.* New York: Macmillan 1925.

-- *Discovery: The Autobiography of Vilhjalmur Stefansson.* New York: McGraw-Hill 1964.

-- *The Friendly Arctic: The Story of Five Years in Polar Regions.* New York, Macmillan 1921.

-- *Hunters of the Great North.* New York: Harcourt, Brace 1922.

-- *My Life with the Eskimo.* New York: Macmillan 1913.

-- *The Northward Course of Empire.* New York: Harcourt, Brace 1922.

-- *Unsolved Mysteries of the Arctic.* New York: Macmillan 1938.

Stone, I.F. *This is Israel.* New York: Boni and Gaer 1948.

Suvenir-program: Folks-konferents far a folks delegatsye keyn biro bidzhan - Souvenir Program: Peoples' Conference for a Delegation to Biro-Bidjan. Los Angeles: ICOR 1936.

Talmy, Leon. "Biro-bidzhan 1928-1931," *Icor yor-bukh - ICOR Year Book 1932.* New York: National Executive Committee of the ICOR 1932: 15-18 [Yiddish section].

-- *Oyf royer erd: Mit der 'icor'-ekspeditsye in biro-bidzhan.* New York: Frayhayt 1931.

Tobenkin, Elias. *Stalin's Ladder: War & Peace in the Soviet Union.* New York: Minton, Balch and Co. 1933.

Bibliography

20th Anniversary of Birobidjan 1928-1948: Second Pictorial Album. New York: American Birobidjan Committee – Ambijan 1948.

"Watches Can Shoot," in *Birobidjan and the Jews in the Post-War World: A Series of Addresses on the Occasion of the Visit to the U.S.A. of Prof. Mikhoels and Lt.-Col. Feffer of the U.S.S.R.* New York: American Committee for the Settlement of Jews in Birobidjan (Ambijan) 1943: 17-20.

We Must Lend a Hand! New York: American Birobidjan Committee (Ambijan) [1945].

Weiner, William. *Unity of the Jewish People: The Answer to Anti-Semitism and Fascism*. New York: Jewish Peoples Committee For United Action Against Fascism and Anti-Semitism, 1939.

Weinper, Zishe. *Birobidzhan*. New York: Kultur tsvayg baym ICOR 1935.

-- *Dos z. vaynper-bukh*. New York: YKUF Farlag 1962.

Weinrauch, Herschel. *Blut oyf der zun (yidn in sovyet-rusland)*. New York: Farlag "Mensh un Yid", 1950.

"What We Stand For," in [Hayim Greenberg, ed.] *Jewish Frontier Anthology 1934-1944* New York: Jewish Frontier Association 1945): 3-7.

Yarmolinsky, Avrahm. "Birobidjan," *Universal Jewish Encyclopedia*, 1941; New York: Ktav 1969 reprint edition: 372-8.

Zhitlovsky, Khaim. *An entfer mayne kritiker*. New York: Cooperative Book League of the Jewish Section, International Workers Order December 1942.

-- "Birobidzhan un erets yisroel," in Isaac E. Rontch, ed. *Icor almanakh: 25 yor sovyetn farband 15 yor biro-bidzhan - ICOR Almanac: 25 Years U.S.S.R. 15 Years Biro-Bidjan*. New York: ICOR May 1943: 38-39 [Yiddish section].

-- *Di yidn in sovyetn-farband*. New York: ICOR 1943.

-- *Hitler oder Stalin? / Hitler or Stalin?* New York: ICOR 1938.

-- "Vegn der sovyetisher yidnshaft," in Isaac E. Rontch, ed. *Icor almanakh: 25 yor sovyetn farband 15 yor biro-bidzhan - ICOR Almanac: 25 Years U.S.S.R. 15 Years Biro-Bidjan*. New York: ICOR May 1943: 17-25 [Yiddish section].

Zukerman, William. "A Jewish Home in Russia," the *Nation* 134, No. 3488 (1932): 540-541.

-- "Soviet Russia Solves the Jewish Problem," *Contemporary Review* 140, 11 (December 1931): 741-748.

-- "The Jewish Colonization Movement in Soviet Russia," *Menorah Journal* 21, 1 (April-June 1933): 74-76, 79.

SECONDARY SOURCES
Articles and Books

Abramsky, Chimen. "The Biro-Bidzhan Project, 1927-1959," in Lionel Kochan, ed. *The Jews in Soviet Russia Since 1917*, 3rd ed. London: Oxford University Press 1978: 64-77.

-- "Russian Jews--A Bird's Eye View," *Midstream* 24, No. 10 (1978): 34-43.

Altshuler, Mordechai. "The Attitude of the Communist Party of Russia to Jewish National Survival, 1918-1930," *YIVO Annual of Jewish Social Science* 14 (1969): 68-86.

Azadovskii, Konstantin and Boris Egorov, "From Anti-Westernism to Anti-Semitism," *Journal of Cold War Studies* 4, No.1 (2002): 66-80.

Bachmann, Lawrence P. "Julius Rosenwald," *American Jewish Historical Quarterly* 64, 1 (September 1976): 89-105

Baron, Salo W. *The Russian Jew Under Tsars and Soviets*. New York: Macmillan 1976.

Bauer, Yehuda. *My Brother's Keeper: A History of the American Jewish Joint Distribution Committee, 1929-1939*. Philadelphia: Jewish Publication Society 1974.

Belfrage, Cedric. *The American Inquisition, 1945-1960*. Indianapolis: Bobbs-Merrill 1973.

Belknap, Michal R. *Cold War Political Justice: The Smith Act, the Communist Party, and American Civil Liberties*. Westport, CT: Greenwood Press 1977.

Bentsur, Eytan and B.L. Kolokolov, eds. *Documents on Israeli-Soviet Relations, 1941-1953*. London: Frank Cass 2000.

Berman, Aaron. *Nazism, the Jews, and American Zionism, 1933-1948*. Detroit: Wayne State University Press 1992.

Berry, Erick. *Mr. Arctic: An Account of Vilhjalmur Stefansson*. New York: David McKay 1966.

Berton, Pierre. *Prisoners of the North*. Toronto: Doubleday Canada 2004.

Blumberg, Esterita "Cissie." *Remember the Catskills: Tales by a Recovering Hotelkeeper*. Fleischmanns, NY: Purple Mountain Press 1996.

Borodulin, Nikolai. "American Art for Birobidzhan," *Jews in Eastern Europe* 3, 49 (Winter 2002): 99-108.

Brent, Jonathan and Vladimir P. Naumov. *Stalin's Last Crime: The Plot Against the Jewish Doctors, 1948-1953*. New York: HarperCollins 2003.

Browder, Earl. "The American Communist Party in the Thirties," in Rita James Simon, ed. *As We Saw the Thirties: Essays on Social and Political Movements of a Decade*. Urbana, IL: University of Illinois Press 1967: 216-253.

Brown, Phil ed. *In The Catskills: A Century of the Jewish Experience in "The Mountains."* New York: Columbia University Press 2002.

Buhle, Paul. "Jews and American Communism: The Cultural Question," *Radical History Review* 23 (1980): 9-33.

-- *Marxism in the United States: Remapping the History of the American Left*, 2nd ed. London: Verso 1991.
-- "Paul Novick: A Radical Life," *Radical America* 17, 5 (September-October 1983): 74-75.

Carr, E. H. *Twilight of the Comintern, 1930-1935*. New York: Pantheon Books 1983.
Caute, David. *The Fellow-Travellers: A Postscript to the Enlightenment*. New York: Macmillan 1973.
-- *The Great Fear: The Anti-Communist Purge Under Truman and Eisenhower*. New York: Simon and Schuster 1978.
Ceplair, Larry and Steven Englund. *The Inquisition in Hollywood: Politics in the Film Community, 1930-60*. Urbana, IL: University of Illinois Press 2003.
Chernow, Ron. *The Warburgs: The Twentieth-Century Odyssey of a Remarkable Jewish Family*. New York: Vintage 1994.
Cohen, Michael Joseph. *Truman and Israel*. Berkeley, CA: University of California Press 1990.
Crowl, William. *Angels in Stalin's Paradise: Western Reporters in Soviet Russia, 1917 to 1937, a Case Study of Louis Fischer and Walter Duranty*. Washington, DC: University Press of America 1982.
Dekel-Chen, Jonathan. *Farming the Red Land: Jewish Agricultural Colonization and Local Soviet Power, 1924-1941*. New Haven: Yale University Press 2005.
-- "'New' Jews of the Agricultural Kind: A Case of Soviet Interwar Propaganda," *Russian Review* 66, 3 (July 2007): 424-450.
-- "An Unlikely Triangle: Philanthropists, Commissars, and American Statesmanship Meet in Soviet Crimea, 1922-37," *Diplomatic History* 27, 3 (June 2003): 353-376.

Denning, Michael. *The Cultural Front: The Laboring of American Culture in the Twentieth Century*. London: Verso 1996.
Devine, Thomas W. "The Communists, Henry Wallace, and the Progressive Party of 1948," *Continuity: A Journal of History* 26 (Spring 2003): 33-79.
Diubaldo, Richard J. *Stefansson and the Canadian Arctic*. Montreal: McGill-Queen's University Press 1978.
Doroshkin, Milton. *Yiddish in America: Social and Cultural Foundations*. Rutherford, NJ: Fairleigh Dickinson University Press 1969.
Draper, Theodore. *American Communism and Soviet Russia: The Formative Period*. 1960; New York: Vintage edition, 1986.
Dubrovsky, Gertrude Wishnick. *The Land Was Theirs: Jewish Farmers in the Garden State*. Tuscaloosa, AL: University of Alabama Press 1992.
Dunaway, David K. "Unsung Songs of Protest: The Composers Collective of New York," *New York Folklore* 5 (Summer 1979): 1-19.

Eckstein, Arthur. "The Hollywood Ten in History and Memory," *Film History* 16, 4 (2004): 424-436.

Emiot, Israel. *The Birobidzhan Affair: A Yiddish Writer in Siberia,* translated from the Yiddish by Max Rosenfeld. Philadelphia: Jewish Publication Society of America 1981.

Engerman, David C. *Modernization from the Other Shore: American Intellectuals and the Romance of Russian Development.* Cambridge, MA: Harvard University Press 2003.

Estraikh, Gennady. *In Harness: Yiddish Writers' Romance with Communism.* Syracuse, NY: Syracuse University Press 2005.

-- *Yiddish in the Cold War (Studies in Yiddish 7). London:* Legenda Press 2008.

-- "Yiddish Language Conference Aborted," *East European Jewish Affairs* 25, 2 (Winter 1995): 91-96.

-- "The Yiddish-Language Communist Press," in Jonathan Frankel, ed. *Dark Times, Dire Decisions: Jews and Communism (Studies in Contemporary Jewry XX).* Oxford: Oxford University Press 2004: 62-82.

Fariello, Griffin. *Red Scare: Memories of the American Inquisition. An Oral History.* New York: W.W. Norton 1995.

Feingold, Henry L. *The Jewish People in America.* Vol. IV: *A Time For Searching: Entering the Mainstream 1920-1945.* Baltimore: Johns Hopkins Press, 1992.

-- *Zion in America: the Jewish Experience from Colonial Times to the Present.* New York: Hippocrene Books 1974.

Fishbein, J. I. ed. *The Sentinel's History of Chicago Jewry, 1911-1986.* Chicago: Sentinel Publishing Co. 1986.

Frankel, Jonathan. "Modern Jewish Politics East and West (1840-1939): Utopia, Myth, Reality," in Zvi Gitelman, ed. *The Quest for Utopia: Jewish Political Ideas and Institutions Through the Ages.* Armonk, NY: M.E. Sharpe 1992: 81-103.

-- *Prophecy and Politics: Socialism, Nationalism, and the Russian Jews, 1862-1917.* Cambridge: Cambridge University Press 1981.

Fried, Richard M. *Nightmare in Red: The McCarthy Era in Perspective.* New York: Oxford University Press 1990.

Friedman, Murray. "From Outsiders to Insiders? Philadelphia Jewish Life, 1940-1985," in Murray Friedman, ed. *Philadelphia Jewish Life, 1940-1985.* Philadelphia: Temple University Press 2003: xxv-xliii.

Geertz, Clifford. "Thick Description: Towards an Interpretive Theory of Culture," in Clifford Geertz, ed. *The Interpretation of Cultures: Selected Essays.* New York: Basic Books 1973: 3-30.

Gitelman, Zvi. *Jewish Nationality and Soviet Politics: The Jewish Sections of the CPSU, 1917-1930.* Princeton, NJ: Princeton University Press 1972.

Glaser, Amelia and David Weintraub, eds. *Proletpen: America's Rebel Yiddish Poets.* Madison, WI: University of Wisconsin Press 2005.

Glazer, Nathan. *The Social Basis of American Communism.* Westport, CT: Greenwood Press edition 1974.

Golan, Daphna et al, "The Jewish Diaspora, Israel, and Jewish Identities: A Dialogue," *South Atlantic Quarterly* 98 (Winter/Spring 1999): 95-116.

Goldman, Michal. "A World in the World: Living in the Coops," *Jewish Currents* 57, 6 (November-December 2003): 24-25, 48.

Goldsmith, Emanuel S. *Architects of Yiddishism at the Beginning of the Twentieth Century: A Study in Jewish Cultural History.* Rutherford, NJ: Fairleigh Dickinson University Press 1976.

Goldstein, Robert Justin. *American Blacklist: The Attorney General's List of Subversive Organizations.* Lawrence, KS: University Press of Kansas 2008.

Gornick, Vivian. *The Romance of American Communism.* New York: Basic Books 1977.

Hallas, Duncan. *The Comintern.* London: Bookmarks 1985.

Hanson, Earl P. *Stefansson: Prophet of the North.* New York: Harper 1941.

Harshav, Benjamin. *Marc Chagall and his Times: A Documentary Narrative.* Stanford, CA: Stanford University Press 2004.

-- ed. *Marc Chagall on Art and Culture: Including the First Book on Chagall's Art by A. Efros and Ya. Tugendhold (Moscow, 1918)*, translations from the French, Russian, Yiddish, and Hebrew by Barbara and Benjamin Harshav. Stanford, CA: Stanford University Press 2003.

Haynes, John Earl. "The Cold War Debate Continues: A Traditionalist View of Historical Writing on Domestic Communism and Anti-Communism," *Journal of Cold War Studies* 2, 1 (Winter 2000): 76-115.

Haynes, John Earl and Harvey Klehr, "The CPUSA Reports to the Comintern: 1941," *American Communist History* 4, 1 (June 2005): 21-60.

-- *Early Cold War Spies: The Espionage Trials that Shaped American Politics.* New York: Cambridge University Press 2006.

-- "The Historiography of American Communism: An Unsettled Field," *Labour History Review* 68, 1 (April 2003): 61-78.

-- *In Denial: Historians, Communism and Espionage.* San Francisco: Encounter Books 2003.

-- *Venona: Decoding Soviet Espionage in America.* New Haven: Yale University Press 2000.

Haynes, John Earl, Harvey Klehr, and Alexander Vassiliev. *Spies: The Rise and Fall of the KGB in America.* New Haven: Yale University Press 2009.

Hemingway, Andrew. *Artists on the Left: American Artists and the Communist Movement 1926-1956.* New Haven: Yale University Press 2002.

Hertzberg, Arthur. *The Jews in America: Four Centuries of an Uneasy Encounter: A History.* New York: Simon and Schuster 1989.

Himelstein, Morgan Y. *Drama Was a Weapon: The Left-Wing Theatre in New York, 1929-1941*. New Brunswick, NJ: Rutgers University Press 1963.

Hoberman, James. *The Red Atlantis: Communist Culture in the Absence of Communism*. Philadelphia: Temple University Press 1998.

Hoffman, Matthew. "From Pintele Yid to Racenjude: Chaim Zhitlovsky and Racial Conceptions of Jewishness," *Jewish History* 19, 1 (March 2005): 65-78.

Horne, Gerald. *Class Struggle in Hollywood 1930-1950: Moguls, Mobsters, Stars, Reds, and Trade Unionists*. Austin, TX: University of Texas Press 2001.

Howe, Irving. *World of Our Fathers: The Journey of the East European Jews to America and the Life They Found and Made*. New York: Simon and Schuster, 1976.

Hunt, William R. *Stef: A Biography of Vilhjalmur Stefansson, Canadian Arctic Explorer*. Vancouver: University of British Columbia Press 1986.

Hurewitz, Daniel. *Bohemian Los Angeles and the Making of Modern Politics*. Berkeley, CA: University of California Press 2007.

Isserman, Maurice. *If I Had a Hammer...The Death of the Old Left and the Birth of the New Left*. New York: Basic Books 1987.

-- *Which Side Were You On? The American Communist Party During the Second World War*. Middletown, CT: Wesleyan University Press 1982.

Ivanov, Alexander. "Facing East: the World ORT Union and the Jewish Refugee Problem in Europe, 1933-38," *East European Jewish Affairs* 39, 3 (December 2009): 369-388.

Jerome, Fred. *The Einstein File: J. Edgar Hoover's Secret War Against the World's Most Famous Scientist*. New York: St. Martin's Press 2002.

Kagedan, Allan L. "American Jews and the Soviet Experiment: The Agro-Joint Project, 1924-1937," *Jewish Social Studies* 43, 2 (Spring 1981): 153-164.

-- "Birobidzhan," *Central Asian Survey* 12, No. 2 (1993): 87-94.

-- *Soviet Zion: The Quest for a Russian Jewish Homeland*. New York: St Martin's Press 1994.

Kann, Kenneth L. *Comrades and Chicken Ranchers: The Story of a California Jewish Community*. Ithaca, NY: Cornell University Press 1993.

Kaplan, Doris C. "Passage to Siberia," in Judy Kaplan and Linn Shapiro, eds. *Red Diapers: Growing Up in the Communist Left*. Urbana, IL: University of Illinois Press 1998: 41-44.

Katz, Lyber. "Around the World," *Jewish Currents* 51, 9 (October 1997): 47.

Kavanaugh, Sarah. *ORT and the Rehabilitation of Holocaust Survivors*. London: Vallentine Mitchell 2008.

Keeran, Roger. "National Groups and the Popular Front: The Case of the

International Workers Order," *Journal of American Ethnic History* 14 (Spring 1995): 23-51.

Kenez, Peter. "Jewish Themes in Stalinist Films," *Judaism* 45, 3 (Summer 1996): 277-284.

Klehr, Harvey. *Communist Cadre: The Social Background of the American Communist Party Elite.* Stanford, CA: Hoover Institution Press 1978.

-- *The Heyday of American Communism: The Depression Decade.* New York: Basic Books 1984.

-- "Immigrant Leadership in the Communist Party of the United States of America," *Ethnicity* 6 (March 1979): 29-44.

Klehr, Harvey and John Earl Haynes. *The American Communist Movement: Storming Heaven Itself.* New York: Twayne 1992.

Klehr, Harvey, John Earl Haynes and Fridrikh Igorevich Firsov. *The Secret World of American Communism.* New Haven: Yale University Press 1995.

Klehr, Harvey, Kyrill M. Anderson and John Earl Haynes. *The Soviet World of American Communism.* New Haven: Yale University Press 1998.

Klepfisz, Irena. "Di Mames, Dos Loshn/The Mothers, the Language: Feminism, Yidishkayt, and the Politics of Memory," *Bridges: A Journal for Jewish Feminists and Our Friends* 4, No.1 (1994): 12-47.

Koch, Stephen. *Double Lives: Stalin, Willi Münzenberg and the Seduction of the Intellectuals.* New York: Enigma Books 2004.

Kolsky, Thomas A. *Jews Against Zionism: The American Council for Judaism, 1942-1948.* Philadelphia: Temple University Press 1992.

Korey, William. "The Soviet Jewish Future: Some Observations on the Recent Census," *Midstream* 20, 9 (November 1974): 39.

Kotlerman, Boris. "Jewish Names on the Map of Birobidzhan," in Aaron Demsky, ed. *These Are the Names: Studies in Jewish Onomastics.* Vol. 4. Ramat Gan, Israel: Bar-Ilan University Press 2003: 109-126.

Krammer, Arnold. *The Forgotten Friendship: Israel and the Soviet Bloc, 1947-53.* Urbana, IL: University of Illinois Press 1974.

Kutulas, Judy. *The Long War: The Intellectual People's Front and Anti-Stalinism, 1930-1940.* Durham, NC: Duke University Press 1995.

Leavitt, Moses A. *The JDC Story: Highlights of JDC Activities 1914-1952.* New York: American Jewish Joint Distribution Committee 1953.

LeBourdais, D.M. *Stefansson: Ambassador of the North.* Montreal: Harvest House 1963.

Lendvai, Paul. *Anti-Semitism Without Jews: Communist Eastern Europe.* Garden City, NY: Doubleday 1971.

Leviatin, David. *Followers of the Trail: Jewish Working-Class Radicals in America.* New Haven: Yale University Press 1989.

Levin, Nora. *The Jews in the Soviet Union Since 1917*, 2 vols., New York: New York University Press 1988.

Lewy, Guenter. *The Cause that Failed: Communism in American Political Life.* New York: Oxford University Press 1990.

Lichtenstein, Alex. "In the Shade of the Lenin Oak: 'Colonel' Raymond Robins, Senator Claude Pepper, and the Cold War," *American Communist History* 3, 2 (December 2004): 185-214.

Lichtman, Robert M. "Louis Budenz, the FBI, and the 'List of 400 Concealed Communists': An Extended Tale of McCarthy-Era Informing," *American Communist History* 3, 1 (June 2004): 25-54.

Lieberman, Robbie. *"My Song is My Weapon": People's Songs, American Communism, and the Politics of Culture, 1930-1950.* Urbana, IL: University of Illinois Press 1989.

-- *The Strangest Dream: Communism, Anti-Communism, and the U.S. Peace Movement, 1945-1963.* Syracuse, NY: Syracuse University Press 2000.

Liebman, Arthur. *Jews and the Left.* New York: John Wiley 1978.

Liebowitz, Arieh. "The Jewish Labor Committee: Past and Present," *Shofar* 12, 3 (Spring 1994): 96-99.

Low, Alfred D. *Soviet Jewry and Soviet Policy.* New York: Columbia University Press 1990.

Lustiger, Arno. *Stalin and the Jews: The Red Book. The Tragedy of the Jewish Anti-Fascist Committee and the Soviet Jews,* translated from the German by Mary Beth Friedrich and Todd Bludeau. New York: Enigma Books 2003.

Lyons, Paul. *Philadelphia Communists, 1936-1956.* Philadelphia: Temple University Press 1982.

-- "Philadelphia Jews and Radicalism: The American Jewish Congress Cleans House," in Murray Friedman, ed. *Philadelphia Jewish Life, 1940-1985.* Philadelphia: Temple University Press 2003: 57-69.

Malmgreen, Gail. "Labor and the Holocaust: The Jewish Labor Committee and the Anti-Nazi Struggle," *Labor's Heritage* 3 (October 1991): 20-35.

McDermott, Kevin and Jeremy Agnew. *The Comintern: A History of International Communism from Lenin to Stalin.* New York: St Martin's Press 1996.

McMeekin, Sean. *The Red Millionaire: A Political Biography of Willy Münzenberg, Moscow's Secret Propaganda Tsar in the West, 1917-1940.* New Haven: Yale University Press 2003.

Medoff, Raphael. "Felix Warburg and the Palestinian Arabs: A Reassessment," *American Jewish Archives* 54, 1 (2002): 11-36.

Mendelsohn, Ezra. "Jews, Communism, and Art in Interwar America," in Dan Diner and Jonathan Frankel, eds., *Dark Times, Dire Decisions: Jews and Communism (Studies in Contemporary Jewry* 20). New York: Oxford University Press 2004: 99-132.

-- *On Modern Jewish Politics.* New York: Oxford University Press 1993.

Meyer, Gerald. *Vito Marcantonio: Radical Politician, 1902-1954.* Albany, NY: State University of New York Press 1989.

Michels, Tony. *A Fire in Their Hearts: Yiddish Socialists in New York*. Cambridge, MA: Harvard University Press 2005.

Mishler, Paul C. *Raising Reds: The Young Pioneers, Radical Summer Camps, and Communist Political Culture in the United States*. New York: Columbia University Press 1999.

-- "Red Finns, Red Jews: Ethnic Variation in Communist Political Culture During the 1920s and 1930s," *YIVO Annual* 22 (1995): 131-154.

Mitsel, Mikhail. "The Final Chapter: Agro-Joint Workers - Victims of the Great Terror in the USSR, 1937-40," *East European Jewish Affairs* 39, 1 (April 2009): 79-99.

Moore, Deborah Dash. *At Home in America: Second Generation New York Jews*. New York: Columbia University Press 1981.

Morgan, Ted. *Reds: McCarthyism in Twentieth-Century America*. New York: Random House 2003.

"*Morgn Freiheit*, April 2, 1922 -- Sept. 11, 1988," *Jewish Currents* 42, 11 (November 1988): 3.

"Morris U. Schappes, 1907-2004," *Jewish Currents* 58, 4 (July-August 2004): 3-4.

Nahshon, Edna. *Yiddish Proletarian Theatre: The Art and Politics of the Artef, 1925-1940*. Westport, CT: Greenwood Press 1998.

Navasky, Victor S. *Naming Names*. New York: Viking Press 1980.

Naylor, John F. *Labour's International Policy: The Labour Party in the 1930s*. London: Weidenfeld and Nicolson 1969.

Nedava, Joseph. *Trotsky and the Jews*. Philadelphia: Jewish Publication Society of America 1972.

Olkhina, Evgenia Aleksandrovna. *Vilhjalmur Stefansson: 1879-1962*. Moscow: Academy of Sciences of the U.S.S.R. 1970.

O'Reilly, Kenneth. *Hoover and the Un-Americans: The FBI, HUAC, and the Red Menace*. Philadelphia: Temple University Press 1983.

Ottanelli, Fraser M. *The Communist Party of the United States: From the Depression to World War II*. New Brunswick, NJ: Rutgers University Press 1991.

Pinkson, Ruth. "The Life and Times of an Elderly Red Diaper Baby," in Judy Kaplan and Linn Shapiro, eds. *Red Diapers: Growing Up in the Communist Left*. Urbana, IL: University of Illinois Press 1998: 231-236.

Pinkus, Binyamin. "Change and Continuity in Soviet Policy Towards Soviet Jewry and Israel, May-December 1948," *Israel Studies* 10, 1 (Spring 2005): 96-123.

-- *The Jews of the Soviet Union: The History of a National Minority*. Cambridge: Cambridge University Press 1988.

Plunz, Richard. "Reading Bronx Housing, 1890-1940," in Timothy Rub, ed. *Building a Borough: Architecture and Planning in the Bronx, 1890-1940*. New York: Bronx Museum of the Arts 1986: 30-76.

Portnoy, Edward. "Modicut Puppet Theatre: Modernism, Satire, and Yiddish Culture," *The Drama Review* 43, 3 (Fall 1999): 115-134.

Price, David H. *Threatening Anthropology: McCarthyism and the FBI's Surveillance of Active Anthropologists*. Durham, NC: Duke University Press 2004.

Radosh, Ronald and Allis Radosh. *A Safe Haven: Harry S Truman and the Founding of Israel*. New York: Harper/Collins 2009.

-- *Red Star over Hollywood: The Film Colony's Long Romance With the Left*. San Francisco: Encounter Books 2005.

Redlich, Shimon. *Propaganda and Nationalism in Wartime Russia: The Jewish Antifascist Committee in the USSR, 1941-1948*. Boulder, CO: East European Quarterly 1982.

-- *War, Holocaust and Stalinism: A Documented History of the Jewish Anti-Fascist Committee in the USSR*. Luxembourg: Harwood Academic Publishers 1995.

Rees, Tim and Andrew Thorpe, eds. *International Communism and the Communist International, 1919-43*. New York: St Martin's Press 1998.

Reiter, Ester. "Secular *Yiddishkait*: Left Politics, Culture, and Community," *Labour/Le Travail* 49 (2002): 121-146.

Resnick, Sid. "The Birobidzhan Controversy," *Outlook* 27, 3 (March 1989): 10-11.

-- "Pesekh Novick: Redakter fun der 'Morgn-Frayhayt'," *Di Pen* 30 (January 1997): 1-8.

Richardson, Peter. *American Prophet: The Life and Work of Carey McWilliams*. Ann Arbor, MI: University of Michigan Press 2005.

Roberts, Geoffrey. *The Unholy Alliance: Stalin's Pact with Hitler*. London: I.B. Tauris 1989.

Roberts, Priscilla. "Jewish Bankers, Russia, and the Soviet Union, 1900-1940: The Case of Kuhn, Loeb and Company," *American Jewish Archives* 49, 1-2 (1997): 9-37

Ro'i, Yaakov. *Soviet Decision Making in Practice: the USSR and Israel, 1947-1954*. New Brunswick, NJ: Transaction Books 1980.

Romerstein, Herbert and Eric Breindel, *The Venona Secrets: Exposing Soviet Espionage and America's Traitors*. Washington, DC: Regnery Publishing 2000.

Rosen, Philip et al, "Philadelphia Jewry, the Holocaust, and the Birth of the Jewish State. Section I: Philadelphia Jewry and the Holocaust," in Murray Friedman, ed. *Philadelphia Jewish Life, 1940-1985*. Philadelphia: Temple University Press 2003: 3-21.

Rosenfeld, Max. "Zhitlovsky: Philosopher of Jewish Secularism," in Morris U. Schappes et al, eds. *"Jewish Currents" Reader*. New York: Jewish Currents 1966: 78-89.

Rosenthal, Jerome C. "Dealing with the Devil: Louis Marshall and the Partnership

Between the Joint Distribution Committee and Soviet Russia," *American Jewish Archives* 39, 1 (April 1987): 1-22.

Rubenstein, Joshua and Vladimir P. Naumov, eds. *Stalin's Secret Pogrom: The Postwar Inquisition of the Jewish Anti-Fascist Committee*. New Haven: Yale University Press 2001.

Rucker, Laurent. *Moscow's Surprise: The Soviet-Israeli Alliance of 1947-1949*. Cold War International History Project Working Paper Series #46. Washington, DC: Woodrow Wilson International Center for Scholars 2005.

Sabin, Arthur J. *Red Scare in Court: New York versus the International Workers Order*. Philadelphia: University of Pennsylvania Press 1993.

Sachar, Howard M. *A History of the Jews in America*. New York: Alfred A. Knopf 1992.

Salisbury, Harrison E. *American in Russia*. New York: Harper & Brothers 1955.

Sanchez, George J. " 'What's Good for Boyle Heights Is Good for the Jews': Creating Multiculturalism on the Eastside during the 1950s," *American Quarterly* 56, 3 (September 2004): 633-661.

Saposs, David J. *Communism in American Politics*. Washington: Public Affairs Press 1960.

Schappes, Morris U. "Paul Novick: In Sorrow and Pride," *Jewish Currents* 43, 11 (November 1989): 4-5.

Schrecker, Ellen W. "Immigration and Internal Security: Political Deportations During the McCarthy Era," *Science & Society* 60, 4 (Winter 1996-1997): 393-426.

-- *No Ivory Tower: McCarthyism and the Universities*. New York: Oxford University Press 1986.

Schwarz, Solomon M. "Anti-Semitism in Russia," *Common Sense* (August 1945): 12-14.

-- *The Jews in the Soviet Union*. Syracuse, NY: Syracuse University Press 1951.

-- "The New Anti-Semitism of the Soviet Union: Its Background and its Meaning," *Commentary* 7 (June 1949): 535-545.

Sebag-Montefiore, Simon. *Stalin: The Court of the Red Tsar*. New York: Alfred A. Knopf 2004.

Shannon, David A. *The Decline of American Communism: A History of the Communist Party of the United States Since 1945*. New York: Harcourt, Brace 1959.

Shapira, Anita. "'Black Night—White Snow': Attitudes of the Palestinian Labor Movement to the Russian Revolution, 1917-1929," in Ezra Mendelsohn, ed. *Essential Papers on Jews and the Left*. New York: New York University Press 1997: 236-271.

Shapiro, Leon. *The History of ORT: A Jewish Movement for Social Change*. New York: Schocken Books 1980.

Shargel, Baila Round. "Leftist Summer Colonies of Northern Westchester County, New York," *American Jewish History* 83, 3 (September 1995): 337-358.

Shkolnik, Leonid. "Birobidzhan: Jewish Autonomy--To Be or Not to Be?" translated from the Russian by Michael Sherbourne, *Jewish Quarterly* 37 (Winter 1990-91): 21-23.

Shneer, David. "The Weakness of the Birobidzhan Idea," *Jews in Russia and Eastern Europe* 3, 49 (Winter 2002): 5-30.

Shuldiner, David P. *Of Moses and Marx: Folk Ideology and Folk History in the Jewish Labor Movement*. Westport, CT: Bergin & Garvey 1999.

Sibley, Katherine A.S. *Red Spies in America: Stolen Secrets and the Dawn of the Cold War*. Lawrence, KS: University Press of Kansas 2004.

Smith, James H. "Red-baiting Senator Harley Kilgore in the Election of 1952: The Limits of McCarthyism During the Second Red Scare." *West Virginia History* 1, 1 (Spring 2007): 55–74.

Snyder, Robert. "The Paterson Jewish Folk Chorus: Politics, Ethnicity and Musical Culture," *American Jewish History* 74 (September 1984): 27-44.

Soyer, Daniel. "Soviet Travel and the Making of an American Jewish Communist: Moissaye Olgin's Trip to Russia in 1920-1921," *American Communist History* 4, 1 (June 2005): 1-20.

-- "The Travel Agent as Broker Between Old World and New: The Case of Gustave Eisner," *YIVO Annual* 21 (1992): 345-368.

Srebrnik, Henry. "'An Enemy of the Jewish Masses': The ICOR and the Campaign Against Zionism, 1924-1935," in August Grabski, ed. *Lewica Przeciwko Izraelowi: Studia O Zydowskim Lewicowym Antysyjonizmie / Rebels against Zion: Studies on Jewish Left Anti-Zionists*. Warsaw: Jewish Historical Institute 2010: 93-116.

-- "An Idiosyncratic Fellow-Traveller: Vilhjalmur Stefansson and the American Committee for the Settlement of Jews in Birobidzhan," *East European Jewish Affairs* 28, 1 (Summer 1998): 37-53.

-- "Birobidzhan on the Prairies: Two Decades of Pro-Soviet Jewish Movements in Winnipeg," in Daniel Stone, ed. *Jewish Radicalism in Winnipeg, 1905-1960 (Jewish Life and Times, Vol. 8)*. Winnipeg: Jewish Heritage Centre of Western Canada 2003: 172-191.

-- "Diaspora, Ethnicity and Dreams of Nationhood: North American Jewish Communists and the Soviet Birobidzhan Project," in Gennady Estraikh and Mikhail Krutikov, eds. *Yiddish and the Left*. Oxford: Legenda Press 2001: 80-108.

-- *Jerusalem on the Amur: Birobidzhan and the Canadian Jewish Communist Movement, 1924-1951*. Montreal: McGill-Queen's University Press 2008.

-- " 'The Jews Do Not Want War!': American Jewish Communists Defend the Hitler-Stalin Pact, 1939-1941," *American Communist History* 8, 1 (June 2009): 49-71.

-- "Leadership and Control Within an American Jewish Communist Front: The Case of the ICOR," *Shofar: An Interdisciplinary Journal of Jewish Studies* 16, 3 (Spring 1998): 103-117.

-- *London Jews and British Communism, 1935-1945*. London: Vallentine Mitchell 1995.

-- "'Next Year in Birobidzhan!' The Messianic Rhetoric of Jewish Communists in the Search for a New Zion," in Ulrich van der Heyden and Andreas Feldtkeller, eds. *Border Crossings: Explorations of an Interdisciplinary Historian. Festschrift for Irving Hexham* (Stuttgart: Franz Steiner Verlag, 2008): 305-317.
-- "Red Star Over Birobidzhan: Canadian Jewish Communists and the 'Jewish Autonomous Region' in the Soviet Union," *Labour/Le Travail* 44 (Fall 1999): 129-147.
-- "Such Stuff as Diaspora Dreams Are Made On: Birobidzhan and the Canadian-Jewish Communist Imagination," *Canadian Jewish Studies* 10 (2002): 75-107.
Stanislawski, Michael. "Introduction" to Israel Emiot, *The Birobidzhan Affair: A Yiddish Writer in Siberia*, translated from the Yiddish by Max Rosenfeld. Philadelphia: Jewish Publication Society of America 1981: vii-xvii.
Starobin, Joseph R. *American Communism in Crisis, 1943-1957*. Cambridge, MA: Harvard University Press 1972.
Steinberg, Bert. "Living a Secular Jewish Life," *Jewish Currents* 54, 9 (October 2000): 19-21.
Steinberg, Isaak N. "Territorialism: A History of the Movement," in Basil J. Vlavianos and Feliks Gross, eds. *Struggle for Tomorrow: Modern Political Ideologies of the Jewish People*. New York: Arts Inc. 1954: 112-129.
Steinberg, Peter L. *The Great "Red Menace": United States Prosecution of American Communists, 1947-1952*. Westport, CT: Greenwood Press 1984.
Stillman, Yankl. "Surviving Stalinism: An Interview with Vladimir Talmy," *Jewish Currents* 57, 4 (July-August 2003): 20-21.
St. George, George. *Siberia: The New Frontier*. New York: David McKay: 1969.
Storch, Randi. *Red Chicago: American Communism at its Grassroots, 1928-35*. Urbana, IL: University of Illinois Press 2007.
Strong, Tracy B. and Helen Keyssar. *Right in her Soul: The Life of Anna Louise Strong*. New York: Random House 1983.
Szajkowski, Zosa. *Jews, Wars, and Communism*. Vol. I: *The Attitude of American Jews to World War I, the Russian Revolutions of 1917, and Communism (1914-1945)*. New York: Ktav 1972.
-- *Jews, Wars, and Communism*. Vol. IV: *The Mirage of American Jewish Aid in Soviet Russia 1917-1939*. New York: privately printed 1977.

Taylor, Nicole. "The Mystery of Lord Marley," *Jewish Quarterly* 198 (Summer 2005): 65-69.
Tobler, Douglas F. "The Jews, the Mormons and the Holocaust," *Journal of Mormon History* 18, 1 (Spring 1992): 59-92.
Tzouliadis, Tim. *The Forsaken: An American Tragedy in Stalin's Russia*. New York: Penguin Press 2008.

Vaksberg, Arkady. *Stalin Against the Jews*, translated from the Russian by Antonia W. Bouis. New York: Alfred A. Knopf 1994.

Walker, Thomas J. E. *Pluralistic Fraternity: The History of the International Worker's Order*. New York: Garland 1991.
Waltzer, Kenneth. "The FBI, Congressman Vito Marcantonio, and the American Labor Party," in Athan G. Theoharis, *Beyond the Hiss Case: The FBI, Congress, and the Cold War*. Philadelphia: Temple University Press 1982: 176-214.
-- "The Party and the Polling Place: American Communism and the American Labor Party in the 1930s," *Radical History Review* 23 (Spring 1980): 104-129.
Walsh, Michael. "Iowa-Born, Soviet-Trained," *Smithsonian* 40, 2 (May 2009): 40-47.
Weinberg, David H. *Between Tradition and Modernity: Haim Zhitlowski, Simon Dubnow, Ahad Ha-Am, and the Shaping of Modern Jewish Identity*. New York: Holmes & Meier 1996.
Weinberg, Robert. "Birobidzhan After the Second World War," *Jews in Russia and Eastern Europe* 3, 49 (Winter 2002): 31-46.
-- "Jews into Peasants? Solving the Jewish Question in Birobidzhan," in Yaacov Ro'i, ed. *Jews and Jewish Life in Russia and the Soviet Union*. London: Frank Cass 1995: 87-102.
-- "Purge and Politics in the Periphery: Birobidzhan in 1937," *Slavic Review* 52, No. 1 (1993): 13-27.
-- *Stalin's Forgotten Zion: Birobidzhan and the Making of a Soviet Jewish Homeland. An Illustrated History, 1928-1996*. Berkeley, CA: University of California Press 1998.
Weiner, Amir. "Nature and Nurture in a Socialist Utopia: Delineating the Soviet Socio-Ethnic Body in the Age of Socialism," in David L. Hoffman, ed. *Stalinism: The Essential Readings*. Oxford: Blackwell Publishers 2003: 243-274.
Weingarten, Aviva. *Jewish Organizations' Response to Communism and to Senator McCarthy*. London: Vallentine Mitchell 2008.
Weinryb, Bernard D. "Antisemitism in Soviet Russia," in Lionel Kochan, ed. *The Jews in Soviet Russia Since 1917*, 3rd ed. London: Oxford University Press 1978: 300-332.
Weinstein, Andrew. "From International Socialism to Jewish Nationalism: The John Reed Club Gift to Birobidzhan," in Matthew Baigell and Milly Heyd, eds., *Complex Identities: Jewish Consciousness and Modern Art*. New Brunswick, NJ: Rutgers University Press 2001: 142-161
Weinstein, Miriam. *Yiddish: A Nation of Words*. South Royalton, VT: Steerforth Press 2001.
Wenger, Beth S. *New York Jews and the Great Depression: Uncertain Promise*. New Haven: Yale University Press 1996.

Ybarra, Michael J. *Washington Gone Crazy: Senator Pat McCarran and the Great American Communist Hunt*. Hanover, NH: Steerforth Press 2004.

Zucker, Bat-Ami. "American Jewish Communists and Jewish Culture in the 1930s," *Modern Judaism* 14, 2 (1994): 175-185.
-- "The 'Jewish Bureau': The Organization of American Jewish Communists in the 1930s," in Michael J. Cohen, ed. *Modern History: Bar-Ilan Studies in History III*. Ramat-Gan, Israel: Bar-Ilan University Press 1991: 135-147.

INDEX

Adler, Stella, 139, 144, 148, 178
Agudath Tarbut La'am (Association for Popular Culture) in Israel, 178, 220
Almazov, Shloime, 7, 14, 235-236; and Ambijan, 129, 239; and American Committee of Jewish Writers, Artists and Scientists, 90; and artwork for Birobidzhan State Museum, 64; and Birobidzhan, 169; and Hitler-Stalin Pact, 83-84; and People's Delegation to Biro-Bidjan, 55, 56, 62, 65, 69-72
Amalgamated Clothing Workers of America (ACWA), 1, 110, 124
Ambijan, xiii-xx, 33, 83; and CPUSA, 194-195; and FBI, 34, 86, 124, 141, 144, 147, 179, 194-197; and aid to Poland, 130, 154, 179, 192, 202, 203, 216, 217-218, 219-221; and Jewish Federations and Welfare Funds, 146-147, 198; dissolved, 204; financial difficulties, 198, 199; headquarters, 33, 108, 204; membership, 108, 141, 147, 153, 172, 201, 215; merger with ICOR, 127; national conferences and conventions, 109-110, 147-148, 153-154, 174-175, 201-203, 220
Ambijan, economic and professional divisions: Agricultural, 111, 122; Furniture, 111; Graphic Arts, 110; Industrial Trades, 103, 110; Metal Trades Machinery, 110, 193; Musicians, 111; Physicians, 111; Produce, 111; Textiles & Wearing Apparel, 110; Women's, 104
Ambijan, major city chapters and divisions: Baltimore, 141, 151; Boston and New England, 123, 140, 151, 201, 218, 222; Bronx and Manhattan, NY, 103, 122; 139, 142, 150-151, 172-173, 178, 216. 221; Brooklyn, NY, 122, 139-140, 144, 151; Chicago, 59-60, 66-68, 71, 123-126, 142, 143, 148-149, 205, 217-218, 222; Cleveland, 143; Detroit, 152, 217; Kansas City, 142, 217; Los Angeles and Southern California, 126-127, 140, 144, 145, 152-153, 178, 218-219, 222; Miami, 142, 217, 222; Milwaukee, 143, 217; Minneapolis, 126, 135n32; Newark and New Jersey, 122, 143, 151, 177-178, 217, 221; Petaluma, CA, 145-146, 178, 222, 156n10; Philadelphia, 140, 151, 217, 221-222; San Francisco, 140, 148, 219, 222

American Commission of Scientists and Experts, 14-15, 33, 38
American Committee of Jewish Writers, Artists and Scientists, 90, 101, 168, 178, 201, 203-204, 230
American Committee for the Settlement of Jews in Birobidjan. See Ambijan.
American Jewish Joint Agricultural Corporation (Agro-Joint), 10-11, 35, 64
American Jewish Joint Distribution Committee (Joint), 10-11, 23n65
Amtorg Trading Corp., 36, 39, 102, 111, 196, 48n37
Anderson, Clinton P., 122, 128, 130
Arbeter Ring (Workmen's Circle), 1
Arens, Jean J., 38, 48n30
Aronoff, Isaac, 109, 129, 198, 203
Aronoff, Jacob B., 72, 123-124, 129, 141, 151, 173, 178, 196, 203

283

INDEX

Aronow, Edward I., 33, 101, 109, 193
Artef (Workers Theater Group), 7, 93
Artwork for Birobidzhan State Museum, 63-64
Asch, Sholem, 90
Association for Jewish Colonization in the Soviet Union. See ICOR.
Association for the Settlement of Jewish Toilers on the Land. See GEZERD.

Bailin, Israel Ber, 7
Bakhmutsky, Alexander, 94, 191, 247n54
Bakst, Fan Groff, 122, 146, 176, 198, 203, 238
Barkley, Alben (Senator), xv, 125, 128, 130, 140, 148, 165
Battle, George Gordon, 40, 43, 44, 103, 105, 107, 108
Bedacht, Max, 5
Ben-Gurion, David, 171, 174
Bernstein, Joseph M., 129, 195
Bernstein, Leonard, 111, 122, 129
Biberman, Herbert, 152, 219
Bick, Abraham (Rabbi), 87-88, 142, 145, 151, 153, 172-173, 192, 204, 222, 230, 232, 235
Birobidzhan, achievements, 130, 139, 145, 149, 151, 214-216, 220; agriculture in, 34, 145, 149; appeal of, xiii, 39; bulwark against Japanese invasion, 12, 30, 32; capital city, 37, 149; climate, 32, 34; history of the project, 12; industry in, 130, 145, 149, 151, 220; as Jewish Autonomous Region, 12; Jewish settlements, 12, 145; movies about, 42-43; place of refuge, 29, 40-42; post-war reconstruction and settlement, 106-107, 109, 144-146, 149-150, 154-155, 220-221; purges and decline, 68-69, 189-190, 231, 232-235, 239; Yiddish culture in, 12, 147, 149, 150, 215, 220
Bittelman, Alexander, 1, 109, 166, 169-170
Brainin, Joseph, 55, 90-91, 168-169, 204, 98n35
Brainin, Reuben, xviii, 9, 15, 55, 230, 236
Bressler, Max, 123
Brin, Alexander, 63
Brin, Joseph G., 123
Browder, Earl, 29
Budish, Jacob Mordecai (J.M.), 33, 36, 42; and Ambijan, 140, 143-144, 153-155, 193-194, 195-196, 197-198, 201, 203, 204-205; 222, and Birobidzhan project, 69, 107, 109, 128, 144, 145, 149-150, 202-203; and death of Shloime Mikhoels, 189; and Holocaust orphans rehabilitation campaign, 108, 123-124, 130; and Israel, 167-168, 171-172, 175, 176, 177-178; and Jewish Federations and Welfare Funds, 146, 198-199; and People's Delegation to Biro-Bidjan, 55, 67-68, 71-72; and Silver Ponds Children's Home, 104, 131; and visit of Itzik Fefer and Shloime Mikhoels to U.S., 105-106; defends Soviet Union, 190, 202; visit to Poland, 216, 217-218; visits to Soviet Union, 37, 66

Cahan, Ab., 1
Cantor, Eddie, 90, 91
Celler, Emanuel (Congressman), 41, 44, 110, 111, 120, 129
Chagall, Marc, xv, 90, 129
Chutzkayev, S.E., 66
Cohen, William W., 33, 37-38, 39, 40,

42, 56, 66, 103, 107, 116n27
Cold War, 179, 189-193, 197
Committee for the Settlement of Jewish Toilers on the Land (see KOMERD).
Communist front groups, 4-6
Communist Party of the United States (CPUSA), Jewish membership in, 3-4, 18n15, 18n16
Cramer, Israel, 203
Crimean colonies, 10-12, 87

Daily Worker, 2, 195
DeWitt, Samuel, 101-102, 104, 110

Einstein, Albert, xv, 90, 101, 125, 129, 130, 154, 168, 169, 201, 203
Eisenstein, Ira (Rabbi), 39, 56
Eppelbaum, Ber, 62,
Epstein, Ab., 13, 15, 55, 57
Epstein, Harry, 151, 178
Epstein, Israel, 221, 225n20
Epstein, Melech, 3, 55, 83

Fascism, 8, 13-14, 31, 61, 62, 83, 87, 108, 109, 142, 165, 198, 203, 204, 229, 236, 79n75
Federal Bureau of Investigation (FBI), xvii, 31, 86, 124, 179, 194-197, 199
Fediushine, Victor A., 101, 102, 103
Fefer, Itzik, 90-92, 105-106, 139, 168, 191, 194-195, 231-232, 245n33
Fel-Yellin, Sarah, 173-174, 218-219
Feuchtwanger, Lion, 90, 140
Fischer, Louis, 29
Fishbein, Jack I., 125
Fisher, Harry M., 58, 60, 123-124, 149, 174
Forverts, xvi, 1, 63, 65, 91-92

Fox, G. George (Rabbi), 58, 59, 63, 125
Frankel, Nathan, 198, 200-201, 203-204, 216, 221
Frayhayt. See *Morgn Frayhayt*.
Frayhayt Gezang Farayn, 7
Freeland League for Jewish Colonization, 9

Germany, anti-Semitism in, 33, 61, 109, 204
Getmansky, Samuel, 193-194
Getmansky, Zina, 122, 172
GEZERD (Association for the Settlement of Jewish Toilers on the Land), 10-12, 37-38, 55, 66, 68, 231
Goldberg, B.Z. (Ben-Zion Waife), xviii, 16; and Ambijan, 33, 140, 203; and American Committee of Jewish Writers, Artists and Scientists, 201, 202; and Holocaust orphans rehabilitation campaign, 142 ; and Israel, 167-168, 175; and Jewish Anti-Fascist Committee, 90, 189; and People's Delegation to Biro-Bidjan, 56, 57, 58, 66; loses column in *Der Tog*, 83, 94n4; and support for Soviet Union, 86, 190-191; and visit to Birobidzhan, 34, 46n21; and visits to Soviet Union, 121, 130, 231
Goldmann, Nahum, 90, 168
Goldstein, Harry, 127, 219
Gousev, M.M., 102, 111
Green, Dwight H. (Governor), 125
Greenbaum, Jack, 129, 148, 192, 194, 203
Gromyko, Andrei, xv, 110, 130, 167-169, 175
Grossberg, Jacob G., 58-59, 67
Grusd, Edward E., 57

Halperin, Aaron, 123-124
Halperin, George, 59, 123
Halperin, Julia, 123
Hammer, Julius, 33
Harris, Franklin S., 33-34, 55, 108, 111, 129
Heimlich, Milton, 110, 193-194
Held, Adolph, 65
Heller, Samuel, 58, 59, 60
Hillman, Sidney, 124, 130
Hitler-Stalin Pact (1939), 83, 101, 129
Holocaust, 89-90
Holocaust orphans rehabilitation campaign, 93-94, 108, 119-122, 124-126, 129, 130-131, 142, 143, 145-146, 147-148, 150-153
Homeier, George Vincent "Skippy," 104, 106
Hoover, J. Edgar, 34, 86, 196-197

ICOR, xiii-xx, 13-17; and CPUSA, 86; and FBI, 86; anti-Zionism, 14; conferences and conventions, 13, 55, 65, 84, 86, 92-93; defense of USSR, 13, 84-87; headquarters, 13, 84; merger with Ambijan, 121
International Fur and Leather Workers' Union, 1, 169
International Ladies' Garment Workers' Union (ILGWU), 1
International Workers Order (IWO), 5-7, 14-15, 121, 196
Isaacs, Stanley M., 145, 148, 198
Isacson, Leo, 150, 170-172
Isenberg, Isadore, 59, 123
Israel, not competitor to Birobidjan 143, 171, 173-174; support for, 170-179

Jenofsky, Abraham, xvii, 235, 245n33; and Ambijan, 129, 142-143, 145, 148, 151, 153, 179, 201-203, 217, 229; and Birobidzhan, 139, 149, 215-216, 220, 239; and Holocaust, 90; and Holocaust orphans rehabilitation campaign, 119-121; and Israel, 171, 172, 174, 175, 176, 177; and Jewish Federations and Welfare Funds, 146-147; and the ICOR, 84-85, 86-87, 92-94, 120-121, 219; and visit of Itzik Fefer and Shloime Mikhoels to U.S., 91-92; defends Soviet Union, 200-201, 202, 218
Jesmer, Solomon, 59, 123-124, 125, 146, 148, 166-167, 174, 189, 196, 200
Jewish Anti-Fascist Committee in the Soviet Union (JAFC), 85, 86, 108, 149, 189, 194, 231-232
Jewish Bureau of New York State CP, 7-8, 195
Jewish colonization in the Soviet Union, 9-11
Jewish Communist movement, 2-3; and anti-fascism, 8; and anti-Semitism, 6; camps, 7, 15; historical background, 5
Jewish Council for Russian War Relief, 86, 87, 105, 123, 152
Jewish Labor Committee, xvi
Jewish People's Fraternal Order (JPFO), 6, 170, 171, 175, 196
Jewish Peoples Committee, 8-9
Jewish Territorialist Organization (ITO), 9

Kahn, Albert, 140, 171, 178
Kalinin, Mikhail, 10, 12, 121
Kaplan, Mordecai (Rabbi), 39, 56
Katz, Moishe, 55, 92, 176, 191-192, 199-200, 201, 204, 222, 229
Kelly, Edward J., 60, 91
Kertman, Aaron, 127, 153, 178, 219
Kibrick, Isaac S., 123
Kilgore, Harley M. (Senator), 111,

124, 128, 143
Kisselev, Eugene (Evgeny) D., 93, 103, 106, 108, 110
Klapperman, Sam, 127
Koenig, Harry D., xviii, 59-60, 66, 71, 123, 200
KOMERD (Committee for the Settlement of Jewish Toilers on the Land), 10, 37, 66, 68
Koval, George, 253-254
Kross, Anna, 88, 104, 108, 193-194
Krupin, Nathan, 60-61, 121, 127, 144, 145, 152, 197, 200-201, 219
Kuntz, Charles, 15, 26n98; and Ambijan, 129, 151, 203, 221, 229, 236; and artwork for Birobidzhan State Museum, 64; and Holocaust orphans rehabilitation campaign, 119, 120; and People's Delegation to Biro-Bidjan, 55, 58; and the ICOR, 13, 14, 84

Lenin, Vladimir, 9
Leof, M.V., 62-63
Levin, Lonnie, 33, 43, 104
Levin, Max, and Ambijan, 33, 38, 107, 109, 129, 148, 198, 203; and Birobidzhan, 108-109, 175; and Holocaust, 90; and Israel, 169, 175; and People's Delegation to Biro-Bidjan, 55, 69; and visit of Itzik Fefer and Shloime Mikhoels to U.S., 105; and Watches for the Red Army campaign, 102
Levine, Sholem, 85, 129, 201, 203
Lieberberg, Joseph, 36, 68
Lipper, Aaron, 66-67, 69, 107
Lipsett, Charles H., 103, 109, 110, 111, 124, 127, 129, 130
Locketz, Louis, 126
Lomakin, Yakov M., 142, 143, 148
Low, Sol, 33, 37, 59

Lowe, Elias A., 122, 129, 148, 203
Lyons, John, 33, 38

Magnuson, Warren (Senator), ix, 128, 130, 140, 165
Mahler, Raphael, 90, 129, 139
Maltz, Albert, 129, 140, 144, 218-219, 224n14
Mandel, William, 222, 237, 246n42
Marcantonio, Vito (Congressman), 8, 41, 55, 120
Marcus, Jacob Raider, 58, 129, 218
Marley, Lord (Dudley Leigh Aman), 30-31, 236, 45n16; and Ambijan, 43, 60, 72, 101, 110; and Birobidzhan, 31-33, 69; and ORT, 31, 72, 51n68
Marmor, Kalmen, xvi, xviii, 6-7, 14
Maud's Summer-Ray, 104-105, 114n15, 114n16
May, Mitchell, 40, 44, 56
McCarthyism, xiv, xvii, 151, 239-240
Medem, Gina, xvi, 16-17, 139, 168, 178, 201, 229, 27n109
Meisel, Nakhman, 87, 92
Melamud, Khayim, 150, 155
Mikhoels, Shloime, 90-92, 93, 105-106, 189, 191, 194, 195, 216, 231
Miller, Moses, 165-166
Morgenstern, Joseph, 63, 111, 120, 127, 143, 150, 175, 179, 203, 185n58
Morgn Frayhayt, 2, 83-84, 235
Münzenberg, Willi, 31
Murphy, Frank A., 128
Murphy, Vincent J., 122, 143
Myers, Eva, 127, 144, 219

Nellis, Leo M, 111, 123, 124
Novick, Paul, 1, 16; and American Committee of Jewish Writers, Artists and Scientists, 90; and

Birobidzhan, 70, 88, 150, 177, 249-252; and Holocaust, 89-90; and Israel, 177; death of Shloime Mikhoels, 189; leaves Communist movement, 235-236; visit to Birobidzhan, 70; visit to Soviet Union, 125, 231

O'Dwyer, William, 111, 130
Olgin, Moissaye, 1-2, 16, 64, 17n4
Olken, Abraham, 14, 55
Olken, Morris L., and Ambijan, 129, 141, 151, 152, 201, 203, 216, 221, 222, 229; and Birobidzhan, 145, 217, 218; and Holocaust orphans rehabilitation campaign, 120, 218; and Israel, 165, 173, 177; and Jewish Federations and Welfare Funds, 141, 198; and the ICOR, 85, 88; and visit of Itzik Fefer and Shloime Mikhoels to U.S., 91, 92
Opatoshu, Joseph, 55
Osri, Ethel, xviii, 123, 125, 142-143, 146, 200
Ostrowsky, William, 61

Pacht, Isaac, 60, 91, 140-141
Palestine, 89, 165-170
Panyushkin, Alexander S., 197
Parelhoff, Bernard, 129, 203
People's Delegation to Birobidzhan, 55-57; 69-71 events in Boston, 58; in Buffalo, 57-58; in Chicago, 58-59; in Cincinnati, 58; in Cleveland, 58; in Detroit, 58; in Los Angeles, 60-61; in Milwaukee, 58; in New York, 57; in Philadelphia, 61-63; in Pittsburgh, 58; in St. Paul, 58
Pepper, Claude (Senator), xv, 102, 125, 131, 154, 175, 198, 204
Picon, Molly, xv, 56

Poale Zion, 178, 231
Posner, Jenny, 85
Pritzker, Nicholas J., 59, 123
Proctor, Hayden (Governor), 143
Proletpen, 7

Recht, Charles, 39-40, 41, 60
Red Army, aid to, 85, 86, 87, 93, 101, 107
Reisen, Abraham, 55
Resnick, Abraham, 123, 201
Revutsky, Abraham, 30
Robeson, Eslanda, 221
Robeson, Paul, 90-91, 104, 129, 216
Robinson, Edward G., 91, 140, 218
Roller, Bernard, 201, 217
Rosen, Joseph A., 11, 64-65, 90, 23n65
Rosenfeld, Samuel, 127, 144, 145, 178, 219
Rosenberg, James N., 11, 35, 105, 110, 111, 130, 229, 242n4

Sabath, Adolph J. (Congressman), 60
Saltzman, Rubin, 55, 175, 196, 203
Sandler, Philip, 61-62, 70-71,
Schaffner, Julius, 59, 123
Schatzov, Lewis, 84, 86, 129, 178, 201, 203, 220-221, 229
Schwartz, Maurice, 90, 91
Serebryanye Prudy (Silver Ponds) Children's Home and Sanatorium in Stalingrad, 104, 110, 122, 129, 130, 131, 194, 137n44
Sherover, Miles M., 33, 37, 42
Shore, Isidore, 151, 218
Sirovich, William I. (Congressman), 8, 44, 55, 63
Small, Sasha, 106, 195-196
Somerville, John, 142, 151, 201, 219, 221

Soviet Union, anti-Semitism considered eliminated, 41, 43, 57, 65, 89, 105, 108, 127-128, 148, 150, 153-154, 169, 190, 191, 192, 193, 236, 207n10 ; anti-Semitism in, 189-193, 230-234
Spertus, Herman, 123
Spertus, Maurice, 123
Stalin, Joseph, 14, 29, 71, 109, 119, 131, 189, 193, 218, 230, 231, 232-234, 235, 242
Stefansson, Evelyn, 35, 104, 110, 139, 238
Stefansson, Vilhjalmur, xv, xviii, 35; and Ambijan, 38, 40, 43, 66, 105, 107, 109, 110, 129, 131, 198, 203; and Birobidzhan, 39, 44, 107; and Congress of American-Soviet Friendship, 101-102; and McCarthyism, 236-238
Stern, Morris, 57, 84, 85, 139, 148, 149, 171, 229, 73n11
Strong, Anna Louise, 36, 48n35
Sultan, Joseph, 8
Supak, Henry, 126

Talmy, Leon, 2, 7, 13, 14, 231-232, 243n9
Territorialism, 9, 31
Thomas, Elbert D. (Senator), 40, 101, 108, 110
Tobenkin, Elias, 11, 68-69
Troyansovsky, Alexander M., 36-37, 38, 40-41, 69, 71, 48n30, 79n75

United Workers Cooperative Colony (Coops), 6, 14, 21n41, 21n42
Uretz, Daniel A., 123, 218, 222

Wallace, Henry (Vice-president), xv, 102, 128, 130, 169, 170, 171, 198, 215, 217
Warburg, Felix, 10-11, 34-35
Watches for the Red Army campaign, 102-103
Wattenberg, Chaika Ostrovskaya, 231-232
Wattenberg, Elias (Elye), 13, 231-232, 243n9
Weiner, William, 5, 9
Weinper, Zishe, 55, 173
Wise, James Waterman, 8, 33, 38, 39, 40, 55, 59, 63, 200, 217, 232, 244n16
Wise, Stephen S., 90
Workmen's Circle. See *Arbayter Ring*.
World Jewish Cultural Union (YKUF), 7, 173, 235, 241
World ORT Union, 10, 11, 31, 65, 71-72, 45n13, 51n68, 80n87
Wronsky, Dora, 222

Yellin, Mendel, 219
Yevsektsiya (Jewish Section of the Soviet Communist Party), 9
YKUF. See World Jewish Cultural Union.
Young, Gerson C., 33, 38, 109

Zacharias, Robert, 123, 124
Zarbin, Harry, 59, 67, 123, 242
Zhitlovsky, Khaim, xviii, 15-16, 70, 85, 88-89, 90, 93, 230, 26n100, 97n31
Zukerman, William, 11, 29-30

www.ingramcontent.com/pod-product-compliance
Lightning Source LLC
Chambersburg PA
CBHW051110230426
43667CB00014B/2520